Camborne Public Library
Lending Department

OPEN DAILY:

Monday,
Tuesday and
Wednesday
11 a.m. to 7 p.m.

Thursday
11 a.m. to 12.30 p.m.
Friday and
Saturday
10 a.m to 6 p.m.

Take great care of this book and do not allow it to get wet. Please inform the Librarian of any defects.

In the event of infectious disease in your house, inform the Librarian. Do not return the books until you hear from the Librarian or the Public Health Department.

All books are issued for 14 days and due for return by the last date stamped on the date label, unless a renewal has been granted. Books can be renewed either personally or by post — in the latter case, author, title, number and date due for return should be given. A book borrowed cannot be changed the same day. A fine of ONE PENNY PER WEEK, or portion of a week, is charged on all overdue books. The guarantor, who has signed a borrower's application for membership of the Library, is liable for loss or damage to any book borrowed.

Books on any subject may be borrowed through the Library.

J. R. BURRELL, Librarian.

'A portrait though a miserable likeness of my dearest husband by
Angelica Kauffmann, when he was at Rome in 1765. The scroll is the
plan of the Temples of Paestum, and there is a view of Vesuvius. But
it's a very, very imperfect likeness of one whose countenance was
benevolence personified, whose smile was to the highest degree captivating, and who had the uncommon beauty of preserving a perfect
blue eye to the last hour of his existence, shaded by the finest eyelashes' – a
note made by Lady Palmerston on 26 February 1803, when drawing up
a list of her late husband's collection of paintings.

PORTRAIT OF
A Whig Peer

Compiled from the papers
of the
Second Viscount Palmerston
1739-1802
by

BRIAN CONNELL

ANDRE DEUTSCH

FIRST PUBLISHED 1957 BY
ANDRE DEUTSCH LIMITED
12–14 CARLISLE STREET SOHO SQUARE
LONDON WI
© BRIAN CONNELL 1957
ALL RIGHTS RESERVED
PRINTED IN GREAT BRITAIN BY
TONBRIDGE PRINTERS LIMITED
TONBRIDGE KENT

To

COUNTESS MOUNTBATTEN OF BURMA

who so generously placed these manuscripts

at my disposal

CONTENTS

CONTENTS

ILLUSTRATIONS

PREFACE

MANY of these papers came to light during the course of reconstruction work at Broadlands, the country mansion on the outskirts of Romsey which was the property of the Palmerston family and has now descended to Countess Mountbatten of Burma. During the nineteenth century the Victorian Prime Minister had built on to the exquisite Georgian house left to him by his father a singularly unfitting north wing. Earl and Countess Mountbatten decided to demolish this excrescence and restore the house to its original eighteenth century form. But first it was necessary to catalogue the contents for retention or disposal. This enabled Mrs Georgiana Blois, who for many years has assisted Countess Mountbatten in this work, to complete the collection she had slowly been accumulating of the correspondence and journals which form the basis of this volume.

Countess Mountbatten's inheritance of the Palmerston estates should, perhaps, be briefly detailed. The third, and most famous Viscount, whom we leave on the threshold of manhood in this book, married at the age of fifty-five, Emily Lamb, sister of his Cabinet colleague, Viscount Melbourne, and widow of Earl Cowper. Lady Cowper had been the third Viscount's intimate friend for many years. When she finally became Lady Palmerston she was already fifty years of age and there was no issue of the marriage. Her elder son by her first marriage inherited the Cowper estates, and those of Lord Palmerston passed, after his wife's death in 1869, to her second son, William Cowper, who took the name of Cowper-Temple, but left no issue of his two marriages. He was created Lord Mount Temple in 1880 and died in 1888.

Lady Cowper's eldest daughter married the great reforming seventh Earl of Shaftesbury, and Lord Palmerston had expressed a wish that his estates should pass to her second son, the Hon. Evelyn Ashley, who, in collaboration with Sir Henry Lytton Bulwer, became his benefactor's first biographer and died in 1907. The estate then passed to his son, Wilfrid Ashley, who

11

became Lord Mount Temple of the second creation, married
Maud, only daughter of Sir Ernest Cassel, and was the father
of Countess Mountbatten.

In presenting this record of the life and times of Henry
Temple, second Viscount Palmerston, my endeavour has been,
with a minimum interpolation of linking passages and historical
background, to give these letters and journal extracts, by
judicious cutting, transposition and juxtaposition, sufficient
narrative force to warrant the description of posthumous auto-
biography. Outside sources have only been quoted where
absolutely necessary to maintain the sequence of events.

The total volume of manuscript material read, and itemised
in the principal appendices, probably exceeds a million words.
The final transcription amounts to less than a sixth of that total.
Nothing has been omitted that could be of interest to an
historian or art connoisseur, but, in order to present the most
colourful picture of the central personality, much has been
retained that an academician might consider trivial. I have
always considered footnotes a hindrance to pleasurable reading;
all the information they would have contained has been incor-
porated in the text.

The reference system can be ignored by the ordinary reader,
but provides specialists with immediate and precise identification of every letter, journal and source quoted. The appendix
listing the manuscript material has been divided into eight
sections, headed A to H. Each group of letters is numbered.
In the reference list at the end of each chapter the letter quoted
is identified and also dated when necessary. All extracts preceding a reference number in the text are from the same hand.

The original phraseology has been totally preserved. Except
in a few instances, where it provides piquant emphasis, the
eighteenth century habit of capitalising nouns has been elimi-
nated, the unpredictable vagaries of spelling and punctuation
have been corrected, and all place and proper names given their
modern form. Round brackets in the original text are retained,
square brackets enclose interpolations of mine. Three dots
indicate cuts.

This whole collection is *inédit*, with the following exceptions:

The second Viscount's journal of his visit to Paris during the debates of the French Constituent Assembly in 1791 was reproduced as an appendix to the *Despatches of Earl Gower*, British Minister at the time, published by Longmans Green in 1888, and some extracts are inevitably reproduced here in their context; A. Michaelis, in compiling his volume on *Ancient Marbles in Great Britain* for the Cambridge University Press in 1882, saw Palmerston's record of his art purchases in Italy in 1764; Sir Henry Lytton Bulwer, the Hon. Evelyn Ashley and Philip Guedalla drew on some of the juvenile letters of the third Viscount in their biographies of the Victorian Foreign and Prime Minister. Otherwise there is no record of this material having been seen, much less read, except by the successive owners through whom the Palmerston estate passed.

My first and most grateful duty is to express my boundless thanks to Countess Mountbatten of Burma for placing these papers so generously at my disposal. Secondly I must thank Mrs Georgiana Blois, who rediscovered these manuscripts, recognised their importance and was kind enough to suggest that they should be entrusted to me. Without her help and tireless research work this book could never have been written.

The final manuscript was submitted for comment to Mr Steven Watson, Student and Tutor of Christ Church, Oxford, who guided me in the historical byways of the times. Mr Charles Mitchell of the Warburg Institute has given me invaluable advice on Palmerston's activities as an art patron and connoisseur.

With his help, and that of Mrs Blois, my wife was able, after months of research, to reduce the scattered and haphazard record of Palmerston's art purchases to some semblance of order. This work was additional to her now accustomed role of unwearied typist, critic, co-editor, disciplinarian and cook. We were both relieved of much of the routine work of transcription and copy-typing by the devoted assistance of Miss Susan Martin and Mrs Jean Mitchell.

London,
April, 1957

CHAPTER I

INTRODUCTION

The second Viscount Palmerston – his close identification with the personalities and events of the reign of George III – the Temple family – Broadlands – his upbringing and education – first travels – enters Parliament for a pocket borough – position as a young Whig aristocrat

UNTIL now the name of Palmerston has evoked only the figure of the jaunty survivor of the eighteenth century, who was Foreign or Prime Minister for most of the first thirty years of Queen Victoria's reign. Yet he was the third Viscount of his line and the branch of the Temple family of which he was the last childless descendant had rendered loyal service to sovereign and country for centuries. The standard biographies dismiss his antecedents in a few paragraphs, presenting him only in the context of the events with which he became associated. Little attempt is made to plumb the attitudes he brought to influencing them, which derived directly from his upbringing. He died as the last representative of the Whig aristocracy which sponsored the incandescent flowering of talent, taste and tolerance during the first forty years of the reign of George III. His own father's active life covered precisely those four decades, and if it was the son who left his mark on history, it was the second Viscount who left his mark on the brilliant heir.

The Young Harry who became 'Old Pam' was in his eighteenth year when his father died in 1802, and a few months short of his majority when his mother died three years later. Yet the pattern of his mind was already formed by the education the second Viscount had devised for him; his political contacts were those to whom his parents had introduced him; his social standing had all the certainty of their established roots; the down of that golden age was on his cheeks and the exquisite grace of its manners were to remain his hallmark. He

was a living link with the Britain of the younger Pitt, Fox,
Burke and Sheridan; of Reynolds, Garrick and Gibbon; of
Topham Beauclerk, Georgiana, Duchess of Devonshire and
George Selwyn. His father had been the intimate of them all.
The second Viscount's range of friendship included an astonishing roster of the great names of his era, from Voltaire at
Ferney, to 'Prinny' in his Brighton Pavilion, Charles Townshend
in the seventeen-sixties and Emma, Lady Hamilton in the
seventeen-nineties. He could give an account of the wedding
of Frederick the Great's 'Golden Boy', the Duke of Brunswick,
to George III's sister, and paid his respects to Louis XVI and
Marie Antoinette in the Tuileries five days before the mob
broke in and massacred the Swiss Guards. He was one of the
outstanding art patrons of his time but, despite membership of
the Boards of Trade, Admiralty and also the Treasury, a
desultory parliamentarian for all his forty adult years. Nevertheless his public career is of notable interest in illustrating the
complexity of political alignments in an age before the full
development of party politics. His attitudes and friendships
epitomised those of many less prominent men and go far to
explain the strength of the régimes of Rockingham, North
and Pitt.

The second Viscount's life provided a microcosm of what is
perhaps the most effulgent period in British history, and in
nearly fourteen hundred manuscript letters and almost a hundred
travel journals and engagement diaries, he left a complete
record of his part in it: exchanges of correspondence with his
famous friends, the love letters of his two marriages, a running
description of parliamentary and political events, an intimate
account of the social world of which he was an ornament,
and tirelessly recorded details of his extensive and repeated
tours in Great Britain and long periods of residence on the
Continent.

The picture he paints fills a vast canvas: the accession of
George III, which occurred in the year of his own majority; a
Europe recovering from the wars of Frederick the Great and
plunging into the holocaust of the French Revolution; the
debates in the House of Commons that ended the war with

America, Fox's India Bill and the ascendency of the younger Pitt; the radical insurgency of John Wilkes, the insanity of George III and the impeachment of Warren Hastings; the marriage of Caroline of Brunswick, and the riot in the Champ de Mars. Palmerston was an eye-witness of them all, and his account is enlivened with the scandals, stories, personalities and gossip that pullulated in the shadow of these great events.

In politics he was without ambition, apart from upholding the Whig traditions of his family. His grandfather, from whom he inherited the title, had received it in return for his staunch support of Sir Robert Walpole, an Irish Viscountcy which took its name from an estate near Dublin. The second Palmerston acquired minor office through the interest of the Marquis of Rockingham in 1765, retained it during the Chatham, Grafton and North administrations, saw his first sponsor into office again in 1872 and then retired to the furthest back bench when Shelburne became First Lord of the Treasury on Rockingham's death. Through the years Palmerston patiently paid his two, three or four thousand pounds for a comfortable pocket borough seat and then, as one of the Whigs who had broken with Fox on the issue of the war with revolutionary France, asked Pitt for an English peerage, a request that was never to be granted, thus ensuring his son's fame in the House of Commons.

He reserved his talents for social life, the arts and travel. He came of age with an income of £7,000 a year and, when his mother died in 1789, this increased to £12,000. Although this did not compare with the wealth of the great Whig magnates, Palmerston made by contrast more fruitful use of it. He was not drawn to the besetting vice of his day, gambling, and only played cards for small stakes which won or lost him not more than thirty pounds a year. Yet his expenditure on works of art during his lifetime exceeded £8,000. He acquired nearly three hundred paintings and three of them, by Sir Joshua Reynolds, sold for twice his total outlay not a hundred years later. He spent £23,000 with 'Capability' Brown and £10,000 with Henry Holland for the embellishment of his houses at Broadlands and in Hanover Square.

He 'was ranked among the most eminent of the connoisseurs of his time'.[1] He became a member of the Dilettanti Society at the age of twenty-six, was one of the early purchasers of classical antiquities from Gavin Hamilton in Rome, one of the first patrons of William Pars and Hugh Dean and placed William Hodges as the artist to accompany Captain Cook on one of his voyages. Rivalling his close friend, General John Burgoyne, as a writer of occasional verse, he became a fellow member of the Literary Club with Boswell and Johnson and was a pall bearer at the funerals of two other intimates, David Garrick and Sir Joshua Reynolds. His patronage of the arts extended from Angelica Kauffmann to Sir Thomas Lawrence and from encouragement of the struggling poet, George Crabbe, to the theatrical entertainments of the Misses Berry at Strawberry Hill.

This *aristocrate moyen sensuel* was equally welcome in the world of philosophy and science. He made himself agreeable to Helvetius and Voltaire, ranged the Alps with Horace de Saussure, the Swiss scientist, who was the first man to climb Mont Blanc, and had his kitchens at Broadlands and Hanover Square built according to the new heat theories of that minor universal mind, Benjamin Thompson, Count Rumford, who was his wife's ardent admirer. Elected to the Royal Society in 1776, Palmerston peered through Dr Herschel's new telescope at planetary nebulæ, travelled the Continent in company with Sir Charles Blagden, the Secretary, and constantly entertained the President, Sir Joseph Banks, who found it in no way beneath his dignity to supply his host with the recipe for a particular form of firework. To the interests of a Boswell, a Baedeker and a Hansard, Palmerston added in his diaries precise meteorological notes for more than twenty years.

His travels were notable: one of the first Englishmen to visit Paris after the Seven Years War, he made two Grand Tours, travelled the Netherlands during the uprisings of 1789, was observer and letter-bearer from Charles James Fox during the debates of the French Constituent Assembly in 1791, and became an ornament of the Neapolitan Court for two years when the first wars of the French Revolution closed Paris to foreigners. He visited every corner of the British Isles, from his estates in Northampton and Yorkshire to his principal land holdings in County Sligo and the academic fastnesses of Edinburgh, where he entrusted his son to the care of the Whig philosopher, Professor Dugald Stewart. Wherever he went he ended each day making exhaustive notes of curiosities seen, descriptions of scenery, travelling conditions, accounts of country houses or establishments visited and the works of art they contained.

The engagement diaries he kept in addition included in the contemporary preface the exhortation: 'As these books may be considered as the annals of a man's life, and may be of use even after his decease, they ought by all means to be preserved.' Palmerston took this so much to heart that it is possible two centuries later to determine exactly with whom he had dinner every night of his life. In later years he abstracted the most important entries into a handsome leather volume, covering the years 1765–95, often adding in this overall diary further comments on events of interest.

From his first appearance on the London scene in the seventeen-sixties, past the turn of the century, there is almost no name of note that does not appear in his guest list: the Townshends, the Spencers and the Pelhams; Newcastle, Rockingham, Fox and Sheridan; North, Mulgrave, Edgcumbe, Ossory, Pembroke and the Paynes; Burke, Horace Walpole and Topham Beauclerk; Pasquale Paoli and the Prince of Wales. . . . With advancing middle age came concentration on the closest friends of his life, James Harris Lord Malmesbury, Gilbert Elliot Lord Minto and Lord Pelham, all three of whom were appointed Young Harry's guardians.

The Royal Society and the Dilettanti Sunday dinners at the Star and Garter were only the more serious of his places of resort. Of a gayer, even raffish, nature were Samuel Foote's Pandemonium Club, Almack's, the Catch Club and the Opera Club. He was indefatigable and his gaiety affected even the most staid guest: 'Dined with Lord Palmerston today; a great dinner of catches', noted Edward Gibbon in 1776.[2] 'Lord Palmerston has not got to his second childhood, but only as far as his second boyhood' Sir Gilbert Elliot wrote in 1786, 'for no schoolboy is so fond of a breaking up as he is of a junket and pleasuring'.[3] Although no libertine, Palmerston enjoyed his share of eighteenth-century gallantry. Between his two marriages he was one of the admirers of the notorious Polly Kennedy, maintained an Italian mistress and became sufficiently involved with an English paramour for her to attempt to blackmail him twenty years later.

These extrovert tastes did not prevent Palmerston from being an exemplary husband and father. He married first, in 1767, Frances Poole, a woman of taste and culture six years his senior and a kinswoman of the Pelhams. Her death in childbed two years later left him a widower for fourteen years before he found a worthy successor. His second wife, Mary Mee, daughter of a City merchant, was clearly a woman of outstanding grace, charm and character, unselfish, a devoted mother to Young Harry, his brother and two sisters, and a gifted hostess. She made her home so attractive to her guests that they did not know how to leave it, 'it was a kind of enchanted castle, where there were regular reunions of the first society, entertained with amusements and splendid hospitality', as Count Rumford's daughter, Sarah, wrote.[4]

Marital duty and fidelity knows no more charming expression than the letters she wrote to her husband in the last five years of the century, when the disasters of the French war were involving him in acute financial difficulties. In return Palmerston had shouldered uncomplainingly the burden of rescuing three members of the Mee family from the consequences of their faulty business acumen. It was a notably happy and devoted marriage, with the children sharing their parents' tastes, travels and harmonious life.

Not only did Palmerston leave a comprehensive record of contemporary public affairs, but also intimate details of his domestic economy. We know what pills he took to cure his colds and how much he gave his postilions. We find him grumbling about his taxes, but paying them honestly; complacent in his attitude to social inferiors, but paying lip-service to the doctrines of Jean-Jacques Rousseau. Lady Palmerston notes the cost of a mahogany table and her husband that of a pipe of port. His life was the private epitome of the privileged few who made the eighteenth century the summit of civilised existence.

The second Palmerston emerges from these papers as a man of warm human sympathies and considerable accomplishments. He was an arch-typical Whig peer, even if the Irish title, membership of the House of Commons and his gravitation to Pitt serve to confuse the description. A bustling, hearty, cheerful man, he was a spectator rather than an innovator in political life, yet his range of acquaintance and catholic taste in the arts made him a person of consequence. There is a marked tone of deference in the letters from his many correspondents, who included some of the outstanding men of his time. The fullness of his life acquires added importance by the fortunate survival of so detailed a documentation, which mirrors through the eyes of a participant not only the momentous era in which he lived, but provides a vivid prelude to the history his son was to make.

* * *

The Temple family traces its line back to Leofric, Earl of Mercia, who founded the Abbey of Coventry, married the famous Lady Godiva and died in 1087. His descendant, Peter Temple, purchased the Manor of Stowe in the reign of Queen Elizabeth and became, through his eldest son, John, the ancestor of the Earls Temple of Stowe and the Dukes of Buckingham. The first born of his younger son, Anthony, who died in 1626, became Sir John Temple the elder, knighted by King Charles I, a member of the Privy Council in England and Master of the Rolls in Ireland. The eldest son of Sir John the elder, was Sir William Temple, the famous statesman and diplomatist of Charles II's reign, who had Jonathan Swift as his secretary and was the correspondent and husband of Dorothy Osborne. The second son, Sir John Temple the younger, knighted by Charles II, became successively Attorney-General and Speaker in the Irish House of Commons. He retired to an estate he had bought at East Sheen, Surrey, and died in 1704.

Sir John Temple the younger's surviving second son, Henry, born in 1673, became the first Viscount Palmerston. A redoubtable Whig family, the Temples had been proscribed by the Irish Parliament that supported James II in 1689, and were only restored to their lands and sinecures after the Battle of the Boyne. With the accession of George I, the Whigs entered into their long tenure of power and the Temples soon obtained further preferment. Already a Member of Parliament, Henry was created, in 1723, a Peer of Ireland, as Baron Temple of Mount Temple, County Sligo and Viscount Palmerston of Palmerston, County Dublin. In 1736 he purchased the estate of Broadlands, near Romsey and continued to sit in the English House of Commons until 1747. He died in 1757.

The first Viscount set the pattern for those generations who sought their spouses in the City of London. By his first marriage to Anne Houblon, only daughter of Abraham Houblon, Governor of the Bank of England, he had two daughters and three sons, Henry, John, who died an infant, and Richard, who married Henrietta, daughter of Thomas Pelham. His second marriage in 1738 to Lady Fryer, widow of Sir John Fryer, Lord Mayor of London, was without issue and the Dowager Viscountess died in 1757, shortly after her step-grandson succeeded to the title.

The boy was the only male survivor of a sorry record of mortality. His father, Henry, was married first in 1735 to Elizabeth, eldest daughter of Colonel Lee. She died of consumption a year later at Montpelier. In 1738 the widower married Jane, youngest daughter of Sir John Barnard, Lord Mayor of London for that year. Henry died at the family's East Sheen house in 1740, a few months after the birth of his son on December 4, 1739.

The records of the heir's earlier years are sparse indeed and he and his mother are not mentioned more than a dozen times in the diminutive engagement diaries which the aged first Viscount kept in his spidery handwriting. Other members of the family appear with greater frequency, but the old man outlived all his male relations. His second son, Richard, died of smallpox in 1749. On March 4, 1750, the shaking hand noted: 'My grandson [Richard's son] Tommy died', and on February 5, 1752: 'My brother [John] died at Bath', with the addition on February 20: 'Was buried in Westminster Abbey, near Sir William Temple'.

In 1754, the septuagenarian settled the bulk of his estate, worth some £7,000 a year, on his surviving grandson, but when Harry came into his inheritance he was still a minor of seventeen. Although the income from it increased with the years, the pattern of the holdings did not alter materially during the second Viscount's lifetime, apart from two forced sales when he found himself in financial difficulties towards the end of his life. Besides stock holdings of £27,000 the income was derived from the following rents:[5]

	£	s.	d.
The house and apartments in St James's Square, at per annum	350	0	0
East Sheen	253	13	6
Great Houghton in Northamptonshire	281	18	0
Fairburn, Yorkshire	188	14	0
Estates in Ireland	3,671	6	0
Hampshire estate	1,239	14	0

His widowed mother had a life interest in further properties, and although the combined total did not compare with the large fortunes of the time, the second Viscount was a very comfortably situated young man.

Apart from the occasional mention in his grandfather's diaries of a Mr Laurence as his companion, there is no evidence of where he spent his school years. His mother, a cousin, John Lord Berkeley, and his maternal grandfather, Sir John Barnard, had been appointed executors, and during his minority Broadlands was let from June 8, 1758, at a rent of £100 a year, to the Whig magnate Lord Powis.

It was already a substantial mansion, but the inventory of every room made at the time, bald as such documents always are, gives no foretaste of the embellishments carried out by the second Palmerston during his lifetime. The contents of the drawing-room were curtly listed as: 'A pair of [fire] dogs; a fire-pan and tongs; one iron back; a pair of bellows, broke;

a marble table on a gilt frame; one mahogany chair with a cushion; ten walnut chairs with blue bottoms and backs and blue linen covers; one firescreen; a chimney glass in a gilt frame; a large looking-glass in a gilt frame; Esquire Temple's picture, in a gilt frame; a corner cupboard and a picture in a black frame.'[6]

The new owner had been sent to Cambridge to improve his mind. On February 2, 1757, he was admitted as a Fellow Commoner of Clare College,[7] being readmitted as a Nobleman on June 1 of that year, after the death of his grandfather. He obtained his degree of Master of Arts in 1759, and an undated note on a scrap of paper in his own hand indicates that academic distinction was not necessarily the primary qualification:

'*Non necessario neque strictim terminorum (ut vocant) numerum, neque usitatus curimoniarum comitiorumque solennitatis, observari debere existumamus.*

The above is the clause in a Statute of the University of Cambridge by which it is empowered to confer degrees on Noblemen, and those related to Noblemen, sooner than the regular time.'[8]

He was still at Cambridge during 1760, and both his diary and account book entries for that year would seem to indicate somewhat sober pleasures for a man of his age. 'Subscribed to relieve French prisoners, a guinea; subscribed to concert, a guinea; charity sermon, a guinea; ticket for the choir at the Installation, a guinea', read some of the notes, although he was clearly a young man of fashion: 'Paid haircutter, £1; paid for laced ruffles, £3 1s. 6d.; to making six shirts and ruffling others, £1 4s. 10d.; paid sword cutter, £1.'[9]

He was in the happy position of drawing £100 a month, but much of this was spent on the extraordinary penchant for travel and observation, which had already developed at this stage of his life and was to fill over thirty journals. There were three such tours in England before he attained his majority; two to the North and one to the South, and his curious eye devoured with equal avidity details of gentlemen's estates, of which he took copious notes for his future guidance, and the first signs of new industrial processes, even before they ushered in a social revolution:

'Holkham [which Palmerston visited in 1758 after inspecting his Northampton estate at Great Houghton], Lord Leicester's, is a most noble edifice, built with a very beautiful kind of grey bricks. It consists of a quadrangular centre and four spacious pavilions, one of which contained Lord Leicester's whole family for some years. There is a simplicity in the building, which has a better effect than any ornaments, and though the inside is extremely magnificent, convenience seems to have been the principal object. The hall, when finished, will be extremely grand, adorned with statues and columns of marble. There are several valuable pictures and a collection of very fine antique statues and busts. . . . The grounds are very prettily disposed, with a very handsome piece of water; there is a menagerie full of curious birds.'[10]

At Lord Stanhope's seat at Chevening he noted that 'one uncommon thing is that the servants do not take any money'. The Duke of Dorset, at Knowle, 'lives in a very hospitable manner, and every week at the latter end of the year gives a ball to the neighbourhood'. Lord Westmorland had rebuilt the church which used to stand near Mereworth House, 'in a very elegant manner at a distance'. In each case he noted carefully the topography of the park, with particular reference to the construction of artificial lakes, cascades and the use of water in landscape gardening. Nor did more prosaic details escape his notice:

'Ramsgate is famous for the pier which is building to preserve the merchant ships from the storms to which they are exposed in the Downs. It was begun about nine years ago, but was discontinued for three years. It has cost about £50,000 and is not near completed.

'Margate is a small dirty fishing town, frequented by numbers of people for the sake of sea bathing, though at the same time they must submit to every sort of inconvenience.

'The Isle of Thanet in general is a great corn country, very open and remarkable for its great quantity of game.'[11]

The long vacation in 1760 found him visiting his Yorkshire

estates: 'Paid for a grey gelding £18', he noted on June 1 before he set out, and keeping a careful note of his expenses on the way – 'Lodgings at York, £2 15s. od.'[12]

'Birmingham is a very large and compact town; well built and the streets in general good. The church is quite modern and the churchyard large, surrounded by rows of very handsome houses. There is also a small square, quite regular and very neat. This town carries on a prodigious trade in iron and other hardware manufactures, and toys in general. Some of the most curious are Mr Tayler's, who deals principally in button making, which is an amazing branch of business, for the number of hands employed, the surprising quickness of the work and the great fortunes raised by it. Those who enamel toys of all kinds. The gunsmiths forges, where the gun barrels are made. The glass pinching, or making – Birmingham diamonds, as they are called. Baskerville's printing office, who deals likewise much in japanning and painting teaboards, waiters, etc. The slitting mills, by which flat bars of iron are slit in order to be made into nails. There is also a sharp instrument which cuts iron bars of an inch thick and 3 broad. The method of gilding metal buttons is very curious, but they are very cautious of admitting strangers to see it. The whole town has an air of opulence, business and populousness beyond almost any except London, and round it are several country houses, built by persons who have raised fortunes in the several branches of business.

'Newcastle is a large town . . . famous for its vast coal trade, in which there are commonly from 5 to 600 vessels employed in carrying coals to all the ports of England and many foreign ports. The town itself is very dirty and the streets very narrow.

'Leeds is a very populous good town and noted for being the centre of the cloth manufacture, which is made in the country about and brought to sale at Leeds market, which is in a very commodious building, twice a week. One remarkable thing is that in this market where there are perhaps 1,500 sellers and buyers, in proportion there is scarce a word to be heard – everything being transacted in whispers.'[13]

Palmerston took careful notes at more of the great estates:

Wentworth Castle, Worksop Manor, Chatsworth and Wentworth House, the seat of the Marquis of Rockingham. Young
as he was, he had an observant eye for the art treasures stored
in these stately homes, an interest which was to develop during
his life into the acquisition of one of the largest minor collections of his time. At Lord Spencer's seat at Althorp he noted 'a
most valuable collection by all the most celebrated masters' and
at Burleigh he particularly liked a painting of Seneca in the
Bath by Luca Giordano. Of the few good pictures remaining
at Belvoir Castle he commented: 'There were many more in a
room built on purpose, but they have been sold on pretence that
it was impossible to keep them from being spoilt by the damp.'

The Temple family had themselves been by no means negligent in their patronage of the arts. The pictures they had
commissioned and acquired had not yet gravitated to Broadlands, where the 1758 inventory listed only nineteen pictures,
but the house at East Sheen, where the second Viscount was
brought up, contained many noteworthy canvases. Sir John
Temple the younger, father of the first Viscount, who had
purchased the house, left at least fifty-five pictures there to
his son.[14]

The first Viscount inherited at least another seventeen Temple
family portraits, which are at Broadlands to this day, six by
Lely, five by Kneller and others by Michael Dahl, Cornelius
Janssen, Jonathan Richardson, William Wissing and Loving.
There is also a painting by Adrien de Vries of Sir Peter Osborne
of Chicksands, father of the famous Dorothy, who married
Sir William Temple in 1654. The successor to the Palmerston
title grew up surrounded by these works of art and during the
course of his life added more than three hundred to their number.

★ ★ ★

Palmerston came of age on December 4, 1760, five weeks after
the accession of George III.

Lord Powis' tenancy of Broadlands was terminated, but the
young squire seemed in no hurry to move from Sheen and had
certainly not yet acquired any lavish habits. On March 24,1761,
he wrote to his agent, John White:

'I purpose coming to Broadlands just to look about me as soon as I conveniently can . . .

'I want to know whether Mrs Liddell, who I understand lives in the house, is able and willing to act in the capacity of house-keeper. Mrs Jocelyn tells me that she lived with the Bishop of London as such. If it be so, I suppose she must be capable of providing a common table, with plain dishes, which is all I should want . . .'[15]

The letter that followed two days later indicated that Palmerston had established himself on the fringes of the political world. White was exhorted to engage his master's influence at Winchester, in the first general election of the new reign, in favour of the man who became Palmerston's first parliamentary patron, Bilson Legge, Chancellor of the Exchequer under the Duke of Newcastle at the Treasury:

'I shall be down myself by the time of the election, but must beg leave to implore you in the meantime to do everything you possibly can in my name to save our Mr Legge. I do not very well know what interest I may have, but be it what it will and desirous to exert it to the utmost in his behalf. . . .'[16]

Palmerston had still to inspect his Irish estates and in the autumn of 1761 he left for Dublin. His first impressions are included in the later chapter on Ireland, which summarises his whole association with that unhappy country, whence he drew more than half his revenues. While he was away he received from his mother an account of the King's Coronation:

'I think you embarked in the afternoon of the Coronation Day; the weather here that day was as fine as possible, which I took great satisfaction in, although I was not there, but to those that were there it was a great benefit, as well as pleasure, as it must prevent the very bad colds that would probably have been catched if it had been wet and damp, and it likewise made the awning unnecessary; but, as it was, the people were deprived of half their view by the procession returning so late from the Abbey that it was too dark to have any pleasure in seeing them pass by. This was occasioned by the neglect of people, whose business it was to get things ready, and who made the King wait a great while before he could set out; some things being

forgot and were to be fetched and what seems very strange,
they made him wait till his canopy was finished which, when
it came, was ill done and had not the proper number of staves
to support it, so that the gentlemen were afraid they should not
have been able to keep it up and it made it very fatiguing to
them. The King's behaviour that day charmed everybody; he
showed such a proper seriousness in the Abbey, so much good
nature and patience when things were wrong, and so much
benevolence in his appearance, mixed with dignity . . .'[17]

On the Continent the Seven Years War was nearing its end.
As soon as he returned to London, Palmerston began to acquaint
himself with the social and political life of the capital, and
was already in correspondence with one of the most celebrated
hostesses of the day, Mrs Howe, sister of the future Admiral
Earl Howe, who wrote to him on February 9, 1761 [1762?]:

'I think I cannot choose a better opportunity to thank your
Lordship for a very entertaining and obliging letter that reached
me before I came to town, than the present one, when, at the
same time, I can send you the result of the Duke of Bedford's
motion made in the House of Lords last Friday for an address
to the King to recall our forces from Germany, which you will
be glad to be acquainted with if your curiosity at all approaches
that of the Londoners upon the occasion. Lord Bute answered
him warmly at first, but subsided. He said, amongst other
things, that by letters he had seen in the morning, he could
prophesy there would be some changes in affairs; insinuated
new alliances and seemed to wish the House of Lords would
not interfere but leave it to the King's own determination, and
ended with proposing a previous question, whether this was
not an improper time to address the King to recall the troops?
. . . The death of the Czarina seems to be a welcome event. The
Stocks have risen upon it. We have yet no account of where
the Brest Fleet are gone, they stole away in the last stormy
weather, when our ships were drove from their stations. It is
supposed Lord Albemarle will set out for Portsmouth next
week, where he is to go, no-one hitherto has pretended to
guess. . . . Lord Howe is going out with a command very soon;
he is now at Plymouth . . .'[18]

On May 27 of the same year he was instructing White to
make Broadlands ready for hospitality:

'As I shall probably come to Broadlands sometime this
summer, I shall be glad if you will give orders to have some
small beer brewed there immediately, as I believe there are the
necessary utensils. The beer must have such a quantity of hops
as that it may be fit to drink in a month. As there are several
rooms at Broadlands that have no curtains, I should be obliged
to you if you would have the windows measured – what is
their height from the floor and their breadth in order that I
may get some made. There is the dining parlour, the drawing-
room and what used to be the dressing room upstairs. I intend
to make them check, either blue or red, with large squares.
If I could get as good at Romsey, I need not send it from
London . . .'[19]

This letter makes no mention of a major development in his
life which occurred the following day, when he was elected to
the House of Commons for the pocket borough of East Looe
in Cornwall. Bilson Legge, although ousted from office at the
general election of the previous year, had prevailed on his former secretary at the Treasury, John Buller, to make available
to Palmerston one of the seats he controlled at Looe, which had
become vacant by the death of the sitting member, Francis
Gashery. John Buller was a political adherent of the Duke of
Newcastle, whose influence was being eclipsed by the rise of
the new royal favourite, the 3rd Earl of Bute. Palmerston's
subsequent parliamentary career provides a picture of the
dilemmas of loyalty affecting Newcastle's political heirs with
the decline of the 'Whig supremacy'.

Palmerston makes a curious error in his overall diary in the
only reference to his election: 'I came in in the third year of the
Parliament', he noted in 1768, at the end of his term, adding,
'upon the interest of Mr Buller at the recommendation of Mr
Bilson Legge'. This cannot refer to any date earlier than 1763.
It may be that not only was he elected *in absentia* – the letter to
his agent on May 27 is dated from East Sheen, which may
reasonably be supposed to be more than a day's stage coach
journey from Cornwall – but that he did not actually take up

his seat until the following year. There is no evidence of any sort. It seems more likely that the overall diary entry, probably written some years later, is a mistake, although Palmerston did spend part of the intervening period abroad.

As fellow Member of Parliament and Hampshire neighbour at Paultons, he had the Rt Hon. Hans Stanley, who played an initial part as British plenipotentiary in the negotiations which culminated in the Treaty of Paris to end the Seven Years War. With the cessation of hostilities in November, 1762, Palmerston took advantage of this friendship to visit the French capital, from which British visitors had been cut off for so long. Just before his return in the following January he revealed, in a letter to his mother, that he had taken some healthy British prejudices with him:

'I have much reason to be pleased with my expedition, having passed my time very agreeably since I have been here and by Mr Stanley's means have made some very good acquaintances. There are several English here who are in general well-received and liked and, indeed, I cannot say that I think they suffer upon the whole by a comparison with the young Frenchmen. We went to Versailles last Tuesday, where we saw the Palace and the whole Royal Family, to whom we were presented. The King's palaces and some of the public buildings in Paris are fine, but in general the town appears to me much inferior to London and the country, as far as I have seen, infinitely inferior to England in point of improvement, populousness or beauty . . .'[20]

His introductions had included many useful and some praiseworthy acquaintances, such as the two rival Paris hostesses, Madame du Deffand and Madame Geoffrin, and Claude Helvetius, the French philosopher, who wrote to Palmerston shortly after his return to thank him for a gift of books:

13 Juin, 1763

'Milord,

J'ay l'honneur de vous écrire pour vous remercier des livres que vous m'avez envoié . . . J'ay devouré l'histoire de "Mr Chime" [?], les deux derniers volumes me paroissent un chef d'oeuvre. Je les trouve même supérieurs aux autres, ce n'est pas que l'auteur les ait plus travaillé, mais c'est que le sujet est bien plus piquant pour les philosophes.... Je me mettray bientot à votre Histoire d'Irlande.... J'ay l'honneur d'être, avec le plus profond respect, votre humble et obeissant serviteur,

Helvetius'

Palmerston's first visit to the Continent clearly whetted his appetite for a further exploration. It was possible to make the full Grand Tour again, and the young Whig aristocrat could afford to neglect his parliamentary duties for higher cultural aims. From June, 1763, he spent the next eighteen months abroad, and laid the foundation of his appreciation of the arts. Before leaving he sent White instructions to keep his political acquaintance sweet:

'I would have Liddell send the pines, as he used to do to Sheen, except that any he may occasionally accommodate my neighbours with, particularly Mr Stanley. As to the other produce of the garden, I should be very desirous that yourself and Mr Norris, and any of my friends, should have any part of it that should be agreeable to them...'[21]

* * *

Much of the lighter relief in the collection of Palmerston papers is provided by the contents of a handsomely bound leather volume in which for many years he noted down current anecdotes, political quips, bawdy stories and contemporary doggerel. There are few famous names whose sallies and misfortunes do not find a place, and in most cases the entries are clearly culled at first-hand. Even these early specimens have the tang of personal experience and were doubtless recounted by his grandfather:

'*An English gentleman, arguing with a Jacobite on political matters, said he had two objections to the Old Pretender's title. The first was that he was not King James's son. "Sir," replied the Jacobite, "you may be assured there is no truth whatever in the reports that were circulated on that subject and that he is really the son of James II." "Why then," replies the other, "that is my second objection and I think it a much stronger one than my first."*

'*In Sir Robert Walpole's time the servants used to have a mock Parliament at a public house at Westminster, where they used to debate while their masters were sitting in the House of Commons. One night, about the time Sir Robert grew to be hard pressed, he asked his man how such a particular question went in their House. "Oh sir," says the footman, "it went against us, though I believe we should have carried it if the Scotch Members had had servants."*

'*Towards the end of Sir Robert Walpole's Administration, Lord Bathurst, who was in violent opposition, came one evening to Lady Thanet and told her, with much joy, that he had got Sir Robert Walpole's head in his pocket (meaning certain papers which he thought would be a ground of impeachment). She answered, "If so my Lord, the best thing you can do is to put it on your own shoulders."*

'*The late King, travelling through Holland, heard a dispute between some of his attendants and the master of a house where he had stopped to take some refreshment in his coach and, on asking what was the matter, was told that the man asked a most extravagant price for some eggs the King had had. On which, he turned to the man who stood by and asked him whether eggs were very scarce in Holland. "No sir," replied the man, "but Kings are."*

'*Upon the King's marriage, when the University of Oxford came to present their address, the Vice-Chancellor, by mistake, offered to kiss Lady S. Bunbury's hand – one of the bridesmaids – instead of the Queen's. The King had been much in love with Lady Sarah, even so as to have had once thoughts of marrying her. Upon which, George Selwyn observed it was no great wonder the Vice-Chancellor of Oxford should mistake the Pretender for the Queen.*

'*One night after Quin had been acting Cato, Rich desired him to go on the stage to make an apology for Signora Campioni, a dancer, who was to have performed after the play. Quin was highly offended and refused. Rich insisted. At last, Quin consented upon condition he might use his own words, which were these: "Ladies and Gentlemen, the manager has insisted on my coming here to inform you that Signora Campioni is unable to dance tonight, having had the mis-*

B

fortune of spraining her ankle – I wish she had broke her neck, by God."

'Colley Cibber carried a play to Quin to ask his advice about bringing it on the stage. Quin, who saw it was a bad one, advised him to keep it. Cibber, who did not relish the advice, asked him how long he would have him keep it and, repeating his question very often, at length Quin said, in a passion, "Why, keep it till the Day of Judgment and then you and your play may be damned together."'

REFERENCES

1. H.37 vol. VI, page 222
2. H.15 20.V.1776
3. H.20 vol. I, page 107
4. H.27 vol. I, page 531
5. F.2
6. F.6
7. H.1
8. F.5(b)
9. F.5(a)
10. A.4
11. A.5
12. F.5(a)
13. A.5
14. G.12
15. C.12
16. C.12 26.III.1761
17. C.17(a) 17.X.1761
18. C.3
19. C.12
20. C.17(a)
21. C.12 26.VI.1763

CHAPTER II

THE GRAND TOUR

The embryo art connoisseur – encounter in Paris with John Wilkes – Madame Geoffrin – guest of Voltaire – news of London from Lady Charlotte Burgoyne and Mrs Howe – travels in Italy with Lord and Lady Spencer – his admiration for the antique – the Temple of Paestum and Angelica Kauffmann – joins the Duke of York's suite at Venice – patron of Gavin Hamilton – acceptance into the great London houses – American affairs in the Commons – elected to Dilettanti Society – appointed to the Board of Trade and Plantations in Rockingham administration – member of Board of Admiralty under Chatham

WITH his membership of Parliament and a respectable fortune, Palmerston, still lacked one qualification before taking his rightful place in the ruling class of the golden age. Foreign travel, the ability to converse in continental languages and personal knowledge of the wonders of the antique world provided the basis for a reputation as a man of culture, and circumstances had so far deprived him of these qualities.

The world of fashionable society and politics had been opened to him. In addition to Mrs Howe, he was welcome in the houses of Lady Charlotte Burgoyne, the daughter of the Earl of Derby who had eloped with the future victim of the Battle of Saratoga, and Mrs Greville, the Frances Macartney who had eloped with Fulke Greville. Palmerston was already an accepted younger member of the Whig faction. The Grand Tour would finally establish him as a man of taste and promise. His second continental journey followed the classic route through France to Switzerland, over the Alps to Rome and Naples, through the towns of Northern Italy, and ended with a circuit of the French provinces, the whole lasting from July, 1763, until the end of November the following year. On the outward journey he painted a sorry picture of Antwerp:

'. . . This town was once in possession of the greatest trade of any town in Europe and famous for the number and wealth of its inhabitants. The civil wars, which laid waste the country for so many years, gave the first blow to its greatness, but its ruin was completed by the Dutch, who, when they had established their republic and possessed themselves of the islands which command the mouth of the Scheldt, resolved to ruin Antwerp, which they effected by prohibiting any trading vessels from coming up the river. It has now no trade, its Exchange covered with grass, and not above a fourth part of the number of its former inhabitants . . .'[1]

He renewed his acquaintances in Paris in August, 1763, and made many fresh ones, although one encounter proved an embarrassment. John Wilkes, the impassioned radical and fellow M.P., whose scurrilous tirades in the *North Briton* had earned him temporary incarceration in the Tower of London during the first week of the preceding May, was also visiting the French capital. The two men met in the street, and were walking in brief conversation when Wilkes was accosted by one Forbes, a Scotsman in the French army, who challenged him to a duel for insulting his country in print. Forbes could find no seconds, but the affair caused a minor scandal. Palmerston must have sent an exculpatory letter to his mother, who passed on his explanation to a relation, William Godschall, of Weston:

'. . . I suppose you observed that Wilkes begun the account he gave of the challenge he received at Paris by saying that he and Lord Palmerston were walking together to Notre Dame when Forbes stopped him. I wrote my Lord word I was mortified at seeing their names together: he answered me that he was not pleased with it, their acquaintance being the slightest that is possible; and that it was quite owing to their being bound to the same place that they were together then; which they had not been above three minutes, when Forbes stopped Wilkes...'[2]

Paris provided the anecdote book with three spirited entries:

'*An actress at Paris, remarkable for not being very orthodox in her amours, asked Mlle Arnaud how she managed so ill as to be continually with child. Mlle Arnaud replied, "Ah! Madame, un pauvre souris qui n'a qu'un trou est bientot pris.*"

'*A great lady at Paris, having bought some of Mlle du Thé's furniture at her auction, was complaining how dear she had been found to pay for it. Upon which, Mlle Arnaud observed that probably she would have been glad to have had the things for the same price they cost Mlle du Thé.*

'*Madame Geoffrin used to say one should never give advice to those who wanted it.*'

Madame Geoffrin also provided him with a coquettish letter of introduction which, from its contents and his subsequent visit to the idol of the age, may have referred to Voltaire:

'Voilà mon cher mylord, une lettre qui vous servira *de passe par tous*. L'Homme à qui elle est adressée a beaucoup d'esprit, et est très aimable et très estimable. Il est un des plus considerables de la République par son mérite, et par sa fortune. Il est mon ancien ami, je lui dis que vous êtes mon coquin, mon vaurien et enfin tous ce qu'il y a de pis. Il vous traitera en conséquence. Si il est à la campagne, je vous conseille d'aller l'y trouver, il le trouvera bon. Je le lui mande.

Je vous assure mon aimable vaurien que je suit bien fâchée de votre départ.'[3]

Arriving in Switzerland at the end of August he found awaiting him a welcome budget of London gossip from Lady Charlotte Burgoyne:

'Her Majesty is so perfectly recovered that our enquiries after her health ceased last Sunday. St James's has been a most admirable coffee house, where everything resorted that was in town and as the hours from seven to nine suited me extremely I used to go almost every night, and am really sorry it is at an end. What little amour was going forward one might see there, and indeed, Lady B[olin]g[bro]ke and Lord G[owe]r afford the town no little conversation; that connection was begun before you left England, and it goes on finely. I cannot feel sorry for Lord B—g—ke, he deserves to be ornamented, and I am only sorry it is not Lord C[o]v[entr]y that does him so great a favour . . . The Duchess of Ancaster has finished herself the most complete figure of affectation and absurdity I ever saw. She now can scarcely walk without shaking off her head, and as to her rouge, it is as deep coloured and as thick laid on as e'er a Duchess in France . . .

'Is it not strange that we must be so very fond of the French fashions that we must even imbibe their vices. I verily believe, in a very little time, we shall be as remarkable for gallantry as they are. You see how much we improve by our connection with that nation. Though I love the French very well and like to live among them I own I am quite angry at our nobility spending so much money in the kingdom. We shall very soon enrich them and are absolutely furnishing them with arms against ourselves, for depend upon it as soon as ever they get up a little again, they will find a pretence for more quarrels and I expect war again in two or three years, which touches me so nearly that I own I hate to hear of so many English people being in France. I dread the consequences. . . .

'Very anxious everybody here is to know who is to succeed Egremont [Joint Secretary of State under Bute and Grenville]. His sudden death, I suppose, would not at all surprise you, for he was the sort of man to expect it from . . . Mr Pitt I hear has behaved very insolently to His Majesty and has determined not to accept the post of Secretary of State, without every man that voted for the peace was turned out. In short, I am sorry to find he holds himself up in that manner. Sure he has no pretensions. I wish it was amicably settled.'[4]

In the draft of a letter to an unidentified correspondent, Palmerston showed that he was finding Switzerland very much to his taste, and also revealed that his reading had included the works of Jean-Jacques Rousseau:

'Among the common people the men seem to be tall and strong and the women handsome. I observe that in general handsome women are to be found where there are tall, stout men. I wonder how it happens; do you think it is by accident or choice? The people here seem to have little amusement but much enjoyment. Their labour is a pleasure to them because what they cultivate is their own. The laws are severe but then they have the comfort of making them so themselves and the man who is to be hanged for breaking them has the satisfaction of knowing that it is by his own authority.

'The town of Vevey, where I am at present, is beautifully situated on the edge of the Lake of Geneva. . . . But what interests and pleases me more than the scenery is the charming simplicity of manners that prevails in this town. I came here unknown, without recommendations, and only one servant and I am treated everywhere as if I was among my oldest and most intimate friends. The instant it was known that I meant to make a stay and wished to associate with the inhabitants I was invited into all their societies, where I go with the utmost freedom and am listened to and admired by persons of more sense and knowledge than myself. The golden age still exists among these good people to whom the feelings of humanity are a stronger recommendation than titles, riches or relationship in other countries. I have met with more worthy, respectable people in this town, which consists of about 3,000 inhabitants, than one should find in half the province towns in France . . .'[5]

In Geneva he composed himself to a long account of his impressions to date, in a letter to Mrs Howe:

'Very soon after I had last the pleasure of seeing you, I went over to Holland, where I stayed near a month. This country answered the general notion I had formed of it, that it was more curious than agreeable. If one considers what the condition of this country was when it first became a refuge from Austrian tyranny, we may at least draw this conclusion, that no hardships are so terrible as a state of oppression and, by considering its present state, we may see that there is no country so miserable but what by the amazing effects of persevering and industry may become at least comfortable. I fear the present inhabitants have degenerated to an uncommon degree from the virtues of their ancestors; the desire of gain seems to have destroyed all public spirit among the superior ranks of people and the lower classes seem to value liberty only as it gives a sanction to insolence and extortion. In short, this Republic appears not likely ever to make a figure again in history . . .

'At Paris I met with an amazing number of English and but

few French, it being just the time when everybody who ever does leave the town was absent. After staying there about a fortnight, I set out for Basle in Switzerland. This is a country I have long entertained a high opinion of and wished much to see; and, indeed, what can be more interesting to an Englishman than a country whose very peasants, without discipline, without generals, and almost without arms, had resolution enough to resist the usurpations of tyranny, and who, after many noble struggles, at length established that system of liberty, which still subsists and is likely to continue because the same spirit continues to preserve it . . .

'I dined yesterday with Voltaire, who lives about four miles from hence, upon the French territory. He is just now 70 complete. He seems feeble and complains of continual pains in his head, but, notwithstanding, seems to have lost nothing of his spirits or intellects and still continues to act his own pieces upon his own stage . . . . He received us with much politeness and attention.'[6]

Voltaire thought well enough of his visitor to invite him to stay at Ferney, an honour he failed to confer the following year on a visitor of smaller fortune and greater pretensions, James Boswell. Palmerston's description of the visit exists only in a draft copy, as indeed do several of the letters at this time, and in this case he gives no hint of the name of his correspondent:

'I passed a day with the celebrated physician and philosopher Haller and had a conversation of some hours on philosophical subjects with him and half a dozen persons of the country, who seemed surprised to hear a young man talk seriously. But notwithstanding their attention and commendation, I could not help feeling sometimes mortified at my own ignorance and thinking that there is a kind of superiority which books give one better than horses.

'I am now settled at Voltaire's house and am regretting the time I wasted in the neighbourhood before I came here. My recommendations to him were such, and from such quarters, as could not fail to procure me civilities, but I believe the real friendliness and cordiality of my reception proceeds from his considering me as your friend and he shows me part of the attention he wishes to show you. He remembers every circumstance relating to you as if he had seen you yesterday, and he loves you as if he saw you still . . . You have no idea of the expense Voltaire is at here and what good he does. He is at once the king and the father of the country where he resides. He makes everybody about him happy and is as good a master of a family as he is a poet. His conversation is enchanting. If he was divided in two, and one had to choose between the man one has read and the man one hears, I should be at a loss. His editors may publish his books as often as they please, but his own edition will always be the best. Madame Denis, his neice, is here and Madame Dupui, the granddaughter of Corneille, of whom you have heard so much. The first seems to have a great deal of natural goodness and of the sort that one loves; the other is one of those common figures and characters, of whom the less is said the better. His house is charming and beautifully situated, with a most magnificent prospect . . . I have been to Geneva, which is a large melancholy town, inhabited by people who don't want understanding or money, and yet seem to make no use of either. I saw nothing pretty there, but the women have a dismal time of it and are as tired as the dead and yet they deserve that somebody should help them to a little amusement. I send you a little sketch I made of Voltaire while he was losing in a game of chess. It is very incorrect because it was done in a hurry by candlelight and through all the diabolical faces which he never fails to make when he knows anybody is drawing his picture, but I think I have hit off his general character, which is the most essential . . . You have no notion how amiable the old man is in private and if he was not one of the greatest geniuses, he would be one of the best preachers in the world. I have seen him receive English, French, Italian and German travellers who all found him equally well acquainted with their country and its literature. His genius is too great to be contained within the limits of his own nation, it belongs to the whole earth. I believe he received from heaven the gift of languages and the knowledge of folio vols, for it is impossible to conceive when he could find time to learn the first, or read the last . . .'[7]

The great philosopher also provided two entries for the anecdote book:

'*Voltaire and Piron were rivals in literature. One day Voltaire asked Piron how he liked his new play; to which Piron answered, "You would have been very glad if I had written it".*'

'*A gentleman at Voltaire's, paying high compliments to Madame Denis on her performance of Zaïre, she modestly said she could not be entitled to them as it was necessary to be young and handsome to succeed in such a part as that. To which the gentleman, with great eagerness and simplicity, replied, "Indeed, Madame, I cannot admit your rule, as you are yourself a striking proof to the contrary".*'

When he returned to England, Palmerston sent Voltaire a book in recognition of his hospitality and received this gratifying acknowledgement, which somewhat nullifies Voltaire's comment in later life that he had been visited by four hundred Englishmen, all of whom forgot him on their return home:

'Milord,

J'ai reçu le petit livre dont vous avez eu la bonté de me favoriser. Ce que j'en ai déjà parcouru me parait porter le caractère de la verité, ce qui est une chose assez rare en livres comme en hommes.

Je suis très sensible au présent que vous me faites; et je l'étais encore d'avantage à votre mérite, quand vous me fesiez quelquefois l'honneur de venir dans ma retraite. Je ne perdrai jamais le souvenir des heures que j'ai passé avec vous.

J'ai l'honneur d'être, avec les sentiments les plus respectueux, Milord,

Votre très humble et très obéissant serviteur,

Voltaire'[8]

Many of the entries in the copious travelling journals that Palmerston kept are bald, factual descriptions of the countryside and towns through which he passed. Occasionally he noted some of the more unusual experiences to which a traveller was subjected in those days. His passage of the Alps in October, 1763, was a most complicated enterprise:

'At Lanslbourg you are at the foot of Mount Cenis and here

you make preparations for passing it. If you have a carriage, it is taken to pieces and carried upon mules. You may ride upon a mule up to the top and over the plain and be carried down by chairmen, or you may be carried the whole way. From Lansl-bourg you ascend two miles to a place called Ramasse (from which place, when the ground is covered with snow, you may descend to Lanslbourg on a kind of sledge in about ten minutes). Here you enter upon a kind of plain, or valley, between the mountains, which reaches about four miles to La Grande Croix, which divides Savoy and Piedmont . . . From La Grande Croix begins a descent of about four miles to Novalese, which is more steep and difficult than that on the side of Lanslbourg, but without the least danger on either side. We found the passage quite free from any snow and, the weather being very fine, were rather troubled with heat than cold.'[9]

Thereafter his notes on Turin, Milan, Genoa and Florence are largely paraphrases of the guide-books of the time, but the beauties of the buildings and art collections laid a firm founda-tion of taste in such matters in his mind. On his arrival in Rome at the end of the year he found awaiting him some crisp comments from Lady Charlotte Burgoyne:

'I shall be glad to hear how you like the Italian society, though I think, in general, it is very agreeable to most men. To me it was detestable. The turn of all women in that country is gallantry, and if one is so unfashionable as to have some notions of honour and virtue one has but a bad chance of passing one's time the least agreeably. I have no idea how anybody can live in Italy that does not give themselves wholly to passion . . .

'You have perfectly cleared yourself with me in regard to having an intimacy with, or friendship for, Mr W.[ilkes]. Indeed, I was persuaded before I had it under your hand, that you could have no connection with so vile a man . . . I am not surprised at Mr W. industriously endeavouring to make the world believe he has some acquaintance who may do him credit in the world, but it shall not avail him when it is in my power to contradict it. I hate the very name of Wilkes, and will not let him employ more of my time at present, nor will I ever mention him unless to say he has been made an example of, which I hope soon to hear of . . .'[10]

Mrs Howe sent a more factual account of his late Paris companion's vicissitudes:

'On the 15th, [of November, 1763] the day the Parliament met, the House was fuller of members than has been known since Lord Orford's time; as soon as they were returned from the Lords, Mr Grenville and Mr Wilkes both begun to speak at the same instant. The first to deliver a message from the King, the other to complain of a breach of privilege . . . Lord North spoke long upon this subject and with great abuse of no: 45 of the *North Briton*. Much debate upon particular words used by him. Wilkes objected to the epithet false, Mr Pitt to that of treasonable. Wilkes took an opportunity to desire leave to waive his privilege that he might be tried by common law. They sat till past 2 and then, having determined that the thanks of the House should be given to the King for his gracious message, they were obliged to defer going upon the breach of privilege. Wilkes' duel with Martin of the Treasury for abuse on the *North Briton*, was the next day, and on that day the address passed without a Division. Wilkes was badly wounded in the body, but is now thought out of danger . . .'[11]

At the end of January, 1764, Lady Charlotte wrote to him again, with a detailed report of the marriage to King George III's sister of the Duke of Brunswick, Frederick the Great's 'Golden Boy' in the Seven Years War, who was to fall, more than forty years later, on the field of Auerstädt:

'His Serene Highness arrived the 13th and his first appearance was at Court on Sunday, the 15th, where you may imagine there was a very great crowd, but as the wedding was to be the next day, and we peers' daughters were admitted to see it, I saved myself a little and did not go to Court on Sunday, as such and such ranks only were admitted, I concluded it would be conducted with some degree of decency and regularity, *mais point du tout*, all was confusion, push as push could. As Lady Di Clavering went with me, we got excellent places. She is a most charming one in a crowd and puts on the best face in the world when she plants herself before a Countess, a thing I could not have done for my life, if I had been even sure that no other method would have procured me a sight of the Prince. The ceremony was performed in the great drawing room, and when the King and Queen came into the room with their attendants, I really thought we should have been suffocated. After the first squeeze we did pretty well, and I must own the Lords were all very polite and good-humoured in making themselves as little inconvenient as possible, and we were close behind the Archbishop, and saw the Prince and Princess very tolerably well. But to be sure, I never repented anything more in my life than the going there. For none of the Royal Family stayed to speak to any of the company, and as to hearing the old mumbling Archbishop of Canterbury repeat the marriage ceremony, it was by no means what I went for . . .

'Saturday was fixed on for their going to the Opera and as the whole Royal Family were to be seen at once, I prevailed with my sister, Mary, to go, as the best opportunity to see the Hereditary. I had likewise promised my daughter an opera and no time, alas! I thought so clever as the present one, when so much was to be seen at once. We dined at three, and I, in my chair, Lady Mary, Mrs Palmer and Charlotte in the coach, sallied forth at five minutes before five, by way of choosing our places. I no sooner got to the Haymarket than I found it full of coaches and chairs and noisier than you can imagine.

'On Tuesday, there was a drawing room at Leicester House, but as everybody passed quite through (as we used to do when the King was Prince of Wales on his birthday), it was without crowd or fatigue. We were presented to the Hereditary Princess by way of taking leave. A-side of her stood her Prince and then the young Princes. At night there was a subscription ball at Carlisle House for the Hereditary Prince, which was very elegant and full of the best company in London . . . There remains only to give you my own private opinion of him. The general one is that he is handsome, has a fine figure, is very genteel and adored for his military character. My own is, that he has a lively eye, a good countenance, but not a good-natured look. He is fair, his person genteel, and though he stoops a little in the shoulders, has a great deal of grace and

looks like a man of fashion. He seemed very lively whilst he
was dancing with the Duchess of Grafton, and when he is
animated, has not that ill-natured look that I fancy I saw in
him at times. He speaks very handsomely of the Princess, I
hear, and therefore I hope they will be full as happy as Princes
and Princesses ever are . . .'[12]

Mrs Howe, who sent him full accounts of the parliamentary
debates on the Wilkes case, had this consolation for him:

'Setting aside political rage, London does not shine this
winter. The opera singers are bad and Mr Garrick's absence
from Drury Lane much to be regretted. No Northumberland
House, nor indeed anything to make you lament your being
out of England, but rather to rejoice that it happened this
year . . .'[13]

She received, in reply, an account dated March 23, 1764, of
Palmerston's excited reactions to the glories of the antique
world. In Italy he had joined the party of Lord and Lady
Spencer, parents of the future Duchess of Devonshire, and
visited most of the Italian cities in their company. The Greek
Temple at Paestum had only just been rediscovered, and
Palmerston's description is, in fact, one of the first records at
the time. So impressed was he with this ruin that when he sat
for his portrait to Angelica Kauffmann while in Rome, he had
himself depicted holding a plan of the Temple:

'I stayed at Naples till the beginning of this month, which
was longer than I intended, but I was tempted to it by the
agreeableness of our society and by the constant amusement
which the place afforded . . .

'We had fine weather and had it not been for one unfortunate
circumstance, our party would have been complete. This was
Lord Spencer being ill the whole time. It is a thousand pities
he has not a better constitution, he seems to be a man whose
value few people know. The bright side of his character appears
in private and the dark side in public; nobody would wish to
change this for its opposite, to which, however, many owe their
high reputation. It were only to be wished that the bright side
were a little more visible; for of the many who see Lord Spencer,
it is only the few who live in intimacy with him who know that

he has an understanding and a heart that might do credit to any man ...

... One of the principal [excursions] I had the pleasure of making in the company of Lord and Lady Spencer ... was to visit the ruins of a very ancient town called Paestum, and now Pesti, about sixty miles from Naples ... I was more struck with them than with anything I ever saw except the first view of Rome. They stand quite solitary upon a deserted plain by the seashore at the bottom of a large bay. Behind them runs the chain of the Apennines. The remains consist of the walls, which are pretty entire, one of the gateways, many foundations of old buildings, and three large public edifices with all their outer columns, with which they were entirely surrounded, and many of the inner ones and the whole entablature standing. The largest has above seventy columns of the doric order of a short and inelegant proportion, which however gives an air of grandeur and solidity and is a proof of their great antiquity. These buildings are the more curious because there are no others of that form with porticos on every side remaining in Italy except we reckon Sicily, where there are some of the same kind, but not so well preserved. The circumstance which often takes away half the pleasure of seeing the remains of old buildings is the number of modern ones which generally surround them, often join them and are often built upon them. When one sees fine corinthian pillars in a narrow dirty street serve to ornament a pigsty, or half an ugly Gothic church tacked to half an old temple, the effect of the scene is destroyed and one loses that enthusiasm which is the pleasantest companion one can carry with one to these spots. There is no mixture of this kind at Paestum and nothing but here and there a solitary cottage appears near the ruins. When one comes into the plain one is struck with the idea of Palmyra, Baalbek or some of those forsaken places; and the scene brought to my mind the answer of a Frenchman as related by Marmontel, who having been among some celebrated ruins and being asked what inhabitants he had found there, replied: *"Je n'ai trouvé que le temps, qui démolissait en silence"* ... Paestum is most famous among the poets for its roses and we found ruins and the space between

them and the sea even now covered with rose trees and
myrtles, which in that part of Italy really grow like the furze
bushes on our commons . . .

'During the latter part of my stay at Naples, that city was
afflicted with an excessive scarcity of corn, which likewise
prevails in a smaller degree in most parts of Italy. But at Naples
and the adjacent country, it was really terrible and we had before
our eyes a scene that really came up to the poetical descriptions of famine. The Neapolitans are not a patient people and
it was as much as the troops could do to prevent insurrections.
Numerous parties of them were constantly posted at the bakers
shops, which, without that precaution, would have been pulled
down. Not a day passed without disturbance and skirmishes
and many were wounded and some killed on both sides. They
have received some supplies, which have restored a little quiet
for the present.

'I am now settled at Rome and regularly going the round of
antiquity. It is deplorable to see what havoc has been made by
barbarians and bigots. Little has escaped but what by its vast
solidity has withstood their efforts, or by being converted to
some use has served the purposes of avarice. One is struck with
astonishment when one considers from the size of the frag-
ments that remain and the nicety of the workmanship, what
those buildings must have been.

'I never had any idea till I came here what a good statue was,
or what effect it was capable of producing. It is grievous to
think what treasures of sculpture are still concealed in the earth,
which, notwithstanding all that has been dug up, is not half
examined even in the most likely places, such as the Palatine
Hill, where the Emperor's palace was placed. Every discourage-
ment is thrown in the way of those who would search, even so
much that no man can dig to any considerable depth in his own
ground without a licence . . .'14

Hans Stanley already trusted Palmerston's taste in the pictorial
arts. Earlier in the year he had written him: 'If you should meet
with a portrait or two of Paul Veronese perfectly fresh and
well coloured I wish you would buy them for me – I leave the
price to you . . .'15

He followed this in May with a splendid piece of London tittle-tattle. Lady Susan Fox-Strangways, daughter of the Earl of Ilchester, had eloped with a handsome, young Irish actor, William O'Brien:

'Lady Susan O'Brien's elopement broke upon us like a thunderstorm, but was not it seems so unexpected to her own family; he grew in this fair maid's favour, and she in his, by acting plays at Holland House, not undiscerned however by the father, who after forbidding all future commerce, had the ill-judged and unfortunate indulgence of consenting to a solemn taking of leave between them. The lover here received a bracelet set with diamonds and her picture in a gold snuff box, more than once theatrically half exhibited, and rapped upon in the green room. These presents were soon followed by the gift of her hand at Covent Garden Church, contrived by what can scarce be called a stratagem, if we consider the very great liberty which young ladies unmarried enjoy in England. The peroration of that sage person Sir Blake Delaval is most worthy of note. Seeing her in tears (wherein she has been most copious), he addressed her thus, "Madam, you have quarrelled with your father and your mother, I advise you not to disgust your husband, who is a pretty fellow, and whom you ought to make the most of". Her cousin Charles Fox had entertained a sort of schoolboy's passion for her, she told him he was too young and gave him a sealed paper containing the name of the person whom she should marry, on promise of never opening it without her leave. This had been two years in his hands, when upon her marriage she sent him word that he might open it. He found therein the name which she has chosen to bear. *Caetera desiderantur*, but will be much better supplied by your female correspondents . . .

'All this neighbourhood are well, and celebrate Lord Palmerston in their potations. Col. Clavering and Lady Di have taken Grove Place. As you probably are acquainted with them I need not say they will be a very good addition to the society of this county . . .'[16]

A note in Palmerston's travel journal on his arrival in Venice at the end of May, 1764, confirms the obvious deduction to be drawn from his copious entries, that he travelled armed with all the available guide books and other travellers' accounts of the time:

'For the remarkable objects, see Keysler, Cochin or Wright. For the Politics and Constitution [of Venice], see Amelot de la Houssaye,'[17] he says. The works in question were Keysler on Germany, Cochin's *Voyage d'Italie* and Edward Wright's *Some Observations . . . France, Italy, etc.*

While there he was accepted into the suite of the Duke of York, brother of George III, whose tour of the Italian states had included an audience with the Pope. Palmerston sent an account of their progress to Mrs Howe:

'I arrived here at Venice a few days before the Duke of York, for whose reception I found everything preparing in the most splendid manner. The Venetians were determined to treat him in no other light than as the King's brother and for that reason put themselves to an immense expense. As to ceremonious dinners, suppers, balls, assemblies, with the long etc. etc. of princely amusements, they are much the same in all countries, with the accidental difference of being, from particular circumstances, more or less disagreeable. All those to which I have the honour of attending His Royal Highness have been so, to so great a degree, that I will attempt no description of them, but by desiring you to imagine the greatest possible misery that a formal dinner or ball can bring with it, and you will then have some idea of what one may suffer when a state is determined to exert itself to the utmost. It is very fortunate that the Duke is not of the same opinion, as his whole time and thoughts seem employed on these objects. However, the Venetians gave one entertainment which is peculiar to Venice and which, for show, exceeds anything I ever saw. This is called regatta, which means no more than a boat race. The magnificence of it consists in the multitude of the spectators and the magnificence of the vessels belonging to the noble Venetians, with which the canals are crowded, and which are so much beyond what can be seen in any other place that I can give no idea of them, but from the description of romance, or the account of Cleopatra's galley in Dryden. The Venetian State has a peculiar facility in entertain-

ing princes beyond any other, because it is a constant maxim
with them to impoverish their rich nobles; therefore, whenever
anything is to be done, which in other countries would be a
public expense, their government, though in a republican form,
being one of the most arbitrary in Europe, they select out a
certain number of nobility, who are obliged to do it out of their
own private fortunes. This has been practiced now. Four nobles
were deputed to receive and attend upon the Duke of York,
and in short to entertain him during his whole stay at their
own expense. He was there three weeks, and in that time they
must have spent three or four thousand pounds each. They
were chosen probably more on account of their wealth than
any other circumstance and, therefore, though their expense
was so very great, they did not, in their own persons, do the
honours of it with dignity and the Duke did not take pains
enough to show them civility, which he ought to have done,
though I confess it required some command of temper, as they
were ignorant and silly and their attendance was often very
troublesome and oppressive . . .'[18]

In a letter to his agent, John White, Palmerston added:
'Our party . . . were the Duke of York, Colonel St John, Sir
William Boothby, Mr Murray, Lord Ossory, Mr Beauclerk,
Mr Turton and myself . . .'[19]

The Spencers had, in the meantime, made their way home
through Austria and Germany, and a letter from Mr Arden,
their travelling companion, from Spa showed that he too had
found the noble Lord something of a trial:

'I sit down with great satisfaction to tell you that our journey
is over and we are all well after it at this place. . . . If you ask
me really whether I had a great deal of pleasure in it I must be
forced to answer in the negative. Lord S's unhappy disposition
to look always on the worst side of things, and if he does not
find a subject for fretting to make one, rendered both himself
and his company insensible to much of the satisfaction which
the circumstances of our journey might have occasioned to
us . . . I have endeavoured during the journey to be as good a
cicisbeo as I could to Lady S. in hopes of gaining some advantage over your Lordship in your absence, but I fear not with

much success. 'Tis true, she has now and then condescended to drink a glass of claret with me, but that has been often to your good health. So all the comfort I have is that I am not the first poor man who has suffered by the introduction of a person of more merit than himself . . .'[20]

By September Palmerston had embarked on his return journey, noting *en passant:*

'The Valais is a fine country to the eye and very fertile. The people have the government chiefly in their own hands and there is no country where a traveller is worse used or more imposed on, or where he can have less redress.

'Marseilles is now a large populous trading town, well built and handsome . . . The French galleys are laid up here, which are very little used as such. As many of the slaves as can practise any trade to get a livelihood are permitted to be all day on shore, in little huts, but always have a heavy chain and are forced to return to their galley at night.'

On a visit to the mausoleum at St Remy he named another of the guide books on which he relied:

'These antiquities are engraved in Montfaucon Supplement, Vol. 4, Chapter 4.'[21]

Lady Charlotte Burgoyne continued to ensure that none of the more piquant details of the London scene escaped his knowledge: 'It was reported when I first came to town that the Duke and Duchess of Grafton were going to part. Various were the conjectures, and as I shall not, I am persuaded, propagate scandal by telling you some of them, I shall go on to give the world's reasons. First that his Grace declared the child she lay in of last was not his. Then that her temper was so bad he cannot dispense with it, and her Grace makes the same objection to his temper. I believe there can be no dispute that the Duke has taken Nancy Parsons into keeping, and that there has long been disagreements between him and his Duchess, and if her temper is not of the most gentle kind, it is not very probably she could submit to such treatment. Some people still believe they will not entirely separate. She is at present at her father's and perhaps things may be accommodated so as to live under the same roof. It is a pity they should not on their

children's account, and it would have a much better appearance
to the world . . .

'The poor Duke of Devonshire died at Spa, where he was
sent to recover from the palsy, and by all accounts it was what
hastened his death. He is a great loss to the world in general
and particularly to his party. He has left one daughter and three
sons. The daughter is to have £30,000 and the two younger
sons £3,000 per annum. What the present Duke's estate will
be, no-one can tell, I suppose, exactly, but they say at least
£18,000 per annum from the Burlingtons and his paternal one,
I believe, is equal to it. Think then what it will come to during
a minority of six or seven years.'[22]

★ ★ ★

Palmerston was much more than an eighteenth century fore-
runner of the despised guide-book tourist. He had the means
and the taste to develop a practical interest in the arts. His first
acquisitions date from this period and he described the mental
processes which led to them in a letter to Mrs Howe:

'The great remains of antiquity (at Rome) such as the
Pantheon, Coliseum, etc., are what naturally attracts one's
admiration first, and their effect depends upon the disposition
of the mind and not upon any particular skill or practice in the
arts. On the contrary, a person not much versed in sculpture or
painting, receives at first but a small degree of pleasure from
pictures and statues compared with what they afterwards give
him when his taste is formed and his eye has acquired by
practice the faculty of readily distinguishing beauties and defects.
Sculpture, though not a more easy art than painting, if one may
judge by the very small number who have attained any great
degree of merit in it, yet is a more natural and simple one. For
this reason the ancient sculpture at Rome generally has its turn
of admiration sooner than the works of the great painters,
many of whose beauties are so obscured by time and others
originally of such a nature as to be quite imperceptible to an
unpracticed eye. It is a new creation that seems to be opened,
and one seems to acquire a new sense to enjoy it. But this
requires more time and application than I could bestow,

therefore you may imagine that what gave me the greatest pleasure were the ancient marbles. Besides their merit, they had the charm of novelty to recommend them. I have seen, before I came to Italy, pictures almost as good as those at Rome, but I never saw a statue worth looking at till I crossed the Alps, or which gave me the least idea of the powers of the art. I believe that in the real comforts and conveniences of life we surpass the ancients and we have many admirable inventions of which they were totally ignorant. But certainly in the arts which they practised and in all the magnificence of luxury, we have nothing to do but wonder and submit . . .'[23]

His enthusiasms were fostered by Gavin Hamilton, a Scottish portraitist of no great talent, who had been settled in Rome for a dozen years and made a very comfortable living out of foisting antique marbles excavated from various Roman sites in Italy on to such avid and budding connoisseurs as young Palmerston. Hamilton had no qualms about 'restoring' his finds, with a nose on a head or a head on a torso to meet the requirements of his clients, who seem to have preferred a botched reconstruction to a mutilated fragment, however indubitable the authenticity.

Palmerston was no exception and during the period he spent in Rome he acquired the collection of marbles and sculpture which still decorates the somewhat chilling entrance hall to Broadlands two hundred years later. For these he paid in 1764 a total of £525, together with a further £55 for unspecified seals, bronzes and casts. He left orders with Hamilton, for which he paid a further £180 during the two subsequent years. He also commissioned Angelica Kauffmann to make a copy of Barocci's Holy Family and Bottani to paint Guercino's Dido in the Spada Palace. Gavin Hamilton was employed as his agent in these transactions, as well as for his colleague Nollekens to model a boy and dolphin, and was himself commissioned to paint the picture of Briseis parting from Achilles which is still at Broadlands.

Hamilton's letters over the next two years exhibit the mixture of effrontery and flattery which enabled him to impose on his patrons:

August 2nd, 1764. 'I have desired Barazzi to send the cameo and intaglio to his own banker and correspondent at Milan, who I hope has by this time safely delivered them to your Lordship. The intaglio don't come so happily as I imagined it would, partly owing to some parts being foreshortened. The drapery is extremely well done, but upon the whole I think he has failed with regard to the dejected character so remarkable in the original. This may be owing to the great diminution in the features of the face, where I suppose it is difficult to preserve those delicate strokes of expression. As to the cameo, I think it one of the sweetest things I ever saw. I was with him a whole forenoon when he gave it the last touches and flatter myself the cameo is not the worse for it. The idea of the head I think a good deal like Guglielmo della Porta's fine statue at St Peter's; as to the stone, it is perfect . . . Cavaceppi has done his best with regard to the marbles, which are now almost finished; the two bronze basso relievos are pretty well advanced and make sweet things . . .

August 2nd, 1765. 'I have the honour to acquaint your Lordship that I have at last concluded a bargain with the Prince Barberini for the fine basso relievo of three bacchante and the triangular altar with three basso relievos on it . . . and heartily congratulate your Lordship in being the possessor of the finest basso relievo in Europe and, as such, I maintain it, it gives me a singular pleasure to think that it falls into the hands of one that has taste to enjoy it, and hope that it won't be placed over a chimney where the smoke may damage it, but rather near the eye, where everybody of refined taste may have an opportunity of doing justice to this exquisite Greek performance . . .

'I should be glad to know what your Lordship thinks of my print of Andromache, bewailing the death of Hector; it is the first of a set of six prints I intend to publish from Homer, and consequently anxious about the success of it . . . The first of these subjects, the Anger of Achilles, I have already painted for the Duke of Bridgwater, but of a size and proportion that would not accompany the rest of my set, so that I intend to paint this subject a second time and have, accordingly begun a sketch – the invention of which, and composition, is entirely different from the former; in short it turns out a favourite composition in so much that I can not help wishing that in place of the Macbeth I was to paint this subject for your Lordship, of the size fixed on for the Macbeth. It is true the work is more extensive and ought to be better paid, but I assure you my Lord that interest is not at all my motive for desiring to have the subject altered, and should be very well contented with £150, which is twenty-five pounds more than agreed on for the Macbeth, or indeed any sum that will be agreeable, so I can have the honour of your Lordship's countenance and protection in a work that I have so much at heart and which, in the end, may prove more a work of honour than interest, from which consideration alone can I hope that your Lordship will forgive me taking so great a liberty . . .

February 10*th*, 1766. 'In case there is any other piece of antiquity at the Barberini Palace that your Lordship would choose to purchase, I beg you would acquaint me soon with your commands, as I am now no longer the only purchaser there. Mr [Colin] Morison and Nollekens have both of them bought marbles and Mr Jenkins has given in a list for the first time, but as I am the oldest purchaser, I shall naturally have the preference. Mr Morison has now in his possession the two famous pictures of C[laude] Lorrain, which I gave up to him, being richer than myself, and in all probability the Barberini collection will soon be dispersed, excepting a few of their most capital pictures, which they still keep up to a very high price. I am still in expectations of having the Magdelene of Guido. I have bought the basso relievo of the Egeia, the sitting figure of the Muse and the sleeping Cupid, for a hundred pounds, and have made this bargain with Morison that if upon the arrival of the above marbles your Lordship should think them dear, he should agree to any discount that your Lordship shall judge reasonable; upon those terms I have bought them, in consideration that your Lordship, having never seen them, trusts entirely to my judgement; the Cupid in particular, I think, the finest boy in all the antique, and, excepting the head, much superior to the boy on the Dolphin; there is a small zoccolo of granite marble which he got made on purpose to correspond to one of your Lordship's granite tables, which he says you bought when in Rome and upon which I imagine it may be placed to advantage. The Muse, he says, your Lordship used to admire when at the Barberini Palace and is, to be sure, one of the sweetest attitudes in the world . . .

April 12th, 1766. 'It gives me great pleasure to hear that my print is likely to meet with success, as a great part of the pleasure of my life depends upon it. I hope soon to be able to get a drawing made from your Lordship's picture of the Anger of Achilles, which is now far advanced and should be glad to know if I could take the liberty to get an elegant frame made for it, as by that means my picture will do me more credit here, and upon its first arrival in England . . .

Undated [*April–July* 1766]. 'It gives me great satisfaction to hear that my print meets with approbation from the public, which will the more encourage me to follow out my plan of six prints from Homer. I have got a companion for it now finished, the Achilles dragging the dead body of Hector, and it has turned out still better than the former, having more force and spirit. As I have not as yet received any money for the sale of my last print, and being now obliged to pay for this plate to print off a sufficient number for sale against next winter, I find myself at present a little put to my shifts for want of ready money, in so much that I have taken the liberty to draw on your Lordship for eighty pounds in part payment for the picture of Briseis, for which I have sent your Lordship my receipt, obliging myself to have the picture finished against the month of November next . . . and shall undertake no other work till that, and my Lucretia, is finished. This last will be done in the month of August. I am quite ashamed of being obliged to trouble you on this occasion, but your Lordship's generosity and goodness to me has made me bold . . .

'My picture of Innocence, which I have finished for the Duke of Rochefoucauld, has done me great honour, this last reason being the best thing that I have yet done. It is some comfort to me that my last picture is esteemed the best. I hope that Briseis will share the same fate. What puzzles me most is the Achilles, to preserve dignity without extravagance in this violent character is no easy task . . .'[24]

It is to be feared that Hamilton's smug satisfaction in his own work was not echoed by contemporary critics. The picture of Andromache bewailing the death of Hector, when shown at the exhibition of the Society of Artists in 1765, was dismissed by Horace Walpole as a 'large piece, very ill-coloured, faulty both in drawing and expression'. Nevertheless, Hamilton did exercise considerable influence, although the value he placed on his restorations has subsequently been completed reversed. The head of Aphrodite he found for Palmerston, who listed it as 'a fragment, damaged', costing only £5, is perhaps the most considerable of the marbles remaining at Broadlands.

On his return to England at the end of 1764 Palmerston was also in correspondence with a fellow collector, Sir William Hamilton, who was to achieve greater fame nearly thirty years later over his acquisition of a flesh and blood beauty. Mr Hamilton, as he still was, had just arrived in Naples with his first wife, to begin his long incumbency as British Minister:

'I am much obliged to you for your kind remembrance of us and for the letter you was so good as to send me; we had indeed a very rough passage and for Mrs Hamilton, to whom the sea was quite a new object, it was dreadful. I found it very unpleasant though I have been more used to it. However, here we are safe in a most delightful climate indeed and now the ceremony of presentations and visitings are over I begin to enjoy the many curiosities of nature and art with which you know this country abounds. I obeyed your commands and have got the drawing of Mausoleum and Triumphal Arch of St Remy from Joli and will send it you the first good opportunity. I am heartily glad you found those ruins as well as I described them, for they pleased me much. When I am more settled and make any new discoveries here I will take the liberty of troubling you with a letter and if there is anything in this part of the world that you think I can serve you in, I hope you will always command me. Mrs Hamilton, (who desires to be kindly remembered to your Lordship) is amazingly recovered since she came here. I am sure this mild climate will re-establish her entirely. I have but just begun to look about me as I was determined to see nothing till I had finished all ceremonials; I admire the bronzes of Herculaneum most exceedingly, and the tour from the point of Micana to Pozzuoli is very classical and entertaining.'[25]

* * *

Palmerston's absence did not appear to have affected his standing as a Member of Parliament. When the House reassembled at the beginning of 1765, American affairs and the imposition of the fatal stamp tax provided the main debate. Palmerston spoke on the subject himself, probably on February 6. The draft of this speech is the only record in his own hand of an intervention in Parliament and for this reason, rather than any intrinsic originality of thought, merits inclusion here. His arguments contain hints of the subsequent Rockingham compromise and a foretaste of Burke's doctrines:

'We have now under our consideration one of those very important points which I think it is a misfortune to a nation to be ever forced to discuss. It is oftentimes so difficult to fix the true and equitable line between the rights of the superior powers on one hand and the claims of liberty on the other, that the attempt generally proves unfortunate. Happy is it for that nation where each are so disposed to keep within bounds as not to make the discussion necessary. When it is once set on foot, happy are those councils where moderation and firmness are so happily tempered as to prevent those bad consequences which are too much to be dreaded.

'As to the general legislative right of Great Britain over her colonies, I believe the most enthusiastic American can hardly be bold enough to dispute it. All such laws as relate to the trade and commerce of the two countries must necessarily be prescribed by the mother country and submitted to by the colonies. But the great question is whether this right of the mother country extends to making internal laws for the policy of her colonies and laying internal taxes? I confess I think it does. I do not conceive how a line of distinction can be drawn between them upon any solid foundation. I think if such a line was attempted it would be always fluctuation backwards and forwards, just as different interests and caprices might prevail in different times. In the next place I think if such a line could be drawn, it would be ruinous and destructive to the interests of both countries. I think it absolutely necessary that such a power should reside in the legislature of Great Britain. I think many cases might happen wherein the exertion of such a power would be absolutely necessary to the very existence of the colonies and to the prosperity of this country so intimately connected with them. Having said this, I must now say that I think this right is founded chiefly upon principles of necessity. I think the frequent exercise of it repugnant to equity and that it is to be reserved only for great emergencies. It does not follow that every right is to be exercised. It does not follow that it is just to exercise it. This, I think, is one of the cases where *summum jus est summa injuria.* Those who impose a tax ought always to be thoroughly informed of the ability, situation and circumstances of the people on whom it is laid to bear it. It is impossible Sir, that the Members of this House in general – it is improbable that even the King's servants – should be so well informed as to be just judges of the proper methods of imposing or proportioning an American internal tax. They cannot see with their own eyes, they are always liable to be, and it is always probable that they will be, misled by the interested or mistaken reports of others. Another very material reason with me why our right of laying taxes on the colonies should be used as sparingly as possible, indeed never but in cases of urgent necessity, is that this right is not built on that solid foundation which alone can induce a free people to submit with cheerfulness to the imposition of taxes. I mean the right of being taxed only by their representatives. No proposition in Euclid appears to me more incontrovertible than that we are not either actually or virtually the representatives of the North American. My idea is that we are the actual representatives of those by whom we are chosen and we are the virtual representatives of all those whose interests are so blended with those of our actual constituents as that no tax can be laid on the one which will not affect the other. We represent the electors who choose us and they represent the rest of Great Britain, so that the whole is linked together and blended in one common interest. Whoever allows this I would leave him to draw his own conclusion with regard to America. How are we, the representatives of a people on whom we lay a tax, professedly in alleviation of the burdens of our own constituents [sentence apparently incomplete]. These are the reasons why I should be against the exertion of this power, except in cases of necessity. The present proposed resolution goes only to an assertion that we have the right in which I agree, and shall give my voice to support it.'[26]

In 1765 Palmerston also started to keep minutely recorded details of his activities in a series of engagement diaries. For the next thirty-seven years it is possible to state precisely how he spent his day, with whom he had dinner and to note to what extent social pleasure took precedence over his public duties. That he was a welcome guest in the great London houses, is testified by the entries for February and March, 1765, alone, when he dined with the Duchess of Ancaster, the Duchess of Marlborough, the Duchess of Bedford, the Spencers, the Speaker and Lord Portland. Also with David Garrick, one of whose closest friends he became. In the later overall diary entry for May 12, 1765, he noted: 'Mr Garrick, Hampton Court dinner, met Mr Charles Townshend and Mr Jepson from Ireland. Garrick, Mr Townshend and Mr Jepson were all excellent mimics and all displayed their talents.' When he was at Broadlands Lady Charlotte Burgoyne kept him informed of affairs in London. In July she sent the welcome news that George III had been obliged to turn again to the great Whig families for his new ministry:

July 11th. 'The new ministry that kissed hands yesterday were the Duke of Grafton and Mr Conway, Secretaries of State; Lord Rockingham, first Lord of the Treasury; Mr Dowdeswell, Chancellor of the Exchequer; Duke of Portland, Lord Chamberlain; Duke of Newcastle, 'tis said and I believe pretty certain, is to be either President of the Council or Privy Seal, and the other for Lord Winchilsea. Lord Barrington, having foreseen the storm early in the day, made his application privately and in person, to the King, declared himself attached to no party, but a faithful servant of his Majesty, that if his employment was necessary for the arrangement, he should quit it with pleasure and be happy to serve in any other station. He is, therefore, to be Secretary at War. Admirals Keppel and Saunders are to come into the Admiralty. The Duke of Richmond to go to Paris and Lord Hertford to Ireland . . .[27]

July 24th. 'The little political news I have heard since I came to Town is now chiefly in the newspapers, except this with regard to Mr Pitt, which you may depend on being true as Mr Shelley tells it everywhere and says it is at Mr Pitt's desire. That he is no way connected with the present Administration, nor does he intend it and that it is very displeasing to him to have hints thrown out everywhere as if he gave his advice. They further add that the Duke of G[rafto]n, went one day to make him a visit and produced some papers which he said he was come to consult him upon and show him the plan on which they purposed acting. That Mr Pitt's answer was that he was always very happy to see his Grace, and had much too great a regard for him to shut his doors to him, but he must excuse him if he shut his lips . . .

July 25th. 'Mr B[urgoyne] has just heard an express has been sent to you to offer you something. From what you wrote, I suppose I may guess at your answer, I wish however that that or anything else might bring you to Town . . .'[28]

But Palmerston had to wait a few months for preferment. In the meantime he continued to savour the provincial pleasures and civic duties of Hampshire, writing dutifully to his mother:

'Southampton is not full of company this year hitherto; last night the Duke of Gloucester arrived and he came at past nine at night and the regular ball would have been tonight, yet he sent on before to desire that he might find a ball ready – which was prepared accordingly. I happened to be at Southampton by chance in the evening, having been out a-sailing all day, so that I was not in dancing trim. I was three days in last week at Winchester for the assizes, to which I was summoned upon the grand jury and as I never had been on such occasion, I thought it proper to go. There was a great meeting of gentlemen, but as there was nobody who took place of me, I was obliged to be foreman of the jury, which just at first seemed awkward; but, as there is no sort of difficulty in the business, it went on very well . . .'[29]

In August and September he set off for a tour of the West Country, savouring again his growing capacity as a patron of the arts. An entry, made later in life in his overall diary, permitted him the privilege of hindsight:

'Chepstow: Here I met with Dean, who afterwards became a landscape painter of some note. He was then a young man unknown, come down to make studies from nature. I carried him on with me in the tour I was making.'[30]

In this instance, Palmerston's patronage was ill-bestowed. He subsequently paid for Dean's journey to Rome, where the painter's marital delinquencies forfeited his patron's esteem.[31]

On his return to Broadlands in October Palmerston received news of his Italian travelling companions from Mr Arden, with an hilarious account of the impact on the hunting field of Palmerston's solicitor, Mr Boehm:

'Last week Lord S.[pencer] and Mr and Mrs Poyntz spent three days with me on a hunting party and as I knew not otherwise how to give them much entertainment, I sent for our friend, the Bohemian, to give them the meeting. He came accordingly, was mounted on horseback and sallied forth a-fox-hunting. Boehm à la chasse, I think you may conceive to be an amazing phenomenon. He pulled off his coat some part of the chase because it was too hot, and rode in a lapelled blue silk gold laced waistcoat without sleeves. He then got two tumbles by his horse turning round a corner to go from one riding to another and returned home wondering very much what sport there was in hunting. However, to make him some amends, Lord S. took him out the next day to an open country and set him on a very staid, sober horse. Here he did very well for some time by following the current of people (as he expresses it), but on our finding a fox, we set off and saw no more of him till we arrived home. The excuse that he then made for himself was, that he really thought there was no hurry when the fox went off and so that he trotted gently on in search of us till he was unfortunately deceived by a herd of cattle, which he supposed to be the hunters, waiting about a wood, as he had observed them doing in the morning. I send you these few traits to show you that our fellow traveller is as diverting as ever. He is now bound for Ireland, where he supposes he shall find himself happier than on any other place of the globe. As he can neither drink nor play at cards, I fear he may be disappointed . . .'[32]

In November 1765 Palmerston received the reward of political virtue. 'Lord Rockingham morning – accepted seat at the Board of Trade [and Plantations]', read his diary entry for the 22nd. The pleasantly light duties of the eight commissioners consisted principally in administering the colonial territories. Palmerston's salary was £1,000 a year. With this elevation, the week before Christmas found him dining with Rockingham, the Speaker and the Duke of York. His diary summary at the end of the year read:

'In the beginning of this year I was chosen a member of the Club at Almacks. The houses I frequented most in London, where I used to dine when it suited me, were Colonel Burgoyne's, Mr Lane's, Mrs Hodges' and Lord Spencer's, as, likewise, General Armiger, while Mrs Armiger lived.'

Early in the new year this political recognition was bolstered by even more welcome acceptance, on the same ballot as Lord Spencer, into the exclusive Dilettanti Society, of which most of the connoisseurs of the day, including the Marquis of Rockingham himself, were members. Joshua Reynolds, not yet a knight, had been elected the previous year and subsequently became painter to the Society. 'Dilettanti Sunday', spent over a gregarious dinner at the Star and Garter Inn, became one of the fixed points in Palmerston's calendar in the years that followed and brought him into contact with many of the personalities who became his intimate friends, Charles James Fox, who was elected two years later at the age of twenty, Sir Joseph Banks, President of the Royal Society, Charles Greville, George Selwyn, Topham Beauclerk, David Garrick and Lord Mulgrave. In addition to the conviviality of its meetings, the Society was one of the principal eighteenth century sponsors of archæological research and artistic talent, and Palmerston remained an active member until his death.

During the summer of 1766 Palmerston embarked on another Continental tour to the Low Countries and France, a journey which was to bring him, *in absentia*, a promotion in office:

'I went from Calais to Dunkirk [he wrote to his mother], where I got Captain Fraser, one of the officers kept there on our part to overlook the demolition, to go about the place with me. If these gentlemen are to stay there till either the spirit or the letter of the Treaty is executed with regard to that place, they are there for life. The state of the matter is, in few words, this: The French have done, and are ready to do, whatever you ask that does not carry with it the destruction of the harbour as a convenient receptacle for large vessels and as this, and this alone, is the object of our demands, you may easily guess that this must afford subject for endless chicanery and contestation, unless prevented by the breaking out of some new war, or our growing wearing of it . . .'[33]

'I just tried the waters [he added from Spa], but fancied they did not agree well with me, so have not meddled much with them . . . I have no accounts from any authority with regard to a change of Boards, but have heard a good deal of it from private hands. Mr Buller's letter I received, which was to say that as there was such a report prevailing very strongly, he thought it right to let me know that in case of such an event my re-election at Looe would be upon much easier terms than the last . . .'[34]

In July-August the Rockingham administration finally perished of its internal discords and the King sent for the elder Pitt. Though Rockingham himself and most of his closest followers left office, some of his friends, including Grafton and Conway, chose to serve with Chatham, as did Palmerston, who noted in his diary:

'In the summer this year there was a partial change of ministry. Lord Rockingham going out of office and Lord Chatham coming in as Privy Seal, but in reality as the head of the administration. While I was out of England I was appointed to the Board of Admiralty; Sir Charles Saunders being then First Lord.'[35]

C

Palmerston's continued absence abroad left him unaffected by the upheaval caused by Chatham's provocative dismissal of Lord Edgcumbe from his post as Treasurer of the Household. Sir Charles Saunders, two other members of the Admiralty Board and several other Rockingham adherents in the administration resigned. Palmerston either acquiesced in Chatham's attempt to attach other Rockingham partisans to himself as individuals, or remained in ignorance of the line to adopt. His only recorded comments were two anecdotes about Edgcumbe:

'*Lord Edgecumbe, commonly known by the name of "Dick Edgecumbe", whose chief passion and employment was play, being appointed teller in the House of Commons upon some division, began as usual calling out the numbers one, two, three, four, five, six, seven, eight, nine, ten, knave, queen, king.*

'*Lord Edgecumbe received his letter of dismission on a remarkable bad day, on which he complained that they turned him out in weather in which you would not have turned a dog out.*'

Palmerston had no intention of interrupting his Continental tour, keeping his mother informed of his progress:

'I had a very pleasant journey from Spa . . . I have no Paris news to send you. I am just come back from L'Isle Adam, a seat of the Prince of Conti, about 25 miles from hence. I was introduced to him when I first came to Paris by Mr Stanley and, somebody happening to mention my being at Paris to him now, I received an invitation to go there. The place is pleasant, being situated upon an island in the middle of a fine river. He has always a large company there, but I cannot say that I much like the French system of living in the country . . . I am obliged to you for your congratulation on my changing Boards, which is certainly an advancement and upon the whole an agreeable one, though in some lights I almost regret the Board of Trade. I have never had any notice of it from anybody and am only informed of it by the Gazette; however, I shall write by this post to Sir Charles Saunders, to let him know where I am and to desire the indulgence of the Board for a fortnight longer absence . . .'[36]

Several of Palmerston's political and private friendships can

be traced to his new office, which he held for eleven years. His
Hampshire neighbour, Hans Stanley, had been a member of
the Admiralty Board at the accession of George III and may
have played his part in recommending Palmerston's appointment. John Buller, to whose family interest Palmerston owed
his seat at East Looe, succeeded Stanley in 1765. The fathers,
and namesakes, of the three closest friends of Palmerston's later
life, Gilbert Elliot, whose son became the 1st Earl of Minto,
Thomas Pelham and James Harris, father of the 1st Earl of
Malmesbury, succeeded each other in another seat on the Board.
In 1770, Charles James Fox became a member for two years.

During Palmerston's stay at Spa an even more gratifying
event had occurred. He made the acquaintance of the lady who
became his first wife, Frances Poole, daughter of a substantial
family of Sussex and Lancashire landowners, who was there
with her friends, Lord and Lady Harcourt. Palmerston's terse
note in his overall diary at the end of the year is his first
reference to the subject:

'During this year the houses I used to frequent most, and at
which I dined when I liked it, were General Burgoyne's, Mr
Lane's and often at Lord Torrington's, particularly at suppers
which he had constantly.

At Spa I lived much with Lord and Lady Harcourt and there
it was my attachment began to Miss Poole, who was with
them.'

The years of his political baptism were about to culminate in
marriage. They had also brought welcome encomiums from
two leading men of the time, the great Chatham and his witty
ministerial colleague, Charles Townshend, Chancellor of the
Exchequer:

From William Pitt to Hans Stanley, June, [1761?]
'Dear Sir,
The information you so kindly took the trouble to convey to
me on the subject of Lord Palmerston is too interesting to me
every way not to express without delay my acknowledgements
to you.

If an opportunity should occur before I can with propriety

myself have any means of assuring his Lordship of my just and
warm sense of the great honour he does me by such favourable
sentiments on my subject, may I beg, dear Sir, the favour of
you to assure Lord Palmerston of my respectful regards.
Pardon this freedom and believe me with truest esteem, dear
Sir,
      Your very affectionate and most obedient humble servant,
                                        William Pitt.'

                                        August 4th, 1767
'My dear Lord,
      I have the honour of your Lordship's letter, and shall have
a real satisfaction in giving Mr Sadleir my immediate and full
assistance. I have no doubt of Mr Sadleir's fair character and
qualifications for the office which your Lordship solicits for
him, but in obeying these or any other commands, which I
may have the pleasure of receiving from your Lordship, I can
have no motive so strong, nor any satisfaction so great as that
of endeavouring to manifest the personal respect and sincere
esteem which I have for your Lordship. I am, my dear Lord,
            Your Lordship's most faithful and
            obedient humble servant,
                                        C. Townshend.'

      The characterful Townshend family had also provided several
entries for the anecdote book:

*'Charles Townshend, asking the name of a gentleman he saw
coming up to take the oath at the House of Commons, was told that
it was Mr Harris of Salisbury, who had wrote upon virtue and upon
grammar. "The unfittest man in the world for this place," says
Charles.*

*'Charles Townshend, being in a large company in the country,
where the conversation turned upon the Robin Hood Society, at
which a baker presided with great reputation, somebody present,
turning to Mr Townshend said, "I hear, sir, that several members of
the House of Commons frequent this baker. It is true?" "Yes, sir,"
replied he, "I believe it is, and I think they judge right. They go to*

the baker for eloquence and they come to the House of Commons for bread."

'*Lord Townshend's wife, having miscarried of twins, it was observed that it was no wonder, for that two Townshends never could agree long in the same place.*

'*After Wilkes had left England, somebody told C. Townshend they heard the Minister intended to outlaw him. "Ay", says Charles, "now's their time, for while he was here he out law'd them all".*

'*Lady Townshend hearing of some certain young ladies who were very ready to oblige their friends with certain manual operations, said she supposed they thought a bird in the hand worth two in the bush.*'

REFERENCES

1. A.6 26.VII.1763
2. C.17(c)
3. C.4
4. C.5 30.VIII.1763
5. C.2 21.IX.1763
6. C.2 15.IX.1763
7. C.2 undated
8. C.8 7.IX.1765
9. A.6 19.X.1763
10. C.5 22.XI.1763
11. C.3 27.XI.1763
12. C.5 31.I.1764
13. C.3 21.II.1764
14. C.2 23.III.1764
15. C.10 7.I.1764
16. C.10 12.V.1764
17. A.6 22.V.1764
18. C.2 undated (June 1764)
19. C.12 24.VIII.1764
20. C.15 15.VII.1764
21. A.6 September–October 1764
22. C.5 16.X.1764
23. C.2 22.VI.1764
24. C.9, see also H.43
25. C.11 19.XII.1764
26. F.11
27. C.5 11.VII.1765
28. C.5 24.VII.1765
29. C.17(a) 23.VII.1765
30. A.2 22.VIII.1765
31. H.39
32. C.15 25.X.1765
33. C.17(a) 28.VIII.1766
34. C.17(a) September 1766
35. A.2 December 1766
36. C.17(a) 8.X.1766

CHAPTER III

COURTSHIP IN FIVE SYLLABLES

Palmerston wins the affection of Frances Poole, a kinswoman of the Pelhams – their love letters – their marriage – congratulations in verse from General John Burgoyne – 'Capability' Brown employed at Broadlands – Palmerston elected for Southampton with the Rt Hon. Hans Stanley – Lady Palmerston dies in childbed

O N her mother's side, Frances Poole was a Pelham, and a kinswoman of the great Whig clan which included the Dukes of Newcastle. Her father was Sir Francis Poole, Bart, who had died in 1763, at the age of eighty-one, and her mother, who had died at the age of seventy a year earlier, was a granddaughter of Sir John Pelham. Frances Poole had two elder brothers, Henry and Ferdinand, and was born in 1733, being rather more than six years older than Palmerston – a factor which caused her serious misgivings when he commenced to declare his affection for her.

She had been something of a protegée of a close friend of the first Viscount Palmerston, Lord Delawar, and a correspondent of his two gifted daughters, Diana, who married General Clavering and figured in all the social chronicles of the time, and Lady Cecilia Johnston, herself a highly intelligent and cultured young woman. Her intellectual attainments had long attracted Lord Delawar's notice: 'I know none of your sex the older by some years that come up to, nor do I see they pursue any probable method of attaining those beauties that adorn your mind', he wrote to her in her late teens and sent her copies of Voltaire's works and Locke's *Essay on Human Understanding*. He was always complimenting her on her good sense and just observation, 'wonderful at your age – go, pursue and be the wonder of your sex'.[1]

Although such comments would seem to class her as a proto-type of the blue-stockings, she had not wanted for suitors, in spite of the heart-whole protestations in her letters to Palmerston.

Lord Edgcumbe and Lord Nuneham [Lord Harcourt's heir] are spoken of in the Delawar daughters' letters as her admirers, and not long before she met Palmerston Lady Cecilia Johnston wrote, 'I hear Colonel Trapeaud is come post from Scotland to enter with you into the holy state of matrimony'. Lady Cecilia had also met Palmerston during his second visit to Paris: 'I thought him the only Englishman there that did credit to his country'.[2]

By the time Palmerston left Spa, Frances Poole was already the recipient of his indifferently phrased verses of admiration. The summer of 1767 found them sufficiently close for the suitor to note in his diary on June 18:

'Dinner at Richmond with Charles Townshend and a large party.

'Miss Poole evening.

'During the preceding winter I had lived a good deal with the same friends as before, but had passed the greatest part of my time at Miss Poole's, to whom my attachment was great and being convinced it was reciprocal, I this evening made her an offer of marriage, which was received as I wished and expected. She was on the point of leaving London to go to her eldest brother, Sir Harry Poole, who was ill at their house at Lewes.'

He had by no means fully persuaded the lady yet. Acutely conscious of the difference in their ages and worried about the fast declining health of her elder brother, she engaged in a courtship by correspondence between Lewes and London which, in its polysyllabic protestations of affection, is both quaint and touching:

From Lord Palmerston: Wednesday, June 24th
'I have waited with the utmost impatience, my dearest Miss Poole, for this day's post which I knew would give me the happiness of hearing from you, which, believe me, is the greatest I can feel in your absence. I had not the least expectation of hearing from you sooner, the fatigue of your journey and your anxious attention to your brother's situation could not allow me a reasonable hope for it . . .

'I will not attempt to describe how melancholy and uncomfortable I have felt ever since you have been gone. I never in any solitude felt so much alone as I have done in this town these last five days, and most of all so when I have been in company; this is not a difficult paradox to explain. My own thoughts and my own recollections have been my best and most entertaining companions, for they have all been employed upon the only object which has been for a long time really interesting to me and severely as I feel even a temporary privation of that object, I protest I would not exchange the melancholy enjoyment of those recollections for the best pleasures I ever experienced from any other source. These indeed, since I have known you, have almost wholly lost their value, and I may safely say, that for months past, I have scarcely felt the sensation of present or the hope of future happiness, without being indebted to you for it, and, at this moment, was you to take from me that hope which I so fondly and fervently cherish of being yours by the tenderest of all ties, you would overthrow the most favourite schemes my heart has ever formed of future happiness. You would take away the spring of every worthy or spirited action and reduce me to that state of languid indifference into which a disappointment in its fondest pursuit and a contempt for every other must throw a warm and feeling mind. . . . The esteem and the affection of a heart like yours is a treasure which, thank heaven, I know the value of and which it will ever be my happiness and my secret pride to possess, and my first ambition to deserve. I cannot, without a mixture of pain and pleasure, reflect on those scruples which set the genuine and unaffected delicacy of your mind in so amiable a light and which, while they make you more estimable in my eyes and would, if not conquered, doubly aggravate my disappointment. But I trust you will not sacrifice my happiness – and may I not almost say your own – to an unnecessary apprehension. It is, as I said before, a great trust, but I am so elated by your good opinion of me that I will not think myself totally unworthy of it. My sentiments of you can never alter because they are founded on what neither age nor sickness can affect. My expectations in a wife are unreasonable, they are infinitely beyond what I am entitled to, but unless they are answered, I never can think of marriage. In you, I find every quality my warmest wish ever asked for and which till I knew you I never had an expectation that I should find and shall I now think so poorly of my own character as to suspect myself capable of ceasing to value what I have so long searched for and found so unexpectedly, or of preferring what I never before thought objects of attention. For if youth and beauty alone could engage my affection, why have I lived so long in the world seeing with total indifference one set of beauties succeed another, without finding one for whom I could entertain a serious thought? I declare if I had a doubt of myself, no present consideration should induce me to risk your happiness, which I know is at stake.

Forgive me for having perhaps at a very improper season entered so much into this subject, but it is ever in my thoughts and will find its way to my paper. . . . I respect too much your feelings and your delicacy to press for any positive decision at this interesting moment of your situation while you have an object before you that must engross your chief attention. I wish you to determine, with your best and coolest judgment, but to remember that you are determining upon the most important and interesting concern of my life . . .

Your ever faithful, P.'

From Frances Poole: Thursday night, June 25th
'If I had time I would endeavour to tell you how welcome your letter was to me, but as I have but just received it, and the post goes out early tomorrow morning, I can only inform you that my brother continues very much the same . . .

My mind is, at present, very full and my time for writing so very short, that I must defer sending a more particular answer to your letter till next post . . .

I trust you cannot doubt of the regard and good wishes of your affectionate, F.P.'

From Frances Poole: Saturday night, 12 o'clock, June 27th
'I was sorry to send you so unworthy an answer to a letter that had my mind been at ease, would have given me as true

pleasure as my heart is capable of feeling; for every line seemed
to prove the sincerity of your too great partiality towards me
and, indeed, your noble and disinterested conduct joined to a
turn of mind so exactly calculated to steal upon my affections,
has put it out of my power to urge a scruple but what is
entirely confined to myself. They are not mere little scruples
of delicacy, at least if they are, my heart feels their force.
Indeed, indeed, my dear Lord, all my fears and all my scruples
arise from the not being able to persuade myself that I am
young enough, or amiable enough to ensure you a lasting
happiness. I say nothing of not being rich enough, for scruples
of that kind may be carried to a degree that is not generous.
Besides, I could not have a serious thought of anybody that
could be influenced by things of that sort. I cannot deny but it
would have been wiser to have thought of all these things when
first I became acquainted with you, but you gained my affections before I was aware of it and not being liable to impressions
of that kind, I had no suspicion of the danger, and consequently
never thought of denying myself the innocent pleasure I enjoyed
whenever I was in your company. I looked upon you as my
friend, and blessed the moment that we became acquainted;
mais ce nom d'ami porta dans mon coeur une tranquillité perfide.
This is the true state of the case and I see not why an affected
refinement should make me conceal an honest and well
grounded affection. An attachment founded on reason and
judgment rarely falls to the lot of anyone, and I never expected
it to be mine, but still the last ten years of my life are perpetually occurring to torment me, and can it be right to
act against these suggestions of my own mind, and what is
worse, perhaps against your own interest and happiness? You
deserve a woman beautiful and young and with every quality
of the mind that can make her amiable, pleasant and com-
panionable. This you ought to have and this I ought to wish
you; but then you so kindly ask me if I ought to risk both
yours and my own happiness for an unnecessary apprehension.
Undoubtedly not, if I could persuade myself that the apprehension is unnecessary, but there lies the difficulty; notwithstanding, I have a confidence in you that I may safely say I

never had in any other man. I am sure of your honour and generosity. I know how impossible it is for you to act inconsistent with either towards any woman who you would honour with a serious thought, but permit me to say that even this is not sufficient for me, nothing but the full persuasion that I could indeed contribute to your happiness could insure mine, and when I consider those things which are against me and, at the same time, think how people of the very best sense and most penetration have deceived themselves in situations similar to yours, I cannot forbear asking you as the greatest of all favours, to take more time to consider this point so essential to us both. This is the only point on which I doubt the coolness of your judgment, but if, after having granted me this, you should still continue in the same sentiments, I should find it hard indeed to disappoint what you so partially call your favourite scheme of life. If it was possible it could cast a damp on one "worthy or spirited action". No, my Lord, your honour and interest I hope, will always be dearer to me than anything else and it is my regard to these that makes me thus doubtful and irresolute . . .

My brother, not being visibly better after so long a time, makes me very full of apprehensions for him. The uneasy and anxious state of my mind I fear will have made this letter very confused, for at present I know nothing very clearly, but that I am your much obliged and affectionate, F.P.'

From Lord Palmerston: June 30th
'You tell me that all your scruples arise from your not being able to persuade yourself that you are young enough or amiable enough to insure me a lasting happiness; this, I hope, it is reserved for me not only to persuade but to convince you of. At least if happiness is the possession at once of all that our warmest passions and our coolest reason can desire, how far lasting happiness is likely to be anybody's lot I do not know, but this I know that I must find it with you, or nowhere. I am sure I have no chance of it with any other woman. To marry another, after so thorough an acquaintance with you, would be insuring a lasting misery to her and myself. Unhappy will

be the day when I have an opportunity of drawing a comparison between my wife and Miss Poole. Was she equal to you, was she superior to you, still it would not do unless she was exactly like you, in short, unless she was you. Not that I would be understood to mean to say that I do not wish you was younger, I do most sincerely. I wish it for both our sakes. We should have a more extensive prospect before us and if it was to be so obtained, I would purchase it with half my fortune. But that would have been more good fortune than ever fell to the lot of any man. What I insist on is this, that with you I have a fairer prospect of happiness than even my fancy ever presented to me before I knew you, for never did it present to me so amiable an object and that it would be folly to give up so fair a prospect because imagination might have added one circumstance more to have improved it . . . My situation in life has long been in some respects unpleasing to me, and yet I have long despaired of mending it, being by birth almost the single remainder of my family. I have few attachments of relationship and though of a disposition, I flatter myself, not indisposed to friendship, yet perhaps from some singularity of temper or concurrence of accidents, it has been my lot to form fewer connections that have gone beyond a common acquaintance than most men. Of the few friends I have had, I have been unfortunate in losing some by death and others by separation. From these peculiarities of situation and the disagreeable sensation of being alone in the world, belonging to nobody, I have long been wishing to form by marriage a connection that should supply that craving void which was aching in my breast, but then the difficulty was to find the object and, strongly as my imagination painted the happiness of a suitable engagement, ten times more strongly did it paint the misery of an unfortunate one . . .

'These difficulties, which I had little hopes ever to get over, arose from my never having met with a woman possessed of the qualities essential to my plan of happiness. My demands, as I have before said, were unreasonable, but yet they were indispensable. For to be married to a woman whom I did not love, esteem and admire, in short, whom I did not prefer to all her sex and to all the world, was and is to me, of all ideas, the most insupportable. At length, in a happy and unexpected moment, this treasure is found. I have met with a woman whose character, temper, disposition and person struck me at once and who has rose in my esteem the more she was known and who, after a long and intimate acquaintance and an attentive examination has left not a doubt or a suspicion in my mind in one of those points where I had so little expectation of being satisfied . . .

'In such a situation can I hesitate? Can I have a doubt? Or can I want more time to consider? No, my dearest friend, my considerations are all concluded and only wait your decision. But at the same time I am willing to wait your own time and will not presume to press too impatiently upon that goodness to which I am already so infinitely indebted . . .

Adieu! Let me hear from you when you have leisure, it is the greatest comfort to your faithful and affectionate, P.'

From Frances Poole: Friday morning, July 3rd, 10 o'clock
'I could wish not to give you pain, but such is my situation at present, that if I give any account of myself, I cannot avoid it. My poor brother has grown visibly worse for some days past and the seeing his sufferings, without the power of relieving him, is more than at times I know how to bear. If there should be any amendment, or even if my spirits should be more composed, I will endeavour by tomorrow night's post to write again. For I fain would thank you for your letter, at present I cannot attempt it. Therefore, adieu! you are the only person to whom I could take up my pen to write even this much . . .

Once more, my dear Lord, adieu!'

From Lord Palmerston: Admiralty, Saturday, July 4th
'I am infinitely obliged to you, my dearest Miss Poole, for your kind attention to me amidst so distressful a scene as you unhappily have before you. You judge indeed right that your letter could not but give me pain. It does most sensibly, and yet I was but too well prepared to expect the contents of it from the account Doctor Jebb sent me after his last visit . . . I will entreat you only to spare yourself as much as you can, not to expose yourself unnecessarily to such fatigues and scenes

of distress as can only serve to wear you without contributing anything to your brother's health or comfort . . .

Adieu! my dearest Miss Poole, how happy should I be to hear a better account of your brother and a good one of yourself.'

From Frances Poole: Saturday night, July 4th, 12 o'clock

'As I find my spirits rather more composed than when I wrote last, I am desirous of endeavouring to thank you for your letter. I do not love to pass over in silence those amiable expressions of kindness which I find in almost every line. For since I have been so happy as to gain your approbation, I would not affect to be insensible to what, at any other time, would have given me the truest pleasure, but then –

"Our dying friends come o'er us like a cloud
        To damp our ardours . . ."

I was struck with a little word or two in your letter in which you seem to doubt if lasting happiness is the lot of any man. I, at this time, feel but too sensibly how much reason there is for suspecting it, but the justness of your reflections must have taught you, what I learn from a severe affliction, but for that, with so much reason as I have to be elated, I should be ill disposed to consider melancholy or mortifying truths, or to think that –

"The spider's most attenuated thread
        Is cord, is cable to man's tender tie
        On earthly bliss, which breaks with ev'ry breeze".

Indeed, my Lord, there are few men "amid the smiles of fortune and of youth whose minds are patient of such serious truths", and I am apt to believe, that the want of friends and domestic comfort is seldom thought of by those that are possessed of so many worldly advantages. What you say of your own family and situation, speaks such sensibility of heart, that no words of mine can tell you how much I was affected by it; nor with what earnestness and sincerity I wished you every blessing you can possibly stand in need of. My fears of your having mistaken the way to find them are not less prevalent than they were; but, the air of coolness and reason in your words makes it difficult for me to know what to answer, and

the delicacy of your conduct makes it impossible for me to
tease you any more with a repetition of scruples that arise from
things which are unalterable. Adieu! my dear Lord!

Adieu, adieu!'

From Lord Palmerston: Admiralty, Tuesday, July 7th
'I have another letter, my dearest Miss Poole to thank you
for . . .

Your image is almost my only companion, for I am often
conversing with that when I am supposed to be present in
other company; and the reading your letters, my favourite
amusement . . .

Your kind and generous wishes of blessings to me are more
affecting to me than I can express, but I have one condition
to add, without which the rest would avail me nothing. May
you be the dear dispenser or the happy partner of every blessing
that fortune has in store for me, and then I shall envy no man.

I often reflect what an uncommon piece of good fortune it
is that neither of us should have been pre-engaged.

Adieu!'

From Lord Palmerston: Saturday, July 11th, 2 o'clock
'It is two or three days, my dearest Miss Poole, since I have
been informed of the unhappy close of that melancholy scene
which has so long afflicted your mind . . .

I cannot, therefore, refrain from writing, though in so
doubtful and anxious a state as I am in at present about you
I really do not know what to say that can be worth your taking
the trouble to read. The common style of letters of condolence
I extremely hate, and I think they are always either quite
unnecessary or quite ineffectual and I am sure you are the last
person in the world to whom I should make use of them. I
trust entirely to your own strong good sense and right judgment to soften down the first violent impressions of grief and
bring it to that calm and soothing sensation of melancholy
which a mind like yours will long feel at times from the
remembrance of a departed friend and which is, perhaps, the
most grateful legacy they can bequeath us . . .

and how entirely I am yours, P.'

From Frances Poole: Sunday night, July 12th, 11 o'clock

'After what has happened you cannot wonder at my not having been in a state of mind that would admit of writing, even to you; to anybody else I have not thought of it for these last melancholy three weeks, and to you, my dear Lord, for this last week, kind and sympathising as you are, it has been utterly out of my power . . .

My dear Lord, do not be uneasy about me, for I am better in my health and at present even more composed in my spirits than I could have imagined, though still not equal to the entering into any detail or even into any particulars contained in your letter. I will write, if possible, by the next post . . .

As there is no post sets out from Lewes tomorrow, I send this by the machine . . .

Very affectionately yours, F.P.'

From Frances Poole: Tuesday night, July 14th, 12 o'clock

'I am infinitely obliged to you my dear Lord for two of the kindest and most soothing letters that could possibly be received in such a situation as mine. At any other time, how eager I should have been to have answered them! At this, it has been entirely out of my power and the little scrawl I sent you the other day has been my only attempt at writing since the melancholy event that has robbed me of a brother that I have but too much reason to bewail . . .

You will not wonder that I am sensibly affected by that part where you so flatteringly congratulate yourself on your having lived hitherto unengaged. With regard to myself, it has certainly been my case, for marriage is a connection in which I saw so many dangers to a turn [?] like mine, that I had but little thoughts of ever entering into it. I was fond of my liberty, happy at home and had never met with that sort of character and disposition that could make me the least inclined to give up those advantages I enjoyed and knew the value of, and to marry as an affair of worldly convenience I ever abhorred the thoughts of, and I knew just enough of myself to be sure that would end in certain misery. Once, indeed, when I was very young I will not deny, but that the attention shown me by one whom you know, had near persuaded me to fancy myself in love, but happily for me, my father was averse to what I soon after found would have been very far from contributing to my happiness; not from any really bad qualities in the person, but from the want of many of those which every woman who thinks must require in one in whom she hopes to find a friend, a guide and a support in every serious occurrence of life; nor that cheerfulness, that liberty, that vivacity of thought which can make common ones pleasurable; and it was long, very long, before I ever saw a man in whom I could think they were all united ... A man undoubtedly risks a great deal; but allow me to say a woman risks still more. . . .

I am very much your affectionate, F.P.'

From Lord Palmerston: Thursday, July 16th
'Your welcome letter by the machine, my dearest Miss Poole, was brought down to me at Sheen the same night it came ...

I was going to have wrote you yesterday, but was prevented and am now not sorry for it, as I have since received yours of Tuesday night, which is everything I could wish it to be and has made me happier than I have been since I have lost your company ...

Allow me to thank you a thousand and a thousand times for the latter part of your letter, it calls forth every sentiment of love, gratitude, esteem and admiration that a warm heart can possibly furnish. It reconciles me to everything that has ever happened to me in the past; it presents me with the happiest prospects in future; it flatters my self love – only take care you do not make me too vain, vain I already feel I am – and, indeed, who can be in any degree worthy of your good opinion who is not proud of it ... In nothing, I fear, can I pretend to come up to the merit you would indulgently give me, but in love and attachment to you; and it is by the sincerity of that alone that I can hope to atone for many faults and defects which I, at this moment, (without the least affectation of false modesty) cannot but know myself liable to. And my comfort is to know that with a generous and tender heart like yours that will atone for much ...

I go into Hampshire tomorrow . . .

I carry ['Capability'] Brown with me and shall now look
with ten times more pleasure upon everything that is doing
there than I ever did before. I shall want your advice in a
thousand things . . .

Adieu!'

From Frances Poole: Tuesday night, July 21st, 11 o'clock
'I have had so much of the headache lately that though I had
the pleasure of receiving your letter on Friday evening, this
is the first day since that I have felt well enough to venture to
take up my pen. I am now tolerably well again and so are my
spirits, which I mention because I am sure it will give you
pleasure to hear it . . .

I received with as much pleasure as my heart is capable of
feeling in its present situation, all your professions of love,
friendship and esteem, and I believe them, flattering as they
are, because I have feelings of my own that teach me to judge
of yours . . .

I shall hope to hear that you found everything in Hampshire
to your satisfaction and in case it proves so I shall have a very
high idea of the clearness with which you give your orders,
for I have been a witness to how little personal attendance
you have bestowed on the alterations that were going on
there.

Adieu, my dear Lord! let me hear from you whenever it is
convenient to you to write, for it is almost the only pleasure
I have not lost the power of enjoying.'

From Lord Palmerston: Broadlands, Sunday, July 26th
'I received yours last night, my dearest Miss Poole, with
that sincere pleasure which everything that comes from or
relates to you must always give me. At the same time, I need
not tell you how sorry I am that you have suffered from the
headache. I cannot say, however, that I am much surprised at it.
I rather wonder you have held out so well through the long
agitation of mind you have undergone . . .

I have found everything going on here as well and I believe
pretty near as fast as I could reasonably expect, though too slow

for my impatience. I do not, however, deserve any part of the compliment you seem inclined to pay me upon the clearness of my orders, having never given any to the workmen, which I believe may be one reason why they have made few mistakes. I have only settled the plans with Brown and then have left everything in the execution of them to him. I am much satisfied with my place upon the whole, and it begins to interest me extremely since I have a prospect of obtaining an almost despaired of blessing without which it would have always been to me dull and inanimate. I cannot help smiling at your congratulation upon the liberty and leisure I enjoy here. I assure you London was a desert, a solitude, compared to it. For what with the quantity of workmen all about me, some business relative to my estate, having just got a new steward, a pretty large and very civil neighbourhood and then, above all, my devoirs to my future constituents at Southampton – to whom I must endeavour to make up by a little attention . . .

Tomorrow I am to have the Mayor and Corporation of Southampton dine with me. I have got two haunches of venison for them, which I hope will do . . .

Adieu my dearest Miss Poole, while I am anything, I am yours, P.'

From Miss Frances Poole: Saturday, July 25th
'. . . we shall arrive in Charles Street on Monday evening, which will be before this letter will reach you, but till today our journey was not absolutely determined . . .

I have enough to make me vain, but yet, my dear Lord, at this time I am not. For every expression that might well raise my vanity, serves only to remind me that those scruples (which you seem to think are not so strong as they were) are but too well grounded; for if I at first thought myself many years too old for you, I now fancy that those years are doubled, so much am I humbled. My affliction has made me feel more sensibly than ever, the force of my scruples; though your behaviour on this occasion has left me less resolution to oppose what you desire and which you tell me you have so thoroughly considered . . .

Your very affectionate, F.P.'

From Lord Palmerston: Saturday night, August 1st

'Your last letter, my dearest Miss Poole, arrived here, unluckily, just as I was gone from home and not returning quite
so soon as I intended, it lay two days unopened, which I was
heartily vexed at as I lost by that means the opportunity of
sending an answer before tomorrow – our post going out but
three times a week. I might now almost as well carry my letter
as send it, since I flatter myself nothing will prevent me from
seeing you on Monday. But as the post may probably get to
town sooner than I shall and as writing to you is the happiest
employment I have here, I will not debar myself of it . . .

I am quite cross with myself for having managed so ill as to
be forced to stay here a whole week after you are in town and
more especially since I find you talk of staying but a short time,
but yet I don't know how I could have avoided it . . .

I cannot express how much I long to see you, the interval since
we parted has been so melancholy and distressful to you and so
anxious to me upon your account, that it seems quite an age . . .

I long to repeat to you again and again my thanks for your
generous kindness and partiality to me and, at the same time,
to endeavour to banish from your mind those undeserved and
unworthy opinions you seemed to have formed of yourself . . .

To one who understands your character and knows how to
value it as it deserves (and if I am possessed of any merit in the
world, it is that), the disproportion of age is nothing. The
consideration with me is not about years but qualities, and I
am fully convinced that no woman in the world but yourself
possesses all those that are requisite to my happiness. And therefore you see, thinking so, which I did from the first moment I
knew you and have only been more and more confirmed in it
to the present, I have no choice left. The desire of passing my
life with you is engrafted upon that desire of happiness which,
from the earliest to the latest moment, prompts and directs the
actions of our lives . . .

I have all this time been considering this matter in the most
selfish light imaginable because I have been led to it by your
generosity which seems to have made you principally think of
my happiness. But when I take in the pleasing thought which

you have permitted me to entertain that it is not an affair of
indifference to you and indulge myself in the hopes that it may
be my lot by a tender and affectionate zeal for your happiness
to add something to the comforts of your future life; all those
motives which before were sufficient to determine me acquire
ten-fold force. In short, to sum up the matter, your image is
the constant companion of my thoughts and the only object
that can much employ the hopes and wishes,

of your affectionate and devoted, P.'³

The six weeks that followed clearly removed all further
doubts and on September 19 Frances Poole wrote from Lewes,
after a visit to Broadlands:

'I have lived too much with you, my dear Lord, not to feel
a strange vacuum whenever I am obliged to be separated from
you . . . In short, my dear Lord, you have had the art of
engrossing my attentions so much, that it has enabled me in
great measure to conquer an uneasiness that otherwise would
have long stuck by me, but endless are my obligations to you,
and I shall never attempt to thank you by words for any of the
marks you have given me of your affection. Indeed, they have
not power to tell you half what I feel. It must be by my truth,
my tenderness, my assiduity to please you, that I must show
my acknowledgements, and even these will fall short. Since
we parted, I have spent a great deal of my time at Broadlands,
which a circle of persons have not been able to draw me from.
Miss Hay, I believe, has often found me wandering there, when
the rest of the company, I trust, have imagined me to be along
with them; not walking by the side of your *belle rivière* [the
Test, which runs through the Broadlands estate], which will
be in high favour if I find you have escaped colds all this damp
disagreeable weather. Pray tell me whether it looks as merry, and
its banks as dry as you have boasted. Has it no hard edges? . . .
My dear Lord! A formal ending is unnecessary as you must
know how entirely I am yours, F.P.'[4]

Although Palmerston's reply contained some highly un-
romantic detail, his protestations were sincere:

'My *belle rivière* was in great beauty and especially the last days when the weather was remarkably fine. It is always merry. I don't remember making the dryness of its banks particularly the object of commendation, they are much like other rivers, but will be made as dry as I should wish them for you to walk upon, and the edges shall be softened and subdued under your own inspection. I assure you the river and its banks and hills have acquired quite a new value and a new interest in my mind since you have made an acquaintance with them and are likely to become an inhabitant there. I am, however, extremely concerned to find that (I suppose from the quantity of dirt and rubbish) the house is grown most excessively full of fleas, who seem to me, at least some I found upon my stockings, to be of the little active kind that used to attach themselves to you at Spa. I am in hopes we shall get rid of fleas and dirt together before next summer . . .'5

On October 6 it occurred to him that perhaps his mother should be informed of developments:

'I should have wrote to you a little sooner but could not have given you any certain notice of the time of my being married, but have the pleasure to tell you that before you read this, you will in all probability have a most amiable daughter-in-law, as I believe we shall be married tomorrow . . .'6

On the next day his overall diary contained this somewhat terse entry:

'I was married to Miss Poole. We remained at Lewes till the 25th of November, when we came to London to the Admiralty. I made an excursion in the intermediate time to Southampton and Paultons.'

But the event brought forth an effusion from a close friend, who revealed himself as another former suitor to his wife:

AN ODE TO LORD PALMERSTON ON HIS MARRIAGE WITH MISS POOLE, *by General Burgoyne, who had formerly paid his addresses to the same lady, but from motives of prudence the match was broken off.*

> While Palmerston, the public voice
> Display's in comments on thy choice
> Praise, censure, or surprise;

Blames thy disinterested part
Or interest finds in worth of heart
Where Fanny's treasure lies.

Fain would my muse, tho' rude, sincere
One humble artless wreath prepare
To bind her lonely brow;
With thee would hail the auspicious morn
Attend the bride she can't adorn
And bless the nuptial vow.

Let the dull claim of due esteem
To lukewarm crowds be claim supreme;
I found pretensions higher;
You know the heart now taught to beat
With friendships sacred temp'rate heat
Has once been tried in fire.

'Twas mine to see each opening charm
New graces rise, new beauties warm
'Twas mine to feel their power
Nature and morals just and pure
For thee have made the fruit mature
Since I adored the flower.

After hard conflict passions cool'd
Discretion, reason, honour ruled
O'er the subsiding flame
Till Charlotte to my vacant breast
With kindred charms and virtues bless'd
A sweet successor came.

Long years of love we've numbered o'er,
And O! to many many more
May heaven the term extend;
To try with thee the pleasing strife
Who boasts the most deserving wife
Who proves the truest friend.[7]

* * *

The anecdote book entries for the period have a distinctly light-hearted tone:

'*At a grand county dinner, given by the Duke of Newcastle, he placed General Mostyn at the head of another table, to take care of the company there, and after dinner, calling continually to the other table that they did not drink enough, Mostyn at last answered him, "I beg your pardon my Lord Duke, we are as drunk as your Grace, only not quite so noisy".*

'*Lord Chesterfield said to Mrs Ann Pitt that he found he was growing quite an old woman. She answered, "I am very glad to hear it. I thought you was growing to be an old man, which is a much worse thing".*

'*Just before Charles Fox left Eton, he was bathing in the Thames and some bargemen coming by, seeing him standing naked in the meadow, were so struck with his excessive hairiness that one of them called out to his companion, "Damn my eyes, Jack, but I believe there's Nebuchadnezzar just come up from grass".*

'*Sir James Marriott, who held the office of Judge of the Admiralty Court, used to come often to the Duke of Grafton when he was First Lord of the Treasury under pretence of business. The Duke grew so tired of him that at last he sent out word he was busy and could not see him. Sir James, offended at this, sent in word that he conceived by virtue of his office he had a right to an audience of the Minister whenever he judged it necessary. To which the Duke sent out word that he was perfectly ignorant of any such obligation when he accepted his office; that he would make immediate enquiry into it and that if it should prove to be so, Sir James might depend upon it he would resign the next day.*

'*All persons who are convicted of any crime are not chargeable with gaol fees. Whereas those who are acquitted are not discharged till they have paid them; which gave occasion to Serjeant Davy to stand up as Counsel for a poor man at a country assize, who was accused of petty larceny, and, at the same time, to say to the Judge he should make no defence notwithstanding. "We have a very good case, my Lord, but we are very poor and have a large family, so that we can't afford to be acquitted. Therefore, your Lordship will be so good as to order us to be whipped and sent home".*

'*A handsome girl, being tried in Ireland before Judge St Leger for a capital offence, the Judge gave a very favourable charge to the jury, who, notwithstanding, brought her in guilty. The judge sent them out again; they returned with the same verdict and, upon the judge showing an inclination to send them out again, the foreman said, "My Lord, if you send us out ever so often, we cannot acquit this woman; our consciences would prick us". "Prick!", says the old judge with contempt, "if you had a P—— among you, you would never have found her guilty".*'

★   ★   ★

It was during the period of his first marriage that Palmerston commenced the refashioning of Broadlands. Over the course of the dozen years that followed Lancelot ['Capability'] Brown laid out the gardens and redesigned and rebuilt the house. Palmerston is distressingly chary of detail. An overall diary note for 1768 says: 'I had begun to build at Broadlands and the old part of the house which was not pulled down was so full of workmen that it was impossible for Lady Palmerston to go there at this time. She remained in London till July and then she went with Sir Ferdinand to Lewes, and I went to Broadlands to look after the work'. Shortly after he arrived he wrote to his wife:

'The account that I gave you of Broadlands was that the work was certainly much advanced and that the house began to wear a more habitable aspect, though as yet not very comfortable. Brown was with me two days last week and brought a man with him who is to direct the out of doors work which we shall begin when the harvest is over . . .[8]

In the following January he had only slow progress to report:

'It has snowed and blowed surprisingly ever since I left London, and yet the ground is as hard and as parched as possible which I fear will do much harm to our new plantation. They have planted all the shrubs they had and several young trees and we shall have time, by the autumn, to settle what more will be wanted. Moving ground and planting are both slow jobs, for which reason I do not say much about their want of expedition, but to be sure they have not surprised me by the progress they have made. However, I see vast improvement to the place in many things they have done . . .

'The joiners are at present chiefly employed in contriving and erecting various sorts of Gothic edifices to ornament Hutchin's room below. What they will make of it, heaven knows, but as they have almost done I have let them proceed. The kitchen building is begun, but not far advanced.'[9]

Lady Palmerston had practical suggestions to make about the interior furnishing:

'I should never have suspected you would have been able to have rummaged out so much upholstery furniture; I assure you I rejoice at the intelligence exceedingly, for it's really vexatious to be obliged to throw away so much money in garrets and places that are never seen. As to the four variegated damask beds, I dare say something may be found to do with them, for if they are too bad in their present state, I should advise in a notable way to have them dyed and then they will do for the common kind of rooms. I am glad to hear so good an account of the mosaic ceiling, for since it contents you I have not a doubt but I shall like it, for your eyes are much more critical than mine . . .'[10]

The history of the Broadlands estate dates back to before the Norman Conquest. From the time of King Edward, the Elder, whose daughter became the first abbess in 907, until the Reformation, its lands, under the title of Romsey Extra, had been the property of Romsey Abbey. When Jane Seymour became King Henry VIII's Queen, her rapacious younger brother Thomas obtained control and sold it to his sycophant Sir Francis Fleming, who built the first house on the site. Through him the estate passed in the female line to the St Barbe family. Sir John St Barbe, who occupied the house from 1661 to 1723, reconstructed and refitted the interior, built the Jacobean stables which subsist to this day, and gave the house

the general appearance described by Celia Fiennes in 1697 in
her diaries as 'half a Roman H'.

When Palmerston inherited Broadlands it still retained many
of the Elizabethan features of its original form. On the east
front, facing the carriage entrance, the entrance hall was recessed
between the north and south wings. On the west front, facing
the River Test and the new vistas laid out by 'Capability'
Brown, a projecting monumental Georgian portico was added.
The records are slightly confusing and it may be that the central
portion of the façade was originally somewhat recessed on
this side too; if so, this was built out flush, giving the west
side a classic, nine-window Georgian façade. Brown's work
was not completed until 1779, and nine years later, Henry
Holland, who became Brown's partner in 1771 and then
his successor, was employed by Palmerston to fill in the
east front with a recessed portico and a new third storey
across the gap.

* * *

The Palmerston reputation for hospitality was fully maintained
in the meantime at Admiralty House. Lord North, Charles
Townshend, Horace Walpole, Reynolds and Garrick are only
a few of the famous names to appear in their guest list. Then
in April 1768 came new elections:

'We remained in London all the winter. A new Parliament
was chosen in the spring, in which I was elected for Southampton, without opposition. I served in the former Parliament for
East Looe. I came in in the third year of the Parliament upon
the interest of Mr Buller at the recommendation of Mr Bilson
Legge, who, being dead, Mr Buller had other views in the
disposal of the seat.'[11]

A fresh sponsor was at hand in the person of his neighbour
Hans Stanley, who invited Palmerston to become his fellow
member for Southampton. The new constituency had over
four hundred voters, compared with forty-nine at East Looe,
and Palmerston had to take some cognisance of his opponent
and electorate. He informed his wife:

'I believe I showed you in town an account of a wild Mr

Maguire, who has been here and who declares his intention of coming down here soon again and bringing such loads of rupees with him as shall buy the town, whether they will or not. In the meantime, he ordered a house to be opened from time to time for the reception of his friends, who met there accordingly the other day in a body, equally respectable both for number and weight. They were from about sixteen to twenty ragamuffins without one single person of character or interest. Nothing can be received with greater contempt than Mr M's proposition is by every man of any estimation in the place. And I am satisfied that instead of doing me any detriment, it will strengthen me exceedingly and that if he was really to spend the £10,000 which he says he would do, I should be chose without £200 expense more than the common election charges. The number of persons at S[outhampton] who are not to be bought with money is very great, and whenever they unite, which happily they do in the present case, the lower sort, though they may make a noise for a time, neither can, nor dare resist them, and even of these three in four are under absolute promise and there are not many that would break a direct engagement. The day before yesterday was the election of a Mayor for the ensuing year who is the returning officer and, therefore, of importance. They were happily unanimous in choosing a man of exceeding good character – and a very good friend of mine – so that I think I have every security I could desire and have only to take care not to lose so fair a prospect by any neglect or want of attention and I have very good friends here upon the spot who will give me notice of what is necessary to be done from time to time . . .'[12]

His wife and brother-in-law, Sir Ferdinand Poole, had been helping Mr Hay in his election campaign at Lewes, and received this sound advice, together with some literary criticism of the first appearance of Dean Swift's posthumous letters:

'Every circumstance you mention about Lewes adds to the triumph of the victory. I saw it mentioned among a list of elections in one of the papers I received last night. I saw likewise an address of thanks from Mr Hampden, I wished to have seen one at the same time from Mr Hay, sure he does not forget it! ... I have got, since I have been here, the last publication of Swift's letters, which I am reading and which amuse me excessively. They contain his very inmost and secret thoughts upon every subject that occurred, serious or gay, and an account of the incidents of his life in a kind of journal, in which nothing is too trifling or too silly to be inserted. However, there is a sort of nonsense which no-one but a man of parts can write and which is not a bit the less nonsense for all that. His is quite of that kind and intermixed with many interesting passages and admirable little strokes. Upon the whole, we are certainly much obliged to the editor of them, though I do not think the Dean himself is; though after the nonsense he sent into the world in his lifetime, he has not much to complain. I can conceive, however, nothing that would have mortified his pride so much as if he had foreseen that these letters would be made public; and that posterity would see the man, of all the most self important, lying in bed to save his half bushel of coals (of which he talks much), and writing whole pages to two women of such kind of language and matter as nurses talk to children. However, he might have consoled himself with one thing, that he appears in a much more amiable light since these letters have been published than he did before. I see in them marks of strong passions, but not that misanthropy which has always been imputed to him and which might indeed grow upon him afterwards from subsequent disappointment. Nothing can be more tender and affectionate than he appears towards Stella, both in words and actions. It is singular that though he mentions the Vanhomrigh family in every page, there is not a syllable that can give the least information about Vanessa. Is it true that poor Sterne is dead? How sorry we shall both be if it is. It was put in an odd way; I am in hopes that it is false, yet not seeing it contradicted last night, I fear it is true. Sure we are wonderfully unfortunate in this country in the mortality of our geniuses. The wits of other countries and the fools of our own live for ever ...'[13]

When Parliament reassembled on May 10, 1768, Palmerston seconded Lord Charles Spencer's motion that Sir John Cust be re-elected Speaker, and took part in the traditional pantomime of dragging him to the chair. During the first four days of February, 1769, Palmerston sat in the House of Commons till two, three and four o'clock in the morning on the business of the disqualification of John Wilkes. The engagement diary for 1768 is one of the only two missing, but the overall diary records an avidly awaited family event. In the autumn he noted: 'About this time Lady Palmerston found herself breeding'. But expectation was the prelude to tragedy. Her correspondence over the years contains many references to headaches and physical malaise, and her charm and intelligence were not matched by good health. In the new year Palmerston was writing to her:

'I am sincerely sorry that though in every great and material point relating to your present situation you are so remarkably well, you are continually prevented from partaking the satisfaction which that consideration gives me by these teasing heartburns and headaches. I most sincerely wish Tomkin's new prescription may succeed better than his magnesia. I am sorry you think the prospect dark before you as I think nobody in your situation (which you must remember is not an uncommon one) can have a fairer . . .'[14]

It was an ill portent. In the overall diary for May 23, 1769, Palmerston had this sad entry to make:

'Lady Palmerston was taken ill with a feverish complaint. Two days afterwards she was brought to bed of a dead child. She was tolerably well for some days, but a fever came on suddenly which made a most rapid progress and on the fatal 1st of June terminated the existence of a being by far the most perfect I have ever known; of one who possessing worth, talents, temper and understanding superior to most persons of either sex, never during the whole of my connection with her spoke a word or did an act I could have wished to alter.'

There had been none of his painstaking entries in the engagement diary from April 9 until Thursday, June 1, when the square reserved for the day was blocked out in black.

Her monument in Romsey Church bears this inscription composed by her stricken husband:

With the nobler virtues that elevate our nature
She possessed the softer talents that adorn it,
Pious, humble, benevolent, candid and sincere,
She fulfilled the duties of humanity,
And her heart was warm with all its best affections,
Her sense was strong, her judgement accurate,
Her wit engaging and her taste refined,
While the elegance of her form, the graces of her manner,
And the natural propriety that ever accompanied her
Words and actions
Made virtue in her seem doubly attractive,
And taught her equally to command
Respect and love.
Such she lived – and such she died,
Calm and resigned to the dispensations of providence,
Leaving her disconsolate friends
To deplore her loss,
And cherish the dear remembrance of that worth
They honoured living and lament in death.

To the memory of the best of wives, the best of friends
He for whom she joined those tender names
Dedicates this marble.

REFERENCES

1. F.8(a)
2. F.8(c)
3. C.1 (a) and (b)
4. C.1(c) 19.IX.1767
5. C.1(d) undated
6. C.17(a) 6.X.1767
7. F.10
8. C.1(d) undated
9. C.1(d) undated
10. C.1(c) undated
11. A.2. 1768
12. C.1(d) undated
13. C.1(d) undated
14. C.1(d) undated

CHAPTER IV

PARLIAMENTARIAN AND POETASTER

Palmerston seeks solace in further travel – Pasquale Paoli at Broad-lands – the host of Admiralty House – aid elicited to obtain pension for Jean-Jacques Rousseau – second Grand Tour with William Pars, the painter – explores the Alps with Horace de Saussure – Almack's, the Opera, Catch and Pandemonium clubs – Reynolds, Garrick and Polly Kennedy – bouts-rimés at Bath – re-elected for Hastings in Lord North's interest – declines a literary dedication – converse with Captain Cook – General Burgoyne's account of Bunker Hill – elected to Royal Society – descriptions of noble houses – appointed to Board of the Treasury – host to Garrick and pall-bearer at his funeral – 'Capability' Brown's account – the fall of North and peace with the American colonies

PALMERSTON sought relief from his distress at the death of his wife in further travel. 'I passed the month of June principally at Sheen', he noted in his overall diary. 'Mr Godschall came and spent a few days with me and I went with him for a few days to Weston. I went to Broadlands at the beginning of July and from thence went with Mr Stanley and Mr Sloane to make a tour into South Wales.'

There is a curious presage of continuity in this brief entry. Mr Godschall, related through his maternal grandmother, was, in fact, the uncle of a young girl named Mary Mee, daughter of a London merchant and sister of Benjamin Mee, who was to become a director of the Bank of England. Fourteen years later she became Palmerston's second wife. The second travelling companion he names was Hans Sloane, the Hampshire neighbour who represented Newport, Isle of Wight.

Their tour meandered through Monmouth – where they landed to see some copper works: 'Very curious and picturesque. We saw the melted ore running out of the furnace into moulds formed of sand to receive it, which gave the most lively representation possible of a lava in miniature'[1] – Newport and

Broadlands, *from a print dated* 1779

Broadlands, 1957

Frances Poole, first wife of Viscount Palmerston

Swansea, and Palmerston kept a dry geographical account of their progress. On their return in August he wrote to his mother:

'I have been returned hither a few days from my Welsh expedition, which answered perfectly well in all the circumstances of weather, company, etc. We went as far as Milford Haven in Pembrokeshire and passed a day in sailing upon it . . .

'The part of Wales we saw is, upon the whole, a much finer, richer and better cultivated country than I expected, but in point of mountains, we were disappointed. It appeared very populous and all the cottages look very neat, being all white, and the inhabitants have a pride in keeping them as white as snow. The towns and villages are bad and put us in mind of the foreign towns in much poorer parts of the world. The roads we travelled were chiefly turnpikes, which have been made in great abundance lately, and we had no reason to complain of the accommodation we met with at the inns . . .[2]

'Southampton is very full and next Thursday Mr and Mrs Pye, who are become inhabitants there, are to give a masquerade to the whole company. I am excessively tired of masquerades and very glad to excuse myself from this . . .[3]

His next letter showed that these parochial pleasures had not erased his loss from his mind:

'I am much obliged to you for your kind letter of enquiry after my health and spirits. The first is very good and the latter indeed better than I could well expect, after so irreparable a loss as I have sustained and which it is impossible for me to forget even for a moment, though I endeavour to submit to it with the best resignation and patience I can, and do not indulge melancholy but try to avail myself of all the best motives and means of consolation in my power . . .[4]

On October 15 he reported an interesting visitor, the Corsican patriot, Pasquale Paoli, who, after the Republic of Genoa had surrendered his island to the French, had sought refuge in England during the summer and had become the lion of the London Season:

'We have had a visit from Paoli, who dined with me today and is gone tonight to Salisbury in his way to Bath, Bristol

D

and Oxford, etc. He came down from London to Portsmouth last Thursday, when I went with Mr Stanley and Mr Sloane to meet him and he came back with us to Mr Stanley's . . . We are all delighted with Paoli and, indeed, I think him one of the most pleasing men I ever met with. He has a very good figure and a very fine open sensible countenance. His behaviour is polite and engaging and, at the same time, perfectly manly. Nobody who hears him converse can doubt his good sense or his information, and he is at the same time extremely modest and yet very communicative where he finds an inclination to enquire into the matters he has been engaged in. There is not the least affectation either in his dress or manner, and he has more the appearance of an exceeding wellbred Englishman, than any foreigner I ever met with . . .'[5]

The new year of 1770 found Palmerston established again at Admiralty House: 'Lord North, Sir Gilbert Elliot, Lord Barrington, Stanley, Jenkinson, Charles Townshend, dined with me', reads the diary entry for January 31. On May 4 comes the even more tantalising list: 'Lord Ossory, Robinson, Charles Fox, Topham Beauclerk, Sir Joshua Reynolds, Crauford, Garrick'. There is, regrettably, no record of the conversational fireworks this company must have engendered, although one of the guests found his way into the anecdote book:

'*Topham Beauclerk, who looked remarkably dirty and unhealthy, having refused to play with a man to whom he used commonly to lose his money and giving for a reason that he was "tied up", the man turned away in a great passion and said, "By God, I should sooner have guessed by your looks you had been 'cut down'*".'

That Palmerston's political influence at this time can by no means have been negligible is evidenced by the letter he received from his earlier host at Spa, Earl Harcourt, latterly Chamberlain to the Queen's household and shortly to become Lord Lieutenant of Ireland. Its subject was Jean-Jacques Rousseau, who had just returned to France, after seeking in England with his friend, David Hume, freedom from persecution on the Continent:

'In consequence of the permission you gave me, I now

trouble you with a letter about Rousseau, which I fear will appear very tedious because I must necessarily enter into a long detail of his present situation, but Lord North [who in January 1770 had become First Lord of the Treasury], being a good-natured man, as well as a man of letters, when he knows the distress Rousseau labours under, will I doubt not feel glad to do himself the honour of extricating him from them.

'His wife has for a long time past been in an ill state of health and incapable of taking care of their small ménage and hitherto, he has himself been her nurse. But his advanced age will no longer permit him to perform that office, besides, not being able alone to clean the house, to go to market, and dress the victuals, he made an effort to keep a servant-maid, but after eight months' experience, found he could not afford it and being now, moreover, both of them unable to do any laborious work, or to attend to their ménage, all they wish is to board in some small family in the country, where they may live free from any care or any trouble and they earnestly desire to return to England; but their miserable income is not sufficient to enable them to live here – unless his pension is paid to him. When Lord Rochford was Ambassador at Paris, Rousseau wrote to him to say that he would accept the pension that the King had granted so generously to him; that he had hitherto only declined taking it through delicacy, as he had left this country so abruptly and had spoken rather disrespectfully of the nation; but that if Lord Rochford would only say that his apology was accepted, he should with great satisfaction receive the annual sums that had been granted. To this letter, Lord Rochford, not I suppose understanding the extreme sensibility of Rousseau's temper and perhaps not feeling what was due to so celebrated a genius, never made any reply, or even took the least notice of it.

'If you could state these circumstances to Lord North and could prevail on him to take the trouble of only writing two or three lines merely to say that the pension formerly granted should be paid to his order, that he had heard that Rousseau's declining to receive it had arisen only from delicacy, and that his motives for that refusal required no apology, such a letter, my dear Lord, would satisfy completely poor Rousseau's sensibility and be the means of his passing the remainder of his days in ease and comfort. So good a work would be a worthy object of your humanity to exert itself in, and I shall be not a little happy if you can succeed. Should you be able to procure this letter, I have means of getting it conveyed to him. The pension is £100 per annum.

PS. Pray do not let this transaction be made public, as that circumstance would perhaps prevent it being of any use, for a thousand eyes [sic] would be told and ridicules given.'[6]

* * *

Travel remained Palmerston's chief pleasure and on June 26, 1770, he set out on a second Grand Tour, this time with a large party, which included his parliamentary colleague, Hans Sloane, Hatsell [probably the John Hatsell who was Clerk to the House of Commons] and 'Pars, a painter' – a landscape artist who achieved considerable renown for his work in water colours. He had recently returned from a journey to Asia Minor on behalf of the Dilettanti Society, where his new patron doubtless met him. Palmerston employed him to sketch bas-reliefs and lake views on this tour, which lasted from June to October and covered most of Switzerland and Northern Italy, returning down the Rhine and through Luxembourg to Paris. Although Palmerston, in the three journals covering this journey, only mentions Pars making one drawing, of a Roman remain at Igel, between Trier and Luxembourg, an account written by his second wife, covering the same ground twenty-four years later, mentions further views which had been taken near the St Gotthard Pass and at Laufenburg and Schaffhausen. Palmerston makes no mention of these drawings at any time, nor is there any record of them having been sold. Many of them are now in the possession of the British Museum.

Palmerston's notes on the journey contain a number of intriguing descriptions:

Chamonix, July 24th. 'Went to some of the peasants' habitations – found their poverty great, but still their air not discontented – most of them proprietors themselves of the land they cultivate. Their lands pay in taxes to the Crown and to the Church about a quarter of what they might let for annually, and money laid out in purchase of land would bring about $2\frac{1}{2}\%$. We were much pleased with the herds of goats going up the mountains to feed regularly and coming down again at night, with a little boy dressed in goat skins to take care of them. We found that these goats were the property of different persons in the valley, who had from 4 to 10 each and who put them under the care of this boy during the summer months, for which they paid him about twopence of our money per goat, for the whole summer, and lodged him by turns . . .

July 27th. 'We were, in general, highly pleased with the behaviour and character of the Savoyards, particularly the people in the valley of Chamonix, whom we found hospitable, civil and obliging, familiar without the least rudeness, very sensible of any attention shown to them and reasonable in their charges which, considering they have been of late years much used to English travellers, is surprising.

'During the whole stay we made in this valley, we did not meet one beggar. The only method they use to try to get money, is by offering something to sell, which, if you do not want or choose to take, they immediately submit and go away.

'The children of the village were chiefly employed in gathering strawberries for us and sometimes, at our return in the evening, we were met by a train of 20 or 30 with each a plate of strawberries in their hands. We generally took them all, and the smallest trifle makes them perfectly happy. We found, by repeated trials where we happened to meet with persons who seemed deserving objects, that the receiving money as a mere gift without giving or doing something in return, was an idea totally new to them, and what they seemed hardly to like . . .

'We began to descend towards Martinach, a town of the Valais near the Rhone . . . The scene continued to improve quite till we reached the bottom and in the same proportion the inhabitants seemed to degenerate, and I never saw so sudden or striking a transition as from the vigorous health and cheerfulness of the mountaineers to the languid and sallow stupidity of the inhabitants of the valley. The swelled throats are very common and among the poorest sort seemed almost universal. All who have this disorder in any considerable degree seem dejected and look sickly and I am informed that it often deprives them of their faculties – but of this I must enquire further . . . I can say from observation that I have seen this evening, in and about the town of Martinach, more idiots than I can recollect to have seen in the last twelvemonth elsewhere . . .'

The party had been joined for a time by the distinguished figure of Horace de Saussure, the Swiss physicist whom Palmerston had met seven years earlier. He was to achieve further renown as the first man to climb Mont Blanc:

Grindelwald, August 3rd. 'Here Mons. de Saussure and I separated, he being obliged to return to Geneva. Mr Sloane and Mr Hatsell, who had stopped a day at the baths of Leukerbad and passed the Mont Gemmi into the Valley of Kandersteg joined me here just as I was setting out for Lauterbrunnen. They stayed at Grindelwald and we agreed to meet the next day at Interlaken.

August 5th. 'There are few executions in the Canton of Berne, as they have an institution resembling the galleys to which the generality of criminals are condemned; the most atrocious for life, others for a time according to the nature of their offence. They are confined in a large building and are employed in labour, particularly in keeping the streets clean, for which purpose they are brought out chained about a dozen together, to a cart, which they drag along and fill with shovels.

'The inhabitants are prohibited from the expensive articles of dress and are under some restrictions with regard to carriages, play, etc., but occasional companies of players have always been permitted, and a handsome room has just been built by subscription for the double purpose of a ballroom and theatre. They dine very early and meet to pass their afternoons constantly at cards, and, as far as I am informed, the polite world at Berne are not at all behindhand with their neighbours in dissipation, etc.

'We passed five days at Berne with Mr Norton, the English Minister to the Cantons, who resides there and who set out with us to make the remainder of our tour. The weather was excessively hot and fine.

August 11th. 'In the Canton of Berne, the people are a plain, strong, healthy looking race; their farmhouses remarkably large and neat. They have the means of living happy as their government is in general mild and their taxes light, and every man knows what he is to pay and what he can call his own – notwithstanding which the state, having no great appointments or pensions to pay, nor any military force but their militia and a small garrison for the city, to keep up, is rich and has a large sum of money beforehand. They have 5 or 600,000 in the English funds.

'The people's dress is odd; the men wear straw hats ornamented with ribbons, and large breeches like Dutchmen, and when they grow old let their beards grow – which makes an old peasant a very respectable figure. The women plait their hair behind with ribbons, which hang down to their heels; they are remarkably strong and large limbed and they tie their petticoat up under their arms, by which means it seldom comes half-way down their legs, which are about the size and shape of a large ninepin ...

August 13th. 'Schwyz is a small town, but neat, and the country about it appears populous and well cultivated. The Governments of this and the other little Cantons, which are Uri, Schwyz, Underwalden, Glarus and Zug, are entirely democratical and lie in the hands of all the people, so that every man above sixteen is admitted to the general assembly, which meets regularly once a year in a field, and is called together at other times when anything extraordinary demands their interposition. They determine all public matters of importance and elect or confirm the council and all public officers ... The council act as a court of justice in criminal matters, and ... when we arrived ... was assembled to try a man for robbery, and the people were waiting in the market place to hear the event. We endeavoured to get in during the trial, but found it impossible. The court soon broke up, which was lucky for us as our landlord was one of the members. They found the culprit guilty of the crime, but did not condemn him to death, which was expected, as he was a notorious offender. They ordered him to be whipped and banished the Canton – the former part of which was put in immediate execution . . .

'The men we saw in the town of Schwyz appeared to us remarkably large and stout made, and the women much the handsomest we saw in Switzerland . . .

August 27th. 'The neatness of the houses has been mentioned before and is very extraordinary all over Switzerland. Another thing has surprised us, which is to see nothing like a labourer's cottage; in 20 miles travelling one scarce sees a house worse than a good farmhouse in England, and in general much better looking. This proceeds from the great plenty of firwood all over the country and as the extent of ground to each house is but small, each owner easily lodges the persons necessary to him for the culture of his farm. In the last two or three days, we have passed much breeding ground and the cattle produced makes a very great article of the Swiss trade with Italy . . .

August 28th, Zurich. 'In the meadow is the place where the inhabitants exercise themselves in firing muskets at a mark. This practice is general throughout Switzerland, and . . . we were informed that every citizen is obliged to come six times in a year to the place of exercise and fire at three butts which are placed there. For this purpose three days in a week are fixed and an officer attends to keep account of those who come . . .

'The inhabitants are not much polished in their manners, nor do they live in much society together. The men assemble to smoke and the women to play at cards, each in separate parties. They are by no means a handsome race and we were all surprised to see so very few well-looking people in the whole town . . .

September 1st, Schaffhausen. 'After having seen the fall of the Rhine, we embarked just below it to proceed towards Basle. The boats made use of for this purpose are most excessively light and slender, consisting of nothing more than three deal planks nailed together. They never think of bringing these vessels back again, and as the workmanship bestowed on them is not costly, they are content to sell them for the value of the wood, or a mere trifle more. They are long and narrow, something like a Thames punt, and they fasten two or more of them together when they have any considerable burden to carry. The Rhine runs in some places with an amazing rapidity and, during the whole of our passage to Basle, we did not go less than 6 miles an hour with two boats tied together, and two men who did little more than steer us in our proper course ...

September 2nd. 'Passed the morning at Laufenburg, where we were much entertained with the variety of dresses in which the country people appeared, who came from the neighbour-hood, and which exactly resembled what we had seen in old portraits. Many of the old women, notwithstanding the season, wore with black dresses those fur caps with gold ornaments which we see in Rembrandt's pictures, and the peasants were in Vandyck dresses, without the smallest difference, from head to foot, except the coarseness of the materials and the want of the costlier ornaments ...

'Basle has some trades, but not so much as it might be expected to have from its situation. It was the residence of Erasmus and for some time of the painter, Hans Holbein – his great friend, many of whose works are preserved here, particularly a Cruci-fixion and some other pictures with it in the town house, which are the best of Holbein's works I ever saw. There is a large library, of which the greatest part belonged to Erasmus, and there are some pictures of Holbein. The most curious thing I saw is an edition of Erasmus' *Encomium of Folly*, with designs done with a pin by Holbein on the margin suitable to the subjects treated of. In one place there is a representation of Erasmus himself, with a note in Holbein's writing to this pur-pose in Latin: "When Erasmus came to this page and saw his picture, he said, 'if Erasmus was like this he would venture to take a wife' " ...

September 5th. 'Sloane and Hatsell, having quitted us here in order to make the best of their way home, Mr Pars and I embarked again on the Rhine to continue our journey to Strasbourg ...

September 12th, Strasbourg. 'Went to see a general exercise of the troops, amounting to about 10,000, of which a considerable proportion were cavalry ...

'The French troops make a fine appearance and are well clothed, but in order to supply the army, the country is depopulated. Whoever looks at the troops would think the French were a remarkable tall well-made people; whoever travels through the country and sees the labourers at work would think they were a nation of deformed dwarfs. Their cavalry in general are poorly mounted, particularly their dragoons . . .

September 15*th*. 'Embarked on the Rhine to proceed to Mannheim. We had now a single boat of a stronger constitution, large enough to carry us with our baggage conveniently, but not so fit for expedition as our former ones . . .

'There is one conveniency in travelling post in Germany, which is seldom to be met with in France, that the postmaster furnishes you with a very tolerable chaise for a trifling sum . . .

September 19*th*. 'Frankfurt is a large imperial city, famous for its trade and its fairs . . . The town has nothing in it remarkable or worth mention, unless it is the goodness of the inns, which are uncommonly large and magnificent. We were there just in the midst of the fair, which, however, did not answer our expectations either as to the concourse of people, the appearance of merchandise or the gaiety of the town. The utmost amusement of the place was a bad German play, and the booths and shops made but a very shabby figure . . .

September 20*th*. 'Went to Mainz in the public boat, which sets out every morning at ten from Frankfurt. It is a vessel as long as a West Country barge on the Thames, and there is a roof over the greatest part of it to keep the passengers dry but yet, on the whole, it is a very inconvenient conveyance, especially at the time of the fair when it is commonly crowded with passengers. Luckily it was fine weather and, choosing to be in the open air, we suffered no inconvenience, and were much diverted with the oddity of the scene. There were on board, to speak within compass, above 300 persons of all sorts, sexes, ages and conditions. The boat itself was like a little fair and there was a band of music, who played most part of the time. About twelve, the boat stopped at a little town called Hoechst, where it stayed an hour, during which time about two-thirds of the passengers, that is to say all who had money to pay for a dinner, went on shore to the public houses in the town, where there were long tables prepared and dinner ready to be served up to all who chose to sit down. At one, everybody returned to the boat and it was a very curious sight to see the train in its procession . . .

September 23rd. 'At Coblenz we took our leave of the Rhine, having followed it almost from its source . . .

September 25th. 'After dinner we set out, intending to lie at Luxembourg, but in passing Igel, a small village within the territory of Luxembourg, we were surprised to see a very fine piece of Roman antiquity, which we had never heard of. It is one of the most capital remains on this side the Alps. It consists of a kind of tower, near 70 feet high, built in a very good taste and highly ornamented with basso relievos and a variety of enrichments . . .

'Having stopped, that Mr Pars might make a drawing of the building, we lay at a small town on the Moselle, called Grevenmacher . . .

September 27th. 'Remained at Metz. Hitherto we had had no carriage, having been supplied at the posts, but as that is not the custom in France, I bought a two-wheeled open chaise for the journey to Paris . . .'[7]

On his return to England Palmerston plunged again into the London social round, which he described thus at the end of the year:

'The houses I used to frequent most this year and to which I had an *entrée libre*, were Lord Nuneham's, General Burgoyne's, Mr Stanley's, Mrs Hay's and Lord Spencer's, besides my mother who had a house in Dover Street.

'When unengaged I dined much at Almack's Club in Pall Mall, where there was a constant and excellent society. On a Saturday I dined at a club at the St Alban's Tavern, called the Opera Club.'[8]

He was also a member of the Pandemonium Club, the raffish institution of which Samuel Foote, the wit and dramatist, was president, and recorded in his book of anecdotes what is probably the original version of the famous quip:

'*Foote and Lord Sandwich were abusing each other in joke, when*

*Lord Sandwich said he should like to know whether Foote would die
by the pox or the gallows. To which Foote answered, "That will
happen according as I embrace your mistress or your principles".*'

Palmerston had also returned with new vigour to his parliamentary duties. On February 13, 1771, he seconded the motion
which Lord Beauchamp proposed approving the Address on
the 'Spanish declaration respecting the seizure of Falkland's
Island'. On March 25 he was at the House until three in the
morning for 'Alderman Oliver's business'. Alderman Oliver,
together with the Lord Mayor, Brass Crosby, both M.P.s, had
joined with Wilkes, now also an alderman of the City, in
resisting the intention of the House of preserving secrecy of
debate by forbidding publication of their proceedings. The
radical City aldermen had discharged an offending printer
from their court and arrested the messenger of the House of
Commons. For this contempt they were both sent to the
Tower, but on their release were hailed as popular heroes. They
were visited in prison by several members of the Rockingham
Opposition, but it seems from a further Palmerston anecdote
that Alderman Oliver had another cross to bear:

'*When Alderman Oliver was sent to the Tower, Sir Charles
Saunders and Admiral Keppel went to visit him. Finding Mrs Oliver
there, Sir Charles began to condole with her on the occasion. She
replied that for her own part she could not lament as she now had so
much more of Mr Oliver's company than she used to have. Sir
Charles, who was a man of few words, said nothing more till he
had quitted the room, when he hurried to Keppel and said what a
damned scrape this poor fellow is got into!*'

On May 19, on a visit more significant than he could foretell
at the time, he went to Weston with Sir Ferdinand Poole and
'found Mr Godschall, Mr and Mrs Culverden [Mary's sister],
Mrs and Miss Mee there'. It is the first mention in the papers of
his future wife, who at that time was a girl of sixteen.

Matrimony was still far from his mind. In the week beginning
June 10 the engagement diary indicates that he was at Ranelagh
on Monday, Wednesday and Friday, and during the following
week he was there again on the Monday and Friday, and at
Vauxhall on the Tuesday and Thursday. We also find him

named by Sir Joshua Reynolds as one of the admirers, with
Lord Robert Spencer and George Selwyn, of the notorious
Polly Kennedy, whose two brothers, convicted of murder, had
their sentence reduced to transportation as a result of her
patrons' influence.[9]

The overall diary for August 2, 1771, contains the short
entry: 'I set out for Ireland with Mr Pars, a draughtsman, whom
I carried with me'. As far as is known, this is the only evidence
of such a journey on the part of the artist, as no further record
of the tour has survived. On his return, Palmerston found that
the future Duchess of Devonshire's aunt required his services
as a linguist and versifier:

'Will you be so good as to translate at your leisure for me
this epitaph of Rousseau's? It is charming in its original, but I
wish *you* to give it me in English: you know, I know how much
you excel in these sort of works, for can I ever forget Iris a
mes feux, etc., which sure is the prettiest translation that ever
was . . .

I have the honour to remain with the sincerest respect, and
esteem, my Lord, your obedient and most faithful humble
servant

Isabella Poyntz'[10]

Ci gisent deux amans, l'un pour l'autre ils vécurent
L'un pour l'autre ils sont morts, et les loix en murmurent;
La simple piété n'y trouve qu'un forfait
Le sentiment admire, et la raison se tait.

This Palmerston translated:
Here rest a pair who by misfortune tried
Liv'd for each other, for each other died.
Harsh laws and stern religion blame their loves,
Reason is silent but the heart approves.

His summary in the overall diary at the end of the year read:
'This year, as before, I used to dine when I pleased, without
invitation, at Lord Nuneham's, General Burgoyne's and my
mother's, who had a house in the winter in Albemarle Street.

'I became a member of the Catch Club, which met every

Tuesday during the Winter season. The Opera Club, Ladies Club, Pandemonium and Almack's as usual.'

Work at Broadlands was proceeding all this time, and the letters from his new agent, Mr Daman, were punctuated with brief reference to the progress of 'Capability' Brown's plans. 'The columns at Broadlands are fixed', he wrote on April 20, 1771, reporting further in October:

'Lush has finished both sides of the river as far as Mr Brown set out, and the piece of the lower meade, late Coles, next to Miss Barker's is taken off, but the earth remains in an heap. He is now preparing the border of the river for turf and levelling the meadow next the old kitchen garden. Pain has finished all the inside of the house and put up the mahogany doors and built the boathouses and is going on with the new building in the front, according to Mr Brown's direction. This building is advanced about six feet above the surface of the court; the painters are employed on all the rooms in the west front . . .'[11]

Daman's letters make it clear that his master was an improving landlord, who had much work carried out on his tenants' farms. Palmerston frequently bought small parcels of land adjoining the Broadlands estate for the purpose, presumably, of straightening the boundaries and slowly, although very slightly, enlarging it, as most of the purchases were in lots of between one and five acres.

The advent of the Grafton administration in 1768 and the appointment of Lord North as First Lord of the Treasury in 1770 had made no difference to Palmerston's official position. Hospitality at Admiralty House included frequent dinners with Charles James Fox, who until this year was a fellow member of the Board, the Duke and Duchess of Gordon, Sir William Hamilton and his first wife, Sir Joshua Reynolds and David Garrick. There were also occasional excursions in the Admiralty barge to Gravesend. The engagement diary for the year contained a number of entries on the right-hand cash pages for two, five and occasionally ten guineas, but the details of the transactions were carefully obliterated at a later date in darker ink. They occur once, twice and even three times a week and occasionally it is possible to decipher a woman's name. It may

well be that with the eyes of posterity in mind, Palmerston
engaged in a little discreet censorship. The following year the
same thing occurs, although there is a supplementary and
additional diary, with duplicate entries, covering his three
months on the Continent between June and October, and here
these over-precise details of a lonely widower's lady companions remain undefaced.

For December 1, 1772, the overall diary contained the
notation:

'India House, being appointed a member of a secret committee of the House of Commons to inspect the affairs of the
India Company; this committee, of which Lord Liverpool,
then Mr Jenkinson, was president, sat at the India House from
day to day.'

Apart from a brief note to Mr Godschall on December 12,
Palmerston left no further record of the committee's deliberations, great though their importance was. Their recommendations formed the basis of Lord North's Regulating Act, which
opened a new chapter in British rule in India:

'My time for this fortnight past has been taken up with the
East India Committee which meets every day at the India
House, and goes on with great assiduity, though I have much
doubt whether we shall be able to make our report before the
holidays...'[12]

July 7, 1773, found him at Oxford to receive an honorary
degree of Doctor of Law. He dined at Queen's College and
attended the concert in the theatre and the ball. At the end of
the month he travelled to Spa with Lord Spencer, and thence
to Brussels and Paris. Received again into the best society in
the French capital, the enviable entry for September 13 noted
that he was at Madame Geoffrin's for dinner and at Madame
du Deffand's for supper; a happy combination of the two leading hostesses. On the 28th of the month he was presented to
the King at Versailles and two days later went hunting with
Louis XV in the forest of Sennart.

His taste for the arts had matured with time. The list of pictures purchased during this three-month period shows the

acquisition of some of the most valuable canvases to grace his collection. Palmerston spent £1,250 in Paris for twenty pictures bought from the great dealer, Dongen, including three Claudes, the Le Nain 'Itinerant Musicians', which is still in the dining-room at Broadlands, and other first-class works by Canaletto, Teniers, Wouwerman and Berghem. He had bought and often re-sold a number of pictures during the ten years after his first grand tour and his choice, in reflection of the taste of the times, fell chiefly on the Dutch school – Backhuysen, Hobbema, Brouwer, Ruysdael, Vandevelde and others. In all these transactions it is to be feared that Palmerston only made a profit on one. The landscape and figures by Berghem bought from Dongen for £208 was sold to Desenfans for £260 and bought back twenty years later for £210.

By 1773 Palmerston had acquired over 150 pictures at a cost exceeding £3,000. His own countrymen were not neglected. He bought Sir Joshua Reynolds' 'Children in the Wood' in 1770 for £52 10s. od., and paid Wright of Derby £200 in 1772 for his picture of an iron forge. Apart from the Berghem, this figure was never exceeded by Palmerston for any picture he bought and his discrimination was already sufficiently acute for them to fetch many times their purchase price when sold by subsequent generations.

* * *

With Britain drifting into war with her American colonies, Palmerston in his engagement diary for 1774 commenced the practice, continued until his death in 1802, of entering the exact temperature and weather of each day; information doubtless of interest to meteorologists, but not of sufficient importance to warrant inclusion here. He did note on January 29 that the Privy Council met to consider the position of Massachusetts Bay, but he found it more entertaining to spend five weeks in March and April at a miniature Parnassus, established by the remarkable Mrs Miller on the outskirts of Bath.

This lady and Captain Miller, her husband, had returned from a long period of residence abroad, to institute a temple of the arts on the banks of the Avon, to which the *beau monde* flocked during the fashionable Bath season. The current craze was for the completion of *bouts-rimés*. Those with poetical pretensions were called upon to complete a series of rhyming couplets, of which they had been given the last words of each line. The manuscripts were dropped into a 'Roman vase dressed with pink ribbons and myrtles' and the kneeling poets were crowned by the presiding muse herself.[13] Such visitors as the Duchess of Northumberland, the Marquess of Carmarthen and Admiral Keppel showed their skill, but of them all Palmerston proved the most adept. These were two of his entries:

To the Spring

To hail thy wish'd return, delightful Spring!
Behold how fair a train their chaplets bring!
Blythe as the feather'd songsters, warbling free,
Who own thy genial power on every tree;
Soft as thy zephyr's wings, when balmy rains
Have scatter'd fragrance o'er the smiling plains;
Oh! ne'er while these adorn the grove and field,
Shall fair BATHEASTON to Arcadia yield.

The Lover's Invitation to May Day

While Nature's warblers fill the trees,
And zephyr wakes his gentlest breeze,
Come forth, my Fair to hail the day,
That ushers in the sprightly May:
Let's twine a wreath with vi'lets blue,
Sweet emblem of affection true!
Come forth, my Fair, nor thus employ,
In fruitless dreams, the hour of joy.

Nevertheless, Palmerston's political fences had to be kept in repair. Although Parliament had not run its full seven-year course, affairs in America were causing serious misgivings and the King was anxious for fresh elections before the situation worsened. The faithful Lord North was able to come to a number of arrangements with borough patrons on behalf of the Court and Treasury party and Palmerston must have profited by one of them. On July 11, 1774, we find him dining with Lord North at Bushey and on August 9 he was there again 'to settle finally about being elected for Hastings.'[14]

Palmerston was still a member of the Board of Admiralty, and his attitude at this juncture is of considerable interest. He did not belong to the group of Newcastle's heirs who coalesced round Burke in their resentment against George III and worked up a party theory of a sort. Palmerston already realised, like most so-called Whigs, and many so-called Tories, that the business of government must go on, and that in politics one First Lord of the Treasury was very like another. If Palmerston had been less in the swim, he would have qualified for the modern historians' classification of an 'independent country gentleman'. If he had been more assiduous, he would have fallen into the category of office-limpets, now described as King's Friends. It is because Palmerston cannot be fitted into either of these attitudes that his political allegiances are so interesting and representative of a whole mass of Englishmen.

It must not be overlooked that North, in spite of the epithets since heaped on him, was also a Whig, a Walpole-character, who tried to ignore all issues and heal all wounds by a moderate taxation policy and *quieta non movere*. The war with the American colonies ruined this, but at the start his American policy enjoyed almost unanimous support. Palmerston wrote to his co-member for Southampton, Hans Stanley, to advise him of his intentions, and received a reply, dated August 6, which illustrates the manner in which elections were still a matter for private arrangements between the interested parties:

'I learnt with very great regret that you continued in the sentiments you formerly mentioned to me with regard to Southampton, as nothing could have been more agreeable to me than to have always had for my colleague one of the men in the world I love the best, and esteem the most; I had indeed hoped, as you had for some time remained silent on the subject, that your reluctance upon that point was diminished . . .

'As you desire to convey my thoughts to Lord North, I will beg of you to say, that I do not at present see any other expedient to prevent infinite confusion at Southampton, than communicating your intention to Mr Fleming, of whose political conduct I have good hopes, but do not pretend to answer for him. If he declines standing, I shall retrench myself upon my own ground, and cannot engage for the support of any second person . . .

' PS. Aug. 7th in the morning.

'Upon consulting my pillow, I think it may be difficult for me to prevent this business transpiring, as in the present temper of people, which is so much upon the *qui vive*, I cannot well avoid being asked about your arrival here, and your intentions, and any evasion of an answer might be resented, therefore if notwithstanding my certainty of your having a quiet, and easy election, you continue fixed in your former opinion, I shall be infinitely obliged to you, if you will come here immediately in order to the bringing my own situation to a speedy and as I think a much more advantageous crisis, but if any serious business (which alone, I flatter myself will delay you), should oblige you to postpone your journey, I beg you will send me by express two letters. The first to the corporation with thanks for past favours, assurances of attachment whenever their interest may be concerned etc., etc., the second to Mr Fleming, "That though it would be improper for you to interfere in the recommendation of your successor, yet thinking the opportunity might be agreeable to him, you have from personal regard, and a wish to cultivate his friendship thought proper to give him the first notice". But if your Lordship should not come, and have no objection to these steps, I ought to explain that I mean the two letters, to be what is called *in retentis* to be made use of or not by me as occasion requires.

'My reason for wishing you to write to Mr Fleming is that his offer may not appear my entire suggestion, which would have the air of my pretending to recommend two members, and occasion a good deal of jealousy.'[15]

That letter arrived on the day Palmerston 'went to Sevenoaks to a cricket match. The Duke of Dorset with six other Kentish men against the Hambleden Club. Kentish men beat easily'[16] However, the political arrangement proceeded according to

plan and Palmerston's engagement diary for October 10 read:
'was at Hastings for the election, having arrived there on the
previous day'.

This sudden flurry of business may have prevented Palmerston
from acquiring a modest measure of literary recognition. With
the date of September 10, he received from Paris a letter from
the French author who had translated Laurence Sterne's *Sentimental Journey* and wished to dedicate his version of *Tristram
Shandy* to Palmerston:

'Je n'ai l'honneur d'être connu de vous que par mon nom.
Vous n'avez point trouvé mauvais que j'eusse eu la hardiesse
de le placer au-dessous de celui de Mr Sterne sur le frontispice
de la traduction de son Voyage Sentimental. Mlle de L'Espinasse,
M. le Marquis de Villevieille, et M. Dalembers m'ont même
dit que vous aviez paru désirer à cette occasion que je fisse
celle de Tristram Shandy. C'est ce que j'ai fait, Milord. J'ai,
tout-à-la-fois, secondé vos désirs et satisfait mon goût. Plus
l'entreprise était difficile ci plus je m'y suis obstiné. Ais-je
réussi? Les personnes que je viens de vous nommer et beaucoup
d'autres me l'ont assuré. Ce qu'il y a de certain, c'est que j'ai
tâché d'identifier ma propre gaieté avec celle de Mr Sterne, et
que j'ai fait mon possible pour que son ouvrage eut parmi nous
le même succès qu'il a eu en Angleterre. J'aurais de la peine à
croire qu'il n'y eut pas la même vogue. Il ne me reste, Milord,
qu'une chose à désirer. C'est que vous me permettrez de vous
dédier ma traduction. Je vous avoue même que ce qui a le plus
contribué à me faire faire tant d'effort, est l'espoir que vous ne
me refuseriez pas cette grace. Je vous supplie donc, Milord, de
me l'accorder, et de vouloir bien, en conséquence, me faire
passer tous vos titres.

J'ai l'honneur d'être avec un profond respect, Milord,
Votre très humble et très obéissant serviteur
          Frenais
          Intendant des affaires de la maison de Néelle,
          Rue de Touraine près les Cordeliers
          à Paris.'[17]

For a generous patron of the arts Palmerston returned a

singularly dusty answer. However, it at least gave evidence of a very tolerable domination of the French language:

'Monsieur,

Je viens de recevoir la lettre que vous m'avez fait l'honneur de m'écrire. Ma mémoire m'avait si mal servi que les circonstances dont vous me parlez m'avaient totalement échappées.

Je vous félicite d'avoir achevé une ouvrage qui aura probablement beaucoup de succès: surtout si vous avez pris la license très permise et très nécessaire d'en retrancher certains passages qui sont fort déplacés dans l'original et qui le seraient encore plus dans une traduction.

Au reste, Monsieur, quoique très sensible à l'honneur que vous voulez me faire en me dédiant votre ouvrage, j'espère que vous ne trouverez pas mauvais si je vous prie très sérieusement de m'en dispenser comme d'une chose qui m'est en général très désagréable et que j'ai toujours fait mon possible pour éviter. Vous ne pouvez pas certainement avoir la moindre difficulté à trouver des personnes dont les noms feront honneur à votre livre et qui ayant l'avantage de vous connaître et d'être connus de vous doivent naturellement s'attendre à ce compliment de votre part.'

Palmerston's membership of the Board of Admiralty gave him the pleasurable privilege of reading the despatches from Captain Cook on his way back to England after the three years of his second voyage of discovery, and, on June 26, 1775, Palmerston sent a short précis to William Godschall. The landscape painter mentioned was William Hodges, who had owed his membership of the expedition to Palmerston's patronage and recommendation:

'Captain Cook is not arrived yet, one of the India ships has brought us a letter from him dated at the Cape and accompanied by his journal, and by several views taken by the landscape painter who went with them. I inspected his journal (which is very full) for about an hour before it went to the King, and found by it that he has not been able to discover any continent and that from his as well as Furneaux' voyage, it is clear that there is none within a habitable degree of latitude.

He has explored everything that he meant to explore and has returned to the Cape of Good Hope after twenty-eight months absence from thence, in very good condition, and without the loss of a single man by sickness from their leaving England. He spent several months after Furneaux' departure in exploring the Pacific Ocean, where he wintered again, and met with several new islands and many others that had been formerly seen by old navigators, but had remained unvisited in their time. In his return, he first made the western entrance of the Straits of Magellan and then accurately surveyed the coast of Tierra del Fuego, hitherto but little known and, likewise, that of Statens Land. In bearing away from thence to the eastward, he fell in with two very large lands, hitherto unknown, in the southern part of the Atlantic Ocean. One of which called by him New Georgia he found to be an island uninhabited, dreary, snowy and horrid beyond anything he had ever seen. He says that Lord Anson's description of Statens Land is that of a paradise compared to this. He found another land of the same kind and while he was examining the northern end, was driven off by a storm without being able to ascertain whether it was an island or a continent. It is, however, equally inhospitable and uninhabited, so that it is of no great consequence. His own opinion is that there is a continent within the ice, and that it advances more northward into the Atlantic than into the Pacific Ocean, as he found the ice and bad weather more advanced there to the northward and his reasoning is that if it were all sea the ice would reach everywhere nearly to an equal degree of latitude. He then satisfied himself that there is no Cape Circumcision, as set down by the French navigators, and then returned to the Cape of Good Hope . . . Kendall's watch made after Harrison's has answered beyond every expectation, and by being now and then corrected by lunar observations, has proved a most faithful guide . . .'[18]

News of an even more momentous event reached him from that thunderbolt of war and old friend General John Burgoyne, who wrote him on June 25 giving Palmerston this account of the Battle of Bunker Hill:

'I take the first opportunity of a safe conveyance of my letter to acquit myself of the duty you enjoined, and which I owe to your friendship.

'But after informing you I am perfectly well, a circumstance from which I am sure you will receive satisfaction, I know not where to find one, which will not give you pain.

'Our prospects on the side of the enemy are gloomy. Enthusiasm, and a combination of artifice on one side, perhaps mismanagement on the other, and accident or both, have produced a crisis that my little reading in history cannot parallel.

'The British Empire in America is overturned without great exertions on your side of the water.

'If the confederacy on this continent is general, as I incline now to believe it, and you determine to subdue it by arms, you must have recourse to Russia or Germany; such a pittance of troops, as Great Britain and Ireland can supply will only serve to prolong the war, to create fruitless expense, and insure disappointment.

'You will hear by these dispatches of a victory of our troops, and perhaps government will be elated with the account. It is glorious to the troops, and important to the nation, inasmuch as the disgrace of the 19th of April [Lexington] is erased, and the superiority of the King's troops over a rebel army is confirmed. It is certain we had the odds of three or four to one, to contend with, assisted with all that nature and art could do to give strength to a post, and inspired (I may so call it), with the fanaticism of a favourite demagogue (Warren) who devoted himself at their head and fell accordingly. But our victory has been bought by an uncommon loss of officers, some of them irreparable, and I fear the consequences will not answer the expectations that will be raised in England.

'I will take the liberty, my dear Lord, to refer you to Lady Charlotte for the picture of the action; it not having been my lot to be personally engaged further then in the superintendance of a cannonade. I had leisure to observe and describe it, and a complication of horrors rendered it the greatest scene that the imagination can conceive. For the time it was most animating; but the private sorrows that followed upon looking round the field, have been more than ordinarily numerous, and affecting . . .

'I have mentioned a plan in my letters to the Great and Powerful, that may carry me home in the course of the ensuing autumn. The enjoyment of your Lordship's friendship will be among the principal pleasures of my return . . .'[19]

The parliamentary recess found Palmerston again on his travels; this time to the West of England. He was wined and dined on board the *Foudroyant* at Plymouth; stayed with Lord Edgcumbe on his estate overlooking Plymouth Sound, and found some curious fishing practices to note in Cornwall:

August 8th. 'Penzance is very pretty as you approach it, but very mean when you are entered into it . . . This is the part of the coast where the pilchard fishing is carried on and it is now in the height. The pilchard is a smaller kind of herring, coming in vast shoals on this coast. When caught, they first press them to extract an oil, and then salt and send them in hogsheads to Spain and Portugal and up the Mediterranean. This fishery employs a very great number of people, who go out in boats with vast nets, called seines and lie waiting till signals are made to them from their comrades on the hills, who can see by the appearance of the water where the shoals of fish are. A seine net is managed by 17 men in three boats, who, on seeing the signal, row away to the spot pointed out and endeavour to enclose the shoal with their net, which they sometimes do so effectually that we were told 300 hogsheads or more are taken out of one seine at a time. Mounts Bay exports about 25,000 hogsheads annually. Vast numbers of single boats go out with smaller nets of a different kind, called driving nets.

August 10th. 'Brixham, a small town within Torbay, is famous for the quantity of fish caught there, from whence the whole country round is supplied. The plenty and cheapness of fish on all this coast is a great luxury to the rich and a most essential blessing to the poor, who are able to purchase, all the year round, excellent fish such as mackerel, whitings, herrings, grey mullet, etc., at a price within the reach of everybody and, in general, at one-third of the price of meat.'[20]

On his return to London he was reasonably assiduous in his

attendance at the House of Commons. Debate on Burke's motion for a bill to give up the dispute with the Americas lasted until four o'clock in the morning of November 17, and was defeated by 210 votes to 105. On November 20 the House considered a bill for prohibiting all commerce with the Americas and for appointing commissioners. The next day, with the members presumably exhausted, Palmerston noted 'there was no House of Commons, for want of numbers for a ballot'. The war certainly had no effect on the habits of the ruling class. February, 1776, found Palmerston hunting near Stevenage with the hounds of Lord Melbourne. In March, Lords North, Sandwich and Lisburne came to dine at Admiralty House with a party of catch singers, and in May Palmerston went, with the Duke and Duchess of Devonshire, Lady Pembroke, Madame de Castiglione, the Prince de Salm, Lords Spencer and Carlisle and Monsieur Champcenet, the King of France's Chamberlain, for a trip in a launch up the Thames. Racing at Newmarket; masquerades at Ranelagh; sailing at Cowes; the Beauclerks; the Beauchamps; Bright[helms]ton[e] – just becoming fashionable; the Duke of Manchester; the Duke of Bolton; Almack's; the Catch Club; the concerts of *antient* music; Garrick at Drury Lane; the diary entries crowded one another in Palmerston's neat copper plate.

On June 8, 1776, Palmerston even found time to dine with Captain Cook, on board the *Resolution* in the Long Reach, just before he set off on his last expedition. There were private parties too, dinners with his future family, Mr and Mrs Culverden, Mrs and Miss Mee, and his mother, Mrs Temple. There were, as yet, no signs of a ripening affection, but the names of Mee, Culverden and Godschall occurred frequently, and he clearly watched his second wife growing up over many years. October 10, 1776, saw recorded the distressingly laconic entry, 'account came of the taking of Long Island; dined at White's; play'. And on November 7 he was elected a member of the Royal Society.

The summer of 1777 found him off on tour again, returning with matured judgment to some of the grand houses he had first visited as an undergraduate:

June 16th. 'Blenheim. Saw the park, house and garden; found everything in high beauty and the place improving continually as the trees that have been planted begin to thrive. The whole plan seems finished and unites magnificence, beauty and comfort beyond any place I ever saw.

June 17th. 'The gardens of Stowe are now as much behind some of the best modern ones in point of good taste as they were before all that existed at the time they were made. The walk round them is rather fatiguing and the entertainment one meets with does not pay one. The water is bad and ill-shaped; the country is ugly and the whole, though very extensive, is destitute of striking beauties. Some of the buildings have been taken down, but there are still too many and yet, though many of them are great and expensive, none that we saw are pleasant or comfortable to sit in ... An immense hall within and some new rooms are not yet completed; some of the old ones have been modernised, but the expense does not seem to have been spared, yet there has been a very great deficiency of good taste and judgment, as we scarcely observed any one part of the house within, or garden without, that was complete in its way, or that was not marked by some striking defect or impropriety ...

June 25th. 'To Carlet Ferry, where we embarked for Liverpool, which is about 6 miles lower down the Mersey on the opposite shore. We were about an hour on our passage and landed about three. The carriage and baggage followed in another vessel, about two hours afterwards. There are several of these vessels employed as passage boats, backwards and forwards between Liverpool and different parts of the Cheshire coast. We walked round the docks before dinner, which are a very great work, begun and completed within a few years past, by which an immense quantity of shipping are received into perfect security and lie at the merchants' doors, to be loaded, unloaded or refitted. We dined at the Golden Lion ... In the evening we went to the playhouse, which is very handsome and spacious and where we found a tolerable good company, among whom were some of the London performers. Liverpool has increased much of late years and is an opulent, thriving, adventurous trading town, and to form some idea of the extent of its commerce, it would be sufficient to see the quantity of shipping in its docks. Its size is very great, but its appearance mean and its streets bad, and except the Exchange, which if it could be well seen would have a fine appearance, we saw no public building of any note . . .

July 2nd. 'About three miles from Ripon is Studley Park, the seat of Mr Aislabie, which is a fine place . . . There are many favourable circumstances belonging to it, such as inequality of ground, wood and views of the adjacent country, but it is ill laid out in point of taste and the water, from its scantiness, formality and badness of its colour, is rather a disgrace than an ornament. There are many buildings and most of them bad. The happiest circumstance is Fountains Abbey, which Mr Aislabie has lately purchased. It is a very noble ruin of a vast abbey and though it appears to have been in a bad style of architecture, yet from its greatness and happy situation it produces a very fine effect . . .

July 4th. 'Wentworth House, Lord Rockingham's, which is an immense house, part new and part old. The new front much resembles Lord Tylney's at Wanstead. The principal apartments are none of them finished and the ornaments are grown to be out of date before they are completed. The hall, which is intended to be a fine one and done with scagliola, in imitation of marble, was begun about four and twenty years ago by an Italian artist, who is still employed there. The apartments which the family inhabit are low and bad. Before the house in the park is a hill, which entirely obstructed all view from the window. This it was thought necessary to remove and, accordingly, it was undertaken about 14 years ago. It is now about half finished, and there are about ten men at work upon it. The stables, which are new built and nearly finished, are very large and magnificent . . .

July 6th. 'To Chatsworth. This place has a very princely appearance. The house is noble, without, and very great within, though it has more of ancient magnificence than of modern comfort. The grounds have been much improved of late years by Mr Brown, who has contrived to make the river a fine object from the garden, from which, before, it was quite concealed.

The gardens themselves have not been much modernised. What remains of the waterworks consists of a very formal cascade and two *jets d'eau*. The latter are the most considerable in England, and from their greatness produce a very noble effect. The plantations on the neighbouring hills are now well-grown and are augmented every year and have so changed the face of the country that Chatsworth no longer presents those dreary prospects it was once reproached with . . .

July 7th. 'To Kedleston. This house, where Lord Scarsdale has built under the direction of Adams, is a very fine one and, at the same time, very comfortable and convenient. The most remarkable thing is the great hall, which is now finished and is one of the most beautiful things, and, at the same time, most magnificent that can be seen. It is ornamented and supported by 20 immense fluted corinthian columns of Derbyshire marble, which have a most noble effect. The grounds are not remarkable for any great beauty, but the park is full of exceeding fine large old oaks.'[21]

During the winter of 1777 Palmerston finally left the Admiralty, after twelve years on the Board, and became a member of the Board of the Treasury, an event chiefly signified by the fact that this obliged him to pay a forfeit of seven guineas to the Catch Club. He was also compelled to find another London residence, and in March of the following year leased a house at 4 Park Street, Westminster, now known as 22 Queen Anne's Gate. He took his reputation for hospitality with him, and the names of Richard Brinsley Sheridan and his wife were added with increasing frequency to the long roster of the guest list.

David Garrick had retired from the stage in 1777, an event signalised by this entry in Palmerston's anecdote book:

'*The clothes in which Garrick appeared for the last time were distributed among the other actors who preserved them as relics. One of them, who received his shoe buckles, returned the following answer:*

"Your buckles, dear Garrick, I'll venture to use,

But who is the man that shall stand in your shoes?".'

In the autumn of 1788 Garrick was writing to his old friend to acknowledge an invitation:

'It happens very conveniently for us that your Lordship will not be so soon at Broadlands. Some friends of ours wished to have passed a few days with us the first week in September, and as we intend taking a peep at the Camp in our way to your Lordship, we will do ourselves the honour, by your gracious leave, to finish the climax of our pleasures at Broadlands about the 13th or 14th. Should this be disagreeable to your Lordship, I shall obey your commands, preferable to any other consideration.'[22]

But the great actor was already failing in health, and on September 10 his wife was obliged to write from Hampton:

'Though at any other time I should have been happy to be the secretary of Mr Garrick, yet at this moment I am very unhappy on many accounts; but he was taken so ill yesterday morning with a pain in his stomach and a trembling cold fit, that he was put immediately into bed, and every assistance was given him that Hampton could procure. He still keeps his bed, and only laments of being disappointed next Sunday of waiting upon you.

'He desires me to present his respects and that he will take the liberty to write a line next Saturday to your Lordship, as we live still in hopes that you might have another leisure day to bestow upon us.'[23]

A few days later, however, Garrick and his friends arrived at Broadlands and at the end of the month Palmerston, Garrick, Sir Joshua Reynolds and Hans Stanley attended the King's tour of military camps at Winchester. After his guests had left, Palmerston reported to his mother:

'Mr and Mrs Garrick have been in this county and passed several days here. He was just recovered from a severe illness and had a slight attack of his complaint one of the days he was with me; however, he was in tolerably good health and spirits on the whole, and seemed highly pleased with this country. They went from me to Mr Stanley's, where they still are, but leave him tomorrow . . .'[24]

Garrick's own letter of thanks had a sombre tone:

'Many things have happened, since I saw you last, worthy of notice. The circumstance of most consequence to me is that I thought I should have never seen Broadlands again.

'A most violent bilious attack almost overset me Sunday morning, but I have luckily got over it and shall leave Mr Stanley in half an hour. Had not Mr Price told me of your Lordship being at Southampton, I should just have called to pay my respects.

'My wife presents hers with mine, and we both assure your Lordship that our reception in Hampshire has made a most lasting impression and for which we beg leave to send our best acknowledgements.'[25]

By the winter Garrick was mortally ill and in January he died. Palmerston's letter to William Godschall on February 1, 1779, gave this account of the last sad scene:

'I am just returned from the melancholy office of attending poor Garrick's funeral, which was a public one and drew together the greatest concourse of people I ever remember to have seen. I was glad to observe so many marks of public respect paid to his memory, as his was a situation which could attract extraordinary honours only by extraordinary merits. The pall was supported by the Duke of Devonshire, Lord Spencer, Lord Hampden, Lord Ossory, Sir Watkin Williams, Mr Stanley, Mr Rigby, Mr Wallace, Mr Patterson and myself. He is deposited in a small vault made on purpose at the feet of Shakespeare's monument. There will be a monument erected to him as near as possible, and I imagine the executors intend to desire Doctor Johnson to write an inscription . . .'[26]

* * *

A new figure in the political firmament made his appearance in July, when a letter arrived from a young aspirant to membership of the House of Commons – two years before he was finally elected, and a year before he attained his majority:

Pembroke Hall, July 18th, 1779

'My Lord,
It being my intention to offer myself a Candidate to represent the University of Cambridge at the General Election, and other Candidates having already entered themselves, I am under the

necessity of submitting my wishes as soon as possible to all the Members of the Senate.

I flatter myself, your Lordship will have the goodness to consider these circumstances as an apology for the liberty I take in troubling you with so early an application, and allow me to assure your Lordship that I should esteem the honour of your Lordship's support on this occasion – a very particular obligation.

I have the honour to be, my Lord,

Your Lordship's most obedient humble servant,

W. Pitt'[27]

On November 17 a letter from 'Capability' Brown, whose account for the thirteen years of his work at Broadlands since 1766 reached the tremendous sum of £23,405, had good reason to express pleasure:

'I have sent your Lordship the amount of the money I have had the honour and pleasure of disbursing at Broadlands, as near as I possibly can, which is the whole of the expense, exclusive of oak timber and red bricks; for the following works (viz:) all the out of door works, in which are included kitchen garden, stoves, dairy, etc., lodges, green house, repairs at Spurshot Farm, or the greatest part of it, some small matter done to the building in the wood. All the necessary men's bills; the whole house – inside and out – the additional offices, etc., and the repairs of the old offices, etc., etc., etc., plans, journey's, commission to myself are included, as will appear on the other side.

'The work was begun in March, 1766, and ended early in 1779, paid by Lord Palmerston.

'There remains due to workmen and myself, under £500, which shall be delivered to your Lordship – with the papers and accounts – when your Lordship comes to town and shall then with an unfeigned heart return your Lordship my thanks for numberless civilities, kind usage and pleasant employment.'[28]

This drain on his resources caused a drastic cut in Palmerston's expenditure on works of art. During the ten years from 1773 until his second marriage, he bought only sixteen pictures at a cost of £300, a quarter of this being spent on four canvases by his protégé Pars. Palmerston was also maintaining a mistress – a Madame Gallina, daughter of an Italian officer of dragoons and wife of a surgeon in Milan. She arrived in London in 1778 and met Palmerston, who installed her in a house in Great Marlborough Street. Within two years he had tired of her and had found her a post as governess with a family, which she left when the husband made improper advances. Palmerston was then deluged with begging letters, and in the end arranged through a Monsieur le Turc to have her fare paid back to Geneva, where she was met 'fortuitously' by her husband. Palmerston had ascertained that he wanted his wife back and instructed le Ture to advise Signor Gallina of her movements – an uncommonly neat solution to an awkward imbroglio.[29]

The engagement diary entries for these years provided evidence of a widening range of hospitality, with the addition of the Duke and Duchess of Devonshire, Lords Ossory and Loughborough, Lord and Lady Jersey, Sir Ralph and Lady Payne, Charles Greville and the Hon. Henry Pelham. Most Sundays in town he called on Mrs Sheridan. Sir Joshua Reynolds was an almost constant companion, and his membership of the Royal Society found him often in the company of Sir Joseph Banks, the President, and Dr Herschel, the famous astronomer. From time to time Palmerston would make a note of some piece of repartee that had pleased him:

'*Lord Stanley, having given a very magnificent, expensive and well conducted entertainment at his house at the Oaks, which was chiefly planned and conducted by General Burgoyne, the weather turned out so remarkably fine that it was observed that it seemed as if General Burgoyne had ordered it and Lord Stanley paid for it.*

'*When Mr Pitt first began to take part in the House of Commons against Charles Fox, Gibbon said he was a very pretty painted pleasure boat, but that if he did not take care he would be run down by the black collier.*

'*Stephen Fox, having a son born by which his brother, Charles, who had borrowed an enormous sum of jews and usurers, was cut off*

The cascade at Lauterbrunnen, Switzerland, drawn by William Pars, during Lord Palmerston's second Grand Tour, 1770

Mary Mee, second wife of Viscount Palmerston

from the prospect of inheriting Lord Holland's estate, Horace Walpole said the child was a second Messiah come into the world for the total destruction of the Jewish nation.'

The unpleasant personality of the son-in-law of the Earl of Bute aroused this comment:

'A person, speaking of the unpopularity of Sir James Lowther, said that the influence his property gave him was so great that with common civility, he might have had the entire command of two counties. "Aye," replied another person, "that he certainly might, or, even with common incivility".'

Palmerston must also take his place as one of the earliest patrons of George Crabbe, who, after working for a period as a day labourer at his birthplace, Aldeburgh, had arrived in London in March, 1781, where he was received by Edmund Burke, who read his manuscripts, helped with their publication and sought the help of others to enable Crabbe to enter the Church. Palmerston received this letter in July 1781:

'My Lord,

If I waited upon your Lordship this day at an improper time, I humbly beg of you to impute it to my earnest desire to return my thanks for the very liberal present which I was honoured with from your Lordship, and my fear that I should not have another opportunity of seeing so kind and generous a benefactor. Your Lordship principally, and some of my other friends, by your unexpected, and I fear unmerited liberality, have given me an opportunity of paying a short visit to a family in Suffolk, very near and dear to me, whom I shall teach to speak of your Lordship with gratitude and the highest respect.

I will presume to call upon your Lordship tomorrow, but fearing that it may not be convenient to admit me, I take the method of thanking your Lordship – not in the manner I ought – but in such as I am capable of; and I humbly beg of you to believe me duly sensible of the favour your Lordship done me, by your bounty and the honour you have conferred upon me, by supposing me an object worthy to partake of it. One so little entitled as I am to your Lordship's notice, from my station in life, and my errors as a writer, must not presume to hope for other favours than I hope I have received, but from what my

E

kind and excellent friend Mr Cholmondeley has told me, and what I have otherwise reason to believe, I can but comment that I am not entitled to your Lordship's advice and correction in the literary employment which my fortune – and since I have met with such friends as your Lordship, I may add, my good fortune – has led me to.

Whatever is my success in future, and however perplexing my difficulties – for the long struggle I have had with poverty and disappointment, cannot be easily got over – I shall ever retain a most grateful sense of your favours, and be proud to see your Lordship at a more convenient opportunity.'[30]

During the dying months of the American war in 1782, and the ministerial crisis that led to the peace, Palmerston made frequent notes on the right-hand pages of his engagement diaries of the debates in the House of Commons – and of political anecdotes concerning the chief protagonists:

February 22nd. 'General Conway moved that an Address should be presented to the King, requesting that the American War might be no longer carried on for the impracticable purpose of subduing the Continent of America by force. Negatived by 194 to 193.

'On Wednesday, February 27th, General Conway renewed his motion with a slight variation in compliance with the forms of the House. The Attorney-General moved to postpone the debate for a fortnight and that a bill should be brought in to empower the King to conclude peace with America on such terms as he should think most beneficial. This motion was not carried, being negatived by 234 to 214. The original motion was then carried and an Address in consequence ordered to be carried up to the King by the whole House.

'On Friday, the 15th [March], a resolution was moved in the House of Commons by Sir John Rous, and seconded by Lord G. Cavendish, to say that Parliament could no longer place any confidence in the Ministers on account of the calamities the country had suffered. This was negatived by 236 to 227. The number of members present with the Speaker and four tellers amounted to 468, besides many who had paired off. This was the largest number since Sir Rob[ert] Walpole's time.

'On Wednesday [the 20th] a similar motion to the last was to have been made by Lord Surrey, seconded by Sir Robert Smith. About four Lord North came to the House and declared that as the purpose of the motion had been made known to the House, he thought it proper to inform them that such a motion was become unnecessary as His Majesty had come to a resolution of putting the conduct of his affairs into other hands; and moved that the House should adjourn till Monday next (the 25th) to give time for new arrangements. This produced noise, altercation and confusion, but was agreed to by the principal persons of the Opposition, with many declarations that if something was not done satisfactorily before Monday they would proceed to something more violent.

'It is generally believed that Lord North has wished to give the thing up ever since the Address was carried against him, but has remained at the King's earnest desire. That upon finding the question of Wednesday likely to be carried against him, he has insisted on giving up before a parliamentary censure was passed on him, rather than afterwards. That the King, even in this extremity, takes it unkindly that he should abandon him and is in the utmost distress at finding himself thus in the hands of all the people he dislikes the most. During the week preceding, negotiations had been carrying on by Lord Chancellor, with Lord Rockingham, to try whether any terms or any coalition could be settled, but without success.

Saturday night, March 23rd. 'Nothing is yet done. Lord Shelburne and Lord Gower have been sent to separately by the King, but nothing seems to have arisen from the interviews. Lord Rockingham, Charles Fox, etc., have received no message or intimation, at which they are much surprised and pretty angry.

Sunday, March 24th. 'The report is that the King has put everything into the hands of Lord Shelburne, who has been with Lord Rockingham today and with the King more than once. Nothing is absolutely settled and the Rockingham Party certainly are very jealous of Lord Shelburne.

Monday, March 25th. 'Everything is arranged. The new Cabinet is named by Lord Rockingham and the House of

Commons have adjourned till Wednesday, for the final settlement of the inferior offices.

'*A little before Lord North went out, Mr Craufurd, who generally voted with the Government, went away and would not vote on a particular motion made by Lord North. This being taken notice of, somebody observed that probably Craufurd did not like Lord North's question. Upon which, George Selwyn, who knew that he had been just making an application in favour of his brother, said he rather supposed he did not like Lord North's answer.*

'*On one of the last divisions during Lord North's administration, as Charles Fox was going out of the House, he said to George Selwyn, "Come George, you had better go out with us", "No," says George, "I can't go out with you tonight, but I shall have no objection to coming in with you tomorrow".*'

'On the 1st July, Lord Rockingham died. This event makes great confusion among the remaining members of the administration who were much disunited before.

Wednesday, July 3rd. 'The King, it is said, has offered the Treasury to the Duke of Grafton, who has refused it, and to Lord Shelburne, who has accepted it. This arrangement is totally disapproved of by Mr Fox and all those who formed Lord Rockingham's Party, who propose to call over the Duke of Portland from Ireland to be at the head of the Treasury. They are labouring today to carry this point, on which it is not probable they will succeed, and if they do not, it is generally understood they will immediately resign.

Thursday, July 4th. 'This day, Mr Fox [he had been joint Secretary of State] resigned the Seals and Lord Keppel and Lord John Cavendish have signified their intentions to quit their situations as soon as the nature of the business will permit. This resignation is a measure of Mr Fox, disapproved of by part of his friends and not very cordially embraced by those that have followed him. It has completely divided the Rockingham Party, as the Duke of Richmond, General Conway and Tommy Townshend do not resign. On which account they are in disgrace with C. Fox and his friends, particularly the Duke of Richmond. Lord Shelburne is making up a new administration without those who are gone, in which it is

thought he will succeed easily as Mr W. Pitt and the Lord
Advocate are likely to join him cordially.

'On Tuesday, the 9th, Mr Fox gave his reasons for resigning,
which were chiefly his bad opinion of Lord Shelburne and his
opinion not being followed with regard to an immediate and
absolute declaration of American Independence. His speech
was very fine, but did not give much satisfaction.

'The new arrangements have taken place. Lord Shelburne
has the Treasury; Mr Pitt, Chancellor of the Exchequer; Mr
Grenville, Eliot and Jackson, Lords of the Treasury; Mr Pratt
and Mr Aubrey, new Lords of the Admiralty; Sir G. Yonge,
Secretary at War; Lord Grantham and T. Townshend, Secretaries of State.'

Although contemporary records suggest that Palmerston left
the Treasury Board with the advent of Rockingham, his own
papers give no clue. The engagement diary notes several visits
to the office between March and June and he dined with his old
patron two or three times. However the appointment of
Shelburne banished him finally to the back benches. The anecdote book entries have a note of asperity:

'*Charles Fox and his friends in 1782, being much piqued at the
Duke of Richmond for not resigning when they did, and the Duke,
having just before refused to fight Lord Rowden, Sheridan said it
was no wonder the Duke would not resign with Charles Fox, for he
was absolutely determined not to go out with any man.*

'*The old Lord Holland used to say that many people were bred
Jesuits, but that Lord Shelburne was born one.*'

The long drawn out peace negotiations betrayed the weaknesses of the Shelburne administration, and by the spring of
1783 another political crisis loomed:

February 17th, 1783. 'The preliminaries of the Peace taken
into consideration. An Address of Thanks to the King was
moved, and seconded by Mr Thos. Pitt and Mr Wilberforce.
An amendment was made by Lord John Cavendish, and
seconded by Mr A. St John, to say the House would
consider them farther. Carried against the Ministry by 224
to 208.

February 21st. 'Motion of Lord J. Cavendish to assure the

King we would preserve the Peace, but that the concessions made by it were too great. Carried against the Ministry by 207 to 190.

February 22nd. 'The weakness of the present Government appears clearly by their divisions and it is concluded Lord Shelburne must go out. Nothing permanent can be established, but by a union of two of the parties. Great speculations are formed whether C. Fox and Lord North, who have acted together and in concert on these points, can unite to form a ministry

February 25th. 'Lord Shelburne has resigned. The Lord Advocate gave notice of this on Tuesday in Parliament, and moved to adjourn till Friday, which was agreed to.

February 27th. 'Nothing is known to be settled. Great endeavours are supposed to be using to make an administration without Charles Fox.

February 28th. 'It is understood the old ministers are out, but nothing done yet towards forming a new administration. The King very unwilling to apply to Lord North or Charles Fox . . .

March 2nd. 'The King sent for Lord North. Wants to separate him from the Rockingham party; without success. Nothing concluded.

March 3rd. 'The King objects to the Duke of Portland being First Lord of the Treasury.

March 5th. 'Many plans in agitation for a ministry with Lord Gower at the head of it. All prove abortive, Mr Pitt refusing to join or support them.

March 7th. 'The King continually sees the Chancellor but nothing transpires.

March 9th. 'The King cannot bring himself to submit to the terms of the Rockingham Party and Lord North.

'The King finds he must give way. Sends for Lord North on Wednesday, the 12th March, and entrusts the arrangements to him.

March 13th. 'Demurs about the Chancellor and Lord Stormont. The first the King wants to keep, the second will take nothing but the Secretary of State, which cannot be complied with.

March 17th. 'Lord North persuades the King to see the Duke of Portland.

March 18th. 'Lord North agrees to be Secretary of State and Lord Stormont then consents to be President of the Council.

March 20th. 'The Rockinghams want to exclude Lord Stormont totally. Lord North absolutely refuses. Each party persisting – the whole breaks off. Duke of Portland goes to inform the King he and Lord North cannot make an arrangement jointly, but offers him one separate from Lord North, which, however, he thinks, Lord North will not oppose. The King declines it.

'On Friday morning, March 21st, the Rockinghams give up their point about Lord Stormont. An arrangement is made of the Cabinet, which the Duke of Portland carries to the King and informs him that he and Lord North are perfectly agreed. The arrangement is as follows: Duke of Portland, Lord of the Treasury; Lord J. Cavendish, Chancellor of the Exchequer; Lord North and Mr Fox, Secretaries of State; Lord Stormont, President of the Council; Lord Carlisle, Privy Seal; Lord Keppel, Admiralty. The King receives this and asks for the whole of their arrangements. The Duke of Portland says he cannot make them till the King shall have approved of the Cabinet and accepted the persons named in it as his Ministers and given them authority to make other arrangements. The King declines this and says he cannot proceed blindfold. So they part.

'On Sunday, the 23rd March, the King sees Lord North and the Duke of Portland separately, still requiring their whole arrangement. They persist on declining to make it till they have the King's authority to act as his Ministers. At night the King informs them the whole negotiation with them is over.

'The King, having seen Mr Pitt twice on Sunday, everybody supposes Mr Pitt has agreed to be Minister and on Monday, the 24th, in the House, Mr Coke calls on him to know whether there is a Ministry formed. Mr Pitt, to everybody's surprise, declares *not*. Mr Coke moves an Address to desire the King would take into his consideration the state of the country and appoint such a Ministry as may deserve the confidence of the people and tend to put an end to divisions. The question passes in the affirmative, without a division.

'On Wednesday, the 26th, the King's answer is delivered, viz; that he is always happy to comply with the wishes of his faithful Commons. Lord Surrey said that the answer, though gracious, promised nothing, and that if something was not done by Monday it would be necessary to pursue the matter farther and that he would move something more.

'On Monday, the 31st March, nothing had passed and though the King had seen Lord North once, yet nothing had passed that seemed to give the least prospect of anything being settled.

When the House met, Mr Pitt being called on as before, declared he had nothing to inform them of except that he had resigned the Seals as Chancellor of the Exchequer. Lord Surrey moved a resolution that the interposition of Parliament was become necessary. This, however, being disapproved of, was withdrawn. He then moved for an Address to be carried up by the House. This, after some conversation, was agreed on all sides, to be postponed for a day or two longer.

'On Tuesday, the 1st April, the King sent for Lord North and told him he was ready to agree to the proposals that had been made and desired the Cabinet ministers might kiss hands on Wednesday (the 2nd April), which they accordingly did.'

North appeared in a sympathetic light in the anecdote book:

'*Lord North, going to his new office of Secretary of State, passed by the door of the Treasury where he had presided so long. Finding there was another flight of steps to ascend, he laughed and said he found the old proverb true, that a man might go farther and fare worse.*'

But it was witty George Selwyn, as in so many other anecdotes, who had the last word:

'*George Selwyn, being very severe in his jokes on the new ministry, who had turned him out of his places, was told by somebody that the ministers would soon find a way to make him change his note. To which he replied that would be difficult as they had not left him a note to change.*

'*Somebody was speaking of some very charitable action done by the present Lady Maynard – formerly Nancy Parsons – and saying she was of a very compassionate and tender disposition. George Selwyn observed it was no wonder she was so tender as she had been kept so long [by the Duke of Grafton].*

'*George Selwyn, being asked whether he had wished an acquaintance of his joy of being appointed equerry to the late Duke of York, said he should as soon think of wishing a canister joy of being tied to a dog's tail.*

'*Somebody telling George Selwyn that Mr Herschel had discovered a new Star, which he had named 'Georgium Sidus' in honour of the King, Selwyn said, "I don't care how many new stars they give him, but I hope they won't find him any more sons".*

'*When Charles Fox attached himself to Mrs Robinson, G. Selwyn observed that nobody was so fit for the Man of the People as the Woman of the People.*'[31]

REFERENCES

1. A.8
2. C.17(a) 10.VIII.1769
3. C.17(a) 20. VIII.1769
4. C.17(a) 12.IX.1769
5. C.17(a) 15.X.1769
6. C.25 1770
7. A.9
8. A.2 1770
9. H.10 pp. 394–6
10. C.26 17.X.1771
11. C.16 19.X.1771
12. C.18(a) 12.XII.1772
13. H.3
14. A.2 9.VIII.1774
15. C.10 6.VIII.1774
16. A.1 8.VIII.1774
17. C.30 10.IX.1774
18. C.18(a) 26.VI.1775
19. C.31 25.VI.1775
20. A.10 August 1776
21. A.11
22. C.34 28.VIII.1778
23. C.34 10.IX.1778
24. C.17(a) 3.X.1778
25. C.34 undated
26. C.18(a) 1.II.1779
27. C.37 18.VII.1779
28. C.36 17.XI.1779
29. C.35
30. C.39 July 1781
31. A.1 and F.23

CHAPTER V

SECOND MARRIAGE

*Mary Mee – their tour to the West of England – the first balloon
manned in England lands on Palmerston's estate – Charles James
Fox's India Bill – Palmerston elected to the Literary Club – purchases
his seat at Boroughbridge from the Duke of Newcastle – birth of
Young Harry, the future third Viscount – a request for help from
Gouverneur Morris – Palmerston's brother-in-law, Benjamin Mee,
sends news from India – one of London's leading hosts – the impeachment of Warren Hastings – views planetary nebulae with Dr
Herschel – Henry Holland employed at Broadlands*

PEACE with America had been overshadowed for
Palmerston by a more personal event, his second
marriage. Like the first, it was a love match. Frances
Poole had been a lady of small fortune, and Mary Mee, of
whose transition from a schoolgirl to a mature woman of
twenty-eight he had been a witness, was no great heiress. Her
father, Benjamin Mee, was a substantial City merchant, with
offices at 34 Fenchurch Street, and her brother, named after
his father, was a partner in the family firm, a director of the
Royal Exchange Assurance Company and of the Bank of
England. However, the males of her family displayed little
financial acumen, drifted slowly into straightened circumstances
and gradually became pensioners of their titled relative, a
circumstance which, to Palmerston's great credit, he met with
affection and equanimity.

The transition from old family friend to suitor occurred on
October 10, 1782, when Palmerston noted in his overall diary:
'Drove Mrs Culverden and Miss Mee in the phaeton. Overturned near Stoneham. Miss Mee's elbow dislocated; set very
soon by Mr Mears.' This mishap was followed by a prompt
peace offering:

'Lord Palmerston presents his compliments to Miss Mee and

hopes her arm is grown better under the present mode of treating it.

'He begs her acceptance of a piece of cloth for a riding habit which Monsr. Scarpelain, the French tailor, assures him is the true Parisian *Gorge de Pigeon* and is to be the most fashionable colour this winter. Monsr. Scarpelain insisted in putting up a piece of silk for the lining thinking it would not otherwise be properly matched . . .'[1]

With this enquiry a warmer note crept into their correspondence over the next two months. The interval of fifteen years had softened the rigid formality of Palmerston's messages of affection:

'Mrs Siddons has sent word she cannot let me have such a box as I wished for Saturday but will take care to keep one for her next benefit; so that my dearest M.M. must reserve her tears till then. That they may never again be called forth but by fictitious distress is the sincerest wish and the fondest hope of her

ever affectionate, P.'[2]

'My dearest Miss Mee,

I have taken the liberty of sending you a muff of the same kind with yours but which the people assure me will not dirty you as that does; so that I hope you may go about London with your nose of its natural complexion and not be obliged to have it either blue with the frost or black with the muff.

I intended breakfasting with you on Thursday morning but find I must be at a meeting at Lord North's at eleven o'clock. What do you do tomorrow evening? Shall you have had an opportunity before that time of talking to your brother? Or shall I come to you on Thursday from Lord North's?

Believe me with the most unalterable affection, my dearest Miss Mee,

ever most faithfully yours, Palmerston.'[3]

'M.M. flatters herself Lord Palmerston will pardon the liberty she takes in troubling him with an enquiry after his health this morning. But the concern she experienced last night at seeing him so much indisposed will she trust plead her excuse.

'Should Lord Palmerston not find himself quite well tomorrow morning, she requests he would not think of calling at her brother's. For she must beg leave to assure his Lordship, however fashionable peace may be at present esteemed, he will certainly meet with a formal declaration of war if he should commit an act so hostile to the repose of M.M.'s as she must deem his running any chance of endangering his health by his kind attention in giving her his society.'[4]

'A thousand thanks to my dearest M.M. for her kind enquiry. My cold is not mended today and as I know going out would increase it I have determined to undergo the mortification of a little confinement in hopes of getting well the sooner . . .'[5]

'M.M. sincerely wishes to hear that Lord Palmerston feels himself much better this morning.

'The family beg leave to unite in kindest enquiries.'[6]

'Lord Palmerston is greatly indebted to Miss Mee for her kind enquiry. He is as much better today as he expected to be and thinks he has reason to hope his cold will not be of very long duration.

'It would have been kind of M.M. to have lengthened her note a little to have told him how she does herself as he feared last night she had a cough coming on.

'Kindest compliments to all the family.'[7]

'There was something in the style of your last note, my dear Lord P., that seemed to imply a desire of being relieved from the importunity of daily enquiries. Influenced by that idea I endeavoured yesterday to suppress the inclination I felt to obtain some account of your health. But to confess a truth, it is too lively to admit of being longer restrained without receiving your wishes on the subject. In that case I should certainly remain silent, but it will not be in your power to make me resign my anxiety . . .

'I feign would flatter myself that I shall soon have the pleasure of seeing you perfectly recovered. In the meantime I trust you will allow me to assure you that I must ever remain yours unalterably, M.M.'[8]

'My dearest M.M.'s kind note found me just beginning to write a few lines to her (though with such a headache that I can hardly see) as I could not refrain from telling her how much I think of her and long for her society and how provoked I am at this tiresome cold that has prevented me from enjoying it . . .

'Adieu, my sweet friend. I would say more but I can really scarce hold up my head and nothing that I could say could express how much I love you and wish for you or how tenderly I am

ever yours, P.'[9]

These stilted counter-enquiries clearly had to lead somewhere. On December 20 Palmerston was writing to William Godschall, Mary Mee's uncle:

'I feel myself much obliged to you for your kind congratulations on an approaching event which gives me the highest satisfaction and from which I have so many just grounds to expect the greatest happiness. Among the many pleasing circumstances of my intended marriage, its connecting me still closer with the House of Weston is, I assure you, not one of the least agreeable . . .'[10]

In his diary the next day he noted: 'Went to Mr Mee's in the morning; signed Marriage Articles'. They were to be married from her mother's house at Bath. The day after Christmas Mary Mee set out, and their brief separation provided the occasion for less inhibited endearments:

From Mary Mee, December 26th. 'Your commands, I am well apprised, will always prove of that pleasurable kind, as to take from me every hope of claiming any merit for my obedience. Of that nature is the flattering one I received the evening preceding my departure, when my inclination had so far anticipated your wishes, that I had formed the design of acquainting you of our arrival ere I obtained your kind orders on the subject.

'From a combination of tiresome circumstances, such as heavy roads, knocked up horses, and dull postilions, we did not reach Reading till an hour too late to admit of proceeding further that night . . . We . . . slept last night at Marlborough and did not enter the city of Bath till five o'clock this day . . .

'In truth I have been so long accustomed to enjoy your society that I feel perfectly unhappy at being secluded from that to me first, and most delightful, of all pleasures. And I must just impart a secret, which is meant only for your Lordship's private information, that if your partiality had not for once gained the ascendant over your judgment and induced you to take me for your endless torment, I should have now found myself the most miserable puss that ever existed. You may believe sincerity dictates my pen, when I assure you I shall think the time long till I again see you . . .'[11]

From Lord Palmerston, December 28th. 'I have just received my dearest Mary's letter and heartily wish I could communicate to her the pleasure it has given me. Indeed my sweet friend, the hearing from you has been the first happiness I have looked forward to since we parted and the only one I have tasted that could in any degree whatever deserve the name. I can scarce believe it is but five days since we parted, the time has moved so slowly and so dull. If I was to live absent from you I should not complain of the shortness of life for I should soon think I had lived as long as Methusalem . . .'[12]

From Mary Mee, December 30th. 'The flattering manner in which you assure me, I still live in your remembrance, gives me a pleasure you may imagine, but I cannot describe. The tediousness of absence no one every more painfully experienced than myself. But I hope I shall have seldom cause to offer a complaint on that subject, for I profess I can form no idea of happiness independent of your society. I trust nothing will prevent our meeting on Saturday. Do you think you will be able to accomplish your design of being with us by dinner? Write me, if you can, a few lines by the return of the post, just to say whether you *hold your resolution* or *desire* to be *off*...'[13]

From Lord Palmerston, December 31st. 'I did not know, my dearest Mary, that I could love you better than I did when I parted from you, or be more thoroughly convinced that I had done the wisest as well as the pleasantest action of my life in prevailing on you to become the partner of the remainder of it, and yet the tender, elegant and delightful letters you have indulged me with since you left London have convinced me that I was very far from seeing the extent of your merits or my own affections ... While I can remember anything, I shall remember, as one of the happiest periods of my life, the sociable and pleasant time we passed at Broadlands after the crowd was all gone. How happy was I in the performance of a thousand little offices which your situation and your kindness together allowed me to undertake, and how selfishly was I ready to bless the accident which enabled me so often to support in my arms and press to my heart what I found gaining such entire possession of it. But the greatest of all pleasures was the idea that I was not quite indifferent to you and that while my affections were all engrossed by you I was not without some little share in yours. I did indeed believe you was not insensible, and found an eloquence even in your silence which could speak without words and which gave me a pleasure only to be exceeded by the charming certainty I have since received that so pleasing a confidence was not groundless ...'[14]

Palmerston arrived in Bath on January 4, 1783, with his brother-in-law to-be, Benjamin, and three days later his diary entry reads: 'Married to Miss Mee in the morning; set out with her and Mr Mee for Broadlands.' Fortunately indeed, for the purposes of this book, Palmerston's comments on his pleasure in his wife's letters were to be amply justified over the years. He had married a witty and enchanting woman and her share of 106 of the 455 letters they exchanged and that remain preserved to us are not only intrinsically delightful in themselves, but inspired her husband to set down in his replies a full and intimate record of his time.

In February he took his new wife to be presented to the King and Queen. But with his new domestic ties and the loss of his seat on the Board of the Treasury the previous year, Palmerston began to lead a much less socially gregarious life. There is a distinctly academic tone to one of his dinners in May, which was attended by Sir Joseph Banks, Sir Charles Blagden and Dr [Sir William] Herschel, the astronomer, fellow members of the Royal Society. In June he had dinner with the new First Lord of the Treasury, the Duke of Portland, but if the occasion was intended to explore the possibility of obtaining another post in his administration, it bore no fruit. With the summer he went off on tour again to the West Country and Wales, accompanied this time by Lady Palmerston and a fellow member of the Dilettanti Society, Sir Henry Englefield. Palmerston's description of the South Wales coal-fields has a curiously timeless ring:

'To Aberavon: Here are some very fine copper works, which are worth looking into as the process is curious and the people very civil. The copper ore is brought hither from Cornwall, for the sake of the coals with which this country abounds, and by repeated meltings is brought to a pure state. . . . In order to be prepared for the process of calcination, it is necessary that the ore should be reduced as nearly to powder as may be. In order to accomplish this, the ore, which after the first melting was run into large lumps, used to be broke by a great hammer and a mill. A much easier and cheaper method has been newly discovered of attaining the same end by letting the melted ore in its highest state of fusion run directly from the furnace into a pool of water, by which means it granulates and is immediately reduced to a proper state for the second calcination. We were surprised to see the melted red hot ore running into water with the utmost quietness, and without producing any violent effect whatever . . .

'From Britton Ferry to Neath, the valley is flat and marshy and smoking with copper works and the fire engines belonging to coal mines . . .

'On the shores of the Tawey above Swansea are several very great copper works with coal pits close to them. The sides of

the hills over them are rendered quite barren by the fumes of
the works continually blown against them . . .

'The people we have seen are stout and well-looking in
general. We have observed a good deal of character on their
countenances and a considerable share of beauty among the
young females. On the article of neatness in their houses – the
less is said the better . . .'[15]

Back in London, on Tuesday, November 25, 1783, he was
one of the witnesses at the launching from the Artillery Ground
of the first balloon to be released in Great Britain, six weeks
after the epoch-making ascent of Pilâtre de Rozier in Paris:
'The balloon let off in the ground about 2 o'clock; was found
near Petworth in Sussex, two hours and forty minutes later',
Palmerston noted in his diary. He also had a vicarious association
with one of the first manned ascents the following year from
London, when the balloon landed on a farm which formed
part of Palmerston's Broadlands estate. The relative entry
read: 'On Saturday, the 16th October [1784], at ten minutes
past twelve, Monsieur Blanchard and Mr Shelden ascended
from Lockie's Academy at Little Chelsea in the balloon belonging to the former. They came down near Sunbury at ten
minutes before one, where Mr Shelden got out, the balloon
not being able to carry them both. Monsieur Blanchard went
on by himself and came down in Spurshot Farm, near Romsey,
at half an hour after four.'

* * *

The great Parliamentary debates in 1783–84 centred round
Charles James Fox's India Bill, and ushered in the long
paramountcy of the younger Pitt. Palmerston's running notes
on the right-hand pages of his engagement diaries from December 15 provide a comprehensive account of this momentous
crisis, and show the extraordinary extent to which George III
was able to resist a majority in the House of Commons:

'The India Bill proposed by Mr Fox, though it passed the
House of Commons by a majority of 114, yet was violently
opposed out of doors by all those who had interests and
connections in India. The King was supposed to be equally

averse to the bill and the ministers who proposed it. A few days before the first question on it came on in the House of Lords, Lord Temple had an audience of the King, who declared to him his disapprobation of the measure, with a declaration that he should consider every Lord who voted for it as his enemy. This, Lord Temple circulated with great industry and the effect answered his expectation. The Lords, of whom a majority had promised to vote for the Bill, negatived it first by a majority of 8 and then by 19. A change of the ministry and a dissolution of Parliament became the immediate objects of expectation. Much warmth and indignation were expressed in the House of Commons. On the 17th, three motions passed: first against those who report opinions, real or pretended, of the King in order to influence votes in Parliament; second for a committee on the state of the nation; third that whoever should advise a dissolution under the present circumstances was an enemy of the country.

'On Thursday night, the 18th very late, the King sent a letter to Lord North [Joint Secretary of State with Fox under the Duke of Portland as First Lord of the Treasury], ordering him to send the Seals by his under-secretary and that he should acquaint Mr Fox to do the same.

'On Friday, the 19th, the seals were both in Lord Temple's custody and Mr Pitt's writ was moved as having accepted the offices of the First Lord of the Treasury and the Chancellor of the Exchequer. Lord Gower was likewise announced as President of the Council. An immediate dissolution was expected . . .

'On Monday, the 22nd, the House met to go into the committee on the state of the nation, previous to which Mr Wm Grenville, Lord Temple's brother, announced that Lord Temple finding himself pointed at by the language and votes of the House, had resigned the seals in order to meet any charges against him as a private individual. The House were likewise assured by Mr Pitt's confidential friends, that he would not advise a dissolution. It was soon known that Mr Pitt and Lord Temple had quarrelled and supposed that the measure of dissolution was one chief cause. The House, however, went

into the committee and without a division voted an Address
to be carried up, viz: the whole House to desire the King not
to dissolve the Parliament in the present state of affairs, which
required the most constant and uninterrupted attention. The
King agreed to receive the Address on Wednesday, the 24th.
The resignation of Lord Temple at first made people suppose
the whole plan of making a new administration was given up.
The contrary was, however, soon known and the Cabinet was
filled up on Tuesday evening. Lord Thurlow, Chancellor;
Lords Carmarthen and Sydney, Secretaries of State and the
Duke of Rutland, Privy Seal. The Address was presented with
a great attendance on Wednesday. The King, in answer, agreed
that the state of affairs required the most vigilant attention,
recommended to the Commons to proceed upon them after
a short adjournment, and promised not to interrupt their
meeting by any prorogation or dissolution. When the House
was resumed, many more writs were moved and an adjournment agreed on to the 12th January [1784].

'In this interval, everybody is busy to conjecture what can
be the plan of the new ministers; how they can hope to go on
with a House of Commons so decidedly adverse to them. It is
supposed they hope to gain over many members during the
recess, in which hope, Mr Robinson, who was so long employed
under Lord North in parliamentary negotiation and who, with
a very uncommon degree of baseness, has gone over to assist
the opposite party, is supposed to encourage them.

December 31st. 'Peerages in plenty have been offered to the
principal persons in the House of Commons, to induce them
to desert their friends. All have been refused and three or four
of the poorest and the shabbiest of the members are the only
proselytes that are as yet heard of...'

On the Sunday evening before Parliament reassembled,
Palmerston dined on his arrival in London from Broadlands
with Lord Beauchamp, who played a considerable part in the
debates, and spent the evening with Charles James Fox, whose
colleague in Opposition he was to remain for nearly eight
years:

'On the 12th January, 1784, the House of Commons met and

was extremely full. The principal debate was whether the order of the day for the committee on the state of the nation, or Mr Pitt's motion for his India Bill, should take place. This, which involved every matter on which any person chose to speak, lasted till 4 o'clock and was then carried for the order of the day by 232 against 193. This majority of 39 shewed on the one hand how diligent the ministry had been, in the interval of Parliament, in getting over proselytes or, in the fashionable phrase *Rats*. On the other hand, it presented such an unpromising prospect as was sufficient to have made prudent men despair of their undertaking. In the committee, Mr Fox moved, in substance, that in case of a dissolution of Parliament before an appropriate act had passed, no person could issue any public money during the interval of Parliament on the authority of any votes of the last House of Commons, without committing a high crime, and that an account should be laid before the House of what money had been issued already, for their information. The second reading of the Mutiny Bill was adjourned till the 23rd of February.

'Lord Surrey then moved that it was necessary in the present difficult situation of affairs, that the administration should be in the hands of persons possessing the confidence of the House of Commons. That the circumstances attending the appointment of the present ministers were such as did not tend to conciliate that confidence. This passed by 196 to 142.

'Most persons who judged of the probabilities of men's future conduct, by reasonings drawn from past events, concluded that after the new ministry had so completely failed in their attempts to gain the House of Commons, they would feel the impossibility of going on without, or, rather, in opposition to it and give up their plan. No such intention, however, appeared and the terror of a dissolution was industriously hung out, to operate on the minds of the members. Mr Pitt, being repeatedly called on to explain the ambiguity of the King's answer and likewise to acquaint the House how far he considered himself pledged by Mr Banks' declaration before the holidays, refused either.

'On Friday, January 16th, Lord Charles Spencer moved in

the committee on the state of the nation that after the resolution before passed, the continuance of the present ministers in trusts of importance and responsibility was contrary to constitutional principles and injurious to the interests of His Majesty and the people. This was carried by 205 to 184.

'On Friday, the 23rd, Mr Pitt's India Bill, after a long debate, was thrown out on the second reading, by a majority of only eight.

'Mr Pitt, after the division, being called upon to explain the King's answer from every side of the House, kept a most obstinate silence, which induced a general opinion that an immediate dissolution was intended. After much violence, the House determined to meet on the next day, being Saturday. On Saturday [the 24th], Mr Pitt, upon being pressed, condescended to assure the House that no dissolution was intended to take place before their meeting on Monday, in consequence of which, they adjourned.

'During the interval the ministers were continually assembled in Cabinet and probably took their final resolution against a dissolution. On Monday, January 26th, Mr Eden, saying that as ministers who had advised the King's answer would not condescend to explain the sense in which they intended it, the House must put such construction on it as appeared to them the true one, and, therefore, moved, in substance, that it appears to this House that His Majesty's speech contains assurances on which this House most firmly rely; that he will not dissolve the Parliament while those important objects before alluded to are depending. On this, Mr Pitt at length assured the House that no dissolution was at present intended and, therefore, wished the motion to be withdrawn. This was not complied with and the motion passed without division.

'On Monday, February 2nd, Mr Coke moved that the continuance of the present ministers after the resolution of the House, before mentioned, is an obstacle to a firm and united administration. This was carried by 223 to 204.

'On Tuesday, February 3rd, a motion was made that the former motions should be laid before the King by such of the members as are of the Privy Council, which was done and on

the Thursday (the 5th) the House was informed that His
Majesty would take them into his consideration.

'Strong wishes were expressed by many members that a
union could be brought about between Mr Pitt and the late
Ministers, and many country gentlemen, and others whose
intentions were better than their judgment, had frequent
meetings at the St Albans Tavern for that purpose, and undertook to negotiate the business. They never, however, could
get so far as to bring the parties together, as the Duke of
Portland declared that till the resolutions of the Commons had
had their due weight by the removal of the ministers, he could
not enter into any treaty whatever, but that if Mr Pitt would
resign or declare his purpose of so doing, he had no objection
to treating with him in order to form a broader and more
extended ministry. This Mr Pitt refused and there the matter
dropped.

'In the meantime, the Lords . . . voted, and carried up, an
Address to the King, approving of the change he had made in
his administration . . .

'On Saturday, the 7th, there was a meeting in Westminster
Hall of the electors of Westminster, to consider of an Address
to the King. This was called by Mr Fox's party, with full
notice, on the ground that the other had been smuggled and
carried up so hastily as not to give time for the people in general
to know of it. The meeting was attended by both parties and
consequently too riotous and disorderly for anything to be
done or judged of. Both parties, as is usual, proclaimed victory,
and prepared their separate addresses . . .

'On Wednesday, the 18th, the order of the day being for the
report of the Ordnance estimate, Mr Pitt was called on to declare
whether he had any information to give the House in consequence of their resolutions having [been] laid before the King,
and his promise to take them into consideration. He declared
himself authorised only to say that the King, on a full consideration of all circumstances, had not thought proper to dismiss his
ministers and that they had not resigned. Mr Fox then moved
to defer the receiving [of] the Ordnance estimates for two days,
to give the House time to consider what ought to be done in

so new a case as that of the King's refusal to comply with the wishes of the Commons and whether they ought to proceed to vote the supplies as usual on such a situation. This was opposed, being called an absolute refusal of supplies and supported as being only a pause in granting them. The question was carried by 208 to 196.

'On Friday, the 20th, Mr Powys moved a resolution that the House still relied on His Majesty's goodness to give effect to the resolutions of the Commons, by removing the ministers which they considered as an obstacle to the formation of such a ministry as the state of affairs required. This resolution was considered as a kind of protest that the House did not relinquish their undoubted right of refusing the supplies if they found no other means of enforcing their rights and it was agreed that if this passed, the House would admit the report of the Ordnance estimate; it was carried by 197 to 177. It was then moved that it should be formed into an address and carried up by the whole House; which was carried by 177 to 156.

'On Wednesday, the 25th, the House attended the King ['went up to St James with the House of Commons address' reads the entry for the day] and received an answer in which he agreed that a more extended administration would be desirable; said he has tried to form such a one on a fair equal footing, without success. Observed that no direct charge is brought against any of his ministers, and that numbers of his people have expressed their approbation of the late changes and for these reasons declined removing his ministers till he sees a prospect of forming such a new administration as is admitted to be desirable.

'On Friday, the 27th, the House met, when the King's answer, being read, it was moved to take it into consideration on Monday and to adjourn all other business till then. This adjournment being opposed, was carried by 194 to 186, many of the majority numbers being absent.

'On Saturday, February 28th, Mr Pitt dined with the Grocers' Company in the City and came back at midnight with a great mob breaking all windows that were not illuminated, till they came to Brooks Club in St James's Street, where the chairmen defended the house and drove the mob away. Those who were drawing Mr Pitt's coach ran away like the others and left him in the midst of the victorious party, by whom he was obliged to quit his carriage and retreat to Whites, but was not otherwise ill-treated. Nobody received any material hurt in the scuffle.

'On Monday, March 1st, another more direct and explicit address was proposed by Mr Fox, and carried by 201 to 189.

'On Thursday, March 4th, the second address was presented to the King, by the House, to which the King gave an answer containing an absolute refusal to comply with the request of the Commons to dismiss his present Ministers. The House, on their return, agreed to take this into consideration on Monday, and on Friday a motion was made to adjourn over the Mutiny Bill, which stood for that dáy, till after the consideration of the King's speech. This was carried by 171 to 162.

'On Monday, March 8th, Mr Fox moved a long representation to be presented to the King in answer to his speech and in vindication of the proceedings of the House, but not praying anything from him. This was carried by 191 to 190, and ordered to be presented by the members of the Privy Council.

'The two parties in the House of Commons being now brought so near, which is owing to the attendance of new votes rather than to the desertion of old ones, it is not advisable to attempt anything farther at present, to give any check to the proceedings of the ministers, but rather to let them proceed their own way with their own measures . . .

Tuesday, March 23rd. 'The Ministry having shewn no disposition to bring on public business, a dissolution of Parliament universally expected as soon as the bills gone to the Lords are passed.

'On Wednesday, the 24th, the King came down to pass bills and afterwards prorogued the Parliament, saying that he meant to call a new Parliament immediately.

'This measure must be attended with great mischief, but from the epidemical kind of spirit that has gone about the country in favour of the King's prerogative against the House of Commons; it is supposed it will answer so far as to produce a large majority in favour of the present ministry.

'On Friday night, the 26th, the Parliament was dissolved and a new one called to meet on the 18th of May.'[16]

In spite of the strain of sitting at the House of Commons until all hours of the morning, Palmerston managed to keep up some semblance of his habits of entertainment. The list of dinner guests on Tuesday, February 10 was made up of the most intimate friends he was to keep in future years: Sir James and Lady Harris [later Lord and Lady Malmesbury], Sir Gilbert and Lady Elliot [later Lord and Lady Minto], Captain Payne and Tom Pelham. A week later, on the 17th, a day which he noted as being, 'Frosty, with some sleet at night', he 'dined at the Literary Club . . . in Sackville Street, being newly elected'. This was the famous coterie founded by Sir Joshua Reynolds and closely identified with Johnson and Boswell. Palmerston had been proposed for membership the previous year, without being elected, in spite of Dr Johnson's support.[17] Apart from three anecdotes concerning its most famous member, Palmerston left no other record of the club's activities:

'*A countryman of Alderman Beckford's was abusing him soon after his death in Dr Johnson's company and among other violent things said he was certain he was gone to hell. "Sir," says Johnson, "I do not know what authority you may have for the assertion. But if it should be so, as the Alderman came from Jamaica, he will probably find no great difference either in his climate or his company."*'

'*Johnson, hearing high encomiums on the simplicity of the old ballads and other poems and likewise of the* Hermit of Warkworth *and some others, wrote in imitation of them, said he thought it very easy to write such all day long and, being called on for a specimen, he began as follows:—*

> "*I put my hat upon my head*
> *And went into the Strand,*
> *And there I met another man*
> *With his hat in his hand.*"'

'*Somebody commending one of Whitehead's odes to Johnson and particularly one line in it which runs thus: "Who rules o'er Freemen should himself be free." "No sir," says Johnson, "there's nothing in this. Billy Whitehead, to be sure, is a pretty tinkling poet, but the line you have mentioned has no merit. The thought is false and I might as well say "who drives fat oxen should himself be fat".'*

News of the progress of Fox's election at Westminster was tempered in Palmerston's letters to his wife during April by references to the first of the financial misfortunes to beset the Mee family. Brother-in-law Benjamin had resigned his director- ship of the Bank of England, sold his £2,000 share holding and was having difficulty in meeting his creditors:

'I hope this will find you, my dear Mary, safe and well at Bath and that you have taken good care of yourself and not suffered by your journey or by a meeting which must neces- sarily have been an affecting one on all sides. I saw poor Ben today who is well in health and somewhat better in spirits than he was. I am to dine with him and Culverden tomorrow. Culverden was with me this morning before I went out, he seems to have better hopes about the affairs and thinks they will be settled with some less unpleasant circumstances than they at first feared. However nothing can be yet known with any certainty. Mr Godschall is come to town and is to sleep here tonight . . .

'I have little or no news to send you. The Westminster election goes on but ill . . . The Duchess of Devonshire and Lady Duncannon and all the fine ladies go canvassing about St Giles's and Clare market with their fine carriages and liveries for Charles Fox but I fear their efforts will not succeed.[18]

'I have just been to see Mrs Siddons play, *Belvedere* which she did with her usual excellence, though she looks ill. If I stay next week I shall be in town at her benefit . . . The Academy dinner will be the same day, but one may go from that as soon as one pleases.

'I saw Ben the day before yesterday; he was well; but I do not learn anything material that is new to inform you of . . . Let the worst happen, though it is unfortunate to begin the world at his age, yet with friends, character and courage much may be hoped for and much may be done . . .

'Charles Fox's friends are in spirits again about Westminster as he has gained above 140 votes upon Sir Cecil [Wray] in the

last three days and is not now much above 170 behind: and as
their votes depend upon influence and compulsion, which
must come to an end, and Fox's upon the spirit of the people,
which certainly increases, I think there is great probability of
his success at last . . .[19]

'Nothing is talked of here still but elections. The Westminster business is carried on with as much eagerness as ever
and no appearance of a conclusion. Fox gained 32 yesterday
and expects to do more today and as Sir Cecil polled only 41
yesterday it looks as if he was almost come to an end. The
numbers of people that are now at work for Fox are prodigious,
as they have got into a method of having great dinners of two
or three hundred people where everybody engages to procure
a vote for him. There are certainly voters enough yet unpolled
and I think he has a very tolerable chance . . .'[20]

The anecdote book carried an echo of the campaign:

*'A butcher in Westminster, when Charles Fox came to ask him
for his vote, made him kiss his greasy wife and daughter and then
told him he might kiss his arse if he liked it into the bargain; but he'd
see him damned before he'd vote for him.'*

Palmerston himself was having far less trouble. An entry in
his account book read: 'Sold £150 out of £1,950 Long
Annuities to pay for my election for Boroughbridge to the
Duke of Newcastle; agreed for £2,625 including all expenses.
Afterwards it was intimated that the Duke would take it well
if I would pay half the expense of the election, amounting to
£60 more! Agreed.' Other candidates unable to count on
powerful Whig connections had fared less well:

'The popular cry in favour of Mr Pitt has run higher during
the elections than could have been imagined. A great number
of the most respectable ministers are thrown out for having
supported the majority at the last Parliament, and an extraordinary number of new and unknown men chose, on no
recommendation but that of declaring themselves friends to
Mr Pitt.'[21]

In the end, Fox was returned. So, of course, was Palmerston.
During the summer months he paid the third of the four short
visits made during his life to his estates in County Sligo, the

details of which are included in a later chapter. On his return
to Broadlands he found his wife pregnant, and on October 4
the family moved to their London home in Park Street,
Westminster. On Tuesday, October 19, the diary entry noted:
'Lady P. ill'. The next day, Wednesday, the 20th, the laconic
note of the birth of the future third Viscount read: 'Mr
Cholmondeley, Mr Mee, Mrs Mee, Mrs Culverden and Miss
Whitworth dined. Lady P. brought to bed of a son at seven
in the evening.'

★ ★ ★

The addition to his family does not seem to have altered the
tenor of Palmerston's activities. The next day he noted: 'Walked
into the City; dined at the Crown and Anchor; Play.' And in
the early part of November he went to spend a week hunting
with Lord and Lady Cadogan at Downham:

'I got to Newmarket the night I left you,' he wrote to his
wife, 'after a dull and slow journey with a mizzling rain most
of the time . . . The Prince was there and afterwards dined
at the club (which is a kind of Brooks's) and played deep
at whist in the evening to the great mortification of his
partner . . .[22]

'I went . . . in search of the coursers but partly from being a
little too late and partly from not readily finding the way, the
chief part of the sport was over before I joined them. I found
several persons I knew, viz. Lord Orford, Sir John Rous, Mr
and Mrs Drake and Sir Charles and Lady Kent. . . . All those
I have mentioned, except Lord Orford, were on a visit at Sir
Henry Peyton's, who lives just by the place where they were
coursing. He seems stupid and vulgar, his wife only the latter,
she is Sir John Rous' sister. All the men went to Swaffham to
dinner where I accompanied them and stayed all night. They
have a club there for the whole week to which I was carried
and dined with about thirty people. They did not give me a
high opinion of the Norfolk country gentlemen. I sat by Lord
Orford who in a wild kind of way is entertaining. The next
day I went out again to course . . . There was to be an assembly
that night but I did not stay for it but returned to dinner at

Lord Cadogan's . . .

'This place answers so perfectly all the descriptions we have
had of it that it is hardly worth while to give any further
account of it. The house is old and bad, except two new rooms
which are good and comfortable. It is in a bottom entirely
surrounded with quantities of very fine growing trees which
prevent you from seeing anything of the desert which spreads
on every side. It seems to be the centre of the frightfulest
country in England and the scene improves, though slowly,
every way in proportion as you leave it at a distance. At the
same time it must be allowed that it has great charms for a
thorough sportsman and a farmer, both which Lord Cadogan
is, and by means of which, with a good dinner and a nap in the
afternoon he has not a moment unemployed . . .'[23]

He returned in time for Harry's christening on Tuesday,
November 23, celebrated at Winchester 'as being more convenient to the country in general'. There was a concert,
followed by a ball, organised 'with great magnificence'.[24]

The winter of 1784 was one of the coldest on record, and on
December 22, Palmerston wrote to William Godschall:

'I hope you have not suffered in your health by the cold
which certainly was severer on the Friday you mention than
has usually been felt in England . . .

'On Friday morning early, when Mr Herschel's thermometer
at Datchet was, I think, two degrees below zero, Sir H.
Englefield's at Petersham was about the same time two degrees
above zero. These were the greatest extremes of cold I had
heard of before yours. The glasses in London were in general
much higher. Mine was seen at 8 o'clock, Friday morning, at
nine degrees, which is as low as any I heard of in town. In
the night, between the last day of the last year and the first day
of the present, Sir H. Englefield at Downham, in Norfolk, saw
his thermometer for about three hours at five degrees below
zero, which is the lowest I ever heard of in England. You
remember probably the observations at Glasgow in January,
1780, when by repeated trials with different instruments in the
presence of the most accurate observers, the mercury in
Fahrenheit's thermometer stood at forty-six degrees below the

freezing point and when laid on the surface of the snow, fell to fifty-five . . .'[25]

Such weather can hardly have alleviated the circumstances of a distinguished visitor to London. Quite what Gouverneur Morris, later to become famous as American Minister in Paris, was doing in London at the time is by no means clear. At the end of the Revolutionary War he had retired from his post as Assistant to the Superintendent of the Finances of the United States and resumed the practice of law in New York and Philadelphia. His brother, Staats Long Morris, had married the Duchess of Gordon and was a general in the British Army, and Gouverneur Morris may have been visiting them, although his own papers make no mention of the fact.

In a letter to Palmerston, written in December 1784, Morris endeavoured to enlist his support for an unfortunate young couple; but the postscript which provides unquestionable confirmation of this otherwise unrecorded visit, suggests that Morris was dodging the duns himself:

'Nothing less powerful than the occasion should induce me to take the liberty of troubling you with this. To render that as little as may be necessary by avoiding too minute detail, however severe and moving these would be. I hasten to acquaint your Lordship that to my sorry certain knowledge, there now languishes, and has languished, for now very near three years, in the King's Bench Prison, a young gentleman and his wife [Mr and Mrs Ravenscroft] both of not barely [*sic*] unexceptional character and morals – but of exemplary ones. He was first a cornet in Lord Pembroke's Regiment of Horse, afterwards a lieutenant in a new-raised regiment; married a young lady, whose personal accomplishments, great as they were, stood only second to her mental ones. Educated by an over-indulgent parent in a line much above the very small fortune he ever would be able to give her, led to this by the young lady being kept almost from her earliest infancy at a distant relation's, a Baronet, who as also his lady, struck by her elegance, etc., scarce ever would let her be from them and who were, of course, supposed intended to provide for her. But alas, the match of the young people proved a pretext for each of their families discarding them on account of the mutual worldy imprudence of it, since both were equally unprovided with anything but the most contracted fortune. The result of this has been an increasing family, a sale of his commission to answer debts, their ignorance of the world and of the use of money brought on; this not sufficing to discharge all their debts, he has been thrown into prison now near three years for a remainder unsatisfied. Her duty and affection led her to accompany him thither, where the far greater part of the time they have lived with two sweet babes and she now near her time, or at least far gone with a third child, in the positive want of every necessary of life. Insomuch as often for weeks, nay months together, to be without more than one change even of body linen and every aggravated circumstance of the utmost want. Their united families allows her £20, and he £10 a year. The far greater part of the first generally is eaten up by the annual expenses of her lying-in and he used to receive the £10 a year every mid-November, but from some cause yet to learn, this year this latter pittance has been witheld and they now, for weeks past, experience the extremity of want in every horrid shape, and had these not met with some little alleviations through my means, now no longer having it in my power myself to afford them and therefore presuming to make this application to your Lordship which hoping will be excused, I remain with great respect and esteem your Lordship's most obedient humble servant,

Valentine Morris

PS. The injustice of government in still leaving my public accounts unsettled and not one shilling either of the whole of my salary as Governor due, or in part of my account, keeps me where such delay placed me and obliged me to request the honour of your Lordship's answer may be directed to me, Mr M. only at No: 2 in the State Apartments, King's Bench, where anyone your Lordship may choose to send to enquire more particularly the situation of the unfortunate family I have named.'[26]

Palmerston's account books of the period contain two items:

'April 27th, 1785, paid Gov. Morris £25', and 'January 23rd, 1786, paid Gov. Morris £20', presumably for the Ravenscrofts.[27]

In February, 1785, Palmerston caught a severe cold, which confined him to the house for most of the month. From the diary note for the week-end of February 12 and 13 it is an open question whether the ailment or the treatment were responsible: 'Forced to take five drops of laudanum on a lump of sugar, or a large teaspoonful of the paragoric elixir to quiet this complaint. Took eight grains of James's powder each night, with a draught containing ten drops of laudanum and a purge each morning.'[28]

However, he was sufficiently recovered by Wednesday, April 13, to make the entry: 'Rode to the City. Called to take leave of Ben Mee, who left London to depart for India.'[29] His brother-in-law had decided to try and recoup his losses in Calcutta, and it was Palmerston who enabled him to make this fresh start. His account book entries at the time included:

'*April* 16*th*, 1785. Sold £50 per annum Long Ann. at 17–1/16 to replace £500 lent to Mr Mee on his bond at his departure for India . . .

'*July* 4*th*, 1785. Signed jointly with Mr Culverden a promissory note to Mr Mee's assignees for £437 15s. 5d. for the repayment of money advanced to him out of the produce of the estate before his departure.

N.B. Both wrote to Mr Mee to let him know we had done so and to desire him to settle it.'

In fact he had assumed larger obligations, as an entry over a year later made clear:

'*September*, 1786. Sold out £200 per annum Long Annuities at 23 years purchase, but half interest being due, which was received before they were transferred, the produce return was £4,550. Of this £2,200 was paid immediately to Barrett for the purchase of the house I live in in Park Street, Westminster. £1,500 was paid by draft to Mr Boehm to pay Mr Mee's bills from India, being the remainder of £2,000 which I agreed to lend him and for which I am in possession of his bonds . . .'[30]

In return Palmerston received a regular budget of news from the exile. Ben's first, somewhat distasteful reactions were, it is to be feared, only the harbingers of his failure to achieve financial rehabilitation, in spite of his hopes and Palmerston's strong recommendation of him to Lord Cornwallis, who arrived in India as the new Governor-General a few months later:

September 11th, 1785, *Madras*. 'This settlement does not appear in any grandeur – to suppose the Company's servants live in style and magnificence is doing them great injustice. Their homes are unfurnished, many much out of repair. Their gardens or grounds more like uncultivated waste lands than land belonging to any person possessed of any property, a few trees planted in different parts to which they pay no attention . . .

'The fronts of the houses beautifully designed, the porticos or verandas magnificent and elegant. The stucco is a composition of shells which when new resemble white marble, but not kept in order for its expense, is become very shabby. I dined with the Governor, who gave us only one course and two sorts wine madeira and claret. The rest of the settlement live in the same style, they drink very little, go to dinner at 2 and to sleep at 5, then visit in the country. The inhabitants are at little expense for carriages, a carriage will last 12 years, their horses are shabby and their appearance resembles such as you see at fairs to let out to children for a ride at $\frac{1}{2}$d. each. The palanquins are very indifferent and I do not see the least appearance of eastern magnificence . . .

September 29th, Calcutta. 'We sailed from Madras with a fair wind and in less than five days arrived in Ballasore Roads. The pilot came on board and gave us little hopes of being at Calcutta in less than a week, as the flood tides were not strong and the wind not favourable. This news disappointed us as we expected to arrive in two or three days. To expedite our voyage . . . engaged a small sloop. We suffered much inconvenience and experienced not the least dispatch. We at last by the assistance of a ten-oared pinnace arrived on the 28th last month. From the time I left England have not felt the slightest

F

indisposition. My ankles from want of exercise at times got gummy but bathing them in cold water and rubbing them with a brush and some goulard, as I should my horses' heels when swelling in the stable, and walking exercise, they are returned to their shape . . .

'I wish I could inform you of some prospect in view for myself. I waited on the Governor, delivered my letters. He desired me to dine with him and after dinner took an opportunity of telling me that he would declare very candidly he would do everything that laid in his power to promote any plan I might pursue, that he should be glad to show every attention to the letters which I had brought, that the dispatches sent out by the *Dutton* had so deranged the settlement that I must have a little patience for the present . . .

'They live very little in Calcutta and the Governor expects no person will call on him in the country unless invited, this inserted in the public papers. The consequence is business is much impeded and the heads of offices and others find great difficulty to transact business with the board . . .

'I am not surprised that those who reside long in this country should be troubled with indigestion. The quantity of buttered muffins at breakfast and tea, puddings, pastry, buttered biscuits, together with butter in the vegetables, is incredible. Plain meats and poultry seldom touched . . . They won't allow that bilious complaints arise from diet or [are] increased by it, but the heat of the sun is the cause. I am considered to have a very insipid taste not eating either fat, butter, pastry or sweetmeats . . .

March 6th, 1786. 'Mr Henchman asked me if I would be a partner with others I knew in a banking house, that he thought government would support it. I told him if he thought I could be of any service he might command me, but as I considered the parties concerned should be such men as against whom no objection could be made, I feared my name from past misfortunes might be objectionable. He replied neither he or those concerned would admit such an idea, and as to capital whatever it might be, he would advance it and that the paper I had purchased I should not be under the necessity of selling but keep till its disposal was for my advantage . . . My engagement will I think be lucrative, certainly honorable, will increase connections here and give me an insight into public and private business and not prevent me receiving any emoluments government might give me as an individual. The parties are men of character and some of very large property . . .

March 22nd, 1786. 'I assure you I feel myself much lighter and easier in mind since my new engagement, as I have, and not without good grounds, reason to think very great advantages may accrue . . .

August 23rd, 1786. 'Many thanks for . . . your early application in my part to Ld. C[ornwallis]. I shall have no reason to lament a change of men, for the present persons in power have never suggested anything to me that even at a future day might lead to my emolument. The whole settlement is suffering for the want of spirited measures being carried on. Little mean jobs are in an underhand manner daily coming to light. The Governor, plausible, smiling and polite, wishes to postpone business till advice is received from Europe. "We will wait a little longer," "Don't choose to be responsible," "Shall be sorry to give offense," such language is constantly held . . . The Genl. has lived out of town till the rains. His society, his mistress, Mrs Knowler, a companion to her, a chaplain with his hair turned up behind fastened with a comb, and his secretary who is attached to him for friendship. He does not visit any person, airs every eve with Madm and thus he supports his dignity. Of course no visitors but by invitation. He has no public day . . .

'I shall most certainly attend to your kind advice respecting personal attachment to Ld. C., particular attentions to be directed to him . . .

'I hope some man of character and abilities well acquainted with the intrigues of the black people will be joined in the council with Ld. C., for this country is inhabited by people full of chicane, lying, political intriguing and deceit . . .

September 17th, 1786. 'I cannot express my feelings for your affectionate and unremitted attentions towards me and indefatigable exertions to serve me. Lord C. arrived last Monday

eve but did not land till Tuesday morn . . . On Wednesday
morn. I went to his house, was introduced to Col. Ross by
Col. Stewart and by Col. Ross to Ld. C. After a little conversation in the room, where there were many waiting to be
introduced, he desired me to walk into a private room where
he expressed himself to me in very open and candid manner
confirming every declaration you communicated to me in your
letters. That for the anxiety of my friends in England for whom
he had a very particular regard, and from what he had heard
of me in this country from his enquiries his wishes and inclination were to serve me. That he made no doubt I must be
sensible that it would require some time for him to be informed
of the situation of affairs in this country. And till then he would
not serve a brother. That when any opportunity offered of
doing me any service which did not militate against the interests
of the Company, he assured me he should readily embrace it,
and he was convinced I would not request him to act otherwise.
When he had got a house and was settled, he desired frequently
to see me, and after bows I retired much pleased with my
reception. The private audience was a singular attention and
implies here so much that I believe I could have borrowed of
some of the rich black people who saw me closetted, a lakh of
rupees on the credit of the notice I experienced. When the two
secretaries were introduced on the Tuesday morn. he took an
early opportunity of enquiring after me of one of them and in
what situation I was in, expressed himself much pleased when
informed I was in a very respectable line of business and with
some of the first people in the settlement . . .

November 14th, 1786. 'I have been several times to visit Ld. C.
whose affability and manners have made him popular. He has
applied much to business and seems much inclined to take up
subjects and carry them through with spirit, dispatch and
liberality.'[31]

★   ★   ★

Palmerston's engagement diary and account book entries at the
end of 1785 contain some interesting detail concerning the cost
of running his Broadlands home:

From July 18th to December 21st above 22 weeks

	£	s.	d.
Butcher	161	8	0
Bread	69	15	0
Fish	28	17	0
Poultry – besides our own	19	0	0
Brookman, Chandlery and etc.	30	8	0
Sundry articles	20	0	0
Charcoal	4	0	0
Grocery from London £50 4 0			
„ „ Southton 4 0 0	54	4	0
Waxchandler	37	1	6
Oilman	17	10	0

The fly leaves of the engagement diaries also carried each year his expenditure in forfeits for non-attendance and subscriptions at the Catch Club, which for 1785 amounted to the relatively low figure of £21 12s. 0d., and also minutely annotated details of his gains and losses at cards. Palmerston at no time seems to have indulged in the fashionable vice of high play, and the figures never exceeded five or six guineas in an evening. In 1785 he showed a distinct profit, winning 72 guineas and losing 50 guineas, and such totals were typical.

Although he ceased to make copious notes of political affairs and parliamentary debates in his engagement diaries from this time on, his permanent relegation to the back benches did not take him out of the orbit of political society. On Saturday, January 28, 1786, his guests to dinner at Park Street were the Dukes of Portland and Devonshire, Lords Cholmondeley, Derby and North and Messrs Fitzpatrick, Fox and Hare, a weighty prelude indeed to the entry for Saturday, February 18: 'Lady Palmerston was brought to bed of a daughter [Frances] at ten o'clock in the morning.'

Palmerston also began to entertain, and increasingly so over the years, the Archbishop of Canterbury, Dr Moore, and his wife, although the item of news in the letter of May 26 to Lady Palmerston was hardly of an ecclesiastical nature:

'When I wrote last night I had not heard of an event which

happened yesterday and has made much talk in London. It was a duel between Mr Fawkener and Jack Townshend from jealousy on Mr Fawkener's part of the other's attachment to his wife. Jack Townshend who is always in love with some married woman and very violent in his pursuit, has, it seems, been some time smitten and so particular in his attentions as to give umbrage to Mr F. who is of a very hot and singular temper. On Friday at Ranelagh Mr F. forbade Townshend's continuing to flirt with his wife, which, being disregarded, he sent him a challenge. They met on Monday, Fawkener fired and narrowly missed, the other fired in the air, seconds then interfered and so it is finished. Fitzpatrick attended Townshend and Colonel Crawford his antagonist. As soon as it was over Fitzpatrick wrote to Lord R. Spencer as follows: Dr Lord Robert, Jack's alive, yours F. I thought you would like to know the truth of this story which sounds so improbable and therefore I write these lines from Chiswick . . .
PS.   Mrs Fawkener is gone to Lady D. Beauclerk's to be out of town for the present. It is a cruel circumstance for her as a thousand ill-natured stories will be raised. One is that she owned to him her preference for Mr T.'[32]

His account book entries for 1786 included: 'March 24th, year's newspapers £12 13s. od.', and 'April 21st, Mr Sloane, for half a pipe of port from Portugal, all expenses and bottles included £28 11s. 6d.'.

The week commencing July 22 was particularly busy. On Sunday he and Lady Palmerston drove to Southampton to visit Lady Spencer and the Duchess of Devonshire, and in the evening Mr and Mrs Sheridan came to stay, leaving on the Wednesday after Lady Spencer, the Duchess and Lord and Lady Duncannon had dined with them.

A few days later Mrs Sheridan wrote to Mrs Stratford Canning, giving the only available evidence of what may have been the main reason for Palmerston's indifferent record as a parliamentarian:

'. . . Broadlands where we arrived to dinner . . . there you would have seen a very beautiful place, a comfortable house, a good natured poetical, stuttering Viscount, and a pleasing, unaffected woman, who, tho' she did squeeze thro' the city gates into a Viscountess, bears her blushing honours without shaking them at you every moment.'[33]

On Friday the 28th Palmerston went to stay at Lewes with his former brother-in-law, Sir Ferdinand Poole, who was host to the Prince of Wales and a large party. Lady Palmerston received these accounts of the Brighthelmstone scene:

'I got here a little after three ... Harry Pelham and Sir F[erdinand] are just come from their bad dinner ... and we are going to the course and afterwards to the ball. It seems the balls are the two first days and none on the third. This is not the fashionable day for Lewes course as the Brighthelmstone people don't come, but I believe some do to the ball. I saw a good many people on the Steyne and among them Jack Payne, who talks of calling on us in his way to Dorsetshire. The Prince, etc. are at Brighthelmstone and Charles Fox and Mr Armistead are coming ...[34]

'The Races are now happily concluded, which as there was no company very interesting and the dust on the course was more inconvenient than anything I ever felt I am not sorry for ... There was a crowded ball the first night which I did not go to ... The Prince of Wales & co. dined here the last day, i.e. yesterday, and the dinner went off very well and pleasantly ...[35]

'I came over to this place [Brighthelmstone] on Monday ... The ball at night which is called the Race Ball was tolerably full but not crowded ... The races began yesterday and by the help of the view and the company form a beautiful scene. Both the evenings have been rainy which has prevented the usual exhibition on the Steyne which I think the prettiest thing here ...

'Mrs Fitzherbert seems in an awkward situation from having no woman to go with her into public and I believe none of the ladies that are here are acquainted with her except Lady R— [?] who lives here and with whom she generally goes to the balls.

'I have enough of Brighthelmstone gaiety and propose going to London tomorrow morning where my stay will certainly not be long and I hope in a very few days to have the very sincere pleasure of finding you and your little companions in perfect health at Broadlands . . .'[36]

Palmerston remained in touch with some of his more sober friends. At the beginning of the year he had been to see Dr Herschel in his new home at Slough and had written William Godschall:

'Mr Herschel has cast his great speculum of four feet diameter, weighing, as I recollect, about 11 cwt and which is to make a telescope of forty feet in length. I understand he is satisfied with its form and is proceeding to polish . . .'[37]

The President of the Royal Society, Sir Joseph Banks, did not seem to regard it as beneath his dignity to give Palmerston a recipe for a trick form of illumination when he wrote him on August 3:

'It is not till this moment that I found the receipt for the blue lights, which I had mislaid, otherwise I should have before now have fulfilled my promise of sending it to your Lordship; it is as follows, the quantity consisted of:—

2 parts red arsenic	½ a pound of red arsenic
7 parts of sulphur	1¾ pounds of sulphur
28 nitre	7 pounds of nitre

'All must be reduced to the finest powder before they are mixed, and mixed together as carefully and intimately as possible. Any common gallipot will serve to contain them, into which the harder they are stuffed the longer they will burn. A little melted or powdered gun powder spread over the surface of the gallipot assists a little the inflamation, but a part-fire held over the pot will, with or without the melted powder, quickly give fire to it.

'We saw these lights the other night most distinctly, 35 miles, and had no doubt had any of them been more distant we could have seen them ten or maybe twenty further.'[38]

Three days later they dined together and paid a joint visit to Slough, where Herschel's sister had discovered a new comet, which Palmerston continued watching from Broadlands through his own telescope during the following three weeks.

In December his account book included the entry: 'Subscribed by Sir Joseph Banks to a man engaging to attempt a journey across the continent of America, £2 2s.'

The year 1787 consisted chiefly of domestic activities. The two children were inoculated against the smallpox, a tantalising diary entry, as it was still nine years before Jenner's successful experiment with his vaccine. Palmerston adds no further details of the treatment apart from an account book entry in May: 'Baron Dimsdale for inoculating Harry and Fanny, £21.' Palmerston attended a very occasional political dinner, but spent most of his time with his relations and the half dozen intimate friends whose names have been noted, although he continued to attend the House when it was in session. Perhaps Lady Palmerston had objected rather more strongly than her mild letter of December 17, 1786 might suggest, to their long periods of residence apart:

'I am quite unhappy about you, and shall not feel the least comfortable till I see you. If you are in any degree afraid of leaving London, and like it better that we should come to town we will set off directly, for place is of no consideration, when your society can be obtained. Let me know your wishes and in this, as in every other instance, I can know no pleasure equal to gratifying them. I am much better, but rather low and comfortless, in short I want to be *dandled* a little.

'The children are perfectly well. Harry never ceases chattering and Fanny, like her Uncle Culverden, is "jig everlasting and dance without end", for she never will be quiet one moment...'[39]

In the summer of 1787 his wife joined him on another tour to the West of England ['expenses... £94 17s.'], with Palmerston taking further notes of the great houses they visited and waxing sarcastic in a letter to his mother at the architectural eccentricities of George III's first Ministerial favourite:

'After we left London we made a very pleasant tour and though we travelled in the phaeton and met with a good deal of rain at times, yet by means of the head, which keeps out the wet, we escaped without inconvenience. We lay one night at Lady Spencer's at St Albans, and three at Sir John Sebright's

farther on in Hertfordshire, and made excursions to visit Lord
Salisbury's at Hatfield, Lord Melbourne's and Lord Bute's at
Luton. The first is very complete and may be supposed to be
everything that it was in Queen Elizabeth's time, with the
addition of all the modern improvements and comforts that
could be introduced without much deviation from the style
and appearance of antiquity which have been well preserved.
What has been done at Lord Bute's is magnificent and comfortable. I think the inside shows more good taste than the
outside. The misfortune and absurdity is that after a sum, not
much less (as is generally thought) than £100,000, has been
expended on this place since the first purchase in improvement,
building, furniture, pictures, *vertu* etc., it is now only half a
house and what is built is so imperfect in appearance without
the remainder, which will probably never be added, that the
general idea of grandeur and magnificence, which must have
been Lord Bute's great object throughout, is lost, after an
expense which, on a judicious plan, would have been much
more than sufficient to have made one of the completest seats
in England. Lord Bute has almost forsaken it and spends most
of his time at a small place he has made on the sea shore near
Christchurch, where he enjoys his health better and Lord
Mountstewart, to whom it will come without any adequate
estate, is not fond of it, so that it is likely to remain a monument
of the injudicious employment of great riches . . .[40]

'Wardour Castle lies just below the downs. The grounds are
extensive – lie well to the house – and are neatly kept. The
present house is new, but the remains of the old castle stand at
one end of the park, rising out of trees and backed by an
amphitheatre of hills, covered with rich woods, and the whole
scene is beautiful from the house. The house has been entirely
built by the present Lord within 14 years. It is a beautiful
structure of stone, 115 feet square, besides the wings. The
apartments are very convenient and comfortable, at the same
time that they are very handsome, and when the whole is
furnished, it will be magnificent. There is a basement story,
but no outside steps to the principal floor, which has not a good
effect without, as the entrance is disproportioned to the general

style of the building. However, the staircase, which carries you up on the inside, is elegant and beautiful. It is in the middle of the house, under a dome, which goes quite to the top, richly ornamented and supported on corinthian columns. The chapel is very fine, grand and yet simple. There are some good pictures . . .

'The great drawing room, which is intended to be the most splendid room, is not yet begun to be fitted up. A very large lake of 100 acres near and in full view of the house was planned by Brown, who laid out the grounds and has done himself credit by them.

'These works are postponed at present, as Lord Arundel is supposed to have distressed himself by the vast sums already expended . . .

'Taunton is a very considerable town, with great appearance of neatness and opulence. There are silk mills and much of the clothing business is carried on . . .

'Enmore, belonging to Lord Egmont, was built by the last Lord (whose hobby horse was the feudal system), directly on the style of the castle of an ancient baron, 500 years ago. It is built of the coarse rough stone of the country, with a deep moat and drawbridge. All the offices, even all the stables and coachhouses are within the moat, or communicate with it by subterraneous passages. The house is dull, very indifferently furnished and little attended to or visited by the present Lord, though the situation and country about it are not bad. There is a kitchen garden, but no pleasure ground . . .

'In our way from Bridgwater to the hills, we passed some copper mines just opened at Nether Stowey, belonging to the Marquis of Buckingham. The ore is uncommonly rich and, if the quantity answers, it will be extremely valuable. The steward told us that some of their ore yielded 70 parts in 100, whereas the Cornish mines yield but 17 and, as he said, the Paris mountain only 3 . . .'

A side-tour which Lord Palmerston undertook alone provided a bucolic note:

'I retired to the inn [at Linton], which proved to be the most miserable hovel of the kind it had ever been my lot to pass a night [in]. I had no place to be in but a wretched hole, which was the common room of the public house, and where I had the company of two farmers and a parson, who were getting as drunk as brandy and noise could make them. The parson, however, did not so far forget his civility as not to endeavour to do the honour of his parish, which he assured me twenty times over, was the most *notorious* and the most *observant* place in the whole creation, as he believed, but he was sure it was so in the north of Devon. I discovered at last that in his vocabulary, notorious meant celebrated and observant worthy of observation. As I did not contradict him, our discourse generally dropped soon, but was continually resumed by him in the same manner. At length, I went out again to take a look at the prospect by moonlight and, before I returned, the farmers having sung all their songs and drunk all their brandy, the whole jovial crew were retired, as I did to a very indifferent and dirty bed, which, however, I found was the pride of the village . . .'[41]

These two years had also seen the beginning of the long drawn out process of impeachment against Warren Hastings. On May 1, 1786, when Hastings had read the first instalment of his reply to the charges made against him in the House, in the full expectation that he would be exonerated, his wife had arranged a celebration party at their house that evening, attended by many of the most famous names in London. Palmerston and Sir Joshua Reynolds were discovered in a corner, being initiated into the game of Twenty Questions.[42] Hastings was to have many more to answer, and at the beginning of 1787 Palmerston noted in his diary:

'Charge against Hastings, on the subject of the Princesses of Oude, made by Mr Sheridan, in one of the finest speeches ever heard in Parliament – 5½ hours in length. Mr Pitt acquiesced in it and the question was carried that there was ground for impeachment in the charge, by 175 to 69.'[43]

It had been Pitt's attitude to the earlier Benares charge, when, after a speech apparently defending the former Governor-General, he had voted for impeachment, which turned the tide against Hastings. This development brought, in the autumn, with the long delay in the mail, a sharp comment from Benjamin Mee in Calcutta:

'The resolutions of the Commons have surprised us much, as it was thought on a general vote of impeachment the business would be done away. Many of Mr Hastings's friends have from personal regard been much hurt at the prosecution being continued and the duplicity of the minister. The popularity of Mr H. is not lessened and general wishes are for his return. Many hope it, some are sanguine enough to expect it as they think proofs will not be produced of Mr H's supposed delinquency. The natives (I mean those of property and connections) express surprise at the measures against him, which however don't lessen him in their esteem . . .

'In England you seem to be very severe against all those in India, and the Company and Board of Control are loading the servants here with opprobrious language and accumulated sufferings as if they had imposed none before on them. The service is not worth holding, and if the distresses of individuals were not too great to admit their return to England a very considerable number would take their departure. Great dissatisfaction prevails and the government here seem to hold the language that to those who have little less shall be given . . .'[44]

In spite of the parliamentary fireworks on the subject, Palmerston's letters to his wife at the end of 1787 indicate that London was not allowing the affair to interfere with the normal round of pleasure:

'I got to town a little after six without stopping. Had there been any dinner going at Brooks's I should have dined there, but as there was not I took some tea and a muffin and went to the play and came back and supped there with a very large pleasant party; which however has had the usual consequence of giving me the headache today, though as I had had no dinner and did not commit any excess I hoped I should have escaped it. My headache however is not very bad and will not prevent me from going to the House.

'The King's speech I hear is a prosing kind of narrative of the Dutch affairs, etc. but does not say anything of any treaty concluded between us and Holland Prussia, which has been expected and was supposed to be the reason of putting off the meeting. I do not imagine there will be anything very material or interesting in the House today. Mr Hastings's business was much talked of. His defence will be given in immediately, which is very voluminous. The House of Commons will not be satisfied with it, and will apply for farther proceedings against him. Of course a trial will be ordered to take place some time after Xmas, and it seems generally thought that it will be in Westminster Hall, but it cannot yet be a fixed thing . . . Fox, Sheridan, Fitzpatrick and Lord John Townshend were at Brooks's . . .[45]

'I hear of nothing but the gaiety of London, suppers, balls and concerts without end. Nobody has less than four princes at a time, and the Dukes of York and Cumberland run about the rooms and play like two kittens. I saw Lord Hampden yesterday who is as happy as possible with it all. He says Lady Hampden is extremely well only *raked to death*. I called today on Lady Caroline Price and have been in her box this evening at *The School for Scandal*. They are determined to stay for an opera which is now deferred till Saturday. The burletta and the dancing I hear are likely to be pretty good as there are some female dancers that are said to have merit . . .[46]

'When I arrived in London on Wednesday afternoon [December 5] I found no House of Commons sitting, there not having been members enough down at 4 o'clock the Speaker went away. Yesterday Mr Gray's motion came on and today is to be the business of the finances and a good deal of conversation about Carlton House . . .

'Hastings' speech did not answer. It was dull, foolish and impudent. In consequence of the reservation he made he is now at liberty to go into such a defence as his counsel shall advise next year.

'I am going to the Levée where I have not been above once this year . . .'[47]

['Cost and expenses of half a hogshead of Hermitage, 12 dozen, £21 9s.' read an account book entry for December 29.]

Palmerston continued to devote most of his time to the affairs of his family, increased on January 17, 1788, by the birth of his second son, William. The summer found him, notebook in hand, on tour again:

'Set out with Lady Palmerston from London. Saw Knowle. The park is fine with inequality of ground and well wooded ... The rooms are melancholy and deserted, all but two or three, particularly a library, which the Duke has filled up in the modern style, and even these have no pleasant view from the windows. The pleasure ground is dull and neglected and rises directly from the house, whose prospect is by that means obstructed ...

'Goodwood, an irregular old house of the Duke of Richmond, with some comfortable rooms, but little worthy of particular notice. The offices form a handsome building near the house, and the Duke is making a dog kennel, which is an object from the house and which both within and without is in a style of elegance unknown hitherto to that species of building. The park is pleasing and in the upper part of it, at some distance from the house, which stands low, is a menagerie now going to decay, but originally very pretty . . .'[48]

He returned in time to assist his friend, Lord John Townshend, in the bye-election at Westminster in August, caused by the appointment of Lord Hood to a seat on the new Board of Admiralty. Hood, who had held the seat with his political opponent, Charles James Fox, since 1784, was ousted by Townshend, to the undisguised joy of the Whigs. On August 2, Palmerston wrote to his wife:

'I have just received yours and am much obliged to you for it. I got to Farnham about 12 on Thursday night and to London about one yesterday. I sallied out immediately for Covent Garden where I found things going well, but voters came in slow on both sides. However, Lord John gained 26 and at the close his majority was 750. Afterwards I went and dined at the Crown and Anchor where there was the second great dinner of Lord John's friends. We were about 450 at dinner and I got to a table with all my acquaintance, so did very well. There was better accommodation and less confusion than could have been expected. The meeting separated early after some toasts and speeches and after agreeing that every-body should endeavour to bring a vote today. I did not much expect to succeed, but I think I have, for Cave has found out a tight little breeches maker in the neighbourhood who is ready to vote and we are just going to the hustings . . .

'Lord Hood's friends had a meeting yesterday at Willis's to imitate ours, where I hear there was a great mob, much con-fusion and no dinner to be got and where they stayed like a pack of fools hollowing and hooting till ten o'clock at night . . .

'Since writing the above I have been with my little friend to Covent Garden and polled him very successfully. The election has not gone so well today, Lord Hood having gained 84 on this day's poll, owing I suppose to great exertion in consequence of their dinner yesterday and to some ill-judged shutting up or at least restraining the expense of houses opened in West-minster for Lord John. This cannot in the least affect the issue of the election, but it somewhat lessens the triumph and may encourage further attempts . . .[49]

'Having done all I had to do and being quite satisfied with London and the election, I am just getting into my chaise to set out and if it is as fine a night as it promises to be may perhaps call on Dr Herschel on my way . . .'[50]

Palmerston was on his way to Ireland for the last visit to his estates he paid during his lifetime, and during the call on Dr Herschel, was shown one of the planetary nebulæ the great astronomer was discovering:

'Visited Doctor Herschel at Slough; came to him at half-past ten and stayed till one. Saw one of his planetary nebulæ, and the nebula in the head of Aquarius, through his 20 feet reflector. The planetary nebula is a very bright object, circular with the edges not very exactly defined and appears like a planet out of focus. Its diameter is about half that of Jupiter and is magnified according to the powers of the glasses used. It is totally invisible to the naked eye, or to anything but a telescope of considerable power. The other nebula is an exceeding fine object. It appears to be a cluster of very bright stars, more thinly scattered about the edge, and thicker towards the centre, where they seem to form a kind of nucleus, which is one blaze of light, and where the separate stars are no longer distinguishable. A star of the 4th magnitude appears in that telescope brighter than one of the 1st in common telescopes. The tube and the whole apparatus of the great 40 feet telescope remains there, and the speculum, which weighs above a ton, is preparing, but I fear it is a very difficult operation to bring it to the right shape and the success very doubtful. I looked through his 10 feet telescope at several nebulæ. This is a fine instrument and perfectly manageable, but the difference between that and the other, when applied to the same object, is excessively great. Indeed, the effect of the great telescope is quite surprising and produces an effect totally distinct from that of any other I ever looked through . . .'51

* * *

Palmerston had decided to carry out further alterations and embellishments at Broadlands while he was away. The diary entry for Monday, March 17, 1788, reads: 'Went with Sir Henry Englefield and Mr Holland to Wyndhams to see drawings.' This is the first mention in the papers of the famous architect, who, ten days later, spent the night at Broadlands, paying three further visits during the year, and producing a written recommendation of the alterations he proposed,52 and a sketch of the suggested decoration of the dining-room ceiling.

Holland was responsible for filling in the east front of the house, joining the two wings by a recessed portico which supported a third storey, thus completing its present rectangular shape. Behind the imposing, but false, new front, an entrance loggia was built in the former courtyard, and the hall redesigned to contain Palmerston's collection of antique statuary. Above it, the wainscoted great chamber of Sir John St Barbe remained the only intact part of the former Jacobean house.

Lady Palmerston kept her husband informed of the progress of the work:

August 6th. 'The three rooms will be finished today, book room, saloon and eating room. The new building goes on very well. The dairy will be finished tomorrow . . .

August 11th. 'The portico all but the pillars done and looks vastly well. The new building comes on very well and the greenhouse, and I should imagine in ten days all the work in the house will be completed. Holland has ordered the bricks for the new work and as we have been at a stand in some places for hands I thought it better to send for more, that it might be finished during the fine weather . . .

September 6th. 'Mr Jagger has worked very hard and his plan will prove very successful I believe, which is to build up the new wall to the chamber floor and lay the floors before he touches a brick of the old one, which will prevent the necessity of taking off the roof to the garden front and save thereby a great deal of expence and trouble . . . The state of the old timbers were very bad indeed . . . The breaking a way through the window in the hall and upstairs will be the last thing done. The eating room into the recess will be 32′ 6″. The place for the chimney was marked out on Friday opposite to the centre window. The maids' hall, steward's room, pantry, Hold's room and the rest of the offices will be completed in the course of next week. The nursery is going on very well . . . The greenhouse seems quite hopeless, I have given it up. The portico and cornice are to be begun this week, a contrivance having been formed to save erecting a scaffold . . .

September 11th. 'The wall of the eating room has advanced rapidly and in three days I believe the timbers will be laid of the bedchamber floor. The recess will be 2 feet 6 . . . One column of the portico is finished and looks vastly well, they are going on but it will prove a long job. The nursery advances. Mr Holland I had a letter from this morning and he has fixed the 19th for coming here . . . After Saturday we shall have but the painters and in a week they will have completely finished within doors, but I think I have told you the same story ever since your departure . . .'[53]

Palmerston, in Dublin, kept a sharp eye on details:

September 13th. 'I have just got a letter from Holland enclosing a plan of the rooms as he intends them. I am very well satisfied with the dimensions of the eating room but I do not at all like his arrangement of the first storey as he means that the inner bedchamber should have only a light closet within it and not a distinct dressing room with a fireplace. Now the getting two bedrooms and dressing rooms was one great inducement to the alteration. The difficulty I know is how to preserve the chimney place in the blue bedchamber which is now contrived and carried up in some very odd and irregular mode and Mr Holland seemed to think neither that nor any other chimney in the wall on that side could well be suffered to exist after the alteration. I shall write to him about it and I mention it now in hopes you may be able to settle something about it on the spot. If a chimney could be procured for both rooms the disposition of that floor was to have been very different from what he has sent me and he has not accompanied it with any observations on that point . . .'

On his return to England he paid particular attention to the final details of the dining room, which remains to this day as he determined:

December 28th. 'I went with Holland when first I came up to Bedford House and saw the room he spoke of which is a very good one. But though it is 2 feet higher than mine I think the cove looks rather small and both Holland and I were clear we had better not have it. He is likewise perfectly convinced that the room will be better without the columns which in the way they were intended, i.e. meaning nothing, supporting nothing, agreeing with nothing in any other part of the room, and only stuck against a wall, I was always averse to. He has made a sketch of that end of the room preserving the recess with pilasters on each side of it and an arch over it that I think will do very well. Indeed the recess is so great an addition to the convenience of the room, which is deficient only in length, that I should have been very unwilling to have parted with it and in the way that is now proposed it will coincide with the ornaments of the doors and altogether that end of the room will look very well . . .'[54]

* * *

The anecdote book entries during these years had also been more social than political:

'*When Mrs Siddons first acted, the people fainted away so*

frequently that somebody said the orange women now cry nothing but, "Hartshorn", and "Lavender drops".

'*Doctor Meade and Doctor Woodward fought a duel in which the former, being disarmed, the latter bad him ask for his life. "No, doctor," said he, "that I never will do till I am your patient."*

'*Mr Cambridge, being in a post chaise with a man who was telling him a very long and dull narrative, called up his son who was riding near the carriage and said he wished to get on horseback and, if the gentleman pleased, his son would come in and hear the remainder of the story.*

'*Mr Woodroffe, a clergyman, having killed a man in a way that he thought not likely to be deemed murder in the eye of the law, wrote to some friends before his trial came on to know how he should appear at the bar – whether in his coat or his gown. Being offended at the unfeeling manner in which he wrote, they answered that they thought it not very material how he was dressed at his trial, but that they advised him, by all means, to be hanged in his coat.*

'*The Duke of Richelieu, who carried on the show of gallantry after his powers began to be much on the decline, being in the company of a lady, whom he had long solicited, but who was under the inspection of a very jealous husband who seldom permitted her out of his sight, she said to him, "Monsieur le Duc, fortune has at length thrown the happy moment in our way. My husband is gone to such a place and it will take him full five minutes to go and return. The opportunity is yours if you make use of it." The Duke, disconcerted at the abrupt call, answered, "Mon Dieu, Madame, me prenez-vous pour un pistolet?"* '

REFERENCES

1. B.1 [?10.X.1782]
2. B.1 October/November 1782
3. B.1 [?19.XI.1782]
4. B.2 5.XII.1782
5. B.1 [?6.XII.1782]
6. B.2 8.XII.1782
7. B.1 [?9.XII.1782]
8. B.2 10.XII.1782
9. B.1 [?11.XII.1782]
10. C.18(a) 20.XII.1782
11. B.2 26.XII.1782
12. B.1 28.XII.1782
13. B.2 30.XII.1782
14. B.1 31.XII.1782
15. A.13 August 1783
16. A.1 December 1783 – March 1784
17. H.14
18. B.1 [8.IV.1784]
19. B.1 15.IV.1784
20. B.1 April 1784
21. A.1 24.V.1784
22. B.1 10.XI.1784
23. B.1 14.XI.1784
24. H.20
25. C.18(a) 22.XII.1784
26. C.41 26.XII.1784
27. A.3(b)
28. A.1
29. A.1
30. A.3(b)
31. C.44(a)
32. B.1 23.V.1786
33. H.45 1.VIII.1786
34. B.1 28.VII.1786
35. B.1 30.VII.1786
36. B.1 2.VIII.1786
37. C.18(a) 1.I.1786
38. C.45 3.VIII.1786
39. B.2 17.XII.1786
40. C.17(a) 26.VII.1787
41. A.15
42. H.10 pp. 491–2
43. A.1 7.II.1787
44. C.44(a) 19.IX.1787
45. B.1 27.XI.1787
46. B.1 4.XII.1787
47. B.1 undated [7.XII.1787]
48. A.16
49. B.1 2.VIII.1788
50. B.1 4.VIII.1788
51. A.16 3.VIII.1788
52. F.14
53. B.2
54. B.1

CHAPTER VI

INSANITY OF GEORGE III

*News of the King's illness from Sheridan and Sir Gilbert Elliot –
the Regency Bill – the King's recovery – death of Mrs Temple –
young Harry's first letter – tour of the Netherlands in revolt – returned
for Newport, Isle of Wight, with the first Lord Melbourne – purchases a new town house in Hanover Square – the trial of Warren
Hastings – Palmerston veers to the support of the younger Pitt –
growth of his family and death of the second daughter*

KING GEORGE III, who had been in ill health for some
time, relapsed into insanity at the beginning of November, 1788. The Whigs saw themselves restored to office
under the Prince of Wales as Regent, and the attempts of Fox
and Sheridan to overturn Pitt provided a parliamentary battle
which lasted the whole winter. Palmerston sent voluminous
accounts of the furore to his wife:

Thursday, November 4th. 'The report of the doctors, though
decisive as to the present state of the King, gives more expectation of a future recovery than is agreeable to the general
opinion or than I believe warranted in sound reasoning. But he
must be a bold man who would hazard an opinion in such a
situation, though he might entertain it, that the King never
would recover. Addington who is eighty-six and was reckoned
an old woman twenty years ago was the most sanguine and
Warren I understand appeared the least so. They said they did
not found their opinion upon the particular symptoms of this
case but upon a general calculation by which it appeared that
much the greater part of those afflicted with these disorders,
including every species, did recover ... It is thought the
ministers are still divided in opinion what measures to take,
and that some of them, particularly the Duke of Richmond,
are for a limited Regency with a Council as a mere temporary
mode of carrying on public business and that they have gone
so far as to propose that it should be offered to the Prince to

be at the head of such a Regency, and if he should refuse it to make one without him. Pitt, however, is certainly too wise to think of this and it is generally thought they will make the Prince Regent, holding out at the same time as strongly as possible the great probability of the King's early recovery, in order to prevent any changes if they can, or if not to weaken and embarrass a new government . . .

'I forgot to mention that the King is going to be put under the care and management of Willis, from Lincolnshire, who I find is considered as skilful in the mode of treating them as well as careful in managing them . . .

'5 o'clock – The House is up. I think the report of the doctors nearly what I have mentioned but rather less sanguine in expectation of recovery than I was told . . . Pitt moved to adjourn till Monday, saying he hoped this evidence would be thought sufficient then to proceed on . . . Fox said he wished it might be found consistent with the dignity and duty of Parliament to take the report as ground of proceeding, as it was certainly more convenient to do so; that he really had not formed an opinion and approved of the matter being reserved to a future day. I was surprised to see him there, he looks ill and spoke rather weak. He is however getting better and I am glad for his sake that no more business or cause of debate arose today.

November 6th. 'I dined yesterday and the day before in company with their Lordships of Huntingdon, Buckingham and Barrington, so I hope I shall be found improved in my breeding. I went away however yesterday time enough to see Mrs Jordan in part of the *Country Girl* and in a new entertainment called *The Pannel*, which has no merit except that she in the character of a waiting maid is a great deal on the stage.

'I have heard nothing new that is material as to public matters though I was some time yesterday morning at the Duke of Portland's who is generally at home on a morning and lets in all men that call, which makes his room a very pleasant kind of coffee house . . . The Prince made his appearance the night before last for a few minutes at Brooks's. He was full dressed, looked well, though I think somewhat paler and thinner than usual.

'Willis is gone to Kew but I have not heard what he says. His opinion is looked upon as a good one, but I hear he refuses to leave the country to take the charge of the King. Charles Fox is not well, though I hope he is likely to be soon. He is weak and has an uncommon drowsiness upon him. Turton gave him the bark which I suppose did not quite agree, as last night he ordered him an emetic. I am afraid he will not be well enough to attend any long debates without risk to himself for some time . . .

November 7th. 'The King is entirely under Willis's care, who I suppose agrees to stay . . . He made him eat some meat for dinner and go to bed at the time he thought proper when, after crying for some time, the King slept for seven hours, being before that quite exhausted with fatigue and watchfulness. The rest he got then seems however to have recruited the disorder as well as the patient, for the accounts since have been that he has been more unquiet and worse on the whole. Today it is that he was uncommonly unquiet yesterday evening, had four hours sleep at intervals and is not better today. Willis I hear says he has hopes of curing him, but does not choose to say anything as to time. Much has been spread of the very favourable accounts Willis gives but I believe what I have said is the truth. Pitt was at Kew yesterday and saw the Queen, I believe for the first time. Reports differ about their intentions, it appears however that Pitt does not mean as has been said to give the King up without some struggle and retire with dignity. The news today is that they mean to propose the Prince sole Regent under restrictions from making peers, granting places for life and dissolving Parliament. If this is the plan much confusion will follow as he will not take it on those terms . . .

November 8th, 5 o'clock. 'The House is again up. Mr Pitt moved for a committee to enquire into the state of the King and named it, consisting of 21 members chose tolerably fairly from both sides . . .

November 20th, ½ past four. 'The House is up. Mr Pitt made a very short speech stating the situation we were in and saying that in such a conjuncture it was impossible to discuss any part of public business and that in all cases that bore the least analogy to this it had been usual to adjourn. But that as it would become necessary in case of the continuance of the King's illness to take measures, he should move to adjourn to this day fortnight and that the House should then be called. The House was excessively full. Nothing was said and the motion passed . . .'[1]

Palmerston was getting inside information on the course of events from Sheridan:

'The news as far as relative to the King's health, has continued so much the same that there has been nothing worth telling.

'The case of our politics is that the Prince has really behaved in the fairest and noblest manner possible. He has very steadily turned aside from all the practices of the ministers, and those employed by them, and has now, in an open and avowed manner, employed the Duke of Portland and Fox to make their own arrangements, in case we'll give him power.

'His conduct to the Duke of Portland, whom he saw at Burlington House on Saturday, has been everything that's right. Desiring him to shake hands, and that they would never again think of the dispute they had about the motion for paying his debts, etc.

'The King is certainly worse than ever – Pitt and Chancellor have both seen him. He abused Pitt like a dog.

'I believe there will be no more adjournment, and that the measure will be to propose a financial enquiry into the King's state.'[2]

Sir Gilbert Elliot also kept him informed. On December 1 he wrote:

'It is hardly necessary to say there is no change in the King's health, although the Court papers and indeed some of the courtiers persist in circulating reports of his amendment and do what they can to keep up an expectation of his recovery. They were five hours on Saturday prevailing on him to get up and he yielded at last to a little show of authority. I understand that the journey to Kew was performed however pretty quietly and when he arrived there he expressed some satisfaction at the apartment he was put into. He was however all this time in the same state of insanity as usual, as one of his fancies soon after he got to Kew will prove. After looking about the apartment and approving of it he insisted on the apothecary's dancing a minuet with him, to which he was obliged to submit and the King danced it remarkably well and with great appearance of strength and activity in his limbs. The Queen is in the Prince of Wales's House at Kew. The Prince came to town on Saturday and went to Burlington House about nine at night. He remained there till about twelve. The Duke of York accompanied him. The correspondence which I believe I mentioned to have taken place between the Prince and the Duke of Portland related to the little difference which had happened between them on the occasion of paying the Prince's debts, and from which many people had apprehended there might still remain some disagreeable impression on the Prince's mind. The day on which Fox first saw the Prince, just as Fox was coming away, the Prince took him by the hand and said nearly to this effect. "Pray shake the Duke of Portland cordially by the hand for me, and tell him that I sincerely hope that everything which is past may be entirely forgot between us. And as a proof that it shall be forgot on my part assure him that as soon as I come to town I will go to Burlington House, and do not desire that it should be considered as a secret that I do so." To this message the D. of P. wrote such an answer as the occasion seemed to require, and the Prince in reply wrote him one of the most gentlemanlike letters that, I dare say, was ever written by a Prince. On Saturday when he came to Burlington House, the D. of P. met him at the door, and as soon as the Prince entered the house he took the D. by the hand, and said, "My dear Duke, I am the happiest man in the world to find myself again in this house, and I have only to desire that what is past may be forgot for ever, and that it may never again be either thought of or mentioned by either of us." The Prince's conduct in this instance has certainly done him infinite credit, and both in the thing itself, and in the manner of doing it has given a very satisfactory proof both of judgment and of heart . . . At this meeting there were Lord North, Ld

Loughborough and a very few others. They talked pretty fully
of business and I understand the Prince was perfectly sound on
all points. He declared explicitly that he would have nothing
to do with the government if it was qualified by any limitation
whatever. There is a dinner today at Burlington House to settle
more particularly our measures for Thursday. Much must still
depend on the proposition made by Pitt . . . He saw the King
on Friday and Saturday and I understand is perfectly satisfied
of his insanity. Indeed, *il est payé pour cela*, for the King abused
him most violently, called him rogue and rascal, and attacked
him strongly about different sums of money which the King
said he had taken from him. Pitt was indeed very unwilling
to go into the King on Saturday, and it was observed that on
some of these attacks about money he showed in his manner
some uneasiness under it . . .'[3]

When Parliament met again Palmerston continued to keep
his wife *au courant*:

December 10th, ½ *past* 5. 'The report of the committee is read.
It is longer but much the same in effect as before. All the doctors
say it is probable he will recover but none of them can say
when. Willis is most sanguine. They all say there are no present
marks of convalescence but some of them say that his general
health being better and his violence being abated are as they
hope forerunners of a recovery. Pitt has moved for a committee
to search for precedents. Fox has agreed to it as a matter of
form but says there are no cases in our history similar as there
are none where there was an heir apparent of full age to take
the place and has advanced it as his solemn opinion that in the
present case the Prince has a claim of right to exercise all the
functions of the King during his incapacity. Pitt has got up in
a great passion says this is little less than treason and that the
government in this case is in the disposal of Parliament and
that the Prince of Wales has no more right to it than any other
individual . . .

Wednesday night, December 10th. 'What I wrote today from
the House of Commons was the substance of what passed
there, though I found when I went back into the House that
I had lost a short but excellent reply of Fox's in which he stated

some strong legal arguments in support of his proposition and challenged the lawyers on the other side to answer them, which was declined. I foresee much violence and ill-blood in the prosecution of this business and probably a weak and uncertain government for many years to come in whose ever hands it may be lodged. The report of the physicians is ordered to be printed so that you will see it. I find Willis remains with the King and is to have the direction of him so I conclude he leaves his house to be managed by his sons, one or two of which are in his line and are his assistants. There seems to be a good deal of the quack about him, as you will probably think when you read his examination, where he says nine in ten of his patients recover, whereas one hears of numerous instances where he has done no good, and in another place where he says the King's disorder proceeds from 27 years' abstemiousness, exercise, application and want of sleep and that he has given him a medicine to counteract all these which began to produce its effect in 6 hours. However I believe he is clever in the management of his patients and keeping them quiet. As to the cure I believe the methods are simple and generally known to medical people. Willis has the character of establishing his authority with less harshness than anybody. By what was said today I think it will be Tuesday next in all probability before the real business comes to be discussed. The Prince is very firm in his purposes but I hear he is much affected and agitated by every occurrence and every report and for his own comfort it were to be wished he had more calmness and steadiness . . .

Saturday morn, hard frost and thick fog [*December 12th*]. 'The King's state I believe continues the same. The people about him have got a perfect ascendancy over him and he is quieter and better in health. His mind I believe just as before. He was taken into the garden yesterday for the first time where however he ran away from Willis but was soon brought back by the attendants. He eats and sleeps better than he did and plays at draughts sometimes with Willis . . .

'The declaration Fox made on Wednesday about the Prince's right seems to have been rather unfortunate, as it has been misunderstood by some of our friends not remarkable for clear

comprehension and misrepresented by all the opposite party.
It became necessary for Fox therefore to bring it up again in
order to explain clearly what he had said, which he did ably.
I agree with him in opinion and understood him before exactly
as he has now stated it, but I am sorry to say it does not seem
to be popular and as we are forced now to contend that the
discussion of such a question is not necessary I am sorry it was
brought up. Pitt whose prudence, at least, I am afraid is not
inferior to ours, thinks he has got some advantageous ground
to stand upon in this question and therefore determines to push
it and will therefore probably move some resolution cautiously
worded in which, without mentioning the Prince, he will
assert in high terms the right of the two Houses of Parliament
in such a case to place the executive government or any portion
of it where they think most conducive to the public benefit.
Our side in such a case will contend that discussions of this sort
are always dangerous and to be avoided if possible and that
the House ought to proceed to take the measures necessary and
proper without delay, rather than sit to moot abstract questions
on constitutional points. In this opinion (though perhaps not
urged with the most weight from those who started the question) I hope we shall be well supported by the most moderate
and neutral part of the House and if Pitt finds that, perhaps he
will withdraw the proposition . . .

Tuesday, December 16th. 'I am just going to the House, where
we shall probably have a long day and I should hope a good
one. If Pitt persists in bringing the question of right to a vote I
hope there is a chance of beating him, as most of the moderate
and neutral people are strong against the decision. The Duke
of York acquitted himself well and judiciously yesterday in the
House of Lords both in matter and manner. The Chancellor,
the day before, gave the Prince the strongest assurances of
support and as I believe his speeches are pretty fairly stated in
the papers you will see what a fellow he is. He has long ago
agreed to give up the seals willingly and take some other good
place under a new government, but this is *entre nous.* The seals
will be in commission, as Lord Loughborough may be first
Commissioner and hold what he has and Speaker of the House

of Lords. I find Lord Malmesbury goes with the Prince and has explained himself fully to Pitt, I mean with regard to full powers and no limitations, which he says is necessary to keep up any credit to this country abroad. I will take my letter with me and put in a word before I seal it up . . .

'$\frac{1}{2}$ past five – Pitt has moved his question of the right and is still speaking. Nothing has been yet said against deciding such a point. The house is now fuller of members than I ever saw it.

December 17th. 'The debate between Fox and Pitt was good, but miserably reported in all the papers, as the crowd was so great that the newswriters were shut out. The division was bad, as you perceive. I was hardly sanguine enough to think we should carry it, but did not expect to be beat by 69, which majority I fear gives Pitt full power in the House of Commons through the business which at present wears no very agreeable aspect. Pitt's popularity seems not be shaken and by that and a majority in Parliament, he will be enabled to carry his own measures which are to make the Prince Regent with limitations to his powers. These limitations probably will be that he shall grant no places for life nor turn out any of the King's House-hold servants nor make peers. The obvious purpose of this is to secure and preserve a majority in the House of Lords at the disposal of Pitt and the Chancellor, to whom they will owe their power and which a dissolution of Parliament (which I believe they find it would be too unconstitutional to prevent) would not do away. This will put the Prince into great difficulties because if he should refuse it, which he would naturally be inclined to do, there is an apprehension lately arisen that Pitt wishes for nothing so much and that he would then offer it to the Queen and prevail upon her to accept it, which as they are both popular might for aught I know go down with the country at large and make Pitt the most established and the most absolute minister this country has ever seen . . . The King is just the same. When exhausted and reduced by physic and want of sleep he is quiet, when recruited he is outrageous. When in his calmest state he was suffered to see the Queen and one of the Princesses, which threw him into such an outrageous frenzy as might have been attended with fatal consequences and they were obliged to put on the strait waistcoat. Most people think Willis a great quack, whose judgment is little to be trusted and whose knowledge extends no farther than to the means of keeping his patients in order and treating them in the common method which is known to all who have the care of persons in that situation. Adieu, I must go to the House ...

PS. Charles Fox has not got rid of his complaint, for which nothing is so bad as agitation of mind. He was very ill and had much difficulty to go on the other night, though he spoke as well as ever I heard him.

Tuesday, December 23rd. 'We had a late sitting last night on the amendment proposed by Mr Dempster to address the Prince to take the administration of government on himself instead of proceeding in Mr Pitt's mode. C. Fox, who has been much out of order two or three days ago, was however down and made an excellent speech, as did Lord North. The speaking on the other side was very indifferent and Pitt made no figure till we came to divide, when contrary to my expectation, as well as that of most people, we were beat by 73, which is by a greater majority upon smaller numbers. Pitt's resolutions being now passed are to be communicated to the Lords today and we are to do nothing more till they have agreed to them, which with the intervening of Christmas day cannot be till the end of the week and we can do nothing more till next Monday. I should have set out today to have come down to you had not the weather been so severe and my cold, which I was in hopes was almost gone, came back again ...'[4]

There was indeed good reason for him to return to Broadlands. Lady Palmerston was *enceinte* with their fourth child and anxious for her husband's company:

Broadlands, December 25th. 'If you do not get well I shall soon follow, for I cannot feel easy when I think you are ill, and there are 75 miles between us. If you have any idea that it will not be in your power to give your daughter Mary the meeting on her first arrival I must come up, as I shall be miserable to go through that trial without your being in the same house. I am perhaps absurd, but I only can answer for my feelings and not for the propriety of them ...'[5]

Palmerston humoured her by return of post:

Friday, December 26th. 'I do not know but that I might come down to you tomorrow . . . However as things now stand I think it is better to remain here a little while longer, during which I take it for granted that the question of the limitations will come on in some shape or other. That appears to me to be the only object now to be disputed and when that is over I shall have done my duty in the cause. If the matter is carried on through a long detail I shall contrive to pair off with somebody and at all events not to stay beyond the time when you are the least likely to want me, when I assure you no consideration should tempt me to be absent . . .

December 30th. 'Nothing is yet done in the House of Commons, which for my own part I do not much regret hitherto as I am better at home than I should be there, but their mode of proceeding seems very dilatory. Today the House is put off on account of the Speaker's [Cornwall] illness, which however I find is thought to be very convenient [as] the ministers are not ready with their plan . . .

January 2nd, 1789. 'I just write a few lines to say that my cold is certainly mending, though slowly and I cannot say that it is yet quite well enough to make me wish to go out, considering the weather. For that reason I do not on my own account so much regret the total stand at which all parliamentary business has been and is likely to be on account of the poor Speaker, who has given a most serious proof that his illness was not pretended by dying this morning about ten o'clock . . . This will occasion new embarrassment and irregularity, as it is one of the most essential rules of Parliament that a new Speaker should be presented to and approved by the King. At least it is so with a new Parliament and I suppose likewise so upon the choice of a new Speaker in the course of a Parliament . . .

'Since I wrote the above Sir Gilbert [Elliot] has called on me. I find the House met today and upon being informed by Hatsell from the table of the event, they adjourned till Monday, when they are to chose a new Speaker. William Grenville is to be the man, who I really think will fill the office well, though it is a bad thing to have a Speaker so decidedly of an opposite party. They must pass over the King's approbation which weakens still more their ground of adhering to all the forms of proceeding. Pitt sent to the Prince with very little ceremony the intended limitations, one of which is that the Queen is to manage the Household, that is to be at the head of a strong faction in opposition to the Prince. The Prince, I understand, is to give an answer, which is a delicate point and I should have thought at least doubtful in point of propriety . . .

'They are labouring hard to get rid of all the physicians but Willis in order to give just such accounts as they please and keep up a constant expectation of a recovery. The King is now said to be better, but since he was last reported so he has been strapped down in his bed for many hours.

'Pitt's plan of getting addresses and thanks does not go on very well. They have failed in Manchester, Liverpool, Norwich, Bristol, Bath and Shrewsbury . . .

'Among other restrictions the Prince is to have nothing to do with the King's real or personal property or revenues. Among these comes the Duchy of Lancaster and that will protect *my friend* Lord Hawkesbury.

January 5th. 'I did not imagine that there was any intention of contesting the Speakership, but this morning I was surprised with the information that it is intended to propose Sir Gilbert Elliot. I am sorry I cannot go there to vote for him but I have totally incapacitated myself for that, having made use of what I thought the last leisure day in taking a little James's powder and some physic. Perhaps they may not divide upon it, as I suppose there can be no chance of carrying it. Sir Gilbert would make an excellent Speaker when he became a little used to the situation, a better one indeed I think (putting all party out of the question) than the other, who has one very strong objection against him, being extremely short-sighted, and is besides subject to violent headaches. Sir Gilbert has likewise been talked of to be Chancellor of the Exchequer, as has also Tom Pelham. Our side are much at a loss for a proper person to hold that situation, as it seems a measure decided that the Duke of Portland is to be First Lord of the Treasury, and Lord John Cavendish who was not very equal to the Chancellorship five

G

years ago, and has been out of Parliament ever since, wishes not to take it again. Whoever stands forward in that department in the House of Commons, with Pitt in opposition to them, ought to be very much used to intricate and difficult business and very ready in debate, and in short ought to be the efficient minister in the House of Commons and there has always been a weakness found when that has not been the case. For this reason I was in hopes that Fox meant now to stand out boldly as First Lord of the Treasury, and that the Duke of P. in some other high cabinet office would have been the ministerial leader in the House of Lords, and I was the more in hopes of this as I do not think we have any person but Fox at all suited to the situation. Whoever takes it must depend upon him for support, which even he cannot give with half the effect and power that he would if the department was his own . . .

'The King is much in the same state. The physicians have a constant dispute with Willis who always wants them to say that he is in a progressive state of amendment, which they are clear is not the case. The state that he is in varies, as in those cases it always must, but in the best state that he has hitherto been in there are (to use the original phrase) no marks of convalescence and this you may depend on it is the opinion of the physicians. The state of his general health likewise varies, and is not very good, but there is nothing that seems to threaten his life . . .

Thursday, January 8th, 5 o'clock. 'I am just come back from the House, which only met to adjourn. The committee of enquiry is going on just as I supposed. They sit morning and night (last night till near 2 this morning) they are this moment separated and are to meet again at eight and they have finished the examination of only one physician though they have had several in . . .

'To stay out the business would be quite impracticable and I believe that in consequence of some measures I took I am now part of one of those happy pairs that Soame Jenyns has celebrated. I think Saturday or Sunday I shall be with you. I can keep myself very warm in the chaise and as to the house, I have no fear of its not being comfortable enough . . .

January 10th. 'As it continues to snow I suppose the roads must be very bad and if I do not set out very early I may possibly not come through in the day . . . As to waiting to see any end either of my cold or the frost or the parliamentary business they appear to me all equally hopeless . . .'[6]

He only arrived just in time. Lady Palmerston was brought to bed of a daughter on the afternoon of Thursday, January 15. This pleasure was alloyed only a fortnight later, when he received a letter to say that his mother had died on Wednesday, January 28, at two in the morning. He immediately set off for Sheen and reported from London on the 30th:

'By the accounts I received it appears that my poor mother, though excessively emaciated and reduced to an extreme state of debility, suffered very little. She had kept her bed since Saturday but it was chiefly from finding herself more comfortable there than up. On that day she was taken out of bed but did not chose to be moved into her dressing room, but after a little while went to bed again. She did not think herself dying nor did Flint think her so near her end till she sank and died with very little pain or struggle . . . Flint showed me the place where she said she saw her put her will which she wrote not above a fortnight ago. I accordingly found a paper wrote by herself not dated nor sealed up. The general purport of it is to leave everything she has to me except some annuities to servants which are not all so clearly expressed as I wish they had been . . .'[7]

Palmerston's own health had been indifferent during the winter, and he spent the next month quietly at Broadlands. However, at the beginning of March he was back in London, making up for lost time. The entries in the engagement diaries for the first week in March included: 'Dined at the Club; Brooks's; ancient music; supper with Mrs Sheridan; dinner at the Crown and Anchor; Play; Devonshire House ball; Oratorio at Covent Garden; the Opera; Mrs Crewe supper and Sir Henry Englefield, Sir Gilbert Elliot to dinner.'

The King had solved the political crisis by being declared convalescent in February. Palmerston remained in London to give his wife an account of the festivities to greet the King's recovery, together with a resumé of a gregarious if not particularly purposeful week:

April 10th. 'As to my history and proceedings they are not very entertaining. Saturday and Sunday you know there were large companies to dinner. The park on Sunday was the most crowded and gayest looking place I have seen for a great while. I totally forgot Lady Hampden's party and so did not go there. Monday dined at Mr Hankey's, very stupid and vulgar . . . I supped at Mr Stanley's with a small party, not very lively. Tuesday I dined at the Catch Club where we had some very good music, from thence I went and played at Loo at the Boehm's and from thence to Lady Archer's, who had a very good assembly, Pharo, sandwiches, etc. It was very pleasant and I think the house beautiful in its way. Lady Margaret invited Harry and Fanny and indeed had sent them cards to a little party of fairies she is to have on Monday next before Lady Elizabeth Yorke's assembly. However I made their excuses and it was agreed that they should not make their entrance into the gay world in your absence . . . Yesterday I dined at Lord Malmesbury's. It was a man dinner with some foreigners and not very pleasant. Mr Hankey's concert was crowded with odd people as you may guess but there was some very good music. From thence to Andrews's which was very pleasant. By having tables round his room he had managed to set down I dare say 60 people very well. There was much good singing till three o'clock this morning . . .

'I shall wish to be back again before Thursday sennight which is the Thanksgiving. It is now announced to both Houses of Parliament that they are to attend the King which will be a ceremony I should not choose to miss and shall by that means have an opportunity of seeing the whole without much trouble. They talk now of Brooks's ball for the day before, which I think a very bad plan and as everybody disapproves it I hope they will alter it . . . It is to be full dress, no uniform and tickets 7 [? guineas] without distinction of ladies and gentlemen . . .

April 22nd. 'In the Herald of today you will see a better account of the ball and its decorations than I could give you. The ornaments were splendid and elegant to the greatest degree and so were in general the dresses of the ladies who attended it. The men were all dressed but in general rather plainly. The Prince was excessively fine but his clothes the most frightful and unbecoming I ever saw. It is surprising how much had been done and how complete the whole was in the very short time since Saturday night but the being obliged to bring it a day forwarder than was intended had cramped them and made some things not so perfect as they would have been. Particularly one of the intended transparencies failing in the machinery which was to let it down just at last they thought it necessary to substitute a board with God Save the King, which would have been a disgrace to Sadlers Wells. However as it was small it was not very conspicuous. The ode spoke by Mrs Siddons in the character of Britannia had not much good effect but it served to fill up the time and to fix people's attention. The supper and wines were as good and as plenty as could be and the attendance far beyond anything I ever saw . . .

April 23rd ['Windy, with some rain. The trees in the Park just beginning to bud']. 'I am just come from the church to Chatham Place where I write this as, I suppose, you will be curious to know what has been done today. Everything has passed off well, the King got to St Paul's about twelve looking, I think, much as usual, did not seem particularly affected nor should I have known from his appearance or behaviour that anything particular had happened to him. I went from home before eight, joined the procession of the House of Commons which was beginning, got to St Paul's about ten. The streets were a fine sight but very quiet though full and great regularity kept up. The entering into the church was very magnificent, an avenue all through it being formed by Guards and Beefeaters in a double row and in the centre under the dome the astonishing mass of charity children piled up quite round. Their singing as the King came in and when he went out had a great effect. The weather was not good but luckily it has not rained since the procession began. The choir was not striking in any respect, the service tedious and a vast deal of common chanting by the ordinary singing men and the organ without any other music. The prayers and sermon could not be heard where I was and the noise in the body of the church so great that there was nothing like devotion or solemnity in the service. The City Guards who lined the streets made the most ridiculous figures possible. The moment the Royal Family were gone all order was at an end and after waiting an hour and a half in the churchyard I walked here by back streets without any difficulty and left the carriage to follow. The cold in the church and afterwards in waiting for the carriages was excessive.'[8]

The anecdote book contained club gossip and some irreverent doggerel:

On two recent melancholy events
>*See the vengeance of Heaven America cries,*
>*George loses his senses, North loses his eyes,*
>*Yet, when they attacked her t'was easy to find*
>*That the Monarch was mad, and the Minister blind.*

Wrote during the King's illness upon the plan of a limited Regency
>*The Rhetoricians fam'd of old*
>*At Witticisms aiming*
>*From Contrarieties we're told*
>*Gave various things a naming.*

>*A non lucendo lucus thus*
>*They called each Grove of Trees,*
>*A non parcendo Parca too*
>*They called the Destinies.*

>*So had they lived in modern times*
>*And seen what modern men do,*
>*Regent they surely would have named*
>*The Prince, a non regendo.*

On the extravagant rejoicings for the King's recovery:
>*Still London exhibits a prospect that's sad*
>*Though the King is recovered the Town is run mad.*
>*This scene of delusion will quickly be over*
>*When the monarch relapses the town will recover.*

'*After great intimacy between the Duchess of Gordon and Mr Pitt, she took offence at something and they did not see each other for some time. At length the Duchess had a mind they should be friends again and, meeting Mr P. said to him in her easy manner, "Well, Mr Pitt, what have you been doing this long time. Do you talk as much nonsense as ever?" "Yes, madam," said Mr Pitt, "but I don't hear quite so much."*

'*A bustling man meeting Lord Abercorn, says to him, "It's uncommonly hot today, my Lord, don't you find it so?" "I am never hot," replies my Lord. "Indeed," says the other, "it may be in some measure owing to my having walked very fast." "I never walk fast," replies my Lord. "But then, I was in a great hurry," says the other. "I am never in a hurry," replies my Lord. And so the conversation ended.*

'*Two gentlemen, listening to a famous player on the violin, one of them observed to the other that the passage the man had just been playing was very difficult. The other answered he was extremely glad of it and that he wished to God it was impossible.*'

★ ★ ★

The children had been far from well. In November of the previous year, Lady Palmerston had written to her husband:

'I am sorry to inform you that poor Harry has got a very sharp attack of St Anthony's fire in the same place as usual. [This disease has disappeared from the medical dictionary and is assumed to be a form of ergotism prevalent at the time.] He was extremely unwell all Wednesday, and I gave him at night 3 grains of James's powder which produced a perspiration, the next morning, yesterday, he took some senna tea, he slept better last night and is in tolerable spirits considering the painful state of his eye and cheek . . .'[9]

By April, 1789, Palmerston, who had the children with him in London, was able to send better news to his wife at Bath:

'We are all well here, I think the children remarkably so. William's cough is quite loosened and almost gone without the emetic tartar which, however, Mr Walker says might be administered if wanted without the least danger of bringing on a return of the fit . . .'[10]

This letter was accompanied, in a round childish hand, by the first appearance on paper of the future third Viscount, then aged four and a half:

'Dear Mama,

I long to see you. My brother and sisters are all well and we shall all be very glad when you come back. I saw Punch yesterday in the street and was much entertained. Give my love to Grandmama and a kiss. Fanny sends her love and a kiss to you and Grandmama.

I am dear Mama
Your dutiful and loving little boy
Harry Temple.'[11]

Palmerston decided that a summer tour of the Rhine would do them all good and on September 17 the family set out from London with Miss Carter, who was Lady Palmerston's companion. In France, the Bastille had fallen on July 14, and the journey was complicated by the spread of revolutionary fervour to the Netherlands. Palmerston's diary pencil was kept busy:

September 19*th*. Arrived at Ostend about eleven in the forenoon, after a good passage, though not a smooth one. Stayed all day to get the carriages landed and the baggage examined, which here as well as elsewhere is rendered very easy by a little money . . .

September 27*th*. 'A short time before our arrival the people of Liège, in imitation of the French, had determined to alter their constitution and make it more free by lessening the authority of their Bishop, or Prince. The people, for this purpose, armed themselves at once and disarmed the small military force which the Bishop kept up. This passed without the least resistance or difficulty. The Bishop acquiesced and promised to confirm whatever the states should determine to be the best form of government. This declaration was received with great applause and the Bishop was carried in triumph to the Hotel de Ville. He took, however, the first opportunity to get out of their hands and went away to Trèves, where he has sent word he shall remain till they are agreed upon their plans . . .

September 30th. 'Aix is very full of French who are obliged to leave their country on account of the troubles. The people of Aix had some disputes last year among themselves, which occasioned the Chamber of Wetzlar (which is the standing Aulic Council of the Empire for settling disputes and maintaining the different constitutions of the whole Germanic body), to send a Commission to sit at Aix and hear and decide the matters in dispute. This is the usual practice in such cases and while the cause is deciding, which is often long and has, in the present case, lasted more than a year, a body of troops sufficient to enforce the decree is sent by the powers who have guaranteed the constitution of the place in question and are to be paid and maintained by the city or state to which they are sent – which is often a heavy burden.

'We have learned here that the Chamber of Wetzlar have notified to the people of Liège that if they do not settle all their business satisfactorily before a day they have appointed in October, they shall proceed in the same manner with them.

October 1st. 'To Berchem, this is a very poor place, with a very indifferent inn at the post. We were obliged to take horses at Aix to bring us this journey as the post master could not furnish us with horses. We had some reason to suspect that there was a combination between the post master and the voituriers, as the price we were obliged to pay was very exorbitant and more than double the regulated price of the post . . .

October 2nd. 'Cologne, a large old town upon the Rhine, like most of the German towns, looks best at a distance, having several buildings belonging to it with romantic, picturesque towers and battlements. The streets are narrow and dirty . . .

October 4th. 'The inhabitants of Coblenz appeared to us to be better looking, better behaved and better dressed than any we have seen for some time, the people of the towns we have lately passed not having much excelled in those points.

'The Post at Coblenz is a very good inn and the master of it remarkably civil and attentive – qualities to which we have not been much used in this journey.

'To Montabaur. We passed the Rhine over a bridge, which is common in this part of the country and is called a "flying bridge". It consists of two large boats joined sideways with a stage built over them both. These are moored to a pile fixed in the middle of the river by a very long cable, supported by eight small boats. When the number of persons, etc. which are to pass are embarked from a quay close to which the stage is fixed, by a particular manœuvre, which throws the vessels into an oblique direction, they are made to swing over, by the force of the current alone, to the other side, where a similar quay receives them and serves to disembark the cargo they have brought over . . .

October 5th. 'We had heard of the difficulties of passing this hilly country in order to go to Frankfurt, or Mainz, and upon the best information we could procure we determined to take the road from Wirges to Königstein and Frankfurt. We had met with so little difficulty as far as Wirges that we began to flatter ourselves that the accounts we had heard were much exaggerated and that we should find the road rather better instead of worse as we came nearer Frankfurt. In this, however, we were much disappointed. The stage from Wirges to Frankfurt is without exception the worst road I ever saw that was reckoned passable for a coach. It crosses a ridge of hills. In some parts it is so rocky that a carriage runs the greatest risk of being broke to pieces and in other parts the ruts are such as make it barely possible for it not to be overturned. The latter happened to one of our coaches, notwithstanding the danger was foreseen and care taken to obviate it, though without effect. The carriage was empty at the time and luckily no material damage done to it. We were forced to stop for the night at Königstein, a small town belonging to the Landgrave of Hesse . . .

October 6th. 'In Frankfurt there is a bookseller of the name of Eslinger, who is a very civil, sensible, intelligent man, who has formed a kind of literary establishment, to which those who are disposed to it subscribe, where they find in different rooms a great variety of books, pamphlets and newspapers in the principal languages of Europe . . .'

Palmerston's passion for accurate detail also found expression:

October 7th. 'At Mainz the Rhine is a very fine river. We omitted to measure the length of the bridge by our steps, but by what observations we made we guessed it to be about 500 yards . . .

October 9th. 'To Coblenz by water, 36 miles . . . Our embarkation consisted of two boats fastened side to side. One of them has two rooms below and a deck above for ourselves, the other is open and conveys the two coaches, baggage, etc. We had generally four men employed in rowing with three oars. The wind was favourable and some part of the time we had a small sail, which helped us on considerably. This sail, however, obstructed our view so much that we soon had it taken down, as we had sufficient time for what we had to perform, and without it we went at the rate of very near six miles an hour . . .

October 13th. 'Walked about Düsseldorf. Town better than any we have seen lately and the streets wider and better paved. The ramparts are pleasant and a little way out of the town are gardens, which are open to the public and are pleasant as walks . . .

October 17th. 'Great riots have happened at Liège since we were there, from no cause but the mere licentiousness of mob government. However, the soberer and better sort of the citizens got the better and some of the rioters have been executed. The time draws near when the decree of the Chamber of Wetzlar, which has been notified in form, must be complied with or enforced by the King of Prussia's troops, who will not be long about it. The decree amounts to a total disapproval of all that has been done, directs that everything shall be put on its former footing, that the free corps shall be disarmed and the cockades and other distinctions laid aside . . .

October 18th. 'To Malines . . . The country of Brabant appears to great advantage in respect to its towns, its roads and the manners and looks of its inhabitants in all which it is greatly superior to the part of Germany we have seen. Germany appeared indeed worse in these respects than I imagined and particularly in the dullness and want of comprehension of the common people and the insolent and brutal character of the postilions. These, added to the very slow progress which could at best be made from the badness of the roads and the inconvenience of the frequent alteration of dialect and money, make travelling there unpleasant ...

October 26th. 'Brussels. The long expected and much talked of attempt to throw off the Emperor's authority, which people began to think would end in nothing, has at length begun to be made. The malcontents being collected in the territory of Holland, near Breda, have at length entered Brabant in force ... The common idea is that if they succeed they mean to make the Prince of Orange sovereign of the low countries, upon proper conditions and with a full security for all their rights and privileges, which it is certain that the Emperor has most grossly and foolishly broke through, though perhaps upon a mistaken and ill-understood idea of improvement. The conduct of the States of Brabant in refusing the necessary supplies for a considerable time was perverse and factious, as it was not called for by any necessity, the Emperor having at that time given up the points contended for. But, on the other hand, his proceeding to dissolve them entirely and to declare himself no longer bound to observe the conditions of the *Joyeuse Entrée*, under which he succeeded to the sovereignty, seems to have been perfectly unjustifiable and impolitic to the highest degree, as it has scarcely left him a friend in the whole country, but those whose immediate interests are concerned in his support. The insurgents are said to have entered the country in two bodies – one advancing towards Ghent, the other towards Antwerp ... They have likewise seized and carried the Chancellor of Brabant, by name Crompapen [?], from his country seat, and mean to keep him as a hostage for the security of any of their party who may be in the hands of the government. The government on their part are active. Great numbers of persons have been taken up and are under confinement and, immediately on the seizure of the Chancellor, five of the principal noblemen of Brabant, who are known to be friends to the insurgents ...

have been taken up and are kept in confinement. The whole
military force that can be collected is in motion and events of
importance are hourly expected. Though this event has been
so much expected, it does not seem that any body of Imperial
troops was collected anywhere sufficient to attack the invaders
on their first entrance. This delay is much in their favour, as
insurrections are daily to be expected all over the country if
the affair remains undecided, and, in that case, the troops,
which in the whole territories do not exceed 14,000 or 15,000
men – though they might be sufficient to quash the attempt in
the beginning – would be totally unable to make head in every
part of a country where almost every individual seems more
or less ill-disposed to the Emperor's cause.

October 27th. 'Set out from Brussels . . . Troops are continually going from Brussels and others are brought in from
Mons, as the town of Brussels is very little to be depended on,
being as much disaffected to the Emperor's cause as any part of
the territory. The gates have been shut these two days and no
persons allowed to pass without a passport, which, however, is
not refused to travellers . . .

October 28th. 'We found the gates of Lille, and the whole
government of the town, in the hands of the National troops,
or armed citizens, who keep very good order and strict police
in the town. Just before they were embodied, considerable
disturbances happened and four or five houses were pillaged,
but all has been quiet since. Our passports from Brussels, from
our own and from the French Minister, were examined at
the gate with great civility and no further trouble given
to us . . .

November 2nd. 'Embarked in the *Lord Hardwick*, Captain
Clark, for Dover. Left Calais at 10 in the forenoon; wind very
scanty at southwest and a good deal of sea. Arrived off Dover
at half past two, a little too late to get into the harbour. Obliged
to land in a great swell in a Dover boat, for which we paid two
guineas, or to remain on board till 10 at night. Landed with
some difficulty and much wetting . . .'[12]

During this tour in the Netherlands Palmerston purchased
nine pictures from Beeckman of Antwerp for £528, including

an excellent Cuyp and a good Ruysdael. His interest in the arts, and his financial position had revived, and during the six years following his second marriage he had been in regular attendance at most of the London sales, acquiring among a score of pictures, two Canalettos, a Hobbema and a reputed Van Dyck, which proved to be a copy. This period also saw the bulk of his purchases of drawings by such artists as Vandevelde, Berghem, Claude, Titian, Veronese and Gainsborough, of which only the Vandeveldes can be traced today.

In the spring Palmerston sent Benjamin Mee a summary of family and political news:

'You will have heard before this reaches you that our scheme of wintering in Italy was changed into that of a short tour on the Continent, which proved very pleasant and entertaining. The expectation of having an addition to our party by the arrival of a new traveller in the midst of it rather alarmed me and made me give up the scheme for the present . . .

['March 30th, 1790, Lady Palmerston delivered of a daughter (Elizabeth) at three this morning; dined at Lord Malmesbury's.'][13]

'We were in some respect witnesses of the beginning of the revolution in the Austrian Netherlands, having been at Brussels when the insurgents entered the country . . . Great confusion is likely to ensue in the country as nothing can be less settled than the plan of their future government. One party wishes to have the supreme authority still lodged in the hands of a sovereign, another to have it in the hands of a council, that is to say to have an aristocratic government, while a third, much the most numerous and I believe much the most powerful, are for a complete democracy. In this they are supported by the example and influence of France and seem likely to pursue the same path of confusion and anarchy that their neighbours are treading.

'Nothing I believe can exceed the wretched state of that country. In the capital they are undoing everything and loosening all the bonds of society, while the horrors that are committed by mobs in various parts of the kingdom are such as would disgrace the most barbarous savages in the wilds of America.

Whether anything like order and government is ever to arise
out of this chaos nobody I believe at present would venture to
predict. Our politicians have been very foolishly disputing and
indeed quarrelling (that is to say Burke and Sheridan) about
the proceedings in France, in our House of Commons, which
seems to be the last place to discuss such a subject. Burke however was very fine upon it and is about to publish a pamphlet
which I will send you when it comes out . . .

'This country happily seems to flourish amidst all the con-
fusions of the world. The King's health is perfectly re-established
and I believe he is free from any symptoms whatever of mental
or bodily disorder. His spirits however are affected by the
perfect consciousness which he possesses of what has passed,
and the apprehension which he must feel of a return; though
I really believe there is as little reason to apprehend it as in any
case whatever of that species of malady. His mind has lost much
of its activity and fondness for business; and ever since the
affair of the proposed Regency the Queen has taken a much
greater part than she ever did before. Mr Pitt possesses her
confidence, while the Chancellor is thought to have a larger
share of the King's. These two go on like cat and dog, but the
Chancellor after much growling is always forced to give way.
The King has a great inclination to go to Hanover and is
supposed to have serious thoughts of doing so this summer.
I believe however it is the wish of those about him that he
should not, and therefore I conclude he will be diverted
from it . . .'[14]

Parliament was dissolved on June 10, 1790, when Palmerston
found it necessary to make other arrangements for his seat. In
April of the previous year he had written to his wife:

'I saw Mr Vernon this morning and am afraid by what he
can learn from Mr Jackson there is but little likelihood of my
coming in for Boroughbridge again as the Duke [of Newcastle]
is not inclined now to bring in any but Pittites.'[15]

His choice had fallen on Newport in the Isle of Wight.
[Electorate: the Mayor, eleven Aldermen and twelve Burgesses;
in all twenty-four, according to a gazetteer of the time.] It was
by no means a cheap procedure: 'Paid for election at Newport

£4,200', read an account book entry for 1790. He was standing, appropriately enough, with Lord Melbourne, whose daughter Emily, after the death of her first husband, Lord Cowper, married Harry, third Viscount Palmerston, Foreign Minister under the Premiership of the second Lord Melbourne. Their fathers' election campaign, as described by Palmerston to his wife, does not seem to have involved an undue expenditure of energy:

June 17th. 'I have received a letter from the Isle of Wight desiring me to attend at the election at Newport which is on Saturday. I do not consider it as any great grievance and therefore intend to go over tomorrow and be at Newport in the evening . . .

'Southampton 3 o'clock – I have been here two hours and given my vote. The election is as noisy and bustling as usual and makes the town very full and gay . . .

June 21st. 'I am just landed from my expedition to foreign parts which has been very successful. I arrived at Newport with my companions [Lord Melbourne and Mr Lamb] on Friday evening at Mr Holmes's house, from whence we were carried to ask the votes of about a dozen shopkeepers who looked as if they thought we might as well have saved ourselves the trouble. The evening concluded with a rubber at whist and a supper of which Mrs Holmes and two other Isle of Wight ladies, tolerably vulgar, did the honours. About eleven on Saturday we were conveyed to the place of election where the ceremony, which was extremely private, took up about an hour, after which we were advised to take a ride to Carisbrook which we did with great pleasure, returned to a dinner of about 80 people and afterwards set out for Cowes, where, as it proved a rainy night, we took up our quarters. Yesterday morning Lord Melbourne, who languished to get back to old England, embarked for Southampton and I for Spithead . . .'[16]

His mother's estate must greatly have improved Palmerston's financial status. An entry in the account book for the year read: 'Paid Lord Cadogan for his house in Hanover Square, fixtures and some furniture, £10,878 7s. 6d.' This is the first mention of the new town residence that Lord Palmerston had acquired.

Contemporary records place it as No. 22, in the modern numbering, on the corner of Brook Street, on the south side of Hanover Square. The site is occupied today by the modern headquarters of a business firm, and all traces of the original building have disappeared. Palmerston continued to use the Park Street house as his London residence for the time being.

When Parliament reassembled it was still saddled with the long drawn out affair of the impeachment of Warren Hastings, which was in fact to drag on until 1795. Palmerston ended the year with a desultory account to his wife of the debates, spiced with details of his social engagements, Harry's health, and the recurring problem of a cook for Broadlands:

November 29th. 'The House of Commons does nothing but swear as yet. I have got through all my oaths this morning which is a tedious business . . .

'Tomorrow the Address will come on, to which I understand little is expected to be said. After that I hear it is intended by Fox and Burke to bring on the business of the impeachment if possible. Tomorrow is the day fixed by the Lords at the conclusion of the last session for resuming it, and though that was only as a matter of form, yet their not having sent any message to the Commons to put it off to a farther day shows that they intend to consider it as over. This question seems likely to be taken up as a constitutional one in the House of Commons and the result will probably be that both sides persevering the Commons will not submit to bring it as a new impeachment and so Mr Hastings will be let off . . .

December 1st. 'I am sorry to find by yours received yesterday and today that poor Harry has so severe an attack of his old complaint. I hope he will soon get rid of it. Dr Blagden just now called here and seemed to think the mode of treating him quite right. He said that if there was any considerable oozing or moisture from the eruption it would be useful to apply powdered starch or common hair powder dabbed on with a swanskin puff . . .

'We had a very full House yesterday which however was soon up, as no objection was made to the Address. On the contrary, it was highly commended as being cautiously and properly drawn up. Fox laid on claims to future disapprobation from the want of precision in defining limits, etc. Burke was much pleased with what the Speaker said on the subject of the impeachment, viz. that he hoped no idea could be entertained in the Lords of its being over and that in the Commons he was confident there could not be two opinions on the subject. Mr Pitt wished to put off the consideration of it, perhaps with a view to endeavour to prevent the Lords from pursuing the plan. I hear however that Mr Erskine is a great supporter of it, and intends to argue it in the House of Commons. Fox ably alluded to the impeachment as one of the principal circumstances that had spread that confidence in the British government among the powers of India, mentioned in the King's speech . . .

'I dined with Burke afterwards at our Tuesdays Club who seemed in very good spirits . . .

December 8th. 'I do not hear any particular news but am going to the Levée and if I hear any will add it. Last Wednesday the King was unusually early and I as usual rather late, so that we did not meet. I may perhaps leave my name at the doors of the Prince's afterwards. I have seen very few fine ladies but have dined a good deal at home and gone to the plays and to Brooks's, both which are better at this time than afterwards. We had a party of very pleasant people at Lord Cholmondeley's, such as Fox, Sheridan, Fitzpatrick, Hare, Pelham, etc. but it did not happen to turn out entertaining, which I believe will be apt to be the case where there is a vast square table filled in the middle with plateaus covered with trees, etc. which seem to put everybody at a distance from each other . . .

December 12th. 'I went afterwards to the Duke of Portland's to an opposition meeting relating to the business of today, that is, the motion for papers and the vote of approbation of the convention . . .

'As to the old subject of cooks I called yesterday to enquire at Daubigny's, where they told me of Mr Talmash's cook who has lately left him and he has been with me this morning. It is

singular enough that he again lived 4 or 5 years with Mr Ellis
before he went to Mr Talmash. It is not very clear by his own
account why he has left their service but what he says is that a
large dinner which was ordered at Steephill at 3 or 4 hours'
notice not being to Mrs Talmash's mind she was excessively
angry and so they parted. He says he left Mr Ellis for the same
reason that it seems others have done, because the business at
Paultons is so great and so constant that it cannot be done
without more help than is allowed. I have no doubt of his
being a good cook, his terms are 80 guineas, allowances
included, but he will not engage without the management of
the kitchen independent of anybody else, which he pretends
he would conduct with more order and economy than if it was
divided. He is a middle-aged man, a Frenchman and has a
stern steady manner which might make him either a good or a
bad servant just as it happened to prove. As he is out of place I
believe he would go down for the time I want him by the
week, if I thought that best, and in that case he seemed to say
he should be ready for that time to take everything as he
found it . . .

ps. If you know of any little things that are portable that
would be agreeable to your little party let me know, that
I may bring them. I have got two maps of Europe and the
World for Harry to play with in the same manner he does
with the map of England and I shall bring him a large good
whipping top . . .

December 16th. 'I have been this morning at the Drawing
Room, so have done my *devoirs* at St James's. The Queen was
graciousness itself and almost invited herself to come to Broadlands. Lady Pembroke was in waiting looking but ill . . .

December 18th. 'I was not at the House on Tuesday as that
was the day I was kept at home [with a pain in his face]. Fox
I understand was very able and Pitt did not speak so well as
usual. They were both excellent on Monday. Thursday was
an entertaining day likewise for a little while by means of a
little sparring between Sheridan and Pitt. You will see by the
papers a little of what passed yesterday. Burke was excellent
in answer to a wild Col. Macleod whom I did not come in

time enough to hear. Every lawyer in the House thinks it requisite to speak on this occasion and so little progress had they made at two this morning that Pitt proposed to adjourn the debate, which was accordingly done till next Wednesday, when I dare say it will take up the whole night . . .'[17]

Lady Palmerston followed events with avidity:

'The reading the debates in the Star takes up all my morning. I dare say the impeachment will be got rid of, for though Pitt speaks with you he will make his forces vote against you. I do think Mr Hastings is particularly unfortunate in having such excessive fools and madmen for his advocates. Indeed he has now got one made friend in Erskine, who may be of service to him, but I think Colonel M'Leod will not prove very useful . . .'[18]

December 20th. 'I hope I may depend on being with you on Friday but do not expect I shall sooner [Palmerston replied]. Everybody allows Pitt to be in earnest with regard to the impeachment and I believe it is settled between him and Burke that when the House of Commons have asserted their right to continue the trial, which it is supposed will be carried by a large majority if the peers are obstinate, the Commons shall, after protesting against the precedent, proceed to a new impeachment rather than let Hastings off . . .'[19]

About this period it is possible to note a softening in Palmerston's staunch Whig aversion to Mr Pitt. Charles James Fox's almost perverse praise of the progress of the French Revolution had already caused much wavering in the ranks of his supporters. After the outbreak of the conflict with France, Palmerston became, as the century drew to its close, one of the body of Whigs who deserted Fox and supported Pitt in his war measures. In a letter to Benjamin Mee, dated April 20, 1791, giving an account of the support of both Pitt and Fox to Wilberforce's motion to prevent the further importation of slaves, debated on the two preceding days, Palmerston referred most graciously to Pitt as 'certainly a man of wonderful abilities':

'The long depending question about the slave trade has come to a determination in the House of Commons and the proposition for immediate abolition has been negatived by 163 to 88.

All the splendid abilities of the House were for it and Pitt and Fox spoke, particularly the latter, with great violence, but I think showed very little of the wisdom or foresight that becomes statesmen. The unqualified and unprepared abolition such as they proposed would I think have been ineffectual and ruinous. A dreadful history (though I believe much exaggerated) certainly does appear in evidence and I hope both the legislature and the parties concerned will exert themselves to make great improvements in the mode of conveying and treating these unfortunate people. The West Indians, though saved for the present from the mischiefs that a blind enthusiastic zeal was preparing for them, have however had fair warning, and if both by law and by general practice they do not introduce some effectual reformation the subject, which neither will nor can go out of peoples minds, will soon be revived and some strong measures be adopted let the consequences be what they may . . .'20

The first day of the Wilberforce debate also heralded tragedy in the Palmerston family. On April 18 William, Mary and Elizabeth, the three youngest children, were inoculated against smallpox, as their elder brother and sister had been a couple of years earlier. During the subsequent four weeks the reaction followed its accustomed course, except in the case of Mary. Her face and parts of her body became badly swollen, she had difficulty in swallowing, and a blister poultice on her neck formed a suppurating sore. On Tuesday, May 17, the poor child died. Palmerston's diary entry read:

'This afternoon poor Mary became worse, and in the night it was perceived that mortifications were beginning. All means to stop them being tried in vain, about eight in the evening this unhappy child, lovely and beloved, after three weeks severe and patient suffering, was snatched from the fairest prospects of life, to fall a selected victim to the practice of inoculation which, though right and beneficial in general, yet in the few cases when it fails, brings a most severe aggravation of grief and anguish of mind on the unhappy parents.'

REFERENCES

1. B.1
2. C.47 November 1788
3. C.48 1.XII.1788
4. B.1
5. B.2
6. B.1
7. B.1 30.I.1789
8. B.1
9. B.2 18.XI.1788
10. B.2 April 1789
11. D.9(b)
12. A.17
13. A.1
14. C.44(b) 12.III.1790
15. B.1 18.IV.1789
16. B.1
17. B.1
18. B.2 19.XII.1790
19. B.1
20. C.44(b) 20.IV.1791

CHAPTER VII

PARIS 1791

Palmerston carries letters from Fox to the Constituent Assembly three weeks after the Flight to Varennes – impressions of revolutionary France – the Jacobins' Club and the debates of the Assembly – the funeral procession of Voltaire – the riot in the Champ de Mars – Paris restaurants and theatres – Philippe Egalité – the Constitution approved – Palmerston's forebodings

PERHAPS the most purposeful journey Palmerston undertook during his life was in 1791. Leaving England just over a fortnight after the flight of the French Royal Family to Varennes, he spent nearly three months in Paris between the beginning of July and the end of September, attending most of the debates of the Constituent Assembly, which had been called to devise a new relationship between the King and the State, visiting and noting with distaste the proceedings at the Jacobins' Club, and witnessing such stirring events as the funeral procession of Voltaire and the great riot at the Champ de Mars.

The most interesting aspect of his visit is the evidence that he was the bearer of letters from Charles James Fox to such Assembly delegates as Lameth and Barnave, counselling moderation in determining the future status of the French King and Queen. His friend Sir Ralph Payne, afterwards Lord Lavington, who had just called at Broadlands with his guest, the Princesse de Thun, during the absence of the owners at Sheen, tried to dissuade Palmerston from making the journey at all. Writing on June 26 he said:

'Perhaps the present state of France, or rather the prospect, since the escape of the King and Queen, will discourage you from pursuing your plan.

'Our party to Broadlands left it with every impression of gratitude to the hospitable landlord and landlady, who have communicated their goodness and friendly attention even to their servants. Were the Tiers Etat of France as worthy, good sort of people as your housekeeper, gardener, and dairy maid. I doubt whether I should be so stubborn an aristocrat as I am.

'We were treated in every respect à la Palmerston; and Caroline de Thun, who has more unaffected naïveté, than any person I ever saw, and who had just been at Blenheim, without even asking to whom it belonged, observed, while she was eating her strawberries and cream in your dairy that, '*Nous n'étions pas si bien reçu, chez Milord Blenheim*' . . .

'If you persist in your Paris plan, will you accept of a letter to the Duc de Richelieu, whom I love very much, who, I flatter myself, has some little regard for me, and who is by much the most accomplished amiable young Frenchman, that I ever knew? He is Premier Gentilhomme de la Chambre . . .'[1]

Palmerston also took letters of introduction from Madame de Boufflers, by then a refugee in England, who begged him to take two boxes of tea to Madame la Comtesse Dupon, and when he left to call at the Hotel de Boufflers, rue de Choiseul, for any letters and packets.[2] Leaving London for Dover at half-past one on July 6, he was at Calais at four the next morning. ['Passage money for self and three servants, a guinea; given mate and crew, a guinea.'] From then on his meticulously kept journal and almost daily letters to his wife provided a comprehensive picture of the scene:

July 7th. 'Set out about two o'clock for Paris by the Flanders road, received a pass from the municipality of Calais which is granted of course without any farther trouble than sending a *laquais de place* for it, but which is examined often on the road . . . We were advised at Calais to put national cockades in our hats which we did, but I believe it was not necessary . . .'

July 8th. 'As far as Péronne the road lies through a fine rich country generally open but beautifully diversified with woods, villages and inequality of ground. We passed several fine abbeys situated on commanding eminences whose appearance is magnificent. All these I was told are broke up and together with their estates are upon sale . . . The present government of France may subsist for a while on these spoils, but it appears to me that the country must suffer as these possessions cannot fall into the hands of such good landlords as the last, and the numerous poor who were assisted by them must either starve or become a charge upon the public. The fortifications which we saw seem going to decay, and we have not seen the face of a Custom House officer who used to stop passengers at the entrance of most of them. Beyond Peronne, which is properly the ancient limit of France, we found the country much worse, less beautiful and less well cultivated. In all the former part of our journey we were much struck with the goodness of the crops of all kinds of grain. We likewise saw much flax and great quantities of poppies, of which they make oil.'

July 9th. 'I found the roads good and the posts well served and as my carriage was light I was driven at the rate of nearly a post and a half, which is equal to 7 miles and a half in the hour . . .'[3]

Arriving in Paris on Saturday, July 9, Palmerston put up at the Hotel de l'Université. ['Lodging, two pairs of stairs, single apartment, four Louis (about £4) per week; dinners at ten livres (eight shillings and fourpence) per day. Much too dear.'] He wrote to Lady Palmerston:

'I arrived here after a very pleasant journey this afternoon about five o'clock, which you know is just three days and four hours from the time I left Park Street, which I think is an expeditious journey, especially considering I have not been out much after nine any night nor till after six any morning. So that you see travelling at least is not rendered worse by the Revolution . . . Paris looks busy and bustling enough but as yet I have seen nobody and therefore can tell you nothing. It is not however for want of exerting myself that I have met with so little, for as I always want to do something immediately on my arrival at a new place, I soon dressed myself and set out to leave my name at Lord Gower's [the British Ambassador]. From thence I went to one of the most fashionable theatres where I saw some good acting and heard some good music but found no creature I knew nor anybody that looked as if I should ever wish to know them.

['Went to the Italians, where I heard a very pretty comic opera as far as relates to the music and the acting. The music is very Italian but the style of singing quite French and a severe strain upon ears that are not in the habit of hearing it,' says the diary note.] 'There was no woman that had any appearance of a gentlewoman and the men were very little better. After the play was over I went to the Palais Royal which at this time of the year is a kind of public place with a covered walk round it full of shops and coffee houses all illuminated and gay. The company there was much as at the play and nobody I saw there but Lord Mountmorris. Pelham is lodged in the same house but is not at home and I fancy I shall not see him tonight.

'Sunday – Tom Pelham has been with me and introduced me to a friend of his, the Vicomte de Noailles, a very agreeable man who is one of the persons that takes a considerable part in the National Assembly. He has carried me there this morning. This day being Sunday is not a day of much business, which I was not sorry for as by that means I got a good place, though we went late and I was better pleased the first time to have an opportunity of looking about at my ease and seeing the appearance and form of their proceedings . . . The great question, what is to be done with the King, is to come on on Tuesday and I hope to hear it. The issue, I understand from Monsr. de Noailles, will be what I have always supposed it must be, to restore him to his former situation and take no notice of what has passed. Any other measure would be heaping difficulties on those they already have to encounter. His going away was not contrary to any existing law, as the decree that says he must not quit the Assembly more than to a certain distance had never been sanctioned. The language therefore is that his flight has made him very contemptible but not guilty. He and the Queen are at present very close prisoners in the Tuileries, no person but the National Assembly or persons with them being admitted into the gardens and soldiers encamped under their windows.

'I am going tonight to the club of the Jacobins where I expect to hear some warm debating. Lord Sheffield is to be introduced in form as a member of the British parliament, a ceremony which I hope to escape as I understand it is not at all necessary.

'I never was more struck with anything than I am in going about Paris with the total absence of everything like people of fashion. Their houses are shut up and not one genteel carriage or person (a very few men excepted) have I seen in the streets . . .

'Sunday night – I have been at the Jacobins and heard a very curious debate. The question was an adjourned one from a former day, whether the King could or should be tried. The Assembly consisted of 8 or 900 people in a room which has been the church of a convent but is now fitted up as a house of parliament. I told you in the former part of my letter that the National Assembly are disposed by a very great majority to determine in the most favourable manner with respect to the King. This is true, but the disposition of the people in general of Paris is extremely violent the other way and from the account I hear and from the addresses that are daily presented to the Assembly, it seems that the same sentiments prevail very generally through the kingdom. When I came to the Jacobins a very dull speaker was making a very tiresome speech in favour of the King which was interrupted at the end of every three or four sentences by a most violent clamour of disapprobation which lasted about five minutes each time and did not tend to shorten the business as the speaker was not to be intimidated. When he had at length done, a Monsr Brissot got up, who is reckoned one of the ablest men of that society, and made a most violent, declamatory and inflammatory speech against the King, concluding that he might and ought to be tried. This was received with as many interruptions as the other but of a different kind, consisting of shouts of applause, clapping hands and waving of hats such as altogether was the most painful thing to the ears I ever experienced. These two speeches took up all the time. The debate was farther adjourned and they concluded by ordering the last speech to be printed and distributed over the whole country. All this flame which is stirring up puts the National Assembly in a very difficult situation, as they must either act against their own determined and declared opinion or against, what appears at least to be, that of the nation in a business in which the utmost violence seems to prevail. Monsr. de Noailles who carried us there seemed very much hurt at Brissot's speech and said he would have given one of his fingers it had not been made at this moment. The Duke of Orleans was there. He is very low in esteem but full of projects. He has declared publicly he will never be Regent but Monsr. de Sillery, a man devoted to him, proposed in a committee of the assembly to depose the King, proclaim the Dauphin and make the Duke of Orlean's son, the Duke of Chartres who is but a lad himself, Regent. This was not well received but only served to show the duplicity of that party.

'I have supped with Lord and Lady Sheffield who are going to Switzerland, as is Pelham to Bourbonne in a few days. Mr Francis is here but have not yet seen him.

'Pray tell Lady Malmesbury that I can conceive no reason for her going round to avoid travelling through France which is perfectly safe and likely to continue so . . .[4]

July 11th. 'Dined with Monsieur de Noailles, Pelham and Tarleton at Robert's, a restaurateur or tavern-keeper in the buildings of the Palais Royal, famous for his good cookery. The dinner was very well dressed but dirty and ill-served . . .

'This afternoon the procession of Voltaire took place, though the weather was very unfavourable, as it was found inconvenient to defer it. It was very long, but a great part of it consisted of very shabby ill-dressed people whose appearance was made worse by the mud and dirt they had collected. Great quantities of National Guards attended, but in disorder and without arms, except such as were on duty. Deputations of different orders of people and among others the Academy. A figure of Voltaire, very like him, in a gown was carried first, sitting in an elbow chair and afterwards came the coffin on a very fine triumphal car drawn by twelve beautiful grey horses four abreast. The coffin was covered and over it a waxen figure was laid on a bed. After having made a great circuit round the town they came to the house of the Marquis de Villette, who is married to Voltaire's niece and where he died. There the figures stopped, a kind of hymn was sung, Madame Villette and her child came down mounted the car and embraced the

figure and then with several other ladies followed it on foot
during the remainder of the procession to the new Church of
St Genevieve where it is to be deposited . . .'[5]

On the 13th Palmerston received an invitation to dine the
following Monday with Antoine Lavoisier, the celebrated
chemist.[6] He also called frequently on the widow of another
eminent friend, Helvetius. Most days he sent a long summary of
events to Lady Palmerston:

July 14th. 'Since my last I have been much occupied and
amused with the various objects which this place affords at
this time. Yesterday the National Assembly went upon the
business of the King's flight. You will very likely see in the
English papers the substance of the report made by the committees, to all of whom united the consideration had been
referred. It was as I told you in my last it was to be, very mild
towards the King and Queen, considering the whole business
as a plot of Monsr. de Bouillé [the émigré Royalist leader]
against the nation, in order to accomplish which it was necessary for him [to] get the Royal Family from Paris, for which
purpose he had excited in the King's mind groundless apprehensions by false representations. They likewise give credit to
his declaration that his intention was only to go to Montmédy
and not to leave the kingdom and though the absenting himself
more than 20 leagues from the Assembly has been declared by
them inexpedient it never passed into a law. Consequently it
would have been a proper subject for remonstrance but ought
not in the first instance to be considered as a crime to be
punished. However they likewise hold that the King's person
is inviolable and that he cannot be made the object of judicial
proceedings. The debate began and I heard Monsr. Pétion make
a flaming speech in opposition to the proposed decree . . . The
minds of the populace in the meantime are greatly inflamed
and neither pains nor money have been spared for that purpose
by emissaries, as it is said of the Duke of Orleans. The Assembly
I believe are very firm in their purpose to agree to their committees' report and I think it very likely this affair may have
very considerable consequences . . .

'I have been very lucky in meeting Pelham here and Lord

Sheffield's family who are very sociable and in the same hotel. I have made by Pelham's means a good deal of acquaintance with the Vicomte de Noailles, who is deeply mixed in all this business, and we have dined three times at a *restaurateurs*, which is the French word for a tavern, of which there are some lately set up in the Palais Royal that pique themselves upon good cooks. As far as I can learn there is very little society in the dining or supping way in private houses, very few women of fashion in Paris, and the men, who are all politicians, run about on foot and dine at these taverns, which is a very different plan from what I remember here. I have not yet found Lord Gower or Lady S[utherland – Lord Gower's wife and a peeress in her own right] at home but had a very obliging message from her to dine there on Saturday [the 16th] with a small party and am likewise to dine there on Sunday at the usual weekly dinner which is commonly on that day. I am afraid Pelham will go the end of this week, which will be a loss to me. Tarleton likewise is in this house and has been of our party. He is much with de Lafayette, who, as well as Noailles, served against us in America, and who both want Tarleton to serve with them if they should have any war. The letters however today from the adjacent countries say that nothing is to be undertaken by force at present. This may perhaps be only to mislead. I believe however that those who wish to destroy the present government of France had best let it alone. The leading men are totally disunited and there are scarcely any who act in perfect concert. This, with the obvious weakness the new constitution labours under in so many respects, does not look like stability . . .[7]

July 15th. 'The Assembly began by reading an insolent petition . . . signed by about 120 names quite obscure and some of them ridiculous. No notice was taken of it and the debate was resumed. Two speeches were made in favour of the report of the committee, one by Monsieur Salle, the other by Monsieur Barnave which were very good and produced (particularly the first) a very great effect on the Assembly . . . The question was put and the proposal of the committee was adopted by a very great majority. Those who were of a different opinion scarcely showed themselves, as it is not the custom to proceed to any division or to number the votes except in very nice cases.

'The members of the opposition, or *côté droit*, of course approved of this measure in preference to any more violent, but, in conformity to their resolution to take no further part in anything but what affects the King personally and only as far as is necessary for his service, none of them spoke in these debates. In the evening great violence was shown by particular people about the town, and great anxiety seemed to prevail among the inhabitants at large as to the consequences. The Jacobins met and came to very violent resolutions against the decrees of the Assembly and voted addresses to the other clubs of the kingdom to join them. Detachments of mob went to the different theatres after the representations were begun in order to stop them . . .'[8]

Sunday saw the discontent inflamed into tumult and Palmerston noted this graphic account of events in his journal:

July 17th. 'This morning early there were gatherings of people in the Champ de Mars, and very unfortunately two men were discovered to have got into the great cavity under the Autel de la Patrie where they had carried their dinner and seemed to have proposed passing the whole day. They were discovered by boring holes through the steps and sides of the place; and the only conjecture that seems to have any probability with regard to their intentions, is that they thought they should see what might happen without being crowded, and that they should have a good prospect of the women's legs who might come up the steps. One of them is said to have been an invalid with a wooden leg, but a young man. This frolic however cost them very dear, for the mob immediately decided that they were placed there to blow up with powder the altar with all the most zealous friends of the Patrie, and seized and carried them before some little inferior magistrates of the Quarter. But finding these doubtful and undecided what they should do, they took them away again and executed them themselves with many circumstances of inhumanity. The Municipality of Paris, having had information the day before that a large body of people were to meet early at the ruins of the Bastille and from thence proceed to the Champ de Mars, had met early at the Hotel de Ville and their chief attention had been directed to the quarter of the Bastille. There however nothing passed nor was any mob assembled. When they received the first information of the murder at the Champ de Mars, they immediately sent some of their body with a battalion of Guards to act as the occasion should require. The accounts they received from these commissioners were unsatisfactory and at length they returned to inform their brethren of the very disorderly state of affairs. That they had met the mob carrying the heads of the two men (which is a favourite amusement) on poles, that one of the bearers had been seized but afterwards rescued, that a man had attempted to shoot Monsieur de Lafayette, but had been prevented, that the man had been seized but released at the desire of Monsieur de Lafayette, that on proceeding to the altar they had found a number of persons signing petitions against the decree of the 15th, that the National Guard had been repeatedly insulted and driven away, that on the commissioners presenting themselves to remonstrate they had been very ill received, but that the mob had insisted on sending 12 persons on their part as deputies to the Hotel de Ville who were waiting without. The Municipality, who had determined immediately before the arrival of their commissioners to hang out the drapeau rouge, which, accompanied with a proclamation is an establishment of martial law, and to proceed in a body accompanied with a very strong force to the Champ de Mars, agreed, however, to stop in order to hear what the mob ambassadors had to offer. These, however, on the sight of the drapeau rouge and of the troops and cannon prepared, had slipped off and were probably gone back to apprise their friends. The expedition now proceeded. It was seven in the evening when they reached the Champ de Mars, in all the environs of which they found great crowds of persons who appeared as spectators. The bank, or *glacis* as it is called, on each side the opening through which they were to enter was covered with people who began to insult them by calling out, "à bas les bayonettes, à bas le drapeau rouge". The Mayor

Frances and William Temple

Elizabeth Temple

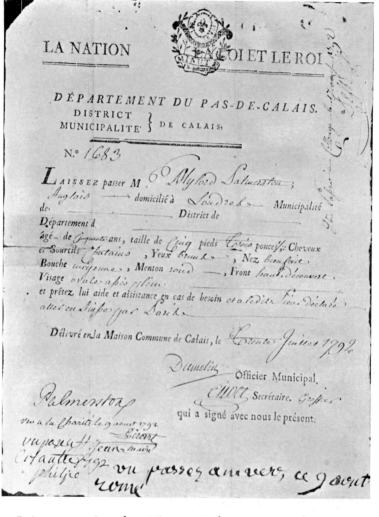

Laissez-passer issued to Viscount Palmerston at Calais, 1792

made a stop just in the entrance, and was proceeding to have
the usual proclamations made when they were interrupted by
a volley of stones from the bank and a pistol fired at the Mayor,
which narrowly missed him and wounded a soldier just behind
him. On this the troops without waiting for orders, as it seems,
began to fire but probably in the air, as it does not appear that
any person was killed by the first discharge though it was a
pretty considerable one. The firing was stopped and the march
continued into the Champ de Mars. The altar in the middle
was now deserted so that the allied corps of civil and military
continued their course between it and the bank which was now
covered with people who had resumed their courage on finding
no one killed, and renewed their attacks with stones and pistols.
A more serious fire then took place from the troops and the
cavalry began to charge with their swords, by which some
execution was done. It is difficult to know the exact numbers
that suffered, but the most probable accounts say about 16
killed and as many wounded who remained behind. Several of
the troops were wounded with stones, etc. and three were
killed who are said to have been single when attacked. A
complete dispersion now took place, the mob all flying into
the town where they threaten the most violent revenge with
fire and sword, that the National Assembly shall be driven out
and Monsieur de Lafayette not suffered to live another day.
Their fire however spent itself very much during their running,
and the people of Paris were so little disposed to be inflamed
by them that (proper guards being posted in various parts of
the town) the remainder of the evening and night passed off
with the utmost tranquillity.

July 18*th*. 'This day the town seems perfectly quiet. The
Mayor and his brethren came to the Assembly to give an
account of the transactions of yesterday. Their conduct was
approved, they were directed to proceed with the utmost
vigilance and firmness to preserve the public peace and punish
the disturbers of it, for which purpose the drapeau rouge is to
continue displayed at the Hotel de Ville . . .'[9]

In his letter to his wife that evening, Palmerston added:
'It is very possible this mask of determination may put a

H

stop to the flame of sedition or it may blow it up. If anything can give permanency to the Revolution and bring it to a good conclusion it must be the perseverance of the Assembly in their plan and their being supported in it. Everything proposed by others is confusion, civil war and misery. The Jacobins' Club, which was always too dangerous an engine to have been countenanced by people of any prudence, has run totally wild and there is nothing violent, absurd or dangerous that is not proposed there in direct opposition to and attack upon the Assembly. In consequence all the members of the Assembly have left the Jacobins except two of the desperate ones. The Jacobins are calling upon the whole country to join them against the decree of the Assembly and to insist on trying and deposing the King. It remains to be seen what part the country in general and the National Guards of the kingdom will take . . .

'The Sheffields and Pelham went away together on Saturday . . . [when] I dined and passed most part of the evening at Lord Gower's with a small and very pleasant French party . . . Yesterday I dined and supped there. We had a large stupid party of English at dinner. Lord Gower is very gentlemanlike and she very agreeable and sociable.'[10]

By the 21st things were calmer:

'I wrote you a hasty account on Monday of what had passed at Paris on the day before. Since that time everything has been perfectly quiet, the seditious proceedings are quite at an end and the authority of the National Assembly perfectly re-established here and as far as yet appears their decrees respecting the King's business are well received in the country. The Club of the Jacobins is sunk in reputation from its intemperate violence and the secession from it of most of the members of the Assembly and a great number of the moderate people will I imagine make it lose its weight. The total silence of Paris at present with regard to the King and the stop put at once to all the republican clamour that echoed in the streets last week shows how few people can make a great noise and how soon they are silenced by a little firmness . . . A great number of people have been taken up in consequence of a decree of the Assembly against those who shall be the inciters or persuaders of violence. A Jew is seized who is supposed to be an agent of the King of Prussia, much is expected to be discovered from him. The Palais Royal, though not less full, is become silent, there are continually troops in it who have a pleasant method of dispersing the groups, which is by constantly marching directly through them. So that you see we are at present under a complete military government, which is a very good one for a stranger at least.

'The King and Queen remain just in the same state of restraint they were and I shall not probably have an opportunity of seeing either of them, which I regret. The confinement is stricter than I could have believed, but they are not kept apart. This is to remain till the committee of revision have made out from the various decrees of the Assembly the best plan they can of the constitution. The intention as now professed is to present it then to the King, who must accept it if he means to continue King, with full liberty at the same time to reject it and retire if he thinks proper. This is at least the common language and it is expected to take place next month, after which a new Assembly is to be chose. I do not find Paris near so agreeable as it used to be in point of amusement and society and I am begin[ing] to be much annoyed with their eternal politics. There are however many objects of curiosity here and in the environs which I have not yet had time to attend to but I see no possibility of my wishing to extend my stay here beyond what I mentioned at first which was a month. I mean to return through Normandy but not to embark there but to fall into the Calais road again. Among other places I shall go to see the Duke of Bouillon's, who lives there and is very fond of the English. He kept Lord Sheffield and his family, who were not acquainted with him before, two days, and as I am acquainted with him I may possibly stay there likewise a day or two, which I should like very well as the style of a grand seigneur in the country is what I have seen least of here.

'I have been to a few of the shops, such as Daguerres and the Angoulême china. I find everything excessively dear, particularly the china, which seems to be at least double the price everything at Christie's sold for. However their being of the

newest fashion is to be considered, though that is not much to
a stranger. Lady Malmesbury's commission shall be executed
immediately. I think she will judge very ill if she takes the road
through Germany instead of travelling through France, which
appears to me to be better than ever as to roads and horses, and
half an hour's trouble at going out of the country about one's
passport is certainly preferable to the journey from Coblenz to
Frankfurt . . .'[11]

At Broadlands Lady Palmerston was proudly showing round
her husband's letters and doing her best to relieve the lot of the
growing colony of French refugees at Romsey. On July 18 she
wrote him:

'Lady Malmesbury declares she will readily give a crown a
piece for your letters and her thanks in addition. You certainly
have the art to make it a doubtful question whether you are
more pleasant, kind and entertaining present or absent . . .

'Saturday Lord M[almesbury], Mr Anthony St Leger and
Monsr. Chansignie [?] and Mr Elliot dined here and in the
evening I had prepared a very pretty fête under the trees for
our Romsey foreigners, three tables spread with fruit cake, tea,
syllabub, etc., when most unfortunately by half past seven,
from the most beautiful evening you ever saw, it changed in
ten minutes to such a thick fog that you could hardly see the
river. It appeared to pour down in thick clouds from the sky.
I never saw such an appearance before at that time of the evening. Our tables were obliged to be brought into the saloon and
my design was lost, but the solid part remained. I had all the
rooms lighted up. They played at cards and at eleven I gave
them a very handsome supper and they were delighted with
my actions though not much entertained with my conversation.
But the Malmesburys performed that part for me. The French
party consist of eight, and two of the ladies seem very elegant
fashionable women and indeed both men and women very
genteel . . .

'I hope you will approve of a little plan I have adopted with
respect to Harry, which is to have Mr Williams to attend him
for two hours in a morning . . . I really felt it was a sad thing
so clever a boy should waste all his hours, and without some

obligation to attend it is impossible to expect children will prefer learning anything to playing about...'[12]

On July 22 Thomas Pelham, now at Bourbonne-les-Bains, wrote a letter which gives the most convincing explanation of Palmerston's presence in Paris. The published papers of James Harris, Lord Malmesbury, make it clear that Pelham himself had also been entrusted with letters, probably from Charles James Fox, to Barnave and Lafayette, interceding for the life of the French King and Queen, and counselling moderation. Malmesbury suggests that Pelham was probably prudent enough to burn them before delivery.[13] Pelham's letter read:

'I am infinitely obliged to you for the very satisfactory and detailed account which I have just received from you, and I sincerely rejoice that your curiosity did not carry you into the Champ de Mars, for I very much suspect that the National Guards will not direct their fire with much exactness and that the spectators will be quite in as much danger as the assailants.

'I am very sorry that Fox's name has been used in the Assembly, though the manner in which you describe it to have been mentioned cannot I think be construed to his disadvantage. Lameth must certainly have alluded to the letters which you brought, and I know that Noailles had very imprudently mentioned to Barnave that letters were expected, the tendency of which were recommending moderation. I shall write to Noailles by this post and also to Fox explaining to him what I conceive to be the cause of Lameth's saying anything about it...

'We hear a great deal of the preparations upon the frontiers and though we cannot depend upon the authenticity of our accounts, I believe that some attempt will be made on the part of the Princes as soon as the harvest is over if not sooner...'[14]

Alexandre Lameth, author of the famous report to the Constituent Assembly on the organisation of the army, and Antoine Barnave, second only as an orator to the great Mirabeau, formed with Adrien Duport the 'Triumvirate' who were largely responsible for the final form of the provisional Constitution. Even in the day-to-day engagement diary entries which Palmerston made in a separate volume during his stay in Paris, there is no mention of any social contact with them, and we are left with nothing but speculation as to what part, if any, he played behind the scenes.

As much as from increasing boredom as from prudence, Palmerston devoted more time over the next few days to the theatre and the arts than to the proceedings at the Assembly, where the delegates were locked in procedural wrangle:

July 23rd. 'Went to see some of their painters,' he notes in his diary, 'David, Vincent and La Grenice, all in the historical line. They seem to draw well and finish with care but their colouring is cold and there is a tameness and insipidity in the whole composition. David is the best.

'Many persons are taken up upon suspicion of being concerned as instigators of the late disturbances, but most of them are found innocent or at least no proof is found against them. The men however who put to death the two unhappy victims in the Champ de Mars are taken up and, I understand, upon clear evidence . . .

July 25th. 'Saw this evening a very pretty French opera at the Italians called *Raoul Barbe Bleu*. It is very interesting and Mademoiselle Cretu, who acts the wife, does it admirably. The present style of music at Paris is very good as the composers have adopted the Italian style, though the performers adhere too much to the old French method of singing.'[15]

On the same day he wrote to Lady Palmerston:

'I have been sometimes at the Assembly and have a ticket which carries me in when I please to a place which is not crowded except on very extraordinary days. I have met with very few of my old acquaintance here but was much indebted to Pelham for introducing me to the Vicomte de Noailles who has been friendly and useful to me both with regard to assistance and information. We dine together sometimes at their taverns, which are very odd places and such a mixture of dirt and elegance and good cookery ill-served and ill-attended as it is impossible to describe. I have met with one old lady who was the first acquaintance I ever had at Paris, the widow of the celebrated Helvetius. She lives at a village about two miles out of Paris. She is a sensible woman and seems to have agreeable people about her. I have dined there once, am invited to come whenever I like it.

'I dined at Lord Gower's yesterday and am to go with Lady Sutherland on Wednesday to see some painters and other things, though I do not very well know what. I have been to an old acquaintance here, the first man for pictures in Paris, and have as usual been making some purchases. I think they are good and cheap so that I need not repent . . .'16

At a cost of £658 he bought eight pictures from Dongen and one from Hammond, both of whom figure in his journal:

July 26th. 'Went to the National Assembly. They were passing a report of 40 articles concerning the manner in which the military force should be called in to assist the civil power. Went to Grandpré's, a picture dealer, who has some of the finest Dutch pictures I ever saw, but most enormously dear, 4, 5 or £600 apiece. I have before been with my old acquaintance Dongen, who is in a very bad state of health. He has some very good pictures and his prices much more reasonable. Lebrun has parted with his collection. Hammond in the Palais Royal has some good ones. Went to see Racine's *Athalie* at the French theatre. It is a finely written piece but heavy in the performance, and rendered more so by the choruses being set to dull noisy French music. The performers of the Italian and French theatres have joined to perform this play, and exhibit it alternately at the two theatres. The music makes it so long that there is no time for any after piece. The theatre was extremely full. It is much the finest theatre at present in Paris in all respects, as the approaches and rooms attached to it are really magnificent. The busts of the principal dramatic writers are in the great room, which is very proper. The front has a large portico and on the stones of the columns, which are numerous, are stuck the titles of favourite plays, which is perfectly ridiculous . . .'17

His letter to Lady Palmerston on the 28th was in the same vein: 'The breaking up of the party who had been here before (with Pelham) was a loss to me as there are no English families here at present and I feel the want sometimes of a place for a rendez-vous after the spectacle which is over about half past nine. As to spectacles, to be sure it is land of clover. It is very difficult to be exact with regard to their numbers but I think there are never less than twenty and some nights more, besides Vauxhalls, fireworks, balls, etc. Since the Revolution everybody may open a theatre and they have increased from 7 or 8 to what I mentioned and there are two more just going to be opened. What is most surprising is that they have all good actors and all seem to have audiences enough to make it answer, though seldom enough to make a crowd . . . Last night I was much pleased with an excellent comedy called *La Coquette Corrigée* in which Mlle Contat, whom I never saw before and who is charming, acted the principal part. I was quite sorry to see an actor called Molé who was a great favourite and whom I have never seen since the first times I was at Paris. He was then a little slim elegant figure and gave the best possible representation of a pert, capering Marquis. He is now the very picture of Sir Ralph Woodford but still goes on making love as if nothing had happened . . .[18]

'Rode in the morning to Montmartre, where the view of Paris and all the adjacent country is extremely fine,' he noted in the diary on July 31. 'It is so near that the town almost reaches to it. Dined with Monsieur Suard at a small house at Fontenay aux Roses about 4 miles from Paris. The country about it is very beautiful and his garden commands a pleasing view over a valley prettily diversified with villas, gardens and woods. Monsieur Suard is a literary man of a moderate and amiable character and as I knew some sensible well-informed men were to be of the party I was in hopes to have got more amusement and information than has hitherto fallen to my share. But in this I was as much disappointed as usual. Eternal politics and political disputes engrossed the whole attention of the party. The French revolution seems to me to level people's understanding as much as their ranks and situations. Blind and violent zeal seems to have taken place of reason, and he who harangues in the Palais Royal garden talks with as much wisdom and clearness on these subjects as the people of the first understandings of the country. Two Monsieur Garats were there, brothers, and both of the Assembly and of very

opposite principles. I was told their politics had no effect upon
their friendship, which I believe is true, but they disputed so
violently that people in England in the same case would
probably have come to an open quarrel. The younger one,
who is a democrat, was quite furious, the other kept his temper
much better and now and then introduced some little stroke
of humour, which served to take off something of the edge of
the dispute. I was diverted with a repartee which was told of
the elder Garat, who being at some ceremony when a new
bishop, who had just taken the oaths and was acquainted with
Garat, said to him with a triumphant kind of sneer, "Bonjour
aristocrate", to which the other instantly replied in the masquerade style, "Bonjour beau masqué". The democrats seem
much out of spirits as they have lately received alarming
accounts of a very serious league that is forming against them
by the neighbouring powers, and feel every day more and more
the weakness of their means of defence and the insufficiency of
their government. The weather is so hot as to be quite inconvenient. At seven in the evening it was impossible to walk with
any sort of comfort and the thermometer, which has been for
these two days above 87, was today very near 89 . . .

August 2nd. 'Rode through the Champs Elysées, which
consists of a wood of young trees planted in rows with an
excessive broad straight road through the middle of it. The
dust is excessive and the soil being like pulverised mortar the
trees themselves are quite white in dry weather. The whiteness
of everything about Paris (except the complexions and linen
of the inhabitants) is a great inconvenience, as all the buildings
are stone and all the soil like mortar, and the very little grass
that is to be seen is generally parched with the sun and whitened
with the dust . . .'[19]

Lady Palmerston's budget of gossip was tempered with
relief at a false alarm:

'You will find that our intelligence about the Duke of York's
marriage was true and that it is now notified in form. *Entre
nous* he did not acquaint the Duke of Portland of it, which was
certainly not right. Lord M[almesbury] has been in constant
correspondence with him and of course informed of the whole

progress of the affair. She is handsome, pleasing but a little
turn to intrigue. She is to have £50,000 for her portion. The
Prince I fancy repents he did not take her himself. He has sent
for Lord M. to attend him at Brighthelmstone, which is a sure
sign he is in some kind of distress as he never sends to Lord M.
if he can help it, for I believe the Prince is very much afraid of
the Lion [Malmesbury] . . .[20]

'You will do me the justice to believe that I long excessively
to see you, yet I think it a pity you should leave Paris till the
King has received the intended proposal and given his answer . . .

'The bells were ringing all yesterday upon your account.
The inhabitants of Romsey have for some time been in despair,
having heard that you with a party of English lords were all
taken up and put into prison, and yesterday the joyful news
came of your being liberated and they testified their happiness
by ringing the bells till two o'clock this morning. I sincerely
congratulate you upon your escape . . .[21]

In his own letter of August 4 Palmerston showed that he had
in fact been more pleasurably occupied:

'Little has occurred here since I wrote last . . . The spectacles
are very pleasant and I sometimes regret that they are so
scattered over the town that I cannot easily pursue my London
plan of going from one to the other. Two new operas of the
same name and founded upon the same story are performing
at two theatres. They are called *Lodoiska*. The scenery in both
is extremely fine with a great deal of old castle and towers
which in the last act are burned and blown up upon the stage
with an effect of fire beyond any representation I ever saw.

'The Assembly are on the point of entering upon their
digested plan of a constitution which I believe will be produced
tomorrow. They say now that the Royal Family are to go to
Fontainebleau before it is presented to the King, in order I
suppose to give a greater appearance of freedom to his determination, and that the change from captivity to liberty may
be less striking and produce less effect than if it took place in
the capital. I think the disposition of the people and of the
Assembly towards the King has taken a very favourable turn
lately. All those who were so violent against him either in print

or in discourse are vanished. Many of them indeed are in prison with the general approbation of the country. The continually declining state of public credit and the very serious prospect of a league amongst foreign powers against the new constitution seem to have occasioned considerable alarm and I guess that there is a general wish of conciliation now prevailing here, for which purpose I understand some confidential persons are dispatched. I am afraid they have gone too far and done or rather undone too much to have left it in their own power to offer anything satisfactory . . .'[22]

In his journal Palmerston wrote:

August 6th. 'Saw a French opera called *Raoul de Crequi*, extremely interesting and admirably acted. The management of their scenery has a great effect, particularly in a method they have adopted and often make use of dividing their stage lengthwise into two parts. Thus in *Raoul de Crequi* there is the dungeon where he is confined and the jailor's apartment, where much of scene passes, both open at once to the audience . . .

August 11th. 'Saw a new piece at the French Theatre, called *Les Victimes Cloitrées*. It is one of those pieces called *drames* which are generally extremely affecting, as this is through great part of its progress, though it ends happily. It is the severest attack that can possibly be made upon the clergy and one can hardly believe oneself in a Catholic country while one sees it. The applause with which it is received is excessive and if there was anything more to be taken from the Church or anything more severe that could be inflicted on the religious orders, such a representation would be sufficient to excite the violence of the people against them.'[23]

Lady Palmerston had further news:

'Lord M. is returned much pleased with the Prince, he has behaved so well on this intended marriage. When he informed the King, by his brother's desire, of the event, the Prince said he by no means relinquished his design of marrying, on the contrary he thought it would be the cause of his being more eager for it, seeing how happily his brother was likely to live. That it had been one of his principal motives in wishing to be permitted to travel, that he might make a choice where his

heart could be given with his hand, for he was of too domestic
a turn to marry a woman he never saw, and if he had been
suffered to have indulged his wish of travelling he might have
been as fortunate as the Duke. He has written in the kindest
way to his brother, but explained to him also his plan of
marrying. In short I find he is just now doing everything
right . . .[24]

'The Empress of Russia wrote in pencil on a piece of paper
enclosed in a despatch to Count Woronzoff that she desired he
would send her a bust of Charles Fox that she might place it
between those of Cicero and Demosthenes, since he had by his
talents and eloquence saved two nations from a war which
must have proved hurtful to both. Woronzoff sent it directly
to Charles Fox through the medium of Sir Ralph Payne and
luckily you know there is a very fine one done by Nollekens.
I think he must feel it and so must Pitt . . .'[25]

In his letter of August 11, Palmerston could only report slow
progress in the Assembly:

'The Assembly entered on Monday on the discussion of their
constitutional code and have gone on with it yesterday and
today. Much debate arises so that they do not make a quick
progress. There is a little knot of republicans who, not finding
it practicable to abolish the monarchy, are trying every scheme
to debase it and take up much time by their efforts to accomplish that purpose . . . In the meantime people's expectations
and conjectures are upon the stretch as to what is to happen at
home and abroad. Twenty different stories prevail about the
long talked of invasion and none to be depended on. There are
certainly troops close to the frontiers but I cannot think enough
to form a considerable army and what are to be added to them
do not seem to be in forwardness enough to act at the proper
season. The country is undoubtedly unanimous to oppose any
attempt, but then they have neither discipline nor officers.
Almost all the latter are gone and the regular troops are by
that means and by the general want of subordination become
nearly as unmilitary as the National Guards and less to be
trusted. Four hundred men and all the officers of the regiment
of Berwick went over a few days ago to join the other party

and I hear that Monsr. Rochambeau, who is the general they chiefly depend on, is very much tired of his situation ...

'I rode yesterday to Bellevue, a house late Mme de Pompadour's and now belonging to the Mesdames who are gone to Italy. It is an elegant house though not fine and well deserves its name, as the view of the Seine, woods of St Cloud, and of Paris is delightful. From thence I went to the manufactury of the Sèvres china which is in the neighbourhood ... The things are beautiful but (as well as at the Angoulême) dearer than I could have conceived. A service of dessert china which though handsome was neither very large nor very fine, 270 guineas. I have bought two or three cups. I mean to bring over some little ornamental things, particularly a chimney clock and I have seen two bronze boys holding each two lights which I think may do for the chimney in the eating room ...'[26]

[The clock by Lépine cost £41 16s. od. and, together with the two bronze boys, now stands on the drawing room mantelpiece at Broadlands.]

August 14th. 'The Assembly continue their discussion upon the constitution which takes up more time and occasions more violence than was expected and every day produces more and more animosity, ill-blood and division among them ... The Duke of Orleans attends constantly and sits in a party of people who are generally considered as having no object or principle but mischief and confusion. It is said that the remainder of the work will go on quicker and that the points of dispute are principally got over. The 25th of this month is the day of St Louis which is always a great day here and it is expected that the constitution will have been presented and accepted before that time and that there will be a kind of gala on the occasion, when the Royal Family will appear in public and resume their situation of outward show and splendour. But to say the truth it is not possible even now to get any information that is to be depended on as to what is to happen. Having stayed so long I shall certainly stay a little longer till I see what the result of this business will be. In the meantime they have continual accounts, which they conceal as much as they can, of the desertion of some regiments, the ill conduct of others and the total want of all energy and power of government in the provinces. Tom Pelham, who you know is naturally very *democrate* in this business, has wrote words that the state of the provinces he passed through on his way to Switzerland is more that of a dissolution than a revolution of government . . .

'The gallant Tarleton is just gone, which I take to have been a wise step though rather late, as he was losing his money and lowering himself in the estimation of the people here, who ever since the American War thought rather highly of him . . .'[27]

August 17*th*. 'Paris is pleasanter to me now than it was sometime ago as there are more people I know, and the arrival of Jack Payne and Hare is an agreeable circumstance, though I have not a wish to prolong my stay beyond the present critical conjuncture. There is very little society now at Paris except for the professed purpose of play and the buildings of the Palais Royal are full of clubs for that only. There is one called the Club Polonais to which Hare, Payne and Tarleton (who has not left Paris) often go, and as they can carry anybody else I went with them today to see the humours of it. The apartments are very good and numerous. There is a constant *rouge et noir* table most part of the 24 hours, the bankers of which are at the whole expense of the establishment, which consists of what I have already mentioned, with an excessive good dinner for a very large company every day, elegantly served, with the best cookery and the choicest wines, to which every member of the club is not only invited but pressed to come gratis as often as ever he pleases. A very gentlemanlike man with a Croix de St Louis does the honours of the table and the company consists of very genteel people. This is very like the system of Pharo in England only more regularly and methodically carried on, and I believe quite as fairly; that is to say that the bankers have no other advantage than what the nature of the game gives them. I sat down to play, just to give a chance of paying for my dinner but fortune decided otherwise, for by setting only single Louis's I brought off 25. But I believe the dinner was well paid by some of our party . . .'[28]

August 21*st*. 'The business here, like all matters of difficulty, goes on very slowly, and though delay seems to be a very

dangerous resource it has been very freely used in the hope of
that it might give time to obviate the various difficulties the
Assembly find themselves involved in. The report of the
articles referred back to the committee and of the additional
ones which they are to propose, though fixed for last Thursday
does not come on till tomorrow, when it certainly will be
entered upon and the business and debates of this week will in
all probability be very interesting . . .

'I fell into company a few days ago with the Duke of
Orleans and was invited with Hare, Payne and Gen. Dalrymple
to dine at his country house about 8 miles from Paris. We are
just returned. We had a small party and I was glad of the
occasion of seeing more of him, and of seeing the place at
leisure, which is a fine one. The house is elegant and the
situation good, with large woods near it, and extensive garden
laid out in the English style. This, though admired here, is the
worst part of it, as they have no gravel and the best lawn they
make is like a rough parched field in England, and at the Duke
of Orleans's there are no old trees in that part of the ground.
He does the honours of his house very pleasantly and without
any ceremony.[29]

August 26th. 'The question yesterday in the Assembly was
the situation of the Princes of the blood royal, whom, because
they may eventually succeed to the crown, the plan is to deprive
of holding any offices or employments or being members of
the legislature. This measure, which seems a very absurd and
unjust one, is evidently dictated by resentment against the
Princes who are absent, and ill will to the Duke of Orleans who
is here. He attends the debates every day and made a speech
in which he declared that rather than give up his rights as a
citizen he would renounce his pretensions to the succession.
The speeches are continually levelled against him and one of
the members yesterday in the course of his argument said he
was for the exclusion, even though the nation must lose the
advantage of having the D. of O. again at the head of its fleets
or employed in its important negotiations in England or elsewhere. This, which was said in his presence, occasioned such an
uproar that it was 10 minutes before the speaker could proceed

and I could not help feeling much for the poor man who sat there the whole time and seemed much disconcerted. They proceeded to determine that the Princes are not to be eligible to any office that is in the disposal of the nation. The two questions remain for today whether they are to be capable of holding offices or employments from the King, and whether they are to have any distinguished titles. In the meantime all the affairs of the country seem to go on very ill. Their taxes are not collected and it is very doubtful whether the greater part of them ever can be, the resource of the assignats will be exhausted and leave the additional burthen of the expense of the religious establishments of the country to be defrayed by the state. The ministers are continually informing the Assembly of mischiefs which they have no means to remedy. Three days ago they were told that their most important colony of St Domingo is in a state of absolute resistance to a decree which they passed in March last in favour of the mulattoes, with as profound an ignorance and as noble a contempt of the consequences as ever inspired the wildest of our advocates for abolishing the slave trade. The probable consequence, as it is now fully stated to them, will be the destruction of the people they meant to relieve and the loss of the colony. The next day they were told by another minister that the political clubs, of which there are many hundreds in the various towns of the kingdom calling themselves *Amis de la Constitution*, are proceeding gradually to take the government of those towns quite out of the hands of the magistrates, whom they will not suffer to proceed against any persons they protect: and yesterday the *Ministre de la Guerre* told them that there were three regiments who were in a state of regular and determined mutiny and whom he had no means in his power to bring back to their duty. All these informations, as fast as they arrive, they refer to their committees, who know as little what to do with them as the Assembly, and seldom do anything. In the case of the colonies and the state of the army they are ordered to make a speedy report. But what can they propose in a country where the people are armed and the government disarmed, where the executive power has neither strength, credit nor support, and the legislature without talents or experience for their business, are in a constant bustle to pass laws which perpetually prove either mischievous or insignificant? The alarm of foreign attack seems to be at present subsided. The negotiators who have been sent to the Princes have done nothing. The decree of yesterday with respect to the Princes of the blood will not help on any accommodation; however, if they should leave them their titles and the power of holding any situations the King can bestow it may give ground for fresh negotiation. It is still impossible to say when this business will be over or what the exact course of it will be but I think a few days must necessarily conclude it.

'I left the Assembly early yesterday to go to the meeting of the French Academy, which is always held on the day of St Louis, for the distribution of the annual prizes for different performances which are then read. Marmontel, who was in the chair, lamented that the fervour of politics had taken off the attention of people of genius from the *belles lettres*, and that not one production had been sent in worthy of a prize. We however profited by it, for instead of hearing inferior productions read, three men of reputation, Monsr. La Harpe, Florian, and the Abbé de Lisle, read performances which were very entertaining and being perfectly well placed I have not been so well amused a great while . . .'[30]

When Palmerston arrived in Paris, he found waiting for him at his hotel a letter dated July 8 from the much cuckolded M. de Flahaut, asking him to spend an evening in their *salon*, in an apartment in the Louvre. The Countess de Flahaut, daughter of a former mistress of Louis XIV, was the acknowledged mistress not only of Talleyrand, but of an acquaintance Palmerston had made seven years earlier in London, the American Minister in Paris, Gouverneur Morris. Palmerston took up this invitation on August 30 and noted in his diary:

'Went to a breakfast at Mr Morris's. He is an American, a gentlemanlike sensible man of property and estimation in America. He was concerned in the line of finance during the war. He has only one leg, having been obliged to undergo an amputation in consequence of jumping from a window in an affair of gallantry. [He had, in fact, lost it in stopping a runaway horse in Philadelphia.] Made an acquaintance with Madame de Flahaut, a very sensible agreeable woman. Her husband and she have apartments in the Louvre where they live much at home and have a small society most evenings. The chief purpose of the meeting was to hear the Abbé de Lisle read some more passages of his poem on the imagination, which he did. They were very beautiful and from what I have heard the poem must be a delightful work. It is hoped it will be published this winter . . .'[31]

The Assembly's business was now approaching its end, and on September 3, Palmerston was able to write his wife:

'I was quite tired of saying time after time that the Assembly were to finish their business in a day or two. In the course of yesterday they went through the whole of it and then proceeded to consider what was to be done next. The committee proposed that a deputation of the Assembly should attend the King to present the constitution to him, to desire that he would give the proper orders and take the proper measures for the security and dignity of his person (which is the form of setting him at liberty), and to desire that if he chose to accept the constitution he would fix the day and the manner when in the presence of the National Assembly he would pronounce his acceptance of the constitutional royalty and his engagement to fulfil the duties of it. The proposal was pretty generally agreed to, but as it did not seem to be their intention that he should propose any alterations it was moved that a declaration should be subjoined to the constitution declaring that the Assembly had finished their work and would admit no alteration to it. This appeared to meet with approbation, but it was observed that as the last articles were but just voted it was necessary that the whole should be put in order and read over, after which the proposed declaration would be proper to be added. This is to be done today, after which it is supposed that the deputies will be named and that they will go tomorrow and that in the beginning of the week the ceremony of his coming to the Assembly will take place, which I shall be very curious to see . . .

'We are a strong party with the addition of Lord Hardwick

and Wyndham. The latter has all the oddity of the family with a great deal of good humour to his acquaintance but has a most unlucky disposition to get into quarrels with the inferior class of people, which must make him an alarming fellow traveller to Mrs Wyndham, who I believe is a very sensible pleasant woman . . .[32]

September 5th. 'At length, after delays that seemed to be endless the constitutional act was finished and carried to the King by a deputation of 60 members of the Assembly on Saturday night [the 3rd]. The King received them with his ministers round him and appeared less embarrassed and delivered his answer better than usual and had rather a cheerful air . . .

'The same night all the guards that were placed as a restraint upon the persons of the Royal Family were removed. The courts and gardens of the Tuileries were thrown open, which were of course very full of people all yesterday, but I do not understand that the Royal Family appeared, unless it was in passing by a window that was open. A number of people went to them yesterday but there was nothing like a Court. None of the foreign ministers have been to them except the Spanish and I believe the Neapolitan, who on account of the relationship of the King's are always on a different footing from the others. I suppose that till the King has declared his acceptation of the crown upon the profferrd terms he does not think it proper to assume any of the functions which had been suspended. It now remains to be known how many days he will think it decent and proper to take before he makes his determination public and with what degree of ceremony he will do it. I hope it will not be long delayed, as it must be obvious to everybody that it is a mere formality, since his determination must undoubtedly have been taken long since. There seems to be no reasonable doubt of his acceptation, though some sanguine aristocrats I met with yesterday at the Spanish ambassador's affected to look significant and gave hints as if he would reject it.

'There has been much movement lately among the aristocrats and several have gone lately to join the emigrants and a good deal of alarm has prevailed here among the opposite party, on account of a supposed union between the King of Prussia and the Emperor which may relate to France. The elections of the members for the next Assembly go on fast and I understand respectable people on the whole are chosen. It seems to me a very curious speculation to judge what turn things will take among them. I understand that the state of their finances is very desperate. If so the new Assembly will declare it and not charge themselves with the future blame. However, the present Assembly are drawing up a state of them which will be published soon . . .'[33]

September 8th. 'I never felt more strongly the misfortune of not being able to be in two places at once than at present, as I most earnestly wish to be with you and yet cannot but rejoice at not having left this place sooner. Nothing very material has passed since I wrote last. The Royal Family are at perfect liberty but I do not know that they have made use of it to go without the doors of the Tuileries. They have Courts three days in the week but do not dine in public. I have seen them once going to chapel, which they do every day through a large crowd of people. If I do not get a more satisfactory view of them I must go on Sunday [the 11th] and be presented. The Queen you may suppose is much changed since Mr Burke and I saw her last. I think her an agreeable looking woman. She seemed to possess herself well and showed no emotion on her countenance. Mme Elizabeth, the King's sister, looked as if she was going to spit in the people's face, which I understand she is almost ready to do upon every occasion. The King himself came rolling along and looked as if he did not care a farthing about it if they would but let him alone . . .

'The elections are going on but are much retarded and obstructed from the badness of the prescribed method of proceeding. Among other inconveniences the excessive length to which they may be carried seems a great fault. In the department of Paris 24 members are to be elected and every single one is a distinct election, so that in a fortnight they have chosen only eight of the number. The electors in some of the distant departments say that they cannot afford to leave their business without being paid and have therefore not only claimed but taken 6 livres per day. This was reported yesterday to the National Assembly, who must of course forbid it. The price of bread was a little raised a few days ago at Paris, though it is still moderate and no appearance of its being otherwise. The consequences of which was some tumult and a proposal to hang Monsr. Bailli, the Mayor of Paris, who came among them to try to quiet them. Luckily for him it was carried against the proposal.

'I conclude the King's answer must be given the very beginning of next week, if not sooner, and when I have been present at that I shall have nothing to do but to leave them settle their affairs as well as they can . . .

'Lady Sutherland carried me a few nights ago to sup at Mme de Staël, the daughter of Monsr. Necker, who is a *bel esprit* by profession. Her husband is the Swedish Minister here. I knew the Necker family when I was last at Paris, but she was then very young. I am glad to have seen her but as far as I could judge I do not like either her appearance, style of conversation or her manners . . .[34]

September 12th. 'I went last night to St Cloud, which during the summer is the resort of the Parisians on Sundays and holidays. Yesterday was the last time of the waterworks playing and was the most crowded of the whole. The scene was beautiful. The gardens are magnificent in the old style with vast walks and a profusion of old trees on the banks of the river. On these days they are full of booths all lighted up. The people were innumerable and quantities of groups dancing in various places. The brightness of the moon with the river and woods together with the quantity of lights glittering among them and the perfect warmth in the air made quite a scene of enchantment. The only thing that a little broke it was the excessive noise, for besides that one Frenchman upon all occasions makes as much noise as five Englishmen, the fashion of the night was to buy little penny trumpets which were sold at all the booths and then to make as great a screeching with them as their lungs would enable them to do. To give you some idea of the quantity of carriages, I was two hours coming back, though the distance is not more than five miles and the road very broad; but there happened to be one place where it was narrowed by a repair and [I] began to doubt whether we should get by during the whole night. Nor I believe should we if there had not been soldiers there to keep some sort of order.

'The night before, coming home through the Bois de Boulogne I met with another scene which looked as much like a fairy tale and was quite unexpected. It is a very forest-like place and there is in it a building where there is a subscription ball for a certain number of nights. The company were just assembled, but as it was a delightful night they were all walking in the wood before they went in to the ballroom, together with great numbers who were not of the ball party. The numbers were very considerable and I have not seen on the whole since I have been at Paris so many genteel, well dressed women as I saw there . . .

'The old Assembly must soon give up to the new, who begin to muster strong. Those who are elected hitherto are not the most violent men, but yet they are people in whom the public have little confidence either as to abilities or character . . .[35]

September 14th. 'The great business here is at length terminated. The King on Tuesday sent a letter to the Assembly, which I enclose. It is well written and was received with much joy. I was there when it was brought in by the Garde des Sceaux in his robes. The Assembly directly voted the general amnesty and sent a deputation to the King to lay that vote before him. Yesterday the Assembly was filled very early and places were very difficult to obtain. By the kind assistance of Monsr. de Noailles, Wyndham and I got exceeding good ones. About $\frac{1}{2}$ past 12 the King arrived. He came with less show and ceremony than I expected and the whole thing was rather flat and awkward. There were two elbow chairs nearly alike, the King sat in one and the President at his right hand in the other. The King's speech was short, he spoke very distinctly and audibly but looked distressed and unhappy. The President, who seemed to assume a kind of equality that to me was disgusting, made a long speech to him in answer as they sat in the two chairs which had a very awkward effect. I did not much admire the composition. The King then withdrew and the Assembly followed him back to the Tuileries. Upon the whole, it seemed to me the last degree of humiliation and had more the air of a triumph over a degraded man than a dignified constitutional act.

'The general joy at this event you may imagine is great as well as the vexation of those who hoped other things, but it remains now to see what be the issue, for it is not everything to have mortified the King and obliged him to swear to support what he detests and to execute what is perhaps impracticable and which by their laws cannot be altered. Some means must be found to modify and to improve the work or nothing but confusion can be the consequence. What the next Assembly will do and what line of conduct they will follow is a matter of much importance and curiosity. I think nobody can pretend to guess what their disposition will be, as they must consist of men in general unknown and unexperienced . . .'[36]

REFERENCES

1. C.58 26.VI.1791
2. C.55 undated
3. A.18
4. B.1 9.VII.1791
5. A.18
6. C.57 13.VII.1791
7. B.1 14.VII.1791
8. A.18
9. A.18
10. B.1 18.VII.1791
11. B.1 21.VII.1791
12. B.2 18.VII.1791
13. H.21
14. C.54 22.VII.1791
15. A.18
16. B.1 25.VII.1791
17. A.18
18. B.1 28.VII.1791
19. A.18
20. B.2 1.VIII.1791
21. B.2 3.VIII.1791
22. B.1 4.VIII.1791
23. A.18
24. B.2 7.VIII.1791
25. B.2 ?11.VIII.1791
26. B.1 11.VIII.1791
27. B.1 14.VIII.1791
28. B.1 17.VIII.1791
29. B.1 21.VIII.1791
30. B.1 26.VIII.1791
31. A.18
32. B.1 3.IX.1791
33. B.1 5.IX.1791
34. B.1 8.IX.1791
35. B.1 12.IX.1791
36. B.1 14.IX.1791

CHAPTER VIII

EMMA, LADY HAMILTON

Palmerston meets Sir William Hamilton's second wife in Paris – the portrait of a bacchante, said to be Lady Hamilton, at Broadlands – Sir Joshua Reynolds presents Palmerston with a painting – Palmerston displeased with its device – Reynolds dies and Palmerston is a pall-bearer at his funeral – Thomas Lawrence commissioned to complete the picture – a family mystery – indifferent health of father and son – plans for residence in Italy

PALMERSTON's final days in Paris were enlivened by a new and most entertaining acquaintance. He had received from Sir Charles Blagden, the Secretary of the Royal Society, a letter dated September 6:

'Sir W. Hamilton, I believe, was this day married to Mrs Hart. The Marquess of Abercorn, who is regarded as the head of the family, I hear, strongly advised the match and was to give the lady away. They intend to set out Thursday for Naples and talk of passing through Paris, where probably you will see them . . .'[1]

Palmerston lost no time in calling on Sir William Hamilton, and as a tailpiece to the letter to his wife on September 14 reported:

'Sir William and Lady Hamilton are arrived at this hotel and are to stay a few days. I have been introduced to her and had the good luck to be the means, by speaking to Monsr. Noailles, of getting them placed yesterday in the Assembly. She is very handsome but not elegant, her face is very much like what I have seen in a fine old portrait and she wears her hair something in that style. She seems very good humoured, very happy and very attentive to him. I am promised an exhibition of her performances that have been so much talked of . . .

'I am now preparing for my departure and think I shall set out on Sunday or Monday next at farthest. I am engaged to go

to the Duke of Bouillon, who sent me a very civil message of
invitation . . .

PS. They have put an end to all necessity of passports but I
think it is better not to be the first to go without as the people
in the country act just as they please.'²

Until he left Paris a week later he was almost continuously
in the Hamiltons' company:

September 18th. 'I am just come home after having been the
greater part of the day on foot endeavouring to see as much as
possible of the shows of the day, the Assembly having decreed
that it should be given up to public rejoicing to celebrate the
termination and acceptation of the constitution. The morning
was chiefly employed in processions and proclamations in
various parts of the town and ended with a general assemblage
in the Champ de Mars and ceremonies much resembling those
of the 14th of July. About six o'clock a very fine balloon went
up with a man in it, which succeeded very well and went
directly over Paris. At night the illuminations of the buildings
and gardens of the Tuileries and Louvre and of the Champs
Elysées, which is a vast piece of ground planted with trees
adjoining to them, were by much the finest of the kind I ever
saw and the whole scene with the immense quantities of people
and music and dancing in every corner exceeded every expectation I had formed. No carriages were permitted to be used in
any part of the town the whole day so that the fatigue was very
considerable to those who wished to see it all. I was all day
with the Hamiltons and Monsr. de Noailles and we succeeded
very well. About ten o'clock Lady Hamilton and the rest of the
party went home after returning from the Champs Elysées,
which are at one end of Paris and I set out by myself to walk
to the ruins of the Bastille which are quite at the other, where
I understood there was to be a very splendid exhibition of
illuminations, dancing, etc. I found something of the kind I
expected but not equal to what I had seen in any respect, yet
as it is a curious circumstance to have been present at I do not
regret my trouble. I saw the King and Queen pass through the
Champs Elysées in their carriage with guards about nine o'clock,
they were received with considerable applause and I dare say

will become very popular. I believe they are to go to the theatre tomorrow . . .

'These circumstances have thrown my departure back a day or two. Whether I set out on Tuesday depends upon a circumstance I am not sure of, but on Wednesday nothing that I foresee can possibly prevent me from taking my departure and in that case I may very well be at London by the 30th of this month . . .

'I perfectly agree with everything I have heard in commendation of Lady Hamilton. She is certainly very handsome and there is a plain good sense and simplicity of character about her which is uncommon and very agreeable. I have seen her perform the various characters and attitudes which she assumes in imitation of statues and pictures, and was pleased even beyond my expectation though I had heard so much. She really presents the very thing which the artists aimed at representing. I have not yet heard her sing which I am told is very remarkably good in its way. I am to do that twice tomorrow. In the morning at the house of an Italian where she is to practice, and in the evening at Lady Sutherland's where there is to be a little music for her . . .'[3]

In the arched alcove of the dining room at Broadlands there hangs to this day one of the most enchanting pictures in the house, reproduced opposite page 256. Both family tradition and the catalogues of art historians describe it as a portrait of Emma, Lady Hamilton as a bacchante, and the classic Grecian features surrounded by a wreath of flowers retain all the freshness of colouring lavished on them by young Thomas Lawrence, who was part-author of this curious canvas.

Family gossip has long suggested that the second Viscount Palmerston was one of this voluptuous lady's less publicised lovers and that the portrait is mute evidence of the liaison. Certainly the later letters from Paris indicate that he was by no means unaffected by her attractions, but the most diligent research can provide no confirmation of this theory. The story of how the portrait came to assume its present form is not for that less curious.

Sir Joshua Reynolds, as we have seen, was not only a fellow

member, with Palmerston, of the Dilettanti Society, but a close personal friend of nearly thirty years' standing. It was Sir Joshua who, little more than a year before he died, presented to Palmerston, as a token of affection, the original canvas – before the supposed portrait of Emma Hamilton was superimposed. The first intimation of the intended gift came from Sir Charles Blagden who, on October 12, 1790, wrote:

'Sir Joshua Reynolds, I find, is now full determined to wait upon you at Broadlands, and as he sets out next Thursday, I intend to accompany him – and he travels with his own horses – and the plan is, to dine . . . with Doctor Wharton at Winchester and proceed thence, either the same night – which will be nearly impossible – or the following morning to your house. Miss Palmer [Sir Joshua's niece] and he propose to make three other visits in your neighbourhood, and Sir Joshua will scarcely be prevailed upon to remain absent from town a fortnight, so that probably your Lordship's share will not be more than four or five days . . .'[4]

On November 8, after they had left, Sir Charles Blagden wrote again:

'Perhaps I am letting out a secret, but Sir Joshua Reynolds is putting into order a picture which he intends for the recess in your new dining room at Broadlands, to be fixed over the side-board. It is a Roman Charity, surrounded with an oval wreath of flowers. He esteems it a fine piece, but does not seem to be certain who was the painter . . .'[5]

Five days later Sir Joshua wrote to Palmerston himself:

'Miss Palmer joins with me in acknowledgement and thanks for the kind hospitality we experienced from your Lordship and Lady Palmerston. Broadlands we shall always think of with pleasure as we left it with deep regret.

'In our journey to Sir John Doyly's, beautiful as the New Forest is, we had rather more of it than at that time we wished or desired. We wandered about it at least eight miles out of our way, which as soon as it was discovered we found in ourselves a much greater disposition to scolding than admiring the beauties of the Forest. This, and losing the little dog which Mr Dance gave us, were the only cross accidents we met with in our grand tour, excepting, indeed, my leaving an old great-coat at Broadlands, and being forced to borrow Mr Dance's. However, that this account of our distresses may not leave too melancholy an impression on the mind, I think it necessary to mention that the way we had lost we found again. The little dog was brought home to us in Leicester Fields by the stage coach-man, and the great-coat will, in all probability, be forthcoming in due time.

'And now, My Lord, to come to the real object of this letter. I should not have thought of troubling your Lordship with our thanks, with the loss of our way, or of the little dog, or of the great-coat, if I had not thought it necessary to advise your Lordship that I have put by the wagon this morning the picture you wot of for the side-board, of which I beg his acceptance in return for the many good glasses of wine which I received from him at Broadlands. To be serious, if I had considered the picture which I have sent as of any value, I should have thought it approaching to impertinence to have to presumed to make a present of it to your Lordship, but I apprehend this is fully within Swift's definition of a present – "that it should be something of small value, but what is not easily procured".

In regard to the emblem, which is added in the middle of the garland, it apparently means something, but what that meaning is, I shall not be in a hurry to blab and destroying the pleasure of the search, by telling beforehand my own riddle . . .'[6]

Within the wreath of flowers Sir Joshua had painted a hand and an eye. Palmerston, totally mystified and not particularly pleased with the device, asked Sir Charles Blagden if there was any explanation. On November 17 Sir Charles replied:

'It was not till last night that I learned the alteration made by Sir Joshua in the picture, which I suppose you have by this time received. Instead of the Roman Charity, which originally occupied the centre of it, he has, I find, put in an hand with an eye, which he declares to be meant enigmatically, but does not give the solution. Probably he intended it as an emblem of liberality, guided by intelligence or discernment. I would rather it was not known that I had mentioned anything to you of the picture before Sir Joshua's letter . . .'[7]

Sir Charles followed this up five days later in more detail:

'After the arrival of the post last Saturday, I called upon Sir Joshua Reynolds, who immediately told me he had received a letter from you, and put it into my hands. He then remarked that he should be sorry if the enigma was so obscure that you would not find it out, but that he could hardly think so, since I had readily divined it. This referred to the conversation of last Tuesday night, when, on hearing what he had painted, I asked him whether the meaning was not liberality directed by intelligence; but he would not then say anything. He now acknowledged that I was right, but used the word "sagacity" instead of "intelligence". Sagacity, however, is commonly typified by the nose, or, rather, by animals remarkable for the excellence of that organ – hounds, for instance. It is evident that Sir Joshua thinks . . . the conception a very happy one, so that it will be rather difficult to lay by the picture without offending him. By the tone of your letter to him, I presume you mean to take the compliment for your ground. Sir Joshua told me that in order to avoid the disagreeable effect of a hand cut off, he had painted it of a marble colour as if it were the fragment of a statue, that he was not sure, however, but it would have been a better idea to have made it a bloody hand, in allusion to your Baronetage . . .'[8]

Palmerston was no better pleased. In a letter to his wife on December 1 he commented:

'I sat an hour with Sir Joshua and Miss Palmer yesterday morning, who are both well. I told him pretty nearly my opinion upon the subject of the picture, resting as much as I could on the unpleasant feel I should have in putting up a picture which must excite so much curiosity and which must be explained into a compliment to myself. He was very good humoured about it and said the hand might easily be rubbed out, and the space left vacant, or anything else put in. I am to dine with him on Saturday . . .'[9]

'I am glad you have got over the picture meeting so well,' was Lady Palmerston's reply. 'I wish Sir Joshua could paint in the middle something like the sketches of Miss Gordon's face.'[10]

Lady Palmerston's reference can only be to the famous studies of the heads of angels now in the National Gallery, by Sir Joshua Reynolds, in which the heads are all portraits of Miss Gordon. This painting had been exhibited at the Royal Academy in 1787. Palmerston was set on having some alteration made, and, on December 6, wrote to his wife:

'We had a great party at Sir Joshua's but he always spoils his dinners by having more people than his table can hold comfortably. There was a small card party in the evening which was melancholy beyond description for want of fire and candle . . .

'Miss Palmer asked me with some eagerness whether I had ordered the picture to be sent to London as she said any alteration might be made in it. So that I believe you had better have it packed up without its frames and sent by the wagon.'[11]

On December 20 Palmerston again wrote to his wife:

'The picture came safe and is gone to Cummins [sic] to have the hand completely removed and the picture cleaned, which I hope will make it brighter. Sir Joshua has just sent me home a picture of his own which I agreed for some time ago and which I think you will like. It is a girl leaning forward on both her arms . . .'[12]

For this Palmerston paid £78 15s. od. It was one of the three canvases by Reynolds acquired by Palmerston during his life – the first was the 'Children in the Wood' and the third cannot be identified. They were sold by the Hon. Evelyn Ashley about 1890 for £16,000.

Comyns was a picture cleaner who did much work for the artists and collectors of the time. The pressure of work at his studio must have been considerable, and during this delay Sir Joshua's health started to deteriorate rapidly. As 1791 wore on he practically abandoned his brushes, and Palmerston seems to have formed the resolution to have the blank centre of his canvas filled in by young Thomas Lawrence, the rising portraitist and a fit subject for his patronage. On October 12 Palmerston wrote to his wife:

'I have been at Lawrence's who has made a beginning which I hope will do very well, but he was not at home. I am to see it again on Saturday . . .'[13]

On October 15 he had bad news of Sir Joshua: 'I called at Sir Joshua's the night before last and was concerned to be told that his eyes were so bad he could not receive me. I sent this morning and did not hear that they were better . . .'[14] But Sir Charles Blagden kept him informed of the progress of the work:

November 8th. 'At Lawrence's lodgings, I was told he was out of town, but would return soon. I shall, therefore, enquire for him again in a few days . . .[15]

November 14th. 'Sir Joshua Reynolds still continues indisposed with his eyes and very low-spirited. It is true that he has sent a letter of resignation to the Academy . . .[16]

November 19th. 'I have seen Lawrence, and he promises to send you the picture in the course of next week. He said it was finished, but the colours being laid on thick, had not yet sufficiently dried . . .'[17]

Sir Charles' next letter at least mentioned the supposed subject of the portrait:

December 8th. 'Be so good as to convey my thanks to Lady P. for her very obliging letter, and inform her that Lady Hamilton is probably before this time presented at the Court of Naples – at least so says the letter I saw yesterday from that country. It states that when Sir William first went to Court, nothing was said about Lady Hamilton, which gave umbrage to both and made Sir William resolve not to attend the Court at Caserta (this perhaps occasioned the report prevalent in town a few days ago, that he was recalled). However, some days after, a messenger was sent importing that the Queen would be glad to see Lady Hamilton, in consequence of which, a time was settled for her presentation and they are both to spend the holiday at Caserta with the Royal Family . . .'[18]

Sir Joshua was now very ill. He lingered for three months and on February 2, 1792, Lord Palmerston wrote to his wife in Bath to tell her:

'Doctor Blagden called just now. I am very sorry to learn by him that poor Sir Joshua is quite in a hopeless state. His constitution is quite broke up and he is going very fast. He has some dropsical symptoms but they seem to be more the effect

of weakness than an original complaint. He is now very little
out of his bed and sees very few people . . .'[19]

On the 23rd of the month Sir Joshua died, and after lying in
state at the Royal Academy was buried in the crypt of St Paul's
Cathedral near the tomb of Sir Christopher Wren. Palmerston
was one of the ten pall-bearers and when the details of the will
were announced found that he had been bequeathed the second
choice of any picture of Sir Joshua's painting, still in the
possession of the executors, the first choice going to the Earl
of Upper Ossory. Palmerston may not have deviated much
from the orthodox in his artistic tastes, but his instincts were
sound. The picture he chose is generally reckoned to be one of
Reynolds' finest – the Infant Academy.

Only two further references in the Palmerston papers have
any reference to the Emma Hamilton portrait. The following
month he noted in his account book: 'Paid Lawrence for figure
added to picture with flowers, thirty guineas'. And in a list of
works of art in his possession, compiled about 1796, he noted:
'A figure of a Bacchante, half length, in the centre of a wreath
of flowers, 3 ft 12 ins [sic, in fact 3 ft 11 ins] by 5 ft 4½ ins,
Baptiste and Lawrence'. Baptiste is identified as Jean Baptiste
Monnoyer (1636–1699), although Palmerston's source of this
information is not known.

It seems a pity to dispose in so cavalier a fashion of the suggestion of this romantic attachment, but on the evidence, and there
is no other available, no confirmation is justified. Palmerston
met and was captivated by Emma Hamilton during that brief
week in Paris, when the position of the French monarch seemed
to have been assured and the city was given over to general
feting and rejoicing. If any attachment was formed he committed no mention of it to paper, although during their two-
year residence in Italy from 1792–1794 the Palmerstons saw
the Hamiltons again and frequently. By then the picture was
completed and occupying the alcove where it still hangs.

★ ★ ★

Palmerston's own health was not too good during the winter
of 1791; he suffered much from severe colds which took him

Emma, Lady Hamilton

Benjamin Thomson, Count Rumford

out of circulation for two or three weeks at a time. However, he kept his wife informed of his social pleasures:

'I have just seen Lord and Lady Hampden, Sir Ralph [Payne] and Mde de Coigny. The Hampdens are to have music on Sunday where I shall go. I am to dine tomorrow at the Culverdens and I am afraid I am engaged on Sunday at the Francis's too much to be off, as am asked to meet Charles Fox at the Payne's, which would be a better thing . . .'[20]

'I was at Lady Hampden's in the evening where there was a very good assembly with a little concert and catch singing. You was much enquired after . . . You are invited to the Duchess of Cumberland's on Thursday, to Mrs Hobart's on Friday and also to the Duchess of Gloucester's every Monday, Wednesday and Friday for ever. I carried home Sir Harry Englefield, who seems vastly well and went in and drank a dish of tea at one in the morning with him and Lady Englefield who is likewise extremely well . . .'[21]

Even on the day of Sir Joshua Reynolds' funeral he dined at the Duke of Portland's and went on to the opera and the play. His parliamentary duties were not entirely neglected. He was in the House of Commons on Monday, April 2, until a quarter before seven in the morning, when a resolution that the slave trade ought to be abolished was carried by a large majority.

The anecdote book entries start to thin out at this period, but Palmerston still had an ear for a good story:

'*A young clergyman, preaching before the University, was much commended by one of the senior fellows of his college for the goodness of his sermon; but at the same time questioned whether he had not taken part of it out of Tillotson – this, he denied. Upon which, the same fellow meeting him again the next day said, "Well, young gentleman, I find you tell me true – that you had not taken your sermon out of Tillotson – for I have looked and found it's all there still".*'

'*A part coxcombe, attempting to be witty on a plain, grave man, told him he did not believe he could say, "Bo to a goose". "Yes, I can", said the other looking steadfastly at him, "and I can likewise say "goose to a Beau".*'

I

'*The author of a new play which had had very great success,
having a dispute with Sheridan about some fact, offered to bet him
the profit due to him from his play which he had never received.
"No," said Sheridan, "that would be too deep a stake for me, but I
will bet you the value of it".*

'*A lady who had granted the last favour to her lover upon the
usual plea that he could not live without her, was afterwards heard
reproaching him for his inconstancy in these terms, "You villain! Did
I not save your life?"*'

Young Harry continued sickly and his mother had another
of the many reports of an attack of St Anthony's Fire.

May 7th. 'Harry, as I told you, was feverish on Saturday
which produced a fresh eruption of St Anthony on his face.
It is not bad nor does it come very near his eye so that that is
not affected by it. Mr Walker attends him and has renewed
the blister and ordered him what he thinks proper . . .'[22]

On May 10 Lady Palmerston received an account of a
remarkable occurrence at the House of Commons:

'A strange incident happened last night at the House of
Commons some hours after it was adjourned. Some clerks
who were writing, smelt a violent smell of fire with smoke
which they could not account for and after much search they
at length found in a kind of cupboard in a water-closet below
the House of Commons a pair of old fustian breeches burning
and stinking at a most extraordinary rate. The way to this
place, which is for the use of the servants of the House, is from
the Lobby, which is shut up when there is nothing doing in
the House or in the clerks' rooms. The place where it was put
is an opening in the wainscot for the purpose of getting at the
pipes and when it is shut it is hardly visible so that several
persons went into the closet before they thought of looking
into this place. There is much deal wood and I should think a
current of air so that perhaps a better place for lodging com-
bustibles could not have been easily found, but on the other
hand nothing could have been devised to put there that was
less combustible than fustian breeches, which upon trial since
made will only smother and cannot be brought to blaze. There

was not much of them consumed but they were a considerable time burning and made a great stink and smoke. I am not inclined to look on this as a serious plot against . . . though I suppose it will occasion a good deal of noise.'[23]

This brought a spirited rejoinder from Lady Palmerston:

'What a very odd incident is this Fustian attack upon the House of Commons. It certainly must be a plot of the *sans culotte* party. Mischief was undoubtedly intended, though the conspirators proved their want of judgment in their choice of the means they made use of to carry with effect through the House their flaming reform. I suppose there never will be any satisfactory explanation of the business . . .

PS. I have been reading the Rights of Women, so you must in future expect me to be very tenacious of my rights and privileges.'[24]

Work had been going on all this time at Broadlands, under the direction of Henry Holland, who seems to have acted as house agent as well as architect. In June, 1792, we find Palmerston making this note of a visit to one of his associates: 'Went to Mr Oddie's to settle about the sale of my house in Park Street'. And in the account book shortly afterwards there is an entry: 'Received in payment for my house in Park Street, Westminster, commission deducted, £2,145', which was £55 less than he had given for it six years earlier.

Holland had certainly found a generous patron. Another account book entry for 1792 notes: 'Paid Mr Holland at various times from May, 1788, to July, 1792, for work at Broadlands and various articles not entered in the accounts, £7,100'. Now Palmerston asked him to turn his attention to the house in Hanover Square he had purchased two years earlier, but which the family had not yet occupied. The work was not started for some time and, in any case, Palmerston was busy with the arrangements for another project. His health had not stood up too well to the two previous winters and only the birth of Elizabeth had prevented the family from seeking a warmer climate two years earlier. With the passage of time the scheme to live abroad had developed on much grander lines and arrangements had been made for the family to embark on the most extensive tour of the Continent that Palmerston had yet undertaken.

Lady Palmerston had yet to see the antique glories of Italy, which had been such a major experience in his own upbringing, and young Harry was of an age when travel might start to broaden his mind. While the Hanover Square house was being altered to suit his own tastes, Palmerston had determined on an extended period of residence abroad, and, on July 27, the whole family, with a caravan of attendants, left London for Dover and Calais, accompanied by their friend Sir Charles Blagden. It was to be their last sight of England for nearly two and a half years.

REFERENCES

1. C.49 6.IX.1791
2. B.1 14.IX.1791
3. B.1 18.IX.1791
4. C.49 12.X.1790
5. C.49 8.XI.1790
6. C.53 13.XI.1790
7. C.49 17.XI.1790
8. C.49 22.XI.1790
9. B.1 1.XII.1790
10. B.2 2.XII.1790
11. B.1 6.XII.1790
12. B.1 20.XII.1790
13. B.1 12.X.1791
14. B.1 15.X.1791
15. C.49 8.XI.1791
16. C.49 14.XI.1791
17. C.49 19.XI.1791
18. C.49 8.XII.1791
19. B.1 12.II.1792
20. B.1 3.II.1792
21. B.1 ?7.II.1792
22. B.1 7.V.1792
23. B.1 10.V.1792
24. B.2 13.V.1792

CHAPTER IX

EUROPE IN TURMOIL

Last glimpse of the French Royal Family – the children's carriage detained by the St Antoine mob – released by the intervention of Santerre – Geneva, a haven – Gibbon, the Duchess of Devonshire, Beckford and de Saussure – the Mont Cenis and the invasion of Savoy – Italy before Napoleon – the Neapolitan Court – King Ferdinand and Emma Hamilton – a tour of Capri – Benjamin Thompson, Count Rumford – summer in Switzerland – the belligerents at Basle – Harry seriously ill – the siege of Toulon and the threat to Rome – the fair of the Ascension at Venice – news of riots in London – Count Rumford their host in Bavaria – excursion to the Duke of York's army in Holland and last sight of Benjamin Mee

PALMERSTON had chosen to travel across Europe in the month that witnessed the massacre of the Swiss Guards in the Tuileries and the cannonade of Valmy. He and Lady Palmerston waited on Marie Antoinette and Louis XVI five days before the mob broke into the royal palace. The family crossed the Mont Cenis the day the French revolutionary armies invaded Savoy. Yet with twenty-two years of war facing their country, the Palmerston family was able to spend twenty-six idyllic, *fainéant* months sampling the joys of the Neapolitan Court and other Italian states.

Palmerston filled no less than twelve journals and diaries during this tour. The vast proportion of their entries is of purely exiguous interest, as, although the detailed descriptions of the landscape through which they passed would do credit to a Baedeker, the pertinent comments on local inhabitants and customs are few and far between, and the exhaustive lists of picture collections seen are only reasonably discerning paraphrases of what was and is available in the better-known guide books of the time.

Fortunately for us these cultural marathons were purgatory to Lady Palmerston, who bewailed their tedium in a series of highly entertaining letter-journals to her beloved brother, Benjamin Mee, who was just returning to Europe from India after again failing in business. Her letters to him consisted of daily entries on a four-page double-crown folio, and as soon as each of these was full she posted them.

Sunday, July 29th. 'At Calais we went to the Hotel de Ville to get our passports, which were made out individually for each of our party, with a particular description of our persons . . .'[1] reads Palmerston's first diary entry. His *laissez-passer*, with all its subsequent endorsements, remains preserved, and is reproduced in part opposite page 225.

They arrived in Paris on August 1 and the next day Lady Palmerston started the first of her journal-letters to her brother:

Thursday, August 2nd. 'I am extremely struck with the magnificent buildings in Paris. The fine hotels and gardens with the number of public walks and gardens, which make a summer passed in Paris as pleasant as the country. The clearness of the air from burning only wood is very singular to anybody used to the smoke of London. I really think it's the only town for a gentleman to live in; but of that description there are few left. The total absence of everything like a person of fashion, or a carriage better than a fiacre is very striking and there's an air of ferocity and self-created consequence in the common people very uncomfortable . . .

'The Royal Family now seldom even walk in the garden and the people have carried a blue ribband along the side of one part and pin upon it every kind of paper filled with abuse. They style it the Austrian ground and not a soul dare pass it for fear of being suspected. Stanley and Mr Weston, who married Miss Tierney, dined with us and we went to the Italian Opera, rue Feydeau, built by Monsieur, the King's brother. We went and walked afterwards in the Palais Royal, which used to be filled with all kinds of elegant people. It was crowded indeed, but with quite a different description. It's the gayest place possible and you might pass your life in it and never want anything but what you might find there. All kinds of shops, coffee houses, taverns – which they call Restauratators [*sic*] – dancing, gambling, politics talking all around you and *Ladies* without number. It

seems now a decided point that they mean next week to depose
the King. The question is to be agitated on Thursday. Several
petitions have been presented on the occasion. His duplicity
and intercourse with the Austrians is alleged as the motive for
this act. A petition is to be placed on Saturday on the altar in
the Champs de Mars, to be signed by all who approve his being
deposed . . .'[2]

On August 5 she sent an account of their presentation to the
French Royal Family, on what must have been the last occasion
that Louis XVI and Marie Antoinette were able to engage in
such a function, barely a week before the mob broke into the
Tuileries and massacred the Swiss Guards:

'Lady Gower wrote to M. Champcenet, my old friend, to
ask him to get us to see the King and Queen go to Mass, and
we received a very polite note saying he would send his servant
to show us the way into the gallery. We went at 12 and were
conducted up the great stairs into a long room, a kind of gallery
hung with tapestry. Here we found the Swiss Guard in waiting
and different gentlemen of the Court, officers, and attendants
on the Court. We stayed sometime, when M. Champcenet
arrived and placed us in an extreme good situation. At length
the poor Queen came in, in her hand the Dauphin, a sweet boy
about the size of Harry, with white hair and dressed quite like
an English child. She was followed by her daughter, a pale,
melancholy girl, about 15; then Madame Elizabeth, the King's
sister; Madame la Princesse de Lamballe; Madame la Princesse
de Tarante and some more ladies I did not know. The Queen
presented the Dauphin to us and spoke very graciously. She
had been up all night, as had the King and all who were in the
chateau. They expected to be attacked and they could last night
have depended upon the National Guard, but they cannot this
evening. When they had passed on to chapel, we went into
another apartment and M. Champcenet showed me where the
mob had broke in the 20th of June. The door we saw was
repaired. They forced into the room where we were sitting
and M. Champcenet persuaded the Queen to go into the next
apartment, where a guard surrounded her. He then went into
a gallery which overlooks the Tuileries, where on the first

attack, after the family were brought from Versailles, the Queen appeared with the Dauphin, surrounded by an inflamed populace, who breathed nothing but revenge and abuse. We remained for some time and then saw the King return with his attendant and the Queen from chapel. The King is so like his pictures, that I thought I knew him perfectly. He was attended by all the Foreign Ministers left in Paris, among them Lord Gower. We did not go into the chapel, as M. Champcenet thought we should see them so much better passing in this quiet way . . .

'From thence we went to the National Assembly. It was extremely full. When we went in there were about ten persons speaking in different parts of the Assembly; a man in the tribune making a speech and the president ringing a bell to gain silence – which never could be obtained, and the people in the galleries hooting, hollowing or hissing just as they approved or else disapproved the sentiment of the speaker. I think I never heard anything in the least like it. Everything which tended to abuse of the King was heard with unbounded applause, but anything in the least of the opposite opinion was received with hisses and groans . . .'[3]

The Palmerstons did not relish the turn of affairs in Paris at all and determined to leave as soon as possible:

'Paris is in the greatest state of fermentation possible [he wrote in his journal on August 6]. The Jacobins, or the violent party, carry everything before them and lay all the blame of the mischiefs that are resulting from their own absurdities on the King and Queen, who are certainly in danger of their lives, from the violence of the people and the little dependence they can have on their guards, who are only National Troops. The Assembly are distracted and seem in a kind of frantic despair and pass their meetings in quarrels and violence and in listening to petitions from various quarters to depose the King. All these they refer to a committee, who are to report them next Thursday, the 9th; it is probable they will recommend the measure of deposition or something like it. . .'[4]

'We went this morning, as soon as we had breakfasted, to the Hotel de Ville to have our passports signed. [Lady Palmerston wrote to her brother the same day.] On going up the steps, the remembrance of all the bloody scenes that had passed upon those steps made me feel quite cold with horror. We took all the children with us. They were extremely civil and detained us as short a time as possible . . .

'We are to go tomorrow, which I regret, though I know it right; but I should like, in days when Liberty is not at such a height, to pass some months here.'[5]

She had an alarming account to give of their departure the following morning:

'We set out from Paris about 12, having been making purchases – a very few, having been sadly hurried away. Passing through the Faubourg of St Antoine, the mob gathered round the carriage in which William and Elizabeth were and Games, Mercier [the servants] and Miss Carter's maid, which happened to be a little behind that in which we were in. Sir Charles Blagden's chaise was likewise stopped. They were very violent in their abusive language, but luckily their object was to make them go to the place where the officers of the Section were sitting. This was willingly complied with and the coach was brought into the court where, however, nobody was at that time, but the greffier. He examined the passports which, being all perfectly regular, he desired them to proceed and an attempt was accordingly made, but without success, for the mob who were, by this time, increased to a great number, would not suffer it and after much abuse and threats obliged them again to return to the Section where they were glad to take refuge. About this time M. Santerre, I believe the Procureur de la Commune, made his appearance among them and after a considerable time, during which he exerted himself with great diligence, he at length, by his influence and by his argument, quieted them so far as to obtain a free passage for the carriage escorted by some of the National Guard, who attended them out of the town, and they came on to join us at Charenton. [Lord Palmerston, in an almost identical diary note, says that the saviour of their children was Manuel, the equally frightening figure who became Mayor of Paris during the Terror.] You may conceive our distress. We were for going ourselves, but the officer who was upon guard particularly requested us not to go as he said it would be the means of detaining us all. He advised us to write a letter to M. Pétion [the Mayor]. We had heard they were safe at the Section, or we should have been quite miserable. Lord P. sent a letter, but the children arrived before the courier got to Paris. The children were not [in] the least alarmed, but the servants were frightened out of their senses. I think I never felt happier than when I saw the coach arrive, the dear things safe. Sir Charles being with them was a great relief . . .

'It was difficult to understand or conceive what were the motives that actuated them, as the few who were the real actors in the business seemed to have lost all sense and to be under the influence of a fury that they could not bear the idea that anybody should leave Paris at this critical moment and having seen our carriage pass grew exasperated at seeing two more and determined to stop them. The conduct and behaviour of the officers, both on this occasion and the preceding day at the Hotel de Ville where we went to get our Calais passports signed, was particularly civil and obliging . . .'[6]

The Palmerstons lost no time in pressing on to Switzerland and safety:

Sunday, August 12th – Lyons. 'When we arrived at the Hotel de Bourbon on the Quay, we found some difficulty in getting apartments as the provinces are in a very unquiet state and the town in peace, the people from the country were arrived and rendered the town so full, accommodation is difficult for a large family . . .'[7]

Monday, August 13th. 'Accounts received this day at Lyons of the attack of the Tuileries by the mob on the 10th; of the massacre of the Swiss Guards who defended it; of the flight of the King and Queen to the Assembly and of the vote passed for the suspension of the King and the assembling a National Convention . . .'[8]

Tuesday, August 14th. 'Tomorrow is a fête and we think it will be as wise to get out of the town as the account of this new Revolution has made much agitation here and the common people seem in their manner strongly allied to the Parisians.

These soldiers are standing about all day and such figures I
never saw – children and old men and ragged and dirty beyond
all description . . .'[9]

Wednesday, August 15th. 'Set out from Lyons. Much incom-
moded in the two first stages by crowds of people going to join
the armies, who, being the very refuse of the mob and under
no discipline, were unpleasant fellow travellers . . .[10]

Friday, August 17th. 'Our passports and baggage were
examined at Collonges, as being a frontier place, but both
with the greatest civility. It is but justice to say that this has
been the case ever since we entered France, and though our
passports have been frequently asked for, no difficulty has ever
been made, nor has one hour been lost by it in the whole
journey . . .'[11]

Safe in Geneva Lady Palmerston found time, on August 18,
to write a more personal letter to her brother. Benjamin Mee
was still on the high seas and had not yet been able to tell his
sister that he had decided not to set foot in England in case his
creditors should seize him. In the end he landed in Ostend and
his involved financial affairs were to keep him out of England
for the rest of his life.

'Shall I own to you that in the midst of all these beautiful
scenes your image ever presents itself? I take you with me
wherever I go and my tears unbidden flow when I think that
you cannot partake with me what in that case would be perfect
pleasure and the regret that every step removes me from
England at the moment you are expected is, sometimes, almost
too much for me. I endeavour, for the sake of Lord P, to bear
up as much as possible, but I am hardly equal to it. When I
hear you are in the arms of your family and friends, I trust I
shall experience a quiet I have not for a long time enjoyed. If
you had been with me I think I should have known no further
wishes. I did not mean to have touched upon this subject, but
at some moments I cannot restrain myself and it's a pleasure to
open one's heart to those we love . . .[12]

'I hear there are a great many people at Lausanne. They have
been very gay, but all festivities have been suspended for 18
days in compliment to the memory of the unfortunate Swiss

massacred in Paris. I believe this country is far from being in a quiet state. The idea of *equality* is gone forth in the world and I doubt will in the end produce much mischief in every country of Europe. I trust England will keep clear, but I fear she will not entirely escape . . .'[13]

While Sir Charles Blagden paid his respects to the many scientists and philosophers resident in this haven of safety, the indefatigable Palmerston was soon hounding his family through the delights of the Swiss scenery, noting in his journal:

August 27th. 'The inns at Chamonix are much improved in consequence of the numbers of travellers who visit these glaciers. We were at the Hotel de Londres, which is very tolerable. For a particular description of these scenes, look into the books of M. de Saussure and M. Bourrit, the first called *Voyage des Alpes*, the other *Description*.

August 28th. 'The ladies who had ascended the Montenvers did not, however, think it prudent to attempt the Col de Balme and, therefore, set out to return to Geneva and I proceeded with mules to pass the Col de Balme into the valley . . .

August 31st. 'At Lausanne. Visited Mr Gibbon, etc. Spent the evening at the Duchess of Devonshire's at Ouchy . . .

September 1st. 'Embarked on the lake in a very good boat, built in the English manner with four men, for which we paid 1 Louis [£1] for the whole day . . .'[14]

Lady Palmerston was more interested in personalities than mountain peaks. Her journal–letters noted:

September 7th – Lausanne. 'We dined at home and went after dinner for an hour to Mr Gibbon, who is in extreme good spirits, but is a good deal altered. We walked on his terrace, from which you have a most delightful view of the Savoy mountains, which are uncommonly fine, and the lake here, being nine miles broad, has a very magnificent appearance. We went down afterwards to Ouchy, a place on the lake about a mile from Lausanne, where the Duchess [of Devonshire], Lady Spencer, Lady Duncannon and Lady E. Foster are living in two houses. They are always at home from 8 o'clock . . .

The Duchess, who has taken extremely to mineralogy, was delighted to see Sir Charles . . .

The Duchess is grown ten years younger, but Lady Spencer seems unhappy and as if she wished to get away from herself. We stayed till 10, and spent an extreme pleasant evening ...

September 10th. 'I do not believe the Duke of Devonshire will come. The idea of some political arrangements may be a reason for detaining him, but he wants but little more excuse than the trouble of setting off. I believe I mentioned they mean to pass the winter at Pisa ...

September 11th. 'Beckford of Fonthill is at Avigoz [Avalligoz?], a small town opposite on the Savoy side. He has a public day once a week where everybody is welcome. He has tents pitched and, I believe, keeps half a dozen cooks and lives *en prince*, but he cannot get any good society. He sends six coaches and six for his company and, in short, his fêtes are like Arabian sales. He has been prevented giving so many fine things by the baillies, who thought the people would be spoilt by such extreme dissipation ...'[15]

On September 15 the party left Switzerland for Italy:

'Set out from Lausanne for Turin, with voituriers engaged from that place. Seventeen horses, seven men and all the expenses of the inns and the passage of the mountain to be defrayed for 85 Louis, [about £85]',[16] Palmerston duly noted.

On the way they called on the old friend who had been Palmerston's travelling companion twenty years earlier, the Swiss physicist who had been the first man to climb Mont Blanc in 1787. He greatly impressed Lady Palmerston:

September 16th. 'We dined today at M. Saussure at Carouge [in fact his house was nearby, at Conches], a very pretty place on the banks of the Arve, a fine rapid bad-coloured water, which, perhaps, appears worse being so near the Rhone. I had a great curiosity to see a man who had enterprise enough to ascend Mount Blanc and genius sufficient to give so elegant and so interesting description of his journey. He is an old friend of Lord P. Madame Saussure is a very well bred woman, but he is quite delightful. He has that sort of piercing eye that Anstey had formerly, but he is perfectly unaffected and unassuming in his manner. You would not conceive he had ever climbed up a mole hill or wrote a line in his life, but you would readily conceive he was equal to all he had achieved . . .'[17]

The passage of the Mont Cenis started inauspiciously:

September 17th. 'To Montmélian, 9 miles, along a broad rich valley, with the hills of Dauphiné on the right. This valley opens at Montmélian into the broader one of the Isère. The Fort of Montmélian is out of the town on a rocky hill. It has been formerly considered as a place of strength, but is no longer so. There is, however, a small garrison there in the present moment, when they are useful at least to watch Fort Barraux, where the French have a strong garrison and a camp which occasions some alarm. However, the people at Montmélian say they are sickly and do not seem to apprehend any attack,'[18] Lord Palmerston noted.

His wife was completely unperturbed:

September 18th. 'As we were on the mountains we met a great many Piedmontese soldiers, cavalry going to protect Savoy. They had all the appearance of bandits. We also met a number of mules loaded with merchandise and heavily laden indeed. It had altogether a very singular appearance and I think the whole journey from Geneva infinitely interesting, replete with wonderful natural scenes such as it's impossible to describe or conceive, and so much beyond my expectations I should have been excessively sorry not to have seen them. But with regard to the difficulty or to the height of the pass of the mountains, I own I was much disappointed . . . It's as easy as going from London to Sheen . . .'[19]

Far off to the north the cannonade of Valmy thundered on the 20th and, as the Palmerstons crossed the pass, the French armies in the south invaded Savoy. Palmerston was fortunate to have no worries beyond fractious voituriers:

September 19th. 'Lanslbourg is a small place with two or three inns, entirely maintained by the passage of Mount Cenis, which begins from hence. The whole of the road we have come is made with great care and expense and is as good as the nature of it will admit. The inns, in general, are not so good as they might be considering the constant business they have and must have. However, to people in health and in tolerable weather, there is nothing worth complaining of . . .

September 20th. 'The noise and confusion, in appearance at least, made by the men who are employed in carrying the party over the mountain, is not to be conceived. They are all, however, under the management of a decent man called the syndic, who finally arranges things with less damage than could be expected. Having made our agreement to have all our expenses defrayed, we have little to do but to take the best care we can of ourselves and things. The bodies of the carriages as well as all the baggage were conveyed by mules. The carriages, when the baggages and bodies were taken off, went upon their wheels, drawn by mules, over the whole mountain, which though from the roughness of the way was not a good thing for them, yet I believe is better than having them carried, as in that case they must be taken completely to pieces.

'The females and the children were all carried in chairs and they have lately got covered ones, which cost more than the common ones and must be paid for extra. The ascent from Lanslbourg is very easy and good and it took me, on a very dull mule, just an hour and twenty minutes to the Ramasse, which is the summit of the ascent . . .

'The actual passage up and down and over the hill took about $4\frac{1}{2}$ hours, exclusive of stopping to dine. When we arrived at Novalese we found our things and carriages got there before us and in about two hours everything was put to rights; our baggage visited for form's sake; the Custom House officers properly fed and ourselves fairly set off for Susa, where we got in very good time. The clamour and importunity of the Lanslbourg people is insupportable. It is proper to give them something as a gratuity, but it is impossible to make them in any degree contented . . .

September 21st. 'As soon as we arrived at Turin we found that the alarm respecting Savoy was revived and accounts were soon received that the French from the camp of Barraux had marched into the country and made themselves masters of it, without resistance. The attack was made the day after we arrived at Turin and five days after we passed Montmélian.

Notwithstanding the length of time that the French have been
threatening Savoy, it seems that no effectual measures whatever
have been taken to secure it. There were a considerable number
of troops in that country, but being dispersed all over it in
various cantonments and destitute of artillery, they were totally
incapable of stopping a large force collected in a point and
supported by a numerous train ... There is great want of
ability in the government of Turin. The King has no able
ministers and is very busy himself with the best dispositions
possible, but very little talents. There has been no attention to
economy for some years past and after so long a period of
peace, the country has neither money nor credit, nor any
military officers fit for service. They are in great apprehensions
for Nice, which they expect to hear is attacked. There is a force
there which is just insufficient to defend it. A body of Austrian
troops have been [expected] to come into Piedmont from the
Milanese, but for some reason or other, probably the expense,
they are not yet come. It is now said they are to march
immediately.'[20]

They stayed for a week in Turin. 'The music of the opera is
exceedingly good and the first woman has a sweet voice, but
the dancing is in the style of Sadlers Wells – they prove their
agility but not their grace ...'[21] Lady Palmerston wrote on
the 22nd.

Transport arrangements for the next part of their journey
were made with the proprietor of the Hotel d'Angleterre,
where they were staying. Lord Palmerston noted:

September 28th. 'Set out for Genoa with Carletti's horses. To
pay 9 Louis each pair to carry us to Genoa, to wait there four
days and to carry us about while there and then to convey us
to Milan, and to bear all our expenses on the road, but not at
Genoa, at the rate of $3\frac{1}{2}$ Louis more per day ...

September 30th. 'To Novi, passed the Tanaro just by
Alessandria, over a temporary bridge of boats, prepared for
the Austrian troops, who are marching into Piedmont to the
number, as is said, of about 8,000 men. Met the first division
of them a little way from the river, amounting to about
2,000 ...'[22]

After a week at Genoa, where they lodged at the Grand Cerf – 'a good inn, with the landlord civil and reasonable', they left for Parma, where Lady Palmerston was not impressed with the opera, but her letters over the next two months gave a colourful description of their experiences, the social chatter interspersed with a wifely sigh at the predestined round of art galleries:

October 15th. 'We found the house a very good one, but the performance very bad and all being a little tired we fell asleep by turns. I find the present Duke as a good sort of man, but he never resides in Parma and the Duchess, who is sister to the Queen of France, is a very odd character. She hunts and shoots and they never live together, inhabiting a country house at some distance from each other, but they visit. She gives a concert this evening, to which he is going to attend . . .

October 16th. 'The want of any person who can clean a picture is much felt in Italy and it's really melancholy to see so many fine pictures suffering from dirt and want of straining, the canvas hanging all in bags . . .

October 18th. 'We intended stopping at Reggio, but when we got there the carriages were surrounded by people that we did not like to get out, it was so very disagreeable. It's very extraordinary that in all the Italian towns the people crowd round you as they would the King in a country town in England. They must see such a number of travellers that one would think they were no sight, but it's really quite a nuisance and the people stink so excessively that it's quite a misfortune to have them near you, and the beggars are without end . . .

October 20th – Bologna. 'We occupied ourselves this morning in visiting some fine churches and palaces and seeing many beautiful pictures, but I will not detail them as nothing is more tiresome . . . A very good box at the Opera . . . and it is a particular comfort as the Bante is now singing and the House is amazingly full and a box not to be obtained. The theatre is a very fine one and as the *nobile* have light in their boxes it makes it look very gay, which is the first theatre I have seen which has the least appearance of gaiety. It was excessively full and the applause is quite wonderful. The instant she appeared the house re-echoed with *eccola*, and the shouts were more like one's idea of the noise of savages in their war dances than the effusion of applause. She is indeed a very fine singer; a good figure, pretty, and an extreme good actress, but the connoisseurs say she is not touching and I am sorry to learn that she takes a glass of brandy always before she begins to make her appearance on the stage. We saw a great many handsome women and all over diamonds . . .

November 30th – Rome. 'This evening we went to the Cardinal de Bernis, where there were the Mesdames of France. They seem perfectly good humoured and one admires their cheerfulness under such a pressure of calamity. The Cardinal, before the late months, was in possession of £24,000 a year; he entertained magnificently, but he is now reduced to less than £2,000. He seems elegant and the manners of that sort of man he is who has lived in the first world, a favourite of our sex as well as the manager of yours. We went from thence to the Duchess of Ancaster, who is always at home of an evening . . .'

[The Palmerstons were employing as cicerone Colin Morison, the Jacobite refugee and art dealer, whom Palmerston had met thirty years earlier with Gavin Hamilton: 'His rule is 50 sequins for one or 30 each for two, he only reckoned Lady P. and me to be paid for', noted Palmerston in his diary.]

December 6th. 'We went this morning to the museum at the Vatican. The cold was excessive, but the magnificence of the collection exceeds everything one can form an idea of. The famous Apollo, the Laocoön breathe a spirit one could scarcely believe marble could convey. The present Pope has increased the collection to an immense extent and is still adding rooms to receive additional marbles. The fine porphyry vases and baths prove to what an extreme of magnificence the Roman had arrived at. The Pope has paid for the re-polishing of one bath, lately, £3,000. I find there is a lottery every year in Rome and the sum which is produced by that plan the Pope appropriates to his improvements and to the purchase of marbles . . .

'The air was quite like a warm bath when we came out of the museum. I never felt cold equal to what I felt this morning . . .

December 23rd. 'As soon as we quitted the Pope's territory

and entered the Kingdom of Naples, we found great difference
in the horses who, from being quite tearing became so weak
that at the first hill they stood stock still. Between Fondi and
Itri we were immovable, and we were obliged to take the
children's horses to our coach to drag us up a very inconsiderable hill. The rain came on most violent, attended by a storm
of thunder and lightning, and when we got to Itri we ordered
fresh horses to go for the children, who were only two miles
from the post, but they provokingly sent those which had
brought us, a circumstance we did not find out till after waiting
two hours. We then ordered fresh horses and in an hour and a
half after poor Fanny and Elizabeth arrived . . .

January 10th. 'Lady Plymouth had been for a few nights at
Caserta to see the Queen, with whom she is quite charmed. I
believe I have mentioned how much I delight in Lady Plymouth.
She is so good humoured, unaffected and pleasant. The Neapolitan men are extremely like the English and imitate their
dress precisely and now ride on horseback and disregard dress
coats just as our young men. The women are pretty, but have
no education and a very pretty woman in describing her way
of life to Lady Plymouth seemed to mention her taking rest in
the middle of the day and rising late as a good way of passing
away the time. "Do you never read?" asked Lady Plymouth;
"No," said the Neapolitan Princess, "I have asked my husband
these two years for a book, and he never will let me have one."

January 12th. 'The King had not had any Court at Caserta;
only a few men went. They are soon to return to Naples to
receive the English, who are arrived since the Court left
Naples. The King's attachment to field sports induces him, at
this season, to live a great deal at Caserta. We had two new
dances, but the Italian style of dancing is to me very bad . . .'

★ ★ ★

Palmerston had renewed his friendship with Sir William
Hamilton, by this time well into his third decade as the British
Minister at the Neapolitan Court. With Paris denied to the
beau monde, Naples was becoming the social capital of Europe.
Lady Palmerston's account of the routs, balls, entertainments

and hunts became increasingly interlaced with a discerning picture of the English Minister's second wife:

January 16th. 'I went first to Lady Douglas, who is always at home of a Wednesday, for all the English and Neapolitans who like to go. We went from thence to Lady Cholmondeley, who gave a ball on her son's birthday, Lord Malpas, who is just one year complete. It was a very pleasant meeting. I there was presented to Lady Hamilton, *pour la première fois.* I find her not so beautiful as I expected, but certainly extremely handsome and her figure uncommonly fine. She was well dressed and there is something in her manner very good humoured and a great desire of pleasing. Sir William looks extremely ill and it puts one a good deal in mind of January and June, for I think she is beyond May. Her voice is vulgar and she and Sir W. are rather too fond, but upon the whole I think her a very extraordinary woman ... It's an odd thing, but there are hardly any of the Neapolitans who open their houses, but the English seem to do the honour of Naples to the Neapolitans ...

January 17th. 'We dined at three o'clock today at Sir William Hamilton's. We sat down 53 and he had received 20 excuses. Conceive that they are 73 strange English at Naples at present, and a hundred more expected from Rome. Sir William has a most elegant apartment, two stories, for in Italy it's generally the way to have an apartment of one floor, but few have the whole house, and the staircases are all open. Sir William has fitted up his upper apartment lately, which has cost him near £2,000. The view from his windows is beautiful ...

'Lady Hamilton looked extremely handsome and really does the honours uncommonly well. She is extremely obliging, without the least appearance of feeling any elevation from the change in her situation. Sir William perfectly idolises her and I do not wonder he is proud of so magnificent a marble, belonging so entirely to himself. We stayed till about 8 ...

January 27th. 'We set off at ten for Caserta ...

'We returned to Sir William, but as they dined at 2, we had no time to see the palace and English garden, therefore left it for another time. Prince Clary and Esterhazy, the Imperial Minister, dined there. In the evening Lady Hamilton sang, accompanied by four musicians, who live in the house, and Paisiello came from the Queen, who luckily did not wish for music that night. He is always with the Court. He sang his own music, which to please me is the best I hear. His countenance is extremely animated and sensible and we had three hours entertainment. Lady Hamilton looked particularly beautiful and her desire to please and her extreme civility is very uncommon. Mrs Cadogan, her mother, looks like a lady you have more often found useful than I could have ever done . . .

February 7th. 'We learn that the sad news relative to the King of France. Surely of such a premeditated murder history has no example of. I cannot say how much this event is felt by all except the murderers themselves. Esterhazey, the Imperial minister, was to have given a fine ball tonight – of course it is put off and he is gone to Caserta . . .'

February 24th. 'We were invited to attend the King's Hunt at Cardetello, about 15 miles from Naples and about 9 from Caserta . . . We arrived at half past ten, which was precisely the right moment. The King received us upstairs in a small room, where there was a very handsome breakfast prepared. The Princess Doria, Lady H[amilton] and ourselves were the only women. There were no English but our party. There were about 12 young men of high fashion who were in the King's hunting uniform, which is extremely handsome – green and gold and a red cape; a very pretty round hat with a feather; a belt round their waist, with a silver boar and two dogs pursuing. The King received us very kindly. His manner is particularly pleasing. In his person he is something like General Patterson and the Duke of Gloucester. There were some Milanese noblemen and we were altogether about 30. After we had breakfasted, the carriage and horses came to the door. The King and those of his hunt mounted their horses and with spears in their hands pranced away. We got into open carriages, which were prepared for us. Our horses were little wild Neapolitans, which I thought would run all ways but the right. We proceeded on about a mile, when we came into an open plain. At some distance from where we were placed was a wood in which were the game. The boars had been previously fed to the sound

of a horn. The King and the hunters took different stations so
that while men were in the wood driving out the game, the
hunters stood on the outside, where the dogs were held – to be
let loose upon the unhappy animals when they issued from
their retreat, and when they were fairly off the hunters pursued
and not till the dogs had brought them down did these valiant
Nimrods attempt to lance their victim. I had the good fortune
not to be obliged to see any of the striking part, as the boars
and the roebucks all took from our carriage and I of course
turned my head away from a sight which could afford me only
pain. To see the course and the riding was very pretty. At
3 o'clock we proceeded to the house which had been all the
time in view . . . we sat down to a very superb dinner, and
were waited upon by soldiers. We had only one course, which
made it so much pleasanter as the dinner was over earlier. After
coffee the King took us to the top of the house, from whence
there is a most extensive view. He then carried us all over his
farm, showed us his dairy and his stables and, in short, was what
few Princes are, desirous you should be quite at your ease, and
doing himself the honours with the civility and good humour
and elegance of a man of true fashion and politeness. I never
passed a pleasanter day and he desired we would promise to
dine with him again at his Belvedere – another house near
Caserta . . .'

Three days later Lady Palmerston was presented at the
Caserta palace to the Queen, who was Marie Antoinette's
sister:

'We ascended a small staircase and entered a dull looking
room, hung with a red paper, out of which a door led to the
Queen's bedchamber, and from whence, in about ten minutes
(for when we arrived she had a Neapolitan lady with her) she
came in. She was very little dressed, of course in mourning.
Sir William presented us, and after some compliments to each
she begged we would be seated and then entered into discourse
on a variety of subjects with exquisite elegance and cleverness
and proved she is extremely well informed and very sensible.
Her figure is small and she has been handsome, but there is an
appearance of sorrow marked upon her countenance beyond

what you often meet with and she looks more worn by grief
than age. She paid the English many flattering compliments
and, indeed, nothing could be more polite and pleasing than
her reception and manner. After we had stayed a full hour, she
took her leave; her eldest son came in. He is a fine looking
youth, about 15. He is married to a sister of the Emperor, who
is 13, but she is not to come for two years, when great fêtes
will be exhibited at Naples . . . We returned to Sir William's
and had tea and music. I like Lady H. too well not to wish that
she had never learned to sing, for certainly her talents do not
lie that way. Her voice is powerful but perfectly without
harmony and I am sure she has no ear. She is, however, a very
extraordinary character, and by her conduct proves how much
she merits her great reverse of fortune. Sir William went to the
King, as is his constant custom, to play at billiards, and he
promised to settle when we were to pass a day with him at the
Belvedere. He returned soon with the King's desire of seeing
us tomorrow . . . and though we did not get home till very
late for Naples, we are to set out tomorrow by half past eight.'

Her account of their excursion the next day gave at least a
contrasting picture of a King whom no historian has failed to
execrate:

February 28th. 'The King received us in the house and carried
us into a saloon, where we reposed a short time and then he set
off, after showing us the house, which is a most elegant villa,
fitted up with infinite taste, to view the manufactory which he
has established about six years. I really feel quite unequal to
describe the scenes which I passed through today. All that I
have ever read in romances of a golden age is here exemplified.
The King has established a school where all the children are
taught to read and instructed in religion. We saw them first
and then proceeded to the different branches of the manufactory, from the winding of the silk from the bags of the silk
worm to the weaving into different species for garments. At
proper ages those who deserve the King's favour are married
to those who may prove the choice of some of the manufacturers. He then settles them in a house (and all the houses are
precisely the same) of four windows in front; two stories high;

completely furnished and in a style of superior neatness, and the man and woman and children, when they have any, all work together. In short, there is a propriety and a comfort in every habitation superior to anything I ever saw and he walks into all their houses, talks to them with the familiarity of a friend, takes the kindest notice of their children, who all come round him without the least timidity and seem to look upon him only as their father. There was one scene I cannot omit telling you of. In going into one of their houses, the King said to Miss Carter: "You may speak French to this woman for she is a French woman," upon which the poor woman burst into tears and said: "Oh, Sir, I wish you could forget I ever belonged to that unhappy country," and the King, who mentioned her being French out of good humour, immediately took her by the hand, assured her he would always be her friend and told her he would send for her mother, who is now in France, and on whose account the poor woman was very uneasy. It affected us all, for it was quite nature. We visited one woman who had only been brought to bed four hours and as she expressed being disappointed at not seeing the King, we all visited her. We found her in the same kind of neat apartment; the child with a silver cap with an artificial flower placed on the side and laced up, as the custom of the country is, in a pink and silver bag (for I do not know what to call it). All the relations were there and the woman appeared much fatigued and ill, but it's the fashion to have the room full of company the instant you have produced an infant or an infanta. We dined at 3 and had an excellent dinner; the view from the Belvedere is beautiful . . . After coffee we walked in the gardens which are cut out of the side of a hill and you ascend from one to another by steps . . . oranges, citrons and lemons . . . wild violets perfumed the air . . . After seeing everything, about 6 we took our departure, after passing one of the most agreeable days possible and seeing a King really making the happiness of his subjects, and his subjects adoring him . . .

March 20th. 'Lady H. is to me very surprising, for considering the situation she was in she behaves wonderfully well. Now and then to be sure a little vulgarness pops out, but I think it's more

Sir William's fault, who loves a good joke and leads her to enter into his stories, which are not of the best kind. She is vastly desirous to please and is very civil and good humoured to all her friends and her attention to Sir William is infinitely amiable . . .'[23]

The Palmerstons also saw frequently General Sir John Acton, the son of an expatriate British physician who had become Prime Minister of Naples. On March 21 he rendered one service to Palmerston's art interests:

'Sir John Acton, Bart., presents his compliments to Lord Palmerston, and in compliance to the desire mentioned in his note of yesterday, has taken the orders of His Sicilian Majesty for the several volumes of Herculean Antiquities following the three which were formerly delivered to his Lordship. Proper directions have been given in consequence to the royal printing office, to present My Lord Palmerston with the several volumes published since the three first. Sir John is glad of this opportunity of doing in obedience to His Majesty's orders, a thing agreeable to Lord Palmerston.'[24]

Ten days later Lady Palmerston was describing a visit to his palace:

March 31st. 'We saw in the first part of the morning General Acton's palace and a most magnificent one it is. It's fitted up with every kind of elegance and comfort, and the best things of France and England are here to be found. I never saw any house so complete and there is not one room in which you could not sit down and feel at home. There is a charming garden and a terrace at the top of the house which extends a great way and which commands a most beautiful view . . .'

She and her husband had also decided to make an excursion in the Bay:

April 3rd. 'At nine o'clock Mr Poore, Miss Carter, Lord P., myself and an Italian architect who had resided some time at Capri, embarked in a felucca rowed by eight men. The weather remarkable pleasant, but there was a great swell, but it did not affect me in the least.'[25]

Even the beauties of Capri barely jolted Lord Palmerston out of the solemn fact-finding tone of most of his diary entries, but as the island was little visited at the time, his comments are of some interest:

April 4th. 'We embarked . . . and followed the coast till we came within a mile of the point of Campanella, and then, finding the weather much improved and the opportunity favourable, we set our sail and stretched over for the island, where we arrived in a very short time and had a very pleasant passage.

'The landing place is on an open beach about the middle of the island on the north side, where there are a few houses. This place is called the Marina of Capri. The town of Capri lies behind it about half a mile inland . . . We had letters from the Bishop of Capri to a person there who would have provided us with lodging in the Bishop's House. We had likewise a letter from M. Hadrava (a person at Naples who is carrying on excavations at Capri in search of antiquities) to the governor of the island, who resides there and has a house where he can receive strangers with convenience . . . We found him and his wife very civil and obliging and their house very pleasantly situated, of which they gave us full possession, with every mark of kindness and goodwill . . .

April 5th. 'The industry and exertion that must have been used in order to destroy all the monuments of antiquity in this island are really wonderful . . .

'In the afternoon we went again on the southern shore rather inclining to the east, where from a point called Tragera there is a very fine view of the bold cliffs below us and particularly of two detached rocks called Monaco and Monacone, which rise out of the sea. These are the great breeding places of a species of bird of the hawk tribe, which destroy the partridges and for the destruction of whose eggs the King, who preserves the breed of partridges with great care, pays two Carlines, or ninepence a piece, and the demand, we were told, amounts to some thousands . . .

'We then visited the Chartreuse convent, which is close on the southern shore . . . Between this and the steep rocks of the western end of the island there is a deep valley, which runs down to the sea and is the only landing place on the southern side. This is called Malo. This is the most favourable place for shooting or catching quails, which come over here in immense numbers in April, in their passage from the African shore. They are reckoned better and more plentiful here than in any other part of the coast and the King generally comes here in April to shoot them and in the autumn to shoot partridges . . .

April 6th. 'In the afternoon the weather proved fine and we set out for the upper country, or Anacapri. The steps to which we soon came are cut in a zigzag manner in the rock, where it is lowest near the sea on the northern side. There are about 520 – most of them high and ill-kept. At the top of these steps we found ourselves upon the level of the upper country and town of Anacapri, fertile and extensive compared with the small extent of the island . . .

April 7th. 'We took our leaves of the Governor, Don Diversi, and his wife, who are very worthy well behaved people. He has a very good house, remarkably pleasantly situated, commanding a full view of the sea towards Naples, with a terrace and garden. He has ten children and the salary of his place is 25 ducats per month – about fifty guineas, English per annum. We were very happy to find there was no difficulty made about receiving a small present, given to the eldest boy, at our departure. Before we embarked, we went to the sea shore on the northern side, just under the hills we had ascended the night before, to visit some remains of old buildings, which appear to have been sea baths, and where there may probably have been a palace. M. Hadrava has lately dug here and found some columns and fine capitals and a large quantity of fine marbles. The most curious thing was a large broad staircase leading down towards the sea – entirely marble – both the steps and the sides, with a vaulted roof ornamented with stuccos. In the middle was a spacious landing place, on which was a beautiful pavement of marble, which has been taken up and brought to Naples, as well as the other things of value found in the islands . . .

April 13th – Ischia. 'We likewise observed large tracts of sea enclosed with strong nets, waiting for the passage of the tunny fish. These nets, which are very large and strong, are something of the nature of a decoy. They are of great extent and the fish who once enter them are led on from one division to another, till they come to an inner one, where they are taken, which, from their great size and strength and indeed numbers, is sometimes a difficult job. Much time is required to prepare these nets and we saw some laying down in the Bay of Baco in February, though the fish are not expected till May. They are so placed as to be fixed with strong cables to the shore and are constantly watched by men in boats, which are moored by them . . .'[26]

Lady Palmerston took up the account of their activities on their return to Naples:

April 21st. 'I called on Lady Hamilton, who had just received the present Sir William has made her of all his diamonds on her leaving off playing at rouge et noir. Her pleasure proved she was worthy of the present and I never saw a gift better disposed. She went with us to some shops. Nothing can exceed Lady H.'s good humour and I must always think her a very extraordinary character . . .

April 24th. 'We have at length determined to leave Naples tomorrow. I must own I never lived in any town which possessed so many charms as Naples and I shall never think of it without pleasure . . .

April 30th – Rome. 'I am quite well today and set off upon my Roman education. We called first on Mr Hamilton who has got a beautiful Cupid stringing his bow and a female figure, a small whole length which he has lately found at Gabia, and a bust of Otho – the only one of the size of that Emperor yet discovered . . .

May 8th. 'We have got very fine weather and Rome is delightful. We live quite a country life; dine at two and go out at four o clock for the evening, which would be charming if you were with me . . . Lord P. thinks he should reach England (if he went this year) not till October and he would have the whole winter to pass through, which might destroy all the advantage he gained by the last. It's some disappointment to me not seeing my mother and the Culs, but I had determined to stay wherever you were and if you do not return to England

I do flatter myself that you will not object to coming to us, for I shall break my heart if I do not see you ere long. We propose going from hence in three weeks and then going to Milan and Venice, from thence into Switzerland, and returning into Italy by the end of September. Pray tell me you will meet me somewhere, I beseech you . . .

May 16th. 'We paid a visit this morning to Angelica [Kauffmann], who is in her manner particularly elegant, and we have agreed that Elizabeth should sit to her . . .

May 17th. 'Elizabeth took her first sitting at Angelica's. I think it will be very like her, and if so you shall have a copy in miniature. We went afterwards to see Mr Greve's [?] collection of pictures, which are very fine. He has laid out an immense sum and as there are very few purchasers at present, he is, I believe, very much distressed. He has bought a most amazing fine collection of Guercino's, but he asks £1,000 for one, but I believe he would take half, but that is not a sum to be had every day . . .

May 23rd. 'In the evening I had letters from Lady M[almesbury] and Lady Stawell but none from you, and one from Lord Malmesbury. They all speak of the real pleasure your appointment will give them . . .'

[Family influence had been brought to bear through Lord Malmesbury and others, and Benjamin Mee had received an appointment as one of the commissaries to the Duke of York's expeditionary force to the Low Countries.]

May 26th. 'We dined at the Websters and went together to the Borghese Villa. We met there the Duchess of D[evonshire] and in the evening went to see Lady Bes[sborough] who makes my heart ache she looks and is so ill. She coughs and spits blood again. She was quite free from either complaint at Naples, but the travelling has brought it on. She is so excessively interesting that one cannot bear to see her in so precarious a state. They will, I fancy, pass the winter at Naples. The Duchess is as enchanting as ever. We looked over drawings of their doings. Lady Elizabeth draws in a most capital style. The Duchess certainly returns to England this summer. The Duke has written a most affectionate letter to desire her to return. Not to adore her seems an odd thing to any person who lives with her . . .

June 18th. 'In the afternoon we set off, passed the Po in a boat and had a very pleasant drive, though extremely dusty, to Milan, where we found Sir Charles Blagden just arrived with Sir Benjamin Thompson, now Count Rumford . . .'[27]

This was the first appearance of the remarkable figure who was to become one of the Palmerstons' most intimate friends. An American Loyalist, Benjamin Thompson had been sent to London with despatches when British troops evacuated Boston during the early stages of the American Revolutionary War. He was appointed as an Under-Secretary of State under Lord George Germaine, but when Lord North's administration resigned, Thompson retired with the rank and half-pay of a lieutenant-colonel. He offered his services to the Austrian army to campaign against the Turks and was introduced to Prince Maximilian, afterwards Elector of Bavaria, whose man of confidence he became. His services included not only sweeping reforms in the Bavarian army and civil administration, but laying out the Englischer Garten in Munich. Knighted by George III in 1783, Thompson was created a Count of the Holy Roman Empire at the request of the Elector in 1791, choosing the title of Rumford from the name of the American township to which his wife's family belonged. Scientist and philanthropist as well as administrator, Rumford was a notable figure of his times and became a devoted admirer of Lady Palmerston, who commented favourably on him in her next letters to her brother:

June 23rd. 'Sir B. seems a great acquisition to our Society . . .

June 28th. 'We had been to the General Hospital . . . All women are received who wish to lie in privately – not married, and they are received without any name being given. Nurses are provided to take care of the children. There are different apartments for different classes of people. There are apartments for people of fashion, to which there is a private door of entrance, a private way to chapel and no-one ever sees them, not even the superintendent of the establishment. They may send in their own furniture if they do not think that which is in the apartment is good enough, and their own servants may attend them. They bring a letter saying who they are, which is placed in the hand of the director or some confidential person, who opens it in case they should die that their friends may be informed of it, but if they recover, it's returned, unsealed, on their departure ...

'This morning Comte de Rumford, Lord P., Miss C and I set off at nine and had a pleasant drive to Como ... After we had dined we took a boat and rowed to the opposite shore. We visited a Dutch gentleman, an acquaintance of the Comte de Rumford, who went with us to the house Prince Augustus had taken and which we had some thoughts of hiring for two months ...

'Comte Rumford is particularly agreeable and a wonderful pleasant addition to our Society. He draws well, takes sketches as we are on the lake and has a thousand resources. His history is a very extraordinary one and not the least surprising part that as a stranger he should have governed the Electorate of Bavaria for five years, reformed numberless abuses in the state and put the army on a most respectable footing, founded manufactories and almost new modelled the system of government, with the whole kingdom against him and no-one to support him but the Elector, who stood by him with the strictest sincerity and gave him the most unbounded confidence ...

July 7th. 'Lord P. has given up all thoughts of taking a place and, upon his return to Milan, we found a letter from Lady M. Blair, with a whole account of her passage over St Gotthard, which appears so easy that Lord P. has concluded to set off from Milan on Tuesday and go again to Como, see the lake completely, then proceed to the Lago Maggiore and so on to the St Gotthard, taking the children with us, settling them at Berne and making our rambles from thence. This plan quite suits me as I long to see Switzerland and I think it is quite a pity to waste our time which we could so well employ this summer by a ramble into that lovely country. We shall leave our carriage on this side of the Alps – take those of the country and as little baggage as possible. I am quite sorry that Comte de Rumford will not go with us, but means to return to Verona for a fortnight and then go to Como. He is a Serving Man and those are never to be depended upon . . .

July 18th – Bellinzona. 'At seven o'clock we set forth as viz: Lord P., Harry, Monsieur Gaetano [Harry's Italian tutor], three men servants and Miss Carter's maid on horseback. Miss Carter in one *portantine* (which is a sedan chair with a horse before and another behind, playing the part of chairmen); three men attended each litter, or *portantine*; 8 baggage horses and William and Fanny in a box each, fastened on each side a horse like chickens going to market, with a tilt over and covered with a fine pink stuff to keep the sun from them; myself in another litter, Games with Elizabeth in a third and Mercier in a fourth. I assure you our cavalcade had a very good effect. Our mode of travelling is to pass three hours in the morning and three hours in the evening, for it's not possible to go out of a foot's pace . . .'[28]

July 19th. 'We dined at a very neat small inn at Ossogno; everything so clean and our cook a Capuchin friar. Near the house is a beautiful cascade. Our dinner consisted of fish, eggs, custard, stewed prunes and pears . . .' Lord Palmerston noted in his journal.[29]

For him this was familiar ground, and from time to time he drew his wife's attention to spots he had visited during his previous journey twenty years earlier, where William Pars had made sketches of the views.

July 20th. 'We set out about 8. I walked upon the bridge [at Giornico] as Lord P. has a view taken from thence. We passed through some little town where they have carried their vines quite across the road that you go quite under shade. We ascended considerably and came to a fine alpine scene. The Ticino tumbling over great masses of rock, we passed over a stone bridge, from which Lord P. had a view taken by Pars of this spot which quite answers all my ideas of romantic scenery . . .'[30]

Switzerland always seemed to excite Palmerston to a greater variety of comment than his normally bald descriptions of places visited, and this occasion proved no exception:

July 21st – Dacio. 'Arrived at the Capuchins, which is a large

building placed nearly about the highest part of the passage in
an open place, perfectly barren and desolate, but where there
is no danger of any snow falling from the tops of the mountains
upon it. It is a kind of great inn, with a small chapel and it is
inhabited by a couple of capuchins, besides other attendants,
whose employment is to assist passengers and supply them with
refreshments. Those who are able, make them always handsome presents and those who are in want are furnished with
what is necessary gratis ...

August 1st. 'Set out for Herisau, a very neat flourishing manufacturing town, or rather village, in the Protestant part of
Appenzell ... Here we left our carriage with orders to go to
St Gall and took horses for ourselves and our baggage to proceed to Appenzell, there being no carriage road to that place
from Herisau, nor indeed from any other place ...

'The road bad, even for horses, but the scenes through which
it passes beautiful in the highest degree, realising all the pastoral
descriptions of poetry and romance. The country is thickly
sprinkled over with habitations, but the appearance of the
people by no means corresponds with the beauty of the objects
around them. The Protestant district in which Herisau is placed,
is full of industry and manufacture, but the Catholic part, of
which Appenzell is the principal place, is destitute of both and
the inhabitants look wretched and are all beggars, as a matter of
course, to every passenger that passes ...

'The people have no employment but the management of
their dairies and their cattle, and are very poor and idle, spending their time and all the money they can get at public houses,
of which, to my great surprise, I was informed there are forty
in a place consisting of less than three hundred houses, and
rarely visited by travellers. The effect of the latter circumstance
shows itself in a strong curiosity to examine strangers and in a
certain frankness and simplicity of manners which is not
unpleasing, except when they are drunk or angry, in either of
which cases they seem very brutal.

'Their houses are much more ornamented with painting on
the outside than any we have yet seen, and their appearance
and customs evidently are different from any we have met with.

K

It was dusk when we entered the place and, passing through the churchyard, we were much struck with two figures in black, with white headdresses and something that looked like red muffs upon their arms, standing in the middle of the graves. They were tall and elegant in appearance and looked like figures in old family pictures. These we found were the near relations of persons lately deceased and it is the custom for them to come in that manner and dress every evening for five weeks, just before the Ave Maria and say a certain number of prayers over the grave, after which they go into the church during the service and burn a certain portion of a large hollow roll of red wax tapers, which was what they had on their arms and which looked like muffs . . .

August 2nd. 'Went up a mountain called Eben Alp, about a league from Appenzell . . . The top of this mountain is covered with coarse herbage, and we found several chalets, or cabins, inhabited by people looking after cows, which are conducted up there to feed for two months in the summer. These chalets exhibited a scene of dirt and poverty that did not agree with the ideas of Rousseau's *Eloise*. The inhabitants of them, how- ever, were simple and cheerful and goodhumoured, and sang the celebrated *Rance des Vaches* in great perfection. It consists of wild simple notes with which they call their cows and resembles in some degree what the keepers in the New Forest make use of when they browse the deer . . .

'We have been much pleased with our excursion into Appenzell, which lies out of the common track of travellers. It is curious to observe how very primitive the manners of these people remain and how effectually the country, beyond Herisau, has been defended against all approaches of luxury. Carriages for conveyance are unknown, the dining hour is eleven or eleven and an half at latest, and at Appenzell and Teuffen, etc., though there are large neat looking houses with gardens, etc. we saw no inhabitant, male or female, whose dress or appearance seemed to put in the smallest claim to gentility, or differ from that of the most ordinary class of people . . .'

[*August 5th.* 'The bridge and town of Schaffhausen have a

very pretty effect. Lord P. has a drawing which is so well
executed that it appeared as if I had seen it before,' noted Lady
Palmerston.]

August 17th. 'The valley of the Grindelwald is very wide and
populous and contains 3,000 inhabitants. We lodged at the
curé's, who is an obliging, intelligent man, has a clean house
and excellent beds, and receives any present it may be thought
proper to make him . . .

August 20th, 21st and 22nd – Berne. 'Visited Professeur Tralles
and M. le Commissaire Manuel, who both dined and supped
with us, as did the Duchess of Devonshire and Lady Elizabeth
Foster. ['They look vastly well and are going very soon to
England', commented Lady Palmerston.] Went to the camp
and drank tea at the Duchess of Bouillon's, who has a house
just by it . . .'[31]

Count Rumford had rejoined them at Berne and on their
arrival at Basle the party was tempted to see an aspect of the
war, by now raging on the Swiss frontiers.

August 24th. 'Stop at Liestal in the Canton of Basle to dine.
Being told that the French, who were within two leagues of
us in the Bishopric of Basle, of which they have possessed themselves, had lately been much in motion and had formed several
camps on the frontiers of the Canton, which, as well as their
camps near Hüningen just beyond Basle, with the Austrian
camps on the other side of the Rhine, might be seen from a
beacon on a hill a little out of the road, called Prattelen, we
resolved to go there. We walked up from the village of that
name, which took us near an hour through very pleasant
scenes . . . The town of Basle lay under us and we could see
at least four camps, French and Austrian, but not so near as we
expected. After returning to our carriages we soon entered a
small district on the Swiss side of the Rhine, called the Fricktal,
belonging to the Emperor. Having been examined with perfect
civility at an advanced post, we proceeded to Rheinfelden . . .

August 25th. 'Having a letter to the Austrian General, Count
Lichtenberg, whose headquarters are about four miles distance,
we sent it by a servant and went to dine at Laufenburg . . .'[32]

'The view of the fall, the town and the castle I know makes a beautiful drawing, for Pars made one from this spot for Lord P.,' added Lady Palmerston, commenting on their arrival in Basle:

August 26th. 'The inn we have got apartments in, Les Trois Rois, is beautifully situated on the Rhine. There is one of the pleasantest rooms, a kind of gallery built over the water, where the table d'hôte is kept at which you may meet Austrian, French and Swiss officers belonging to all the different Cantons, emigrants, English, Danes, etc. The Austrians and French meet continually. The officers are permitted to enter the town with their swords, but the soldiers leave their arms at the gate . . .

'We met two French officers riding. I felt as if I had seen two savages who, if they had an opportunity, would scalp us with pleasure. They never touched their hats, a civility no other gentleman on the Continent ever neglects . . .'[33]

Palmerston duly noted the civilities of the following day:

August 27th. 'Went to the Heights of Haltingen over the bridge of Basle, where we found Count Lichtenberg. He conducted us to his batteries, which command Hüningen and serve to keep the French in some sort of order, as he has constantly fired into the place and done execution there, whenever they have commenced hostilities across the river. They were then at work in great numbers on throwing up some works before Hüningen towards and very near Basle, which must give umbrage to the Swiss who last year by their remonstrances put a stop to a similar attempt. The French are now weak in the part of their frontier and are probably alarmed lest the intention of the Austrians should be to violate the Swiss neutrality and attack them on the side of Basle. The Austrians, however, do not seem to be formidable in numbers, and nothing serious is likely to be attempted by either party. We saw two small camps near the batteries, of Hungarian and Croatian troops, who made a good appearance . . .'[34]

Basle was the furthest point in the Palmerstons' Swiss tour and they retraced their steps in leisurely fashion to Italy while Sir Charles Blagden made his way back to England. Lady Palmerston concentrated on family and social gossip:

September 5th – Fribourg. 'In the town . . . are 2,000 emigrants, among them the Princess de Condé and the Princess Louise de Conti. It's a most melancholy circumstance to see so many people of fortune and fashion reduced to such extreme indigence by the reign of these barbarians . . .

'We had a very fine drive to Berne . . . had the extreme pleasure of finding all the children quite well. They have got a country house consisting of a room and a portico upon a hill, which overlook the town, the river, the bridge, the public walks and on the other side a field, which leads to a kind of common, near which is the camp. Here they breakfast, dine and sup and Harry takes his supper after riding. I never saw them look so well in my life, but they are burnt like gipsies . . .

September 16th. 'We arrived [at Lausanne] in time to visit Lady Cholmondeley and enquired after the poor Duchess [of Ancaster] who I find is as ill as possible . . .

September 18th. 'I took a walk with the children down to Ouchy. The Lake was very rough and extremely fine; we walked round by Cour, where the Duchess of Ancaster lives. Saw Miss Followes, who told me that the Duchess wishes to see us. Poor soul, she is in one of the most dreadful states to be conceived, afflicted by a thousand sad complaints and yet never utters a repining word. Her patience, resignation and good humour is perfectly extraordinary and she is the express image of a saint. I fear there is not a hope of her recovery.'[35] [The Duchess died before the end of the year.]

Passing over the Great St Bernard, Palmerston made his usual careful notes:

September 21st. 'St Pierre is a poor place with a bad inn. It is from here that the actual passage of the mountain begins and is only practicable for mules. We agreed for a sufficient number to convey our party and our baggage quite to Aosta, where the carriage road begins again, and which is called nine leagues, at the rate of 17 French livres for each mule, including the attendants. The two youngest children were carried on men's shoulders in baskets, called hotes, made for the purpose of carrying burdens.

September 22nd. 'Set out about ten, the weather pretty good . . . What wind there was came down upon us in eddies in some particular places and brought drifts of the fresh snow in our faces, enough to make us conceive the dreadful effects of the hurricanes of wind to which those elevated places are exposed and which are sometimes so severe as to obliterate all appearance of a track, while the traveller can hardly see any object by which to shape his course, on account of the quantity of dust or snow with which the atmosphere is loaded. At such moments the inhabitants of the convent are active in giving assistance to any passengers who may be engaged in the upper parts of the mountain, and to do this with effect they make use of a very large fine breed of dogs, whom they carry out with them, who soon discover whether there are any persons near and who, in spite of darkness and the deepest snow, can always find with certainty their accustomed track.

'In about $3\frac{1}{2}$ hours we arrived at the convent, which is at the highest part of the passage. Just before arriving there you mount up a hill of perpetual snow, which lasts through every season. To us it was all alike, everything in this part being covered to a great depth. The buildings of the convent are extensive, the apartments good and some of them quite handsome and convenient. There are generally from 12 to 18 monks resident there, with a large number of attendants, whose chief employment is to assist, entertain and lodge passengers. Their hospitality is at everybody's service, without reward, but from those who are able and willing to give it they receive whatever is offered, which goes to the general funds towards which, likewise, they send out persons to collect in the neighbouring countries. Their expenses must be great, as everything made use of must be brought from below. Their baker lives at 18 miles distance and all the fuel they use, of which the quantity must be very great, is brought to them during the summer months upon mules backs. They take it by turns to receive and entertain strangers. Those whom we saw were polite and obliging. Their church is a much handsomer building than might have been expected in such a situation . . .'[36]

Lady Palmerston had more of an eye for the behaviour of the inhabitants:

September 24th. 'At Verres we made an acquaintance with a

blacksmith, who having finished his day's work was enjoying
the fine evening and a little comfortable repose and conversation after his day's labour. He had a most spirited intelligent
Italian countenance (the way the sudden change the short
journey over the mountains produces is infinitely curious in
climate, persons, manners and intelligence. The Swiss are the
useful cart horse breed, the Italians the elegant race). The man
was surprised we could admire mountains, but he said the
English were for ever changing about. No nation ever loved
travelling like them. I was not much surprised at his being
weary of his enclosure, for certainly to live in a more level
country is to be preferred . . .

September 28th – Milan. 'There is a very pretty buffo opera
performing and a most excellent man, Viganoni, who leaves
Milan on Monday for Venice. Marchese has been singing at
Bergamo during the fair and had a thousand sequins [about
£500]. It's immense what musical performers are paid in Italy
for their performance. The opera very full. The music charming and Viganoni really a most excellent and pleasing singer . . .

September 29th. 'There is an excellent female serious dancer,
who certainly brings her leg out of her pocket. I never yet saw
anybody lift it so high and stand so long upon the other, except
a stork in a garden at Basle . . .

October 4th. 'This being the Emperor's name day, there was
a grand gala at Court. I took all the children; we found the
room extremely commodious; we looked into the place where
we saw all the fine carriages and they are vastly well appointed
with fine liveries, volantes and chasseurs. At two the Archduke
and Duchess entered the salle, which is a most superb room,
followed by the Court, who had paid their *devoirs* previous to
their entering the room. The Archduke handed the Duchess
to her seat. There were two under a canopy, and they set down
to a small table with two covers. They had a magnificent
dinner, served up and a fine dessert. They scarcely eat anything,
to the great surprise of our children who wished to have
assisted them in performing that part of the ceremony, with
less form but with more nature. They kept calling up people
to speak to the whole of the dinner time. The ladies were

infinitely well dressed and the men also, magnificently, and yet with good taste. The music played the whole time. The ceremony took up about an hour, when they rose and departed. The Archduchess was extremely well dressed; the Duke was in a uniform; I could not help turning my thoughts to his poor captive sister [Marie Antoinette].'

At Verona an untoward event halted their progress. 'You will perceive a chasm in my journal', Lady Palmerston wrote on October 28, 'but I have had nothing to tell you to give you pleasure. Since I wrote, Harry has been extremely ill. A fever came on. We gave him James' Powders, and emetic tartar without success. We sent for Doctor Farga, the most eminent physician of Verona. He found it to be a fever of the country; a kind of intermitting [sic] which in the autumn the inhabitants are extremely subject to and particularly after a hot summer. He gave him the bark [quinine] as soon as he possibly could take it. It has agreed with him extremely. He has kept his bed a week; he rose last night. Thank God his fever seems quite conquered and he still takes small quantities of the bark. His appetite is returned and strength is all that is wanting, I trust, to complete his recovery . . .

November 11th – Florence. 'In the evening we visited the Beckfords, who live in Lord Cooper's house, which is a most magnificent palace and for which they only pay £60 a year. Mr Beckford has furnished it. I hear Lady Cooper talks of returning next year to Florence. Miss Beckford is extremely handsome and the son a fine youth . . .

November 19th. 'The Beckfords dined with us. Mr B. is extremely agreeable and gentlemanlike. He puts me a little in mind of Lord St Helens.

November 21st. 'Lord P's cold remains so much the same that I do not think we shall get away very soon. I wish we had been settled at Naples, but Harry's indisposition at Verona put us back three weeks . . .'[37]

On December 10 they left Florence for Rome and Naples, but before they departed Lady Palmerston received a note from her admirer, Count Rumford, who was at Pisa:

'If ever there was a spoilt child I am one, and it is all your fault. I have been so long used to your agreeable company that I really feel quite awkward when I am deprived of it, and going from you is so like going from home that it makes me feel quite lonesome and melancholy. It fills my mind with sentiments to which alas! it has long been unaccustomed. What a train of reflection does that word Rome call up, and what inexpressible sentiments does it excite in the mind of a person like me, an exile doomed to roam in the wide world, without a home and without a friend? . . .'[38]

In Naples, Lady Palmerston found it difficult to reconstitute the carefree social round:

December 16th. 'I first visited Elizabeth at Angelica's and I am delighted with the picture and I am so pleased with it that I am going to have it copied in miniature . . . [reproduced opposite page 224]

December 23rd. 'I find half my Neapolitan acquaintances shut up; some for state offences, but more for imprudences in love affairs. I never will marry an Italian till convents are out of fashion, for being shut up for life is a horrid thing and I never can approve this fashion of being shaped up [?] by fathers and husbands . . .

December 24th. 'I went to Lady Plymouth and Lady Bessborough in the morning. The latter sees company on Mondays and Thursdays and Lord Grandison on Tuesdays and Saturdays . . .'[39]

The atmosphere of the previous year had changed. The portentous figure of Napoleon had imprinted itself on world events for the first time, and Count Rumford gave her the first intimation of it from Rome:

'As I know you will feel more concern at the news which arrived here yesterday and which has thrown all Rome into consternation, than I do, I wish I were with you that I might have it more in my power to persuade you that the evil is not by far so great as you imagine – and to own you the truth – but, this must be *entre nous*, I don't think it any evil at all. An army at Toulon, merely for the sake of keeping possession of that port, with a fleet at Toulon merely to be ready to carry off that army in case of accidents, was, in my humble opinion, disposing of any army and a fleet in a manner very disadvantageous to Great Britain They might both be better employed elsewhere. And as to Italy, half a dozen ships and a few frigates will be quite equal to defending it now that the naval force of the French is so effectually destroyed in the Mediterranean . . .'[40]

Ominous events obtruded increasingly in her tittle-tattle to Ben:

December 29th. 'We finished the evening at Lord Grandison's, where we met a large party. Soon after we arrived Sir William Hamilton received a note from General Acton to inform him of an account he had just obtained of the combined army having evacuated Toulon, that the French having been joined by the Nice army amounted to 80,000 men, that our force not amounting to more than 18,000 effective men, there was no chance of making a safe resistance and that in consequence of the danger to which our force would be exposed without a possibility of success it had been decided to abandon the town and burn the arsenal and shipping. Everything was carried on with so much secrecy that even the soldiers had no suspicions of the intention and that after three days preparation and embarking 300 Royalists and our united troops, they set sail for [blank in the original] and that the Neapolitans were in the Port of Spezia. The sight of the flames was not lost for two days . . . Two men were stabbed yesterday in the streets, but this makes no more sensation in Italy than picking of pockets in England, though there is less of this business in Naples than in any other Italian town, except Florence. Eight people were stabbed in Rome on Christmas night . . .

January 3rd, 1794. 'Last night Mr Quintin [son of a former governor of the Tuileries] arrived and we have got him an apartment in the house, as we have for Comte Rumford, who comes today. They both dined with us . . .

January 4th. 'We dined early in order to attend Lady Hamilton's Prima Sera, where I was glad to see Lady Bessborough; Sir William is gone with the King hunting to Monte Dragone for four days and it's said is to proceed to Mola de Gaveta [?] to meet his troops from Toulon and return them his thanks for their spirited behaviour. It seems agreed on all hands

that the Neapolitans have behaved singularly well. We were
all to proceed with Lady Hamilton to pay a visit of condolence
to the Princess Belmonti, whose husband died three days ago
and it's the fashion for the widow to sit up in a room with the
hangings taken down, with hardly any light in the room and
all in the deepest black, to see all her acquaintances. Luckily
few people care for their departed half, or it must be the most
wretched ceremony for the survivor possible. In this case they
had been separated lately, after living ill together for 40 years.
We went from grief *à la mode* to the *Matrimonia Segreta*,
which is very pretty music. Lady Plymouth and I have a box
together at the Florentine. It was over early and when we came
home we drank tea, played at chess and trick-track with the
Count and Mr Quintin till late. It's vastly pleasant having those
agreeable men in the house . . .

January 5th. 'We dined a large party today with Lady
Hamilton . . . Nothing could do the honours better than Lady
H., and few so well. The more I see of her, the more I admire
her and think her a very superior woman . . .

January 10th. 'Sir William Hamilton came early and read to
us Sir Sidney Smith's account in a letter to him of the event of
Toulon and of his share in the business. He certainly was of
infinite service and without his assistance we should have had
more to regret . . .

'I do not attempt to give you any detail of Sir Sidney's letter
as long before this you will be in full possession of the whole
transaction. A combined force will never have equal energy
with an army belonging to the same nation. The jealousies, the
variety of language and the contempt and aversion different
sets of people entertain for each other is a wonderful disadvantage, which must attend the present heterogeneous army
now opposed to the herd of wild barbarians united in the great
principle of self-defence, and a mad enthusiasm which pervades
alas! too many minds for the peace of Europe . . .

January 13th. 'This has been a day full of engagements. At
two we went to dinner at General Acton's, where there was a
diplomatic meeting. No English except for Sir William and
Lady Hamilton and ourselves . . . Our dinner was . . . superb

and I never saw anything so well served; in short, it had all the
splendour of a prince's entertainment with the ease of a private
dinner. He himself is a thin genteel looking man; not handsome, but neat and quiet and gentlemanlike . . .'41

Visits to Pompeii and Vesuvius, where Count Rumford was
nearly killed by a sudden eruption of stones, provided additional
occupation; another excursion to Capri with Lady Spencer,
and increasingly aimless tours about Naples served to while
away the spring, but significant gaps and a sense of boredom
in the family journals provided ample reason for their decision
to return home. Moreover, French incursions over the frontier
were threatening the north of Italy and cutting off any line
of retreat for English tourists in the south; it was obviously
time to leave, and by the end of May, 1794, the family had
reached Venice, with Palmerston noting details of their return
journey:

May 26th. 'Arrived at Venice. Lodged at the Lion Blanc on
the great Canal, near the Rialto. Good apartments; table ill-
served. Paid for the apartments 85 sequins [about £40] for the
season of the Ascension, which is considered to be about a
month . . .

May 27th. 'Went on board a galley ready for the sea, which
is to accompany *Bucentaur* in tomorrow's ceremony. Saw the
Bucentaur which is brought out and lies opposite St Mark's
Place. It is a cumbersome unwieldy barge with two stages of
apartments. It is loaded with much carved work and dirty
gilding . . .

'The principal time of assembling is from eight till eleven at
night, which is the hour at which the opera begins . . . Before
the opera the Venetian ladies likewise make visits to each
other's casinos, which are apartments they have here and fit
up very neatly, but not expensively. In these apartments, which
are all in the neighbourhood of St Mark's and generally consist
of two or three small, low rooms, the Venetians assemble and
receive their friends and amuse themselves without ceremony,
seldom or never receiving company in their great houses . . .
The opera lasts till two, after which many of the Venetians
assemble to sup, so that the hours are very late . . .

May 29th. 'This was the Ascension day, but there being some wind and the weather thought unfavourable, the ceremony of the Doge going out in the *Bucentaur* to espouse the Adriatic is postponed till Sunday, as it must always be on a holy day. As the *Bucentaur*, which is the worst sea boat that can be devised, goes upon this occasion quite out at one of the openings by which the lagoons communicate with the sea, having on board the Doge and nearly the whole of the Government, there are four persons dignified with the title of Admiral, who are entrusted with this valuable charge and are answerable for the event. Of course they have power to put off the ceremony and it never is performed till a day happens when there cannot be a doubt entertained of its security. Besides which it is popular to put it off once or twice if there is the least pretence for so doing, under an idea of keeping strangers at Venice . . .

June 8th. 'At length the ceremony of the Doge going out to espouse the sea took place. The *Bucentaur*, when filled with company, was a showy sight. It moved fast, being towed by 14 large rowing boats. It has likewise oars of its own. A large concourse of boats, full of company, attend on this occasion, but it was generally said they were fewer and less splendid this year than usual. The number of persons on board was about 200. The Doge is seated in the state cabin in the stern. He sits in an elbow chair very close to the window. On steps elevated at the head and stern, two at each end, stand in a very conspicuous manner the four Admirals in scarlet gowns with great wigs and caps on their heads. The procession moved across the lagoon to the Lido, one of those long narrow islands by which it is divided from the sea . . .

'The *Bucentaur* was towed into the passage, or port, of Lido and being turned round with her stern to the sea, the Doge rises up in his Chair of State, the back of which lets down, and turning himself round throws the gold ring, which is provided, into the sea, repeating these words: "*Desponsamus te Mare in signum vere perpetuique Dominu*". After this the whole company go on shore at Lido, where the Doge hears Mass and then returns in the same state to Venice. The whole ceremony is attended with great acclamation; music and firing and if the day is bright, which it was on this occasion, the sight is gay and amusing . . .'[42]

Their erstwhile travelling companion, Sir Charles Blagden, sent news, in a letter dated June 10, of the display in London of one of the art treasures which had been found in the ruins of Hadrian's villa at Tivoli, and acquired by the great collector, Charles Townley:

'Mr Townley has set up his Discobolus in the dining room at the end towards the Park, where the antique well formerly stood. It is a very fine figure and the ancient quoit remains in the hand, but no-one can tell in what manner he was to throw it. Mr Townley himself fancies it was to be rolled on the edge along the ground, but the figure holds it in a very awkward manner for this purpose. Mr Knight thinks it was to be thrown in the air and brings abundance of quotations from the ancient authors to show that the discus was not bowled but tossed or flung. The manner of holding it, however, is just as awkward for this motion as the other. Whatever may have been the play, the motion was extremely well expressed, without exaggeration, yet conveying the full idea of strength. Mr Townley particularly admires the head and especially the manner of working the hair, which he thinks equal – if not superior – to that of any known statue. The hair is represented as curling, cropped very close all over the head so as to be nowhere more than about two inches long and divided into a great number of locks which bend with the curling in all possible directions, and a fine variety of forms. The arm holding the quoit was broken off – it is supposed at the Customs House here – but Nollekens has repaired it. This figure is one of the many things found at Tivoli. You will recollect that it was got out of Rome with some difficulty by Mr Jenkins. Mr Townley does not say what he gave for it . . .'[43]

Sir Charles also sent political news of a not particularly encouraging nature:

'The account of Lord Howe's naval victory [the Glorious First of June] did not arrive last Tuesday (the 10th), till late in the evening . . . In consequence of the victory, there have been two nights of illumination, and perhaps there will be a third tonight. The first night, which was Wednesday, but few people expected it, and consequently most were not prepared, a very disorderly mob took advantage of this and broke a vast number of windows, the greatest part through mischief, though in some instances their outrages were directed toward particular persons who were supposed to be disaffected. Among these Lord Stanhope was the principal object. They broke most of his windows – even to the destruction of his window-frames – and evidently aimed the stones at the persons who endeavoured to put out lights. In short, they were bent on personal mischief, and probably would have murdered Lord Stanhope if they could have caught him. Fortunately the whole family were at Chevening. Mr Wilkes' house in Grosvenor Square suffered much. They were all gone to bed, consequently could not be very expeditious in putting out lights, and the mob, not pretending to suspect his loyalty, seemed to think him a proper subject for their amusement. The illuminations last night were splendid, but not equal to those we had on the King's recovery. They differed from all I remembered before in this circumstance, being accompanied with more discharge of fire-arms; frequent reports of guns and pistols – almost amounting to volleys – were heard in every corner of the streets, and it was to me a matter of unpleasant reflection to observe so many of the ill-looking men who paraded the streets had fire-arms of some sort or other in their hands. Their intentions at that moment were loyal, but how soon may they be turned to mischief when they find they have the power!! ...'[44]

However, they were certain of a warm interim welcome at Munich. Count Rumford wrote Lady Palmerston on June 22 with instructions for their journey:

'If you should conclude to come here from Innsbruck by the way of Benedict Bayern, Lord P. must get permission from the Governor of Innsbruck, otherwise the post masters will refuse to give horses for that road, but if his Lordship makes his application in person, and if he informs the Governor that he has particular reasons for wishing to take that road, I have no doubt but that permission will be readily granted ... Enclosed

I send you a letter of introduction to the Abbot of Benedict Bayern which you will deliver in case you should arrive there before me . . .'[45]

They stayed a fortnight in Munich, with visits to the Bavarian alps at Berchtesgaden, Traunstein and Bad Reichenhall, where Palmerston made exhaustive notes on the underground salt mines. By the middle of the month they were on their way north again, with Lady Palmerston enchanted, after so many years of separation, at the prospect of seeing her beloved brother again. Palmerston compressed the account of the last phase of their journey into a few lines in his engagement diary after his return:

'To Ratisbon, Nuremberg, Bamberg, Coburg, Cassel, Hanover, Osnaburg and to the Hague, where we stayed near a month, including an excursion to the Duke of York's army near Bois le Duc [Hertogenbosch] and Gorcum [Gorinchem]. We embarked at Helvoetsluys and arrived in England in [October].'[46]

In one of his many letters to Lady Palmerston after their departure Count Rumford counselled caution:

September 7th – Munich. 'I am quite charmed with your heroic resolution to share the dangers of the campaign with your beloved B., but I own I hope to hear of your being packed off for England, however contrary it may be to your wishes. I should be very uneasy to hear you were left behind, however safe you might think yourself in Holland . . .'[47]

There is, regrettably, no record of her meeting with Benjamin Mee, except for a diary note, made eight years later by Lady Palmerston after her husband's death, when she engaged in cataloguing the works of art in his houses. She records a picture by Zoffany of 'B.M.' sent from India by Mr William Hickey, 'a great friend of my dear brother's. It arrived in Hanover Square only three weeks before I wept my dear husband's loss! The likeness struck me most painfully and yet pleasurably – it seemed as if I had found my dear brother once more – though grown uncommonly large – the climate of Calcutta had that effect – an effect cruelly changed when we met in 1794 at Gorcum! Alack, we met to part for ever!'

Their long tour had cost the best part of £9,000. Palmerston carefully noted the details in his account book:

Various expenses on journey from July

27th 1792 to April 10th 1793	£2,190	15	9
from April 1793 to April 1794	£4,537	19	0
from April to October 1794	£2,122	0	0[48]

Their momentous tour closed with this prosaic comment from Lord Palmerston on the fly leaf of his engagement diary for the following year:

'Landed at Harwich from Helvoetsluys after having been abroad with my family for more than two years, on October 2nd (1794). Came to the house in Hanover Square. Stayed in town till about the 10th of November, including a week passed at Sheen. Then went to Broadlands. Parliament, which was to have met on the 25th November, adjourned to the 30th December. Came to London about the 6th of December; stayed till the 16th; returned to Broadlands. Hard frost set in about Christmas. Having a cold, I did not go up to the meeting of Parliament on the 30th.'[49]

REFERENCES

1. A.19(a)
2. D.5
3. D.5
4. A.19(a)
5. D.5 6.VIII.1792
6. D.5 7.VIII.1792
7. D.5
8. A.19(a)
9. D.5
10. A.19(a)
11. A.19(a)
12. D.5 18.VIII.1792
13. D.5 20.VIII.1792
14. A.19(a)
15. D.5
16. A.19(a)
17. D.5
18. A.19(a)
19. D.5
20. A.19(a)
21. D.5
22. A.19(a)
23. D.5
24. C.61 21.III.1793
25. D.5

26. A.19(b)
27. D.5
28. D.5
29. A.19(d)
30. D.5
31. A.19(d)
32. A.19(d)
33. D.5
34. A.19(d)
35. D.5
36. A.19(d)
37. D.5
38. D.6 29.XI.1793
39. D.5
40. D.6 27.XII.1793
41. D.5
42. A.19(f)
43. C.49 10.VI.1794
44. C.49 13.VI.1794
45. D.6 22.VI.1794
46. A.1
47. D.6 7.IX.1794
48. A.3(d)
49. A.1

CHAPTER X

HARRY GOES TO HARROW

Palmerston completes his art collection – the Malmesburys, the Crewes, the Pelhams, the Paynes and the Sheridans – war in the Netherlands – Princess Caroline of Brunswick marries the Prince of Wales – Harry sent to Harrow school – Palmerston the Pittite – Count Rumford in England – Palmerston blackmailed – Holland and the Hanover Square house – financial embarrassment

During the family's residence abroad Palmerston made the last major art purchases of his life. By the time he returned to England he had spent over the course of thirty years well over £8,000, but in the years remaining to him the occasional pictures he acquired at the London auctions and galleries cost him only 134 guineas, and, apart from Canaletto's Arsenal at Venice, included nothing of consequence.

His taste continued heavily to favour the artists of the Dutch school. With riots breaking out in Paris, on August 6, 1792, he bought for £216 from Dongen, the Parisian dealer, 'Pontius Pilate Washing His Hands', attributed to Rembrandt, and a landscape by Cuyp, and on his way back through the Hague in September, 1794, bought two Van de Veldes and a Van der Neer. In the interval he acquired in Italy, through various agents, including James Durno and his early acquaintance Gavin Hamilton, a number of works by such artists as Veronese, Barocci, Carracci and good copies of Titian and Correggio.

During the Italian tour he also made a number of miscellaneous purchases of alabaster and marble, some of which were lost when the ship carrying them was sunk.

On his return to London Palmerston slipped effortlessly into the well-worn pattern of his social round. All the familiar names reappeared in his guest book, the Malmesburys, the Crewes, the Pelhams, the Paynes and the Sheridans. Additional to the roster were a number of titled French refugees, both in London and at Broadlands, where Lady Palmerston dispensed

hospitality to the large emigré colony which had settled at
Romsey, reinforced by the officers of the Marquis du Dresnay's
Corps, who were training in readiness for the ill-fated expedition to Quiberon Bay. From London, Palmerston kept his wife
informed of events there:

'I went to the opera where the performance I think is good
and better at least in all respects than what we have been used
to; but I think the style of ornament of the house worse than
anything I could have supposed, and I was the more surprised
as I had understood it was rather handsome. The paintings are
clumsy and bad to the extreme and the whole appears the most
singular union of tawdry and dismal I ever met with . . .

'I have sent by today's post two venison warrants to Col.
Heywood and begged the favour of him to order one of them
to be served immediately as they are on the New Forest . . .

'Today I am just going to dine at home on a boiled fowl
and shall go to the play where I see the Royal Family are
to be . . .'[1]

'I have seen Pelham who came up yesterday from Reading
where his regiment is. Lord and Lady P. and Mrs H. Pelham
are in town for the latter to be presented and they are all gone
to Court today . . . Pelham has seen the Duke of York, who
is very well. His coming to England was quite unexpected to
himself but he was coming to the Hague . . .

The play was very full and very loyal. In the list of names of
places taken there was not one that I knew . . .'[2]

The Duke of York, at Pitt's insistence, had just been relieved
of the command of the British forces in the Netherlands, where
on January 4, 1795, the French forces had launched their attack
on the line of the Waal. Poor Ben was literally in the wars
again and wrote to his brother-in-law:

'I am sorry to inform you that Holland is to be abandoned
by our army. We are posting to Amersfort, Deventer, etc. I
have a great charge still here . . . I shall do all I can to save a
great part, but as our wants of assistance to remove stores
increase, the disposition and means of the Dutch to relieve us
decline, I think it is not improbable that the next excursion I
am sent upon will be to Bremen or Hamburg. The cause of

this disastrous business and the reasons of its effect will (if not smothered from political or partial motives) be satisfactorily explained to the nation. I suppose the Hanoverians are worn out and tired of this service. The new Austrian subsidised troops are not zealous in the cause, thinking themselves disgraced by being hired. The British are worn down with fatigue and sickness. Under all these circumstances you may naturally suppose the war is against us, however great our pecuniary resources. And how a numerous army with all its contingencies will be foraged in the impoverished country of Westphalia, bad roads, no water carriage, remains to be unfortunately experienced I fear . . .'[3]

Palmerston passed on to his wife the somewhat cold-blooded reaction of the City merchants in his budget of London news:

January 22nd. 'I see the City have done very handsomely. I have met with some speculators who do not think the loss of Holland so very fatal a blow to us as others do. They think it will get us out of a war on the Continent which does not seem to succeed; that it will do more harm to Holland than good to France; that it will ruin the trade of Holland which has always in a general view been more an object of rivalship than of benefit to this country, and that the trade of England will in consequence receive a very great increase; that the Dutch seamen, supposing even that Holland should be made to take part against us, will be too unwilling to fight with France to be of much use to them, and that if, as it is hoped by many, the Stadtholder and the Dutch Admiral should bring off a large fleet our Navy will be the first at least to be benefited. I find . . . that the people in the City particularly connected with Holland have had so much time to prepare themselves and secure their property that no considerable failures are expected, and that immense property is every day pouring into the country from thence which must be of immediate use at least to keep up the funds, and much of which may perhaps ultimately remain here and increase the general capital. How much of this may be true I do not know but when a great apparent misfortune arrives it is good at least to look round it and try whether we cannot find some view of it less black than that which first presents itself . . .

February 24th. 'Mr Pitt got through his budget yesterday without much animadversion. His taxes in general do not seem to be much objected to. If the guinea per head for wearing powder is collected, which I think must be difficult, it will produce far beyond what he computes it at.

'I went to Mrs Crewe's last night who had told me she always sups at home about eleven and supped with her *tête à tête* and had a long batch of politics in which we agreed very well as she is not at all bigoted to Charles Fox's politics, though Crewe cannot bring himself to vote against him . . . She looks fat and jolly and laments your absence . . .

March 3rd. 'I dined yesterday at Crewe's. We had no women but Mrs Crewe who, poor dear woman, talked as much as half a dozen and got more puzzled and talked more nonsense than it has been my lot to hear for a great while. We did not dine till almost seven, which always makes me sick, and after dinner Pelham and Tom Grenville got into a long debate of above an hour about the trials of contested elections which put me to sleep. So there is an account of a party that should have been pleasant manquée . . .

March 6th. 'I am just come in from my walk and have been this noon [?] looking at Sir Joshua's pictures which are upon view. There is an immense number of them of all sorts but not a great many that are remarkably captivating, though several very fine . . . Sir Joshua's drawings are likewise upon private sale at another place but they set high prices on them and will not sell many I believe . . .'[4]

Lady Palmerston also had some gossip about an old friend:

March 6th. 'I suppose Emma (Godfrey) has told you that there is a report of her former lover Sir Charles B[lagden] marrying Caroline Grote. I think she is a bold girl, though he may think her a *delicious girl* and feel for her most *tender emotions* I should fear after a very short period she may find a very worthy man, a man of strict honour, a man of learning and science and a man of the truest principals a most unpleasant husband. I wish I may be mistaken but as I know we should fight in less than a week I own I am sorry for Caroline, who has everything to make her life comfortable and ought not to exchange that state without she was sure of *bettering herself.* All this however is *entre nous* . . .

'I called on Lady Malmesbury who had a most charming clever letter from Canning with the history of the times . . .

March 10*th.* 'Lady M[almesbury] has just been here, she desires her love and hopes that you have been to see Nagel's pictures . . .'[5]

Palmerston's account of London art sales was punctuated by the problem of how to get his unfortunate brother-in-law back to England without his being arrested by his creditors:

March 13*th.* 'I have received yours with Boehm's [their solicitor] enclosed. I shall see him in a day or two and will talk with him on the subject. I understand his meaning I think and am sorry to say that I fear what he says is true, that no paper signed by any of the creditors of the Bengal Bank could at present give any personal security to Ben in England, because as the creditors of a bank are extremely numerous, the number in England and the powers transmitted from India unknown, it would be impossible to get it executed by the whole and the greatest danger would perhaps arise from obscure people with small demands who might think that by a sudden arrest they should get paid. And I fear the danger would be the greater if it was known he was here, on account of the situation he is at present in, which in the minds of the generality of people is connected with the idea of great profit . . .

March 14*th.* 'I have been today at Sir Joshua's sale where I bought two little things of no great consequence. Pray make Lady M[almesbury] easy and assure her I will see Nagel's pictures as soon as they are to be seen, which will be in 3 or 4 days at farthest. I would have gone before now but they are in the house where he still remains . . .

March 16*th.* 'I have but a moment to say we are all well. I am just come in from Sir Joshua's sale and the party who are so good as to carry Fanny to the play desire her early . . .

'I have seen Nagel's pictures, of which some are very good. By they are most amazingly eclipsed by Calonne's collection which are now on view and all the most beautiful collection as well as the finest and in the best order of any I have seen for a great while . . .

March 16th. 'I am just returned again from Sir Joshua's sale so late that I have only time to say that we are all well . . .

'Sir Joshua's pictures have sold well and have fetched more than £10,000, which I understand is a good deal more than the last valuation.

'Our play turned out well and Fanny was much pleased . . .'[6]

In her gratitude for her husband's efforts on behalf of her brother, Lady Palmerston, who was at Bath, did not neglect news of their friends, the Elliots, who were in Corsica, where Sir Gilbert was functioning as Viceroy after the capture of the island by the British during the campaign of 1794:

March 16th. 'I think we may say of our poor B[en] that misfortune hath marked him for her own. I now plainly perceive that he must remain for ever exiled from his family, from his friends and from his native country and the fond hope I had indulged that we had some happy days in store that we might yet pass together in England must be entirely relinquished. Alas! my poor mother, her disappointment will be extreme, she had looked forward to the hour of meeting as at no very distant period. The hope of which happiness has supported her through ten long years of absence. Perhaps you will kindly represent the risk he will run by attempting to return (for he means to take the first opportunity). I know you will convey the mortifying intelligence with a delicacy of manner I do not think his other friends are equal to and which you so eminently possess. Forgive my continually tormenting you with my misfortunes . . .

'Lady M[almesbury] has had a very entertaining letter from Lady Elliot. She still remains enchanted with the country around Bastia. She describes the advantages that the Corsicans might derive from trade if they knew how to benefit themselves by the riches of their country in wine, oil and silk, in which she coincides with Boswell in his sentiments on that subject. General Stewart was going away, to the Elliots great joy, as the General and Viceroy had disagreed exceedingly, the general insisting he ought to have the rank and command of Commander-in-Chief, which the Viceroy considers as residing with him. This however is only between you and I. It may be no secret but as I had it from Lady M. I should not like to mention it but to you. Lady E[lliot] is sighing for England or Scotland. She says the weather is fine, but not yet summer the 1st of February. I think her ladyship was rather unreasonable to expect that season so early.

'What a difference to us between this March and the last. You were visiting the Governor of Capri and I was dining out of doors in some excursion within view of the Bay in such weather as I fear we shall not be indulged with even in June. This country ought to possess many advantages, for the truth is the climate is detestable . . .'[7]

Palmerston could find no solution to his brother-in-law's troubles:

March 17th. 'I have had some conversation with Boehm and with Henchman about Ben's affairs. They and Culverden and, I believe, everybody who knows the nature of the business, seem to agree that he could have no permanent security here as things stand at present and that nobody could advise him to risk even a short visit, for though very probably the persons from whom danger is to be apprehended might not be apprised of his arrival for some time, yet every day that his stay was prolonged would be full of anxiety and apprehension . . . I do not imagine that there is the smallest chance of Ben's having it in his power to come over at present. It seems generally thought that the British cavalry are to remain and as Mr Watson has upon all occasions expressed so much satisfaction with Ben's conduct I cannot doubt of his being continued in employment, and if so, the season of action is too near at hand to admit of absence. Had the army gone into long and undisturbed winter quarters he might very likely have got leave of absence for a short time in the dead part of the season, but now I look upon all ideas of that kind as at an end if he continues in his present situation, which as I before said, I conclude he is to do. I am the more confirmed in this as Culverden tells me that in a letter just received, which he has sent to you, he makes no mention of coming over. I do not know therefore whether there is any occasion for my writing to him on the subject you mention. It is not a pleasant one and one would not wish to enter upon it unnecessarily but if you still wish me to do it or think it material, I will . . .

March 27th. 'There have been above £5,000 worth of Calonne's pictures sold today. Tomorrow is the great day when there will be sharp bidding. I do not however think it certain that the whole produce will amount to what they refused, which is 25,000 guineas. There has not been yet more than £9,000 produced by the sale and yet most of them have sold well. I bought 3 pictures at Sir Joshua's sale, none at Nagel's nor as yet at Calonne's.

[At Sir Joshua's sale Palmerston bought a landscape by Mola for 14 guineas, a view of the Rhine by Van de Heyden for 7 guineas and a landscape by Wouwerman for 91 guineas.]

March 30th. 'I came home so late from Calonne's sale on Saturday and was to dine at Lord Ossory's that I could not write a word. Everything went at fine prices the last day. They say some of the best were bought by a Mr Cox of the City for the Empress of Russia, particularly two pretty Claudes which sold for near £1,100. I bought nothing in the whole sale and I am very glad I was wise enough to keep my money.

April 1st. 'I am very happy to send you a letter from Ben which, as you gave me leave so to do, I opened and rejoice that he is well. I was the more desirous of opening in order to see what his plans might be in consequence of a note received this morning from Mr Rose . . . by which I find that Mr Watson and the person next to him are coming over to settle accounts, etc. and that Ben has been selected from among the assistant commissaries on account of his good conduct to be the next in trust to a Mr Le Mesurier who will be in Watson's place. This I am very glad of, as it will be very advantageous I hope both in point of salary and credit and future claims and pretensions. I suppose as the army is so much reduced that Mr Watson will not return any more and in that case therefore Ben's situation will last as long as any of our troops remain and I hope by this a better half-pay will be settled for him at the expiration of the time, besides future expectations.'

Such hopes were over-sanguine. Benjamin Mee died at Bad Pyrmont, still an exile, on August 2, 1796.

*   *   *

Even the defeat and distress of a British army could not compete in London with the interest aroused by the arrangements for the Prince of Wales to marry Princess Caroline of Brunswick. In spite of the assistance accorded him by Parliament in 1787, the Prince had not mended his ways and his debts now amounted to over £600,000. Even his Whig supporters had fallen out with him, and in order to escape from his difficulties he had agreed to his father's demands to make a dynastic marriage, in spite of the secret ceremony he had gone through with Mrs Fitzherbert. Lord Malmesbury had been sent to bring the Princess over to England and Palmerston kept his wife fully informed of developments:

March 3rd. 'Crewe has been persuaded by the Prince to be one of a committee whom he has named to examine into the state of his affairs. He gets rather laughed at about it by some and pitied by others. Among them by Pelham who has been upon that duty before and does not seem to think it will be very satisfactory. It will most likely end in doing something he does not like or quarrelling with the Prince. The others are Mr Lambton, Nesbitt, Macdonald and Sir Richard Heron . . .

March 10th [?]. 'The Princess is expected very soon. The Prince and Lady J[ersey] are at Kempshott. The P. is highly offended on two accounts because Lady J. is not invited to the private parties at B[uckingham] House and because he is not promoted to the rank of Major-General in the Army! The gentlemen who were to examine his debts have somehow or other got off. I do not know how but everybody wishes them joy . . .

April 4th. 'Her Royal Highness is at Gravesend and was in some degree expected in town today, at least everything was in readiness to receive her and the carriages and guards went for her. I was down at Westminster where many people were waiting to see her pass. An account however soon came that she remains on board the *Jupiter* where she is tonight. To-morrow she is to come up in one of the yachts and will be at St James's about three o'clock . . .

April 6th. 'It was unlucky the day was so bad yesterday as it spoiled the show. She came rather sooner than I thought she would have done. I just saw a glimpse of her at the window but too little to judge. The report of her is good. All the men say she would be a pretty woman if not a princess. She is well made, with a good person, rather plump, but not too much and her height is between Lady Jersey and Mrs Aston, between whom Lord Cholmondeley saw her standing and therefore could compare. She is lively and talkative, not at all nervous nor alarmed at her situation and upon the whole I understand she answers better than was expected . . .

April 7th. 'The marriage as you will see by today's papers is at length fixed for tomorrow and the presentations and galas for Wednesday and Thursday sennight. I am sorry there is to be so long an interval as I feel almost inclined not to wait for them and yet upon consideration I believe it will be better and certainly righter so to do. It will be a good thing to have it over at the right time to avoid the fuss and trouble of after presenta-tions and I suppose if it was long delayed the coat I have made which is perfectly right now would be out of date . . .

April 8th. 'The day smiles upon the business and I hope it will prove a good omen.

'I saw Lord Malmesbury last night. I think he looks very well and in good care. He speaks very highly of the Princess's good temper and good spirits. She seems to feel herself quite at home and among her own family and is as free with them all as possible. She has been kept rather strict at home and is quite like a girl got loose for the first time among her uncles, aunts and cousins . . .

April 9th. 'Those who were admitted to the drawing rooms assembled between seven and eight. It was difficult to get there in a carriage. I was glad to take to a chair at the top of St James's Street. The three rooms were considerably full of very finely dressed people who soon began to ask each other what they

were come for, having nothing to do with the marriage ceremony, the procession even of which could not be seen by more
than 20 or 30 of them as it only passed along one end of one
room. The rooms were extremely dark and oppressively hot
as there were great fires made to supply perhaps that great
deficiency of every other light. A duller or more discontented
meeting I never saw and as there were no seats and a prospect
of remaining there at least four hours in that hole without a
possibility of retreat, most of the ladies sat down in their fine
dresses upon the floor. In short it put me in mind of a gala in
the black hole. What with the lateness of their going to the
chapel, there being three separate processions, the number of
ceremonies when they got there and an anthem of $\frac{3}{4}$ of an hour,
it was more than half past ten before it was over. The procession then came slowly up the three drawing rooms and after
staying ten minutes or a quarter of an hour at most in an
immense crowd at the upper end, they marched back again in
order to go away to supper at Buckingham House. The Royal
Family spoke to those who happened to be within their reach
while they went up and down as well as while they remained
at the upper end. I had a very good view of the Princess, who
was led by the Prince. You may suppose she could not appear
to the best advantage in such a moment of hurry and fatigue.
They have taken away the heels which it seems she wore rather
high when she came, by which, and by her head not being
dressed like other people's she looked more diminutive than I
expected. It was proper, it seems, that she should have on her
head a little crown of excessive fine diamonds, which though
very valuable was not at all becoming and made no figure in
the midst of the lofty plumage with which she was surrounded.
She seemed well made, very fair, with regular features and I
dare say a pleasing character of countenance, but in the hared
and frighted state in which one saw her little could be judged
more than she seemed very desirous of being civil and doing
everything right . . .'

The one thing the poor creature had not been able to do was
to please her husband, who treated her shamefully. Within a
month her position had become intolerable:

May 11th. 'Everybody I hear is in the highest indignation at the proceedings at C[arlton] H[ouse]. She is quite shut up and not permitted to see any person but such as are approved of. She complained to Lord M[almesbury] that she never saw him. He said he had called almost every day but never could be admitted. She then begged he would come the next day at two. He thought it right to tell the Prince, who appeared to approve it highly, but when the time came the answer at the door was as usual, she was not very well. He met her at night at a ball and was reproached for not keeping his appointment and it appeared she had been expecting him. The two attendants she brought with her, who are mere servants, are ordered away . . .

May 12th. 'The call of the House and all business is adjourned as you will see for some days on account of the Speaker's illness. I did not get down till the adjournment was over, so that I did not hear anything there. Lord S. [?] at dinner fancied it was a pretence in order to make some other arrangement about the debts, as it was found that the House would not agree to the propositions which were to be made. I do not know how that may be but I should not wonder if it was so, as the public mind is highly irritated and all reserve seems to be laid aside. Lady J[ersey] is hissed and insulted and I hear is afraid to go to C[arlton] H[ouse] in her own chair . . .

'The story I mentioned yesterday about Lord M[almesbury] is true nearly as I stated it. The P[rince] when informed of the appointed visit said nothing would always give him so much satisfaction and when Lord M[almesbury] came the message was given to him in the Prince's name, that he could not be admitted for reasons which she told him afterwards with tears in her eyes were not true. Nothing can be so unkind as the whole system of his manner and conduct towards her and whenever she does see any of those whom she was in intimacy with before she came over, if she has any opportunity of speaking to them privately she cannot refrain from tears, though I do not find that she makes any direct complaints. All the harsh things are put upon him [Malmesbury] to do and the Lady affects great kindness with a degree of familiarity in public that has more than once disgusted all the spectators . . .'[8]

Lady Palmerston was incensed by this news:

May 13th. 'I quite lament over our poor captive Princess. She must sadly regret Hanover ... She will I dare say agree with you in the opinion that winter was to her the season of hope and spring that of disappointment.

'I cannot comprehend the motive which induces Lady Jersey to behave so injudiciously ill and what advantage she can derive by making the Prince behave not only like a fool but as a complete brute. I thought Lady Jersey was as cunning as a serpent, though not quite as harmless as a dove, and that she would have done everything to conciliate not to disgust the wife and the world. Her worst enemy cannot wish her to pursue a line of conduct so destructive to the stability of her empire. She must feel like her cousin Robespierre (for I am sure they are related) and that ere long she may not be murdered but she will be driven from society. How silly not to be content with cajoling and dressing Lord Carlisle. She might have gone out to the end of their days in a quiet respectable attachment ...'9

Palmerston replied with an account of the settlement of the Prince's debts:

May 14th. 'I was yesterday at the King's Levée and at the Princess's Drawing Room. The first was crowded, the latter, being made up only of odds and ends who had not been before, was very thin. She is really rather a prettyish little woman though we passed her so quick I had hardly time to look at her. The rooms are all fitted up and are very beautiful.

'I understood that the Speaker will be able to attend and that the business of the Prince's debts will come on today, but the proceeding of today will not lead to much discussion it is said ...

May 15th. 'The business of the Prince's allowance was carried by majority sufficient, but the turn of the debate was very mortifying to him. Mr Grey strenuously opposed giving him more than £100,000 and was for letting him settle his debts as he could. There is to be a parliamentary commission to enquire and examine witnesses upon oath as to the nature of his debts, in order to see whether they ought to be paid to the full extent.

He will have £100,000 to spend, £25,000 to pay the interest
and £13,000 to pay off the principal which by compound
interest will take 27 years to discharge them.'[10]

* * *

In the same month Palmerston had a much more pleasant
duty of a family nature to perform. On May 26, 1795, Harry,
at the age of ten and a half, was sent to Harrow. It was certainly
not too soon as far as his spelling was concerned, which, in the
two batches of childish letters up to this date to his mother and
father, was execrable. However, his studies had not been neglected during his European tour with his parents and from time
to time he wrote very passable letters in French and Italian to
his mother, a facility which was to last him all his life, thanks
to his father's insistence:

'Pray give my best love to all your party and tell Harry I am
glad he likes Camilla [a new pony]. Pray likewise tell him that
I hope he does not omit to apply himself in the afternoon to his
French and Italian with Mr Gaetano [the tutor they had brought
back from Italy] as it would be a pity to neglect them,'[11]
Palmerston wrote to his wife shortly after their return from
the Italian tour. When Lady Palmerston went to Bath in
January he had all the children to live with him in Hanover
Square, sending regular domestic news, which has a remarkably
modern ring:

January 22nd, 1795. 'Harry is vastly well and if it was not for
the disagreeable remains of his disorder upon his face could
hardly be called an invalid. I should think that now it would
not be worth while to move Willy. I had not the least idea of
its being a catching disorder or I would have had him moved
at first. They are all very well and I never saw Lilly look better
or seem more lively ...

February 11th. 'The children are to be here this evening. They
will have had wet and windy weather but as it is very warm I
hope they will not suffer. Their rooms are ready for them. I
have moved into my room upstairs which is much more convenient to me for having all my things about me than staying
below and full as warm. Lilly's picture [by Angelica Kauffmann]

is come in perfect preservation. It is a nice portrait and more like her than your copy ...

February 23rd. 'Yesterday morning Fanny, William and Lilly all showed signs of having got the prevailing colds, particularly Fanny who had a headache and was rather hot. Willy had some headache but Lilly had little more than a sneezing. Mr Walker came to them and gave them some medicine in the course of the day and ordered them all to take James's powder at night which seems to have answered perfectly well ...

February 24th. 'I do not know very well what dentist to employ ... perhaps such a man as Spence would be best for the children ... Is not Jenkins that Scotch dancing master who teaches nothing but that jig that Harry used to dance with his knees bent and his shoulders up to his ears?

March 9th. 'If you remain at Bath at Easter I always intended to come to you and will with great pleasure bring the children down. It will be an agreeable jaunt for them and will I dare say do them good. They are very well upon the whole, though in this weather little remnants of colds will sometimes show themselves They have but a dull time of it here for the weather is so bad that they can seldom get much amusement abroad. Yesterday was fine and I sent them to walk in the Green Park. Today is as cold and wet as ever. I fancy I must bring Mr Jones down as Harry must not just now lose the opportunity of pursuing his studies ...

March 12th. 'I am going to dine with the Payne's today and I am going to send Harry and Willy with Messrs Jones and Gaetano to see the *Wheel of Fortune* and *Alexander the Great.* Fanny is to go the first day ...

'A boy at Harrow had died of a very rapid scarlet fever and all the boys are come away and are not to return till after Easter, which will be the middle of April, but I never meant Harry should go till May ...

March 13th. 'The two boys were delighted last night at the play, though Willy was a little tired till the dance began, but then he was all alive ...

March 17th. 'I have had a letter from Mr Bromley [the housemaster at Harrow] to say that as the school has separated

L

so much sooner they will meet on the 10th of April, which is rather sooner after Easter than the usual time. I think however the beginning of May, which is the time we always talked of for Harry to go, will be soon enough as he will not be losing time in the meanwhile ...

'As to masters, I believe upon enquiry the man who teaches Miss Johnson music will be the best we can have, especially as he can attend both here and at Sheen, as he lives at Richmond but attends scholars in London. I think it would be of no great use to begin before Fanny returns from Bath ... As to the dancing master, it may remain till you come. The dentist I hate the thought of and as nothing seems to press particularly and I did not well know whom to employ, I have done nothing. However, I will have their mouths looked into to see whether there is anything necessary ...'[12]

In a letter to his mother on March 23, Harry told her: 'I went out today on horseback in Hyde Park on Camilla, who went very well. There was hardly anybody there, and I saw Mr Fox for the first time; as I remember. But when I saw him, how very much surprised I was, for I had formed an idea of his being rather lean, but I never saw a man so fat in all my life.'[13]

His father could also send good news about Fanny:

March 27th. 'I am very happy to tell you that poor Fanny mustered up a great deal of courage today and has had one tooth out, which is what Spence thought most immediately necessary, and she says it did not give her near so much pain as she expected and that she shall not much mind having the others out when it is necessary ...'[14]

On April 30 Mrs Bromley sent Lady Palmerston a letter with a timeless note:

'We shall be very happy to receive Mr Temple ... If your Ladyship sends the following things to school with Mr Temple it will be sufficient.

2 suits of clothes, a great coat, 10 shirts, 10 pocket hand-kerchiefs and 6 or 8 pr of stockings. As the stockings are washed every week a large quantity is not necessary, indeed I could wish not to have more linen than is sufficient to change three times a week ...'[15]

It was Lord Palmerston who shouldered the final details:

May 16th. 'The boys are well but I never see them but for a moment as our hours are so different that I have no means of doing so, not dining at home, without deranging their studies or their amusements, either of which I should be sorry to do.

'I shall go to Harrow in a day or two and settle for Harry to go there to stay about next Saturday which will be as soon as his things will be ready . . .

May 18th. 'I drove down to Harrow yesterday and had some conversation with Mr and Mrs Bromley. She seems very intelligent and notable and I dare say will take very good care of Harry. She wished to know in case of his being a little indisposed what medicines and in what doses he had been used to take, which I shall accordingly tell her and if you have anything to direct on the subject you will let me know between this and Saturday, which is the day at present fixed . . . I forgot to ask them about night shirts but I am persuaded they are quite out of the question and would only make him the joke of the other boys . . . As to a bed, I understand what is there is a very good one and as the room is small its turning up in the day is a very convenient circumstance. As I suppose the servants would not be fond of making it more than once a day it will be much more comfortable for him to go into than if it had been tumbled about upon and had everything thrown upon it during the day . . .

'Harry will have a little more than two months to stay there at present, as the next holidays begin the latter end of July and last 5 or 6 weeks . . .

May 26th. 'I carried Harry to Harrow yesterday evening and left him there in very good spirits and perfectly happy in staying there. Willy desired to go and help put Harry to school, which he accordingly did. I dare say Harry will be quite happy there if he can but keep his health. I am very sorry it happens to be so very cold again just at his going, but I recommended to him and to Mr and Mrs Bromley for him to be careful just at first. He is to have a nice little bureau to fit a nook in his room, made after the pattern of one he saw there which did stand there. Some shelves are to be put up for his books and he has two cupboards with locks and keys. The maid who attends on him seems a very active pleasant servant. I found there are two boys who wear nightshirts, so at present, at least, for fear any change might give him cold he has his. As to the bed, there is nothing done about it. You may do what you please when you come, but a turn-up bed is so much more convenient in so small a space and the other sort of beds are so ill used by the boys who come in, that unless there is some real advantage which I do not know of, there are many reasons for preferring that which is there . . .

May 29th. 'I have had a very pleasant letter from Harry today . . . I shall be in London on Sunday night, dining at Sheen on my way. I intend going down to Harrow on Tuesday to see Harry and hear the speeches, which is always a compliment to the masters and what they like . . .

June 3rd. 'I went yesterday to Harrow and found Harry very well and very happy. The day was a very good one. I got there about ½ past 12 and found the heath before arriving at Harrow full of the boys, who were come out to meet their friends, among them I soon discovered Harry and the Ponsonbys. I took up Harry and carried him back. He looks clear and is in very good spirits and does not seem to have got any fresh cold during the severe weather he had at first going. On the contrary, the cough he had when he went is lessened. The town was full of people who came to see their children and to hear the speeches, which were by the upper boys and which lasted near two hours. I could not have believed so many boys could have been found who would have spoke so ill as most of them did. The last was a son of Lord Harrowby's who is the captain of the school and is going to Cambridge. He spoke tolerably quiet and well . . .

'Harry seems quite at home and at his ease and Mr Bromley says he never saw a boy become a schoolboy so immediately. Indeed he spoke very handsomely of him before him in every respect and says that as he finds him very quick at his book and that he has made good progress, he shall keep him some time unplaced and under his more immediate inspection, in order

to place him the better a little while hence and more according
to his age and parts . . .'

Bright scholar though he was, Harry missed none of the fun
of school. In a letter dated June 20 he told his mother that all
the boys are making cross-bows and complains to her of the
high cost of whalebone. A mind broadened by foreign travel
and sharpened by tutors soon earned its reward. By February 22,
1796, his father was able to report:

'I went yesterday to Harrow and found Harry looking very
well and in very good spirits. He has a little cough but it is
not a bad one, much less than he has been often used to have.
His nose has a little tendency to be sore but that likewise is
slight. The Bromleys seem to take good care of him. He is
placed in the 4th form which makes him very happy and gives
him new consequence as he is nobody's fag and need not
answer when anybody calls Boy! . . .'

★ ★ ★

Palmerston spent the summer of 1795 quietly at Broadlands
entertaining near relatives and close friends. He was back in
London in October for the reopening of Parliament, giving
Lady Palmerston an account of the demonstrations against the
King and expressing himself for the first time as a whole-
hearted admirer of William Pitt, in spite of the unsatisfactory
course of the war against France and the collapse of the
Quiberon expedition:

October 29th. 'I arrived last night in London just at the proper
time to stop at the Cockpit, where there was the usual meeting
to hear the speech and Address. You will have seen them both
in the papers. The pacific part of it so much talked of does
not amount to much. Indeed it was improbable anything
material could be said unless some treaty was in great forwardness and in the present very critical moment of affairs in France
it seems quite impossible to suppose that any could be begun . . .

'I finish this at the House of Commons. Sheridan has just
spoke and made a violent speech against the King's speech and
the conduct of the war but has moved no amendment to the
Address but declares he will vote against giving any supply to

carry on the war. Jenkinson, whom he attacked in his speech, is just got up to answer him . . .

'PS. The King was I fear insulted coming down to the House. It is said something was thrown at the coach and broke the window but I do not know it. I was told just now he was shot at, but I dare say that is not true.

October 30th. 'You will have seen the issue of last night's debate in the papers. Pitt's speech was the finest I ever heard him make and is generally esteemed so. There was nothing remarkable in the speeches on the other side except the intended mischief of Sheridan's. Pitt made a very explicit declaration that if the government of France as established by the new constitution could enter upon its functions and become efficient, he should no longer consider the state of France in itself, and independent of other political considerations, as any bar to concluding a treaty of peace with them. Fox declared himself so far satisfied with this as to defer any motions respecting peace till the event of the commencement of the new government in France should be known.

'The outrages offered to the King were very serious and alarming. He was hissed and pelted with dirt and stones, some of which came into the carriage both going and returning and in going, when he was nearly opposite the entrance of the House of Commons, something passed through the glass of the coach which from all the circumstances the King himself and the persons with him are convinced was a bullet, which must have been discharged from a wind gun as no fire, smoke or report was perceived. He was again attacked and his coach nearly stopped in going from St James's to Buckingham House and the state coach extremely damaged in its return to the mews. Both these circumstances happened from the confusion and want of attention of the persons about the King, who had given orders for guards to attend both himself and his coach. The Lords entered into an examination of this matter last night and voted an address which they sent to the Commons for their concurrence. The House are just now going to hear the evidence of the facts and will then join in the address . . .'[16]

Since their return to England, Lady Palmerston had received

a number of letters from her admirer, Count Rumford, who was enjoying a respite from administrative duties in Bavaria, to further his philosophical and scientific studies. His main preoccupation for some time had been with the behaviour of heat and light, and he did not disdain the practical application of his theories. A new form of stove which cooked large quantities of food cheaply was his latest hobby-horse and he visited England at the end of 1795 to propagate his ideas, a project temporarily clouded by the theft of a trunk containing all his papers from the back of his coach. Part of the active encouragement he received from the Palmerstons was the installation of his new-fangled cooking ranges in the kitchens of Broadlands and the Hanover Square house:

November 3rd, 1794 – Munich. 'My situation in this country is not become more agreeable of late; on the contrary, I never saw the absolute necessity of retiring more strongly than at present. I am now quite sure that I can never expect one moment's quiet and satisfaction in this country, whatever line of conduct I may adopt. It is in vain that I keep a roof and avoid every appearance of having anything to do with public affairs. I am suspected of having a hand in everything of importance that happens and am as much exposed to attacks and to solicitations as if I were actually at the head of the administration. But why should I tire you with this disagreeable subject? As soon as my fate shall be finally determined, I will inform you of it once and for all. In the meantime, you know enough of the situation I am in to form a tolerably just idea of what must be going on. I am going on most successfully in my experiments upon heat and have lately made some improvements in my machinery which have produced quite marvellous effects. I lately roasted one hundred pounds of veal in six large pieces at once through and through, with thirty-six pounds of the very cheapest (pine) wood which cost just three creutzers – or something less than one penny farthing English – and several persons who were witnesses to the experiment declared they never tasted roasted meat more delicately done. What renders this experiment peculiarly interesting is that meat may be roasted by this contrivance with sea coal as well as with wood, or even with charcoal or with turf. If a pound of coal gives as much heat in combustion as a pound of wood – and I believe it does more – upon that supposition, knowing the price of coals by the chaldron and the number of pounds in a chaldron of coals – you may easily calculate the expense of roasting a hundred pounds of meat in London by my contrivance. Pray inform yourself and let me know how much a chaldron of coal weighs and how much it costs at a medium. What a fortune I could make by coming to England, taking out a patent for my new inventions relative to the economy of fuel and entering into partnership with Boulton . . .

June 13th, 1795 – *Munich*. 'You have no idea, my dear Lady P., how exquisitely beautiful my garden [the Englischer Garten] is this year. I have been constantly at work upon it, almost ever since you left us and have made many improvements. I have just finished a most magnificent amphitheatre, built in the form of a half circle, with five rows of seats rising one above another, composed of earth and covered with verdure and crowned above by twenty-five boxes, each ten foot wide in front, covered with a roof; the whole, especially when filled with people, forming a very magnificent view. It holds about 2,000 persons and was filled the other evening when fireworks were given for the amusement of the public and when the Elector was present . . .

'I am much flattered by the obliging manner in which you mention my intended visit to England. I have already spoken seriously to the Elector upon the subject and I really think you will see me before the end of October, perhaps sooner. I cannot describe the impatience I feel to see you. Nothing, surely, could afford me so much delight. You may perhaps have found out that I am in love with you, for that is what could not be hid. But neither you nor anybody else beside myself can form an adequate idea of the affect. regard I feel for you, or of the heart-felt pleasure it affords me to reflect upon your kindness to me and to know that you are really and truly my sincere and affectionate friend. It comes to the share of few to have such a friend, and if I do not deserve it, I am at least grateful for my good fortune . . .

'I am lodged in quite a princely style and my concerts are the most magnificent assemblies you ever saw. I have literally all the world at them – at my best I had near one hundred ladies. I have fitted up my great apartment in front of the house which, as you may remember, consists of a very grand hall and three handsome rooms adjoining to it in an elegant manner. The hall and all the rooms are bordered by Turkish sofas, which completely surround them on every side. My concerts are given in two acts and between the acts the company retire to another handsome apartment consisting of three large rooms on the opposite side of the court, where they find tables spread for tea, punch and other refreshments. I wish you were here to see in what a style your friend does the honours of Munich . . .

August 15*th – Munich*. 'I shall leave Munich in about four weeks and hope to be with you at Broadlands about the 20th October. Everything relative to my journey is finally settled to my unspeakable joy and satisfaction and if my friends in England receive me kindly, nothing will be wanting to my perfect happiness. My health seems to be perfectly confirmed, and I do not fear even the November smoke and fogs of London. My leave of absence is till the end of April and I mean to spend the whole winter in London – unless you should order otherwise – I beg you would order bricks [and] mortar to be prepared for the new kitchen wash-house and hot house at Broadlands, Sheen, etc. I mean to put you to a very heavy expense in indulging my foolish passion for introducing new improvements . . .

Royal Hotel, *Pall Mall*, *October* 14*th*. 'I am at this moment in such a state of mind as renders me totally unfit for all society. I have met with such a loss as nothing can ever repair. I have been deprived of the fruits of all the labours of my whole life. Coming into town last night at about a quarter of an hour after six in the evening in my post chaise and four, I was stopped by St Paul's Church by a gang of villains and in a moment a large trunk containing almost all the papers of any consequence I possess in the world was cut off from behind my carriage and carried clear off. What I lament most is the loss of all my philosophical papers – the result of whole years of intense study and of innumerable experiments – is lost for ever. I feel myself poor for the first time in my life and I am so much disheartened by this heavy blow that I almost doubt whether I shall ever entirely recover from it. It does not appear to me to be possible for anything to ever make me smile again, or to remove the sad gloom which overspreads the whole universe. I never felt so indifferent as to life, or rather, life was never so insupportable to me. A collection of political memoirs and essays (to me invaluable) the plans, the original plans of all my operations in Bavaria – all my original proposals as they were made (in writing) to the Elector – all the returns and other details of the Establishments for the Poor – all these are gone. I went immediately to Mr Bond's office in Bow Street and by the advice they gave me there I have offered a reward of ten guineas to any person who shall bring or send back my papers, but I have very little hope of recovering them. I was at the Levée today, and must stay here to be presented to the Queen. I came home after the Levée and have seen nobody. When you get back to Broadlands you will let me know it, and I will come to you for a few days, but pressing affairs of a very disagreeable nature will oblige me to spend more time in London than I could wish. My agent here has thought proper to make difficulties in complying with a request I made him three months ago by letter to lay out for me in the stocks about £1,600 he has in his hands, of mine. It seems it is inconvenient to him to give me my own money. I must see how I am to get it; as I am not rich £1,600 more or less is an object to me. Luckily I brought between £1,500 and £1,600 with me from Bavaria, otherwise I might have found myself in serious distress. Judge, if in this moment, I should make an agreeable companion . . .'[17]

A fortnight later Lord Palmerston was able to give his wife rather more encouraging news about Count Rumford's loss. The letter also mentioned, for the first time, a project that was to occupy Palmerston's attention for the next seven years. Having veered to the support of Pitt's policies, he had formed the intention – partly as a means of avoiding the continued expense of getting himself elected to the House of Commons – to ask for an English peerage. Lord Lavington, formerly Sir

Ralph Payne, who was influential in Court circles, had undertaken to sound out the ground for him:

November 3rd. 'I dined on Saturday at Lord Lavington's, where I met Count Rumford and Sir Charles Blagden; the former had been down to St Albans. I think he looks thin but seems in pretty good health. He has had a man with him who brought him an assortment of small parts of many of his papers saying he found them in the street. They would have been of no use as they were and therefore Count Rumford did not take them but gave him great encouragement to try to *find* the whole of them which therefore I am in hopes there is a good chance he may succeed in. What seems to be the greatest loss is what he calls his common place book. The others I understand may in a little time and with some trouble be replaced and some of his most valuable papers were not in the trunk.

'I had a good deal of conversation with Lord Lavington upon the subject that has been so near bringing me up to London before. He has been extremely friendly about it and said it was a thing he had longed to speak to me about but did not know whether it would be agreeable to me that he should. He is certainly much *au fait* of these kind of things and in very intimate connection with all the parties, having been the person chiefly trusted and employed on both sides in all the late transactions. He desired to be permitted and has undertaken to sound the ground a little for me and felt with me that the other mode would have been a little more abrupt than would have been quite pleasant or perhaps quite expedient. At least what he does will not prevent the other . . .

December 19th [?]. 'I rode yesterday morning to Chiswick where the Dowager Lady Spencer has been for this last week. She was not at home when I went but I stayed and looked about the place till she and the Duchess [of Devonshire] came. The additions they have made are I think well done, as they make it a good villa and it is all in one house without much hurting the elegant appearance of the outside. Count Rumford was there waiting for them likewise. He is so called for everywhere that he is quite distracted and I really think the perpetual agitation will at last make him ill . . .'[18]

Count Rumford was indeed enjoying a great welcome and wrote exultantly to Lady Palmerston a few weeks later:

February 12th. 'You can hardly form any idea of the enthusiasm with which my schemes for making the poor comfortable and happy have been received by many of the most worthy and benevolent characters in this town. Mr Wilberforce has come to a resolution to move heaven and earth and, what is still more, the House of Commons, to get my system adopted throughout the kingdom and to show that, if it is possible, he will himself undertake to introduce it in London. He has been with me to ask my assistance and assures me that nothing shall prevent his making the attempt . . .'[19]

Palmerston was equally smug about a small social success the next week:

February 19th. 'I was at Court yesterday which was very brilliant. There were so many princes and princesses that people said it was like going to see the waxwork. The Princess of Wales looked very well and seemed to acquit herself with great propriety. She remembered me, which I did not much expect, and made me a curtsey quite across the room. I afterwards got near her and had a little conversation . . .'[20]

No headway had been made in Palmerston's project to obtain a seat in the House of Lords, and with an election due he had to take steps to conserve his seat in the Commons. There is no record of the monetary consideration involved, but he persuaded Mr Penton, a Pittite, and one of the sitting Members for Winchester, to stand down in his favour, and obtained the Prime Minister's approval for the arrangement:

February 18th. 'I had some conversation with Mr Pitt yesterday, chiefly respecting Mr Penton's business, which I had communicated to him by letter before by Lord M[almesbury]'s advice, who thought it would please him and prevent the possibility of his making any other engagement. Pitt was extremely civil and seemed much pleased with the circumstance; the more so I dare say as I think I am pretty sure by his manner that the other object will hardly succeed . . .'[21]

The 1796 engagement diary gives a straight-faced account of how simple the procedure thus became:

May 5th. 'Mr Penton and Sir R. Gamon called a meeting and dinner of all the voters, at which Mr Penton declared his inability, on account of health, to attend Parliament, and proposed me in his place, which was accepted and all the voters, being separately applied to, promised. There are 36 resident voters, 27 or 28 were present, those who were absent were applied to and all but 4 promised.

May 6th. 'Went round to those who did not attend the meeting: dined at Sir Richard Gamon's, with the Mayor and Aldermen. Went away in the evening.

May 23rd. 'Came.to Winchester to Mr Penton's and was sworn in – a business – having been elected after I left the last time.

May 25th. 'Went to a breakfast, which Sir R. Gamon and I gave at the White Hart. Went from thence at eleven to the Town Hall. The Mayor, after the writ and precept were read, declared the purpose of the meeting. Acts of Parliament against bribery read – Mayor sworn – Mr Penton stated to the meeting his inability to attend and proposed Sir R. Gamon and me. Mayor asked if anybody proposed any other candidate. None being proposed, he declared us duly and unanimously elected. Sir Richard Gamon and I returned our thanks separately and Mr Penton likewise, for the kindness done him in taking his recommendation.

'Election being over, we returned back to the White Hart, where the breakfast was continued and some of the voters took some cold meat. Sir Richard and I went round to the house of the Mayor and Aldermen and visited such as were at home.

'Sir Richard called me at Mr Penton's to go to dinner. Some men were collected who wanted to take off the horses and to draw us to the inn, which we declined. N.B. They applied to us while at dinner for something to drink – sent them a guinea. About 60 people dined. Such of the non-residents as live near the town and several of the townspeople, not voters, being invited. Stayed till half past seven, when Mr Penton, being an invalid, took his leave and we went away at the same time. Many toasts, but no compulsion about drunkery and no

notice taken of those who avoided it. Two or three hogsheads
of beer given to the people in the street. Very little noise or
disturbance. Went to Sir R. Gamon's house from the White
Hart, where my chaise was waiting and from thence to
Broadlands.

'Expenses of the election day between Sir Richard and me.
The Mayor undertook to settle them and Sir Richard to pay
my share of them with his own. My share amounted to
£87 12s. od., including fees to Town Clerk 25 guineas and to
[blank] 10 guineas.'

★   ★   ★

A distinctly disagreeable reminder of the past – probably dating
back to the erased diary entries in the 1770's – had been sent on
April 13, 1796, in the shape of a blackmailing letter from a
former lady friend:

Lisbon, April the 13th '96
'This letter, My Lord, being of the greatest importance to
your subsequent – domestic – happiness – I must, therefore, beg
leave to call forth your most serious attention to the contents
of it.

I am persuaded this intrusion will not be deemed *impertinent*,
when you are informed of my *reasons*, and *motives* for having
thus addressed you: – and in order to trespass upon your Lordship's time as little as possible – I will immediately come to the
point, and explain the business – in as few words as the nature
of the subject will admit of –

From *long*, and *extreme ill health* – with a variety of *other
distressing* circumstances – (a repetition of which, would be as
painful for me to recount as your Lordship to peruse) – am
I driven to the disagreable necessity – of Publishing – *The
Memoirs of My Own Life*. 'Tis in order to procure myself *a
little bread!*

From the very first moment, My Lord, in which I made my
appearance in the gay world, I have ever kept a *regular* and
correct journal – of those occurrences and events – in which either
my Friends or *myself* were at all concerned: – and *by this journal*,

I am thoroughly enabled to give *the world* a very great variety
of *little anecdotes*, and *particulars* – of those Gentlemen, with
whom, I have been at all acquainted.

I have been already offered, (by a gentleman from England
to whom I had shown a few introductory pages of *my memoirs*)
for the *entire* copyright of my manuscript either the sum of
five hundred pounds in ready money, or an annuity of fifty
pounds a year for the remainder of my life, – but notwithstanding the *pressing necessity* of my *exhausted finances*, I was
determined *not to accept the money* without having first made
known to *my friends* the *unfortunate situation* in which I am
placed and in consequence thereof *my unalterable determination* –
to *publish my memoirs immediately* – *unless* assisted *by them* in the
extricating myself from my present difficulties.

All I request of *my friends*, is the contribution of a sufficient
sum of money to enable me to *purchase* myself an annuity for
my life. *In that case*, I will adhere, – *most sacredly* – *to the promises
I now make* – of *destroying* not only the whole of *my manuscript*
but, likewise – every *letter, note* &'. &' – which may *hereafter*
lead to a *discovery* of the *names* or *circumstances* of my respective
friends. But, – on the contrary – should *I not* receive an answer
by the *return of* post, – and *that to the purpose;* – The *anecdotes*
and *particular occurrences* of *every gentleman* – whose *name* may
be inserted in *my journal* – *must*, and *will*, in the course of a very
few weeks appear before the awful tribunal of *the public*.

As *this letter*, My Lord, (provided I am not honoured with
an *immediate* answer to it) together with many others, possibly –
upon the same subject – will be *published* and *prefixed* to *my
memoirs, the world* will then perceive the *generous* conduct *I have*
observed towards my friends and that, the *publication* or *sup-
pression* of their *names – weaknesses – meannesses – frolics – vices*
&c. &c – *entirely* depended upon *themselves*.

Your Lordship – I most sincerely hope – will not oblige me
to the disagreable office of presenting to the critical eye of an
impartial public – a *correct* and *chronological* account of our *several
meetings* at the house of *your friend Mrs Weston*'s (in Berkeley
Street Piccadilly).

It is my *penury* and *ill health*, my Lord, which alone *could* have *extorted* from me these *important secrets*, and I do *assure* you it can be *no otherways avoided* – than, by your *immediate acquiescence* in my present requests. It is impossible, (from my *engagements* respecting *the manuscript* with the above mentioned gentleman) that I can *defer* the time of *settlement* for a *longer* term than that of the *return of post*.

There is one *particular* and *important* circumstance of which I wish to inform and apprise your Lordship. It is this – that (*at present*) no person whatever (*Your Lordship*, *Mrs Weston* and *myself* excepted) has the least knowledge, or suspicion, of *our former clandestine connexions:* – nor is *anyone* at all acquainted with the *purport* of this letter. You will, therefore, act just as you please. I have done *my duty*, and it only remains for *you* – to *do yours:* – what *your own* reflections may determine *that duty* to be I *know not*, but should I receive *no answer* to this *friendly* address, I shall be perfectly aware of your Lordship's sentiments, and proceed accordingly: – though I can hardly suppose you would *wish the world* to be so well *acquainted* with your *private intrigues* as *my journal must* occasion them to be: – and let it be remembered, though it may be an easy matter to *prevent* this publication, yet to *recall* it, – when *published* – will be *impossible*.

I have the honour to be, your very humble servant

Anna Crewe (Anna Pitt)

PS. This letter (together with several others) I have enclosed to a gentleman in Wales, who will forward them to their respective destinations, and any letter directed to Mrs Crewe, Lisbon, in a *blank cover* – addressed to Mr Countney, St Althan, near Cowbridge, Glamorganshire, will be duly forwarded to me by the first packet that sails for this port.

He is totally ignorant as to the *contents* of these letters, and has no reason but to believe me to be, a *married woman!*

N.B. The enclosed is a list of the names of those gentlemen to whom I have written by the present opportunity. *Your name*, however, my Lord (in the *list* presented to my *other friends*) I have *entirely omitted:* – being thoroughly convinced that, your *subsequent* conduct *towards me*, will *not merit an exposure!* Once more adieu! –'

In his reply Palmerston showed himself a better diplomatist than the reputation of his public career would seem to warrant:

Draft letter to Mrs Pitt, May 16th, 1796

'Madam,

On my return to London after a few days' absence I found your letter stating your distressed situation and your intention of procuring some relief by publishing the memoirs of your life. In answer to this as far as regards myself I have only to say that anything that ever passed between us was of so trifling and unimportant a nature that I feel very little interested about the publication of it. I am sorry that the mode of application you have adopted makes it impossible for me with propriety to afford you any assistance at present. All I can say is that when your book appears, if I find you have omitted mentioning my name, I shall look upon it as a mark of delicacy and attention on your part which would give you a just claim to some pecuniary assistance from me, which in that case I should not refuse to afford you.'

The lady was not to be put off:

Lisbon, Wednesday June 8th, '96

'My Lord,

I confess myself not a little surprised at the contents of your letter (with which I am this moment honoured) dated the 16th of May last.

That my *mode* of application should have proved displeasing to your Lordship is a circumstance of which I was by no means aware, but acknowledge myself most essentially hurt when, at the moment in which I was labouring to adopt the most delicate, and satisfactory, plan of conveying the account of my unfortunate situation, and intentions, to my friends in general – that Lord Palmerston, *alone*, should reprobate the idea, and, *negatively*, tend to the *extinguishing* [of] that flame of approaching happiness, and competency, for the completion of which, the *whole* of my *other* friends have, with the utmost humanity – and unexpected liberality, respectively, promoted my, otherwise, feeble attempts in realising that state of *existence* to which

I had directed my most sanguine hopes and moderate wishes. – Yes, my Lord, I have received, not only their pecuniary assistance, but, likewise their best thanks, and warmest praise, for the handsome manner in which I had treated them respecting my intended publication: – and many of these friends, my Lord, as *slightly* known to me, as yourself: – and though they could not (had they conducted themselves with *propriety*) have contributed to my relief – still, recollecting (perhaps) that (*in regard to Mrs Pitt*) it would not be the *first* time of their having overstretched that emphatic line, they (in the present instance) have once more overlooked the exact observance of that *freezing* thought, and contributed their assistance to an unfortunate and penurious *female* – remembering, that the education, generally appropriated to the formation of *their* understandings doth entirely preclude the possibility of their being so competent a judge of *strict decorum*, in the framing and drawing up a case of *real* distress – and poverty – as those of the other sex – whose understandings having been assisted, and informed by academical tuition – and whose avocation in life so frequently demanding *this* trial of their skill, renders the task of solicitation, and appeal, not only an *easy*, but likewise a *natural one*.

Indeed, my Lord, such a letter from *you*, (of whom I never before had reason to think but with the utmost pleasure and satisfaction) has made the deeper impression upon my mind from the circumstances of having ever conceived you to be possessed of the greatest humanity and fellow-feeling. Had any person told me that such an appeal to your Lordship's philanthropy (even by *a stranger*) had been attended with un-success, I must, from the opinion I had ever formed of my Lord Palmerston, have received the intelligence as I would the grossest violation of *truth*. 'Tis true, my Lord, the conclusion of your letter promises me your pecuniary assistance at a subsequent period: that is to say – after the publication of my book. Does your Lordship mistrust *my gratitude?* Can your Lordship suppose, for a moment, I should first receive your donation and *afterwards* make public those little anecdotes *I now* have the power of doing? Thank God, the gratitude of *Anna Pitt*, hath not been entertained in so unfavourable a light by any *other friend* whatever.

Your Lordship, will, I am persuaded, do me the justice to believe that, what I am now about to say, has not the most distant allusion to a doubt of *your own scrupulous* adherence to the voluntary promise made in your former letter: but, my Lord, suffer me to assure you, that had I not relied too much upon the promises of the great, I need not now have bent myself to supplicate for Bread! I might have swam in affluence and splendour, but (at the moment) knowing nought but the sunshine of fortune, I *then* disregarded those promises I have since found to have consisted in air. What was the consequence? I vowed never, again, to abide by them, – and was your Lordship to put the case home, you would not only *commend*, but *applaud* me for that determination. For let us suppose (but which I know to be impossible) that after the publication of my work, I received either a five or a ten pound note from your Lordship? Where should I obtain redress for such a mockery. Should I not be laughed at, and told I had deserved it, after the innumerable instances I had received of the instability of those promises which had been made me – By Great Men! – to trust them ever again. I could, in that case, make no other reply than this – that though deceived myself I would take pretty good care that the rest of the world should (in future) be well guarded from a like misfortune: – for I would instantly add a postscript to *my work*, to convince the many poor wretches who may come hereafter – *by real letters* and concurring circumstances, – of the cruel and unavoidable fallacy of worldly dependance.

And now, my Lord, after having informed you, that I have heard from every friend to whom I had written by the same opportunity with your Lordship (excepting five) and that in the most satisfactory manner imaginable, I can only say that so pleasing a circumstance has so far reduced the bulk of *my book*, – and, in course, its value to the intended purchaser, that I have declined the gentleman's offer (the particulars of which were fully explained in my last letter to your Lordship) and shall myself published the *two Vols* now remaining in order to return my grateful thanks to all contributary friends – and that in a general way, without making mention of *any names:* – and at the same time to bring forth to public view those few remaining persons who have so materially injured me: – and for the exclusion of whom no *pecuniary* consideration whatever, could induce me to give assent.

With every apology, my Lord, for having thus, *again*, intruded upon your valuable time – and the hopes and expectations of once more being honoured with a line from your Lordship –

I have the Honour to be, Your most obedient, very humble servant

> Anna Crewe, formerly Anna Pitt.

PS. Since I last wrote to you, my Lord, I have brought my recollection to your *domestic address* – but – as my former packet reached your Lordship so very safely, I conceived it more prudent (and that it would be more satisfactory to the wishes of your Lordship) to transmit my present letter by means of the *same conveyance* – rather than that of forwarding it immediately to *Broadland!* [*sic*] a seat that forms, at once, so beautiful and respectable a prospect, from the elevation of *Rumsey Bridge*. Once more adieu!

N.B. Upon second thoughts, my Lord, I again transmit you my address – Mrs Crewe, Lisbon – enclosed in a blank cover and addressed to Mr Countney, St Althan near Cowbridge, Glamorganshire – fearful that you may either have destroyed, or forgotten it.'[22]

In spite of the implied threat in the postscript, Palmerston merely annotated this letter at the bottom in his own hand: 'Not answered'.

* * *

Count Rumford had stirring news in his letters to Lady Palmerston on his return to Munich:

August 19th, 1796. 'We [his daughter had joined him from America] arrived here at 3 o'clock in the afternoon and at 4 I saw the Elector, who received me in the kindest manner possible; as did also the Electrice whom he went and called into his room to see me. The young Countess of Rumford was presented to their Electoral Highnesses and was (really) most graciously received. We found their Electoral Highnesses on the eve of their departure for Saxony. The Austrians are retreating in all directions and we expect the French here in a few days. I am determined to stay here and share the fate of a country to which I feel myself attached by the strongest ties of gratitude and affection. Perhaps being present, I may have it in my power to be of use, or I certainly should not. My first visit to my garden drew a flood of tears to my eyes. The monument the public have erected to commemorate my services in this country is such as I dare not describe and the inscriptions on it – which are engraved in Bavarian marble – are such as I cannot read without blushing. To think how little I have deserved them. I wish you could have seen my daughter – when they were translated to her – as she stood with her eyes swimming in tears, gazing on her father's bust . . .'

He needed all his reputation to deal with the looming crisis. The French armies under Jourdan and Moreau which had invaded the German states were locked in fierce combat with the Austrians under the Archduke Charles. As the fortunes of war swayed, Rumford had delicate duties to perform:

September 25th. 'I found everybody here in the greatest consternation. The Elector had packed up and sent off to Austria all his most valuable effects and held himself in readiness to leave the country himself at a moment's warning and to retire into Saxony. He actually left us on the morning of the 22nd, upon the arrival of the French upon the frontiers of Bavaria, and he is now at Lokwitz, a country seat belonging to Count Schall – his Minister at the Court of Saxony – situated five English miles from Dresden. As to myself, according to my own proposal, it was settled that I should remain at Munich and hold myself in readiness to act in case an opportunity should offer where my active services should be wanted. In the meantime, that I should have an eye to what should be going on, that I should correspond constantly and confidentially with the Elector and that in case the French should come to Munich, I should endeavour to display and make the most of my new establishments and try to interest the feelings of their generals in their preservation and in the preservation of the town and the country. I was, however, in the sequel, called upon to act a more conspicuous and ostensible part. On the 23rd August, the French crossed [the] Lech near Augsburg and attacked the Austrians at Friedburg, under the command of General La Tour, and drove them from their position and obliged them to fall back to Dachau, which is in sight of Munich and only four leagues distant from it. In consequence of these events, the army of Prince Condé, which was posted on the Bavarian side of the Lech at Landsberg, fell back towards Munich to cover the left of the Austrians in their new position and give time for the baggage of both armies (the Austrians and that of Condé) to pass the Isar at Munich. This passage lasted two whole days, during which time all the roads in the neighbourhood of Munich were full of wagons. On the 26th and 27th the armies followed and passing over the bridge at Munich took post on the bank of the river opposite the town where, as you may remember, the ground is high and commands most completely not only the bridge over the Isar but also the whole city. Upon this commanding eminence several batteries were erected. The bridge was barricaded and every measure taken, as well to defend the passage of the river as to awe the town. Some days before the arrival of the Austrians in our neighbourhood, all the Bavarian regiments which had been called in from their several garrisons and cantonments in the different parts of the country were assembled at Munich, so that the garrison of the town consisted now of more than 10,000 regular troops besides the militia of the city, which amounts to 2,000 men.

'This force had been collected in order to protect the capital and prevent it being occupied by either of the armies in its neighbourhood and also to prevent our troops being insulted or disarmed or forced to act contrary to the orders and intentions of the Elector. Some of our battalions had been disarmed by the Austrians in the Palatinate and we were determined that the same insult should not be offered to the Bavarian regiments. Consequently, when the Austrian army approached Munich in their retreat from the Lech, the gates of the town were shut and the garrison put under arms. The Austrian general was told (and unfortunately for us, in language rather too gross and insulting to be borne with patience by the general of a formidable army) that he might pass round the town and over the bridge, but that a passage through the town would not be permitted, and if it should be attempted force would be opposed by force.

'It was certainly right not to permit the Austrian army to pass through the town. They had no right to do so, on the contrary, by the laws of the Empire, all cities which are the residence of the sovereign of that country, have a right to refuse a passage to all foreign troops, even to those of the Emperor. Added to this, there was a road round the town without the walls. As the Austrians were not pursued in their retreat by the French, and as it was the side of the river opposite the town which they meant to defend, there was not even a pretext for their insisting on a passage through the town. Politeness, however, as well as prudence required that all offensive language and unfriendly demonstrations should be avoided, which, I am sorry to say, was not the case.

'Not contented with refusing a passage to the troops, the gates were shut against officers who singly presented themselves and politely asked leave to go into the town on their private affairs and even the Prince of Condé and General La Tour were positively refused admittance, though they desired to stay in the town but a few moments and offered to leave their escorts behind them at the gates. This is not all. When General La Tour came before the town at the head of his army (which he conducted in person) a detachment of Bavarian cavalry went out to meet him and, with their swords drawn, conducted him (I blush to say it) like a prisoner round the town, to the scandal of all those who were witnesses to the scene, and to the eternal shame of the officer who commanded in Munich at that time.

'This treatment, as is easy to conceive, exasperated in the highest degree the Austrian general and, after he had crossed the river with his army and planted his artillery and posted his troops on the commanding height over against the town, he lost no time in making us acquainted with his sentiments on the subject, and those whom the Elector had left at the head of the affairs of state (the Council of the Regency) began to see the dangers into which the unaccountable conduct of the officer at the head of the troops had plunged them. Under these embarrassments they thought proper (in consequence, as I have reason to believe, of private instructions left them by the Elector) to call me to their councils. Till this moment, I had been living at Munich as a private man, contenting myself with merely superintending the several public establishments that had been formed here under my direction, and amusing myself with the direction of workmen employed in the public garden. I had not even put on my regimentals since my return from England, except when I went to Court, and I did not foresee any event that could render my active services in the line of my profession of any public utility, much less could afford a general officer an opportunity of acquiring reputation, I studiously avoided taking part in what was going on and kept myself as retired from the world and from all public business as possible. What tended to increase the alarms of the Regency greatly was the consternation that reigned in the town, which was general among all classes of the inhabitants, and was painted in every countenance and as the public had never much confidence in the officer who commanded the troops and soon perceived by his agitation (which was so apparent as to be noticed by everybody who saw him) as well as by the confusion and uproar into which he had contrived to throw the troops in the garrison by his unmeaning and contradictory orders and arrangements, that he had quite lost his head, every step he took was watched in anxious expectation of the dangers that might follow from it, and served to increase the apprehension of the frightened inhabitants. The whole garrison was under arms two whole days and nights – eight regiments of infantry, five regiments of cavalry and above a thousand horses with a complete battalion of artillery which filled all the streets and public squares – cannon were drawn out of the arsenal and planted at all the gates and nothing was heard, night or day, but the clashing of arms, the clattering of horses upon the pavements, and the confused noise of a multitude of people moving in haste in all possible directions. Other sounds, still more alarming, began at last to mix in this din. The murmurings of the soldiers grew general and loud, and even the very horses had been exposed (unnecessarily) the whole time to the utmost violence of the storm. In short, the situation of affairs within the town began to be really critical and alarming, to say nothing of the hostile preparations of the Austrians on the opposite bank of the river, though their cannon were pointed against the town and, though I knew they were much exasperated against us, yet I did not imagine they would fire into it – at least not till the arrival of the French should give them a new and better pretext for doing so. I had not the smallest doubt, however, of their beating our houses about our ears the moment the Republicans should make their appearance in the town, and I was much afraid the proper measures would not be adopted and pursued with firmness for keeping them out of it. This was the situation of affairs when I was called to assist at the deliberations of the Council of Regency. I will not add to the length of this long epistle by giving you a history of all the measures that have since been adopted under my direction. I will only tell you shortly that the town of Munich has been preserved and the honour of our troops has received no stain. I might add (to you) that from the moment I took command of the army, the apprehensions of the inhabitants began to subside and that I never pass through the streets without receiving the most flattering proofs of the public gratitude and affection. The first step I took after I had taken the command of the army was to go myself to General La Tour to make our excuses for the improper manner in which he and his army had been treated; and at the same time to assure him that the French army should not be permitted to enter the town and, if they should attempt it, such attempts would be opposed by force . . .

November 18th. 'It gave me uncommon pleasure to receive a letter from you dated from my own room at Broadlands. Pray write to me from thence often. Was it to flatter me, my dear Lady P., that you desired to have a continuation of my history of our military transactions? – or would those details really amuse you? I can treat you with no battles of our own, though we were witnesses to several sharp engagements within pistol shot of our walls, and great numbers of bullets of all dimensions whistled over our heads. Perhaps at some more leisure moment, I may sit down to write a detailed account of all that happened during the short time that the environs of Munich were the theatre of war. It will serve to fix in my own memory events that were peculiarly interesting to me, and it may perhaps at some future period afford amusement to a friend. I received yesterday a most flattering compliment from the Duke of Berkenfeld, the next heir to the Elector's dominions, after the Duke of Deux Ponts. He had been residing at Ansbach, in the King of Prussia's dominions, during the time the French were in Bavaria, from whence he is just returned to Landshut, the place of his ordinary residence, and is now here on a visit to the Elector. He came up to me at the Levée and loud, so as to be heard by the whole Court, returned me his thanks for the important services I had rendered the Elector and the country. He said that not only Munich, but Bavaria and the national honour had been preserved by my prudent and spirited exertions. That is for you – and for you alone. I should be sorry to be thought vain and ostentatious; you, I know, will not think me so . . .'[23]

* * *

During the whole period since the family's return from the Continent at the end of 1794 the alteration and decoration of the Hanover Square house had been continuing, with a fair degree of disorder, of which Palmerston sent his wife full details:

February 9th, 1795. 'We are in fine confusion here with litter and cases of all kinds which I am getting out of the way as well as I can. I hope the house may be made comfortable in time but I cannot say much for it at present. It never has been possible to make the rooms warm during the cold weather and now that is over all the chimneys seem disposed to smoke . . .

October 30th. 'I have had Holland with me this morning. Various reasons are given why much greater progress could not have been made, though it is certain some might. In about a fortnight or a little more everything will be so nearly finished

that it will be a good time to chose furniture and therefore I
believe it will be worth while for you to come up then and
I hope to go down with you afterwards, though I foresee that
there will be no adjournment till near Christmas . . .

December 12*th*. 'I have been in the City and called at the two
carpet warehouses. I see nothing better than the two patterns
we chose and therefore think I shall take that with the ovals
for the two drawing rooms. The man from Carpenters Hall is
to come to measure the rooms in a day or two. I called likewise at Gillows, who thinks he shall have no difficulty in
supplying any quantity I may want of the vine leaf linen . . .

February 18*th*, 1796. 'Your apartment seems finished and is
very pretty. I shall get the grate home and put up the pictures
and books as soon as I can. I shall have the green of the pedestals
of the columns altered to a plain green as I do not like the
imitation of wood. I am afraid they have made but a bad job
of the chimneys as I found the inner room smoking yesterday,
which would be a cruel circumstance and spoil all the furniture.
Mr Holland desired I would let him alone for a day or two and
he would effectually prevent it . . .

February 22*nd*. 'The chimney in the inner drawing room
smokes when the fire is first lighted, which is very provoking
and must not be suffered as it will spoil everything. The proper
grate is now brought home and may perhaps do better than
that which was made use of as it is a little higher. They are
going likewise to set it a little farther back. If this does not
answer we must either try Count Rumford's plan entirely or
have a close stove. The carpets, tables and chairs are all within
a few days of being ready as the people say . . .'

By the end of the year, he was introducing a note of economy:

December 5*th*. 'As to furniture and carpets I am quite at a loss.
I suppose one cannot do without an expensive carpet under
one's green cloth. I am very doubtful whether I shall cover the
whole room. I rather think I may as well not do it as the floor
is all new or as good as new, nor do I suppose it is material to
have a fine carpet upon the floor of the outer room which can
at present be nothing but a passage and which therefore I
should think might do with green cloth only and something

of sailcloth for the servants to walk over to my room door, or perhaps as it is a small room a moderate carpet in the middle and no green cloth would be the best. I suppose I shall keep the same sofas and chairs that I had before, only having them new repaired and covered, but with what and what are the curtains to be? . . .

[Undated] 'As to furniture, the old distracting subject, I think it will be best to keep the old cabriolet chairs for the outer drawing room. Shall I have them new gilt and painted or only painted? I think the sofa will be best in your dressing room and I find Ince has been altering it as to the stuffing and making cushions, etc. according to directions you left with him. The question now will be, will you have those eight chairs of his which will match very well with the sofa or will you have new ones? You may have his new painted for 2 guineas or perhaps something less, so that the difference of price is trifling, as those I mentioned would not be quite so cheap as I understood, the only thing is which you would prefer.

'I have been this morning at Bedford House with Holland, but did not see much there to the purpose except one curtain which is handsome enough, it is lined with green tammy. The fringe is a mixture of worsted and I believe cotton with some silk. If you think it better I can have cotton fringe but I thought when you was here you decided to have the fringe part worsted with silk head. Green worsted does better than any other . . .'24

Their attention to the expense involved was very much a sign of the times. The collapse of Pitt's first coalition in the war against France was the prelude to a bad period of internal stress and depression in England. The funds were down to almost half their face value, ready money was short everywhere and Palmerston found that he was in process of over-spending himself. He had already paid Holland £1,100 on account of the alterations and works at the Hanover Square house, plus another £350 for minor work done at Broadlands and Sheen and still owed him another £1,560, which was not paid off for nearly two years.

In November, 1796, Palmerston had received an additional account from Ince, Holland's associate, the cabinet-maker, for

£700, of which £250 was paid on account, although he had to wait for another six months for the rest. Palmerston clearly considered his bill excessive and must have complained about it in a letter to Lady Palmerston, which is not extant, but which elicited this reply:

November 11th. 'I am much surprised and truly sorry to hear that Ince persists in making out such a bill, and I own I think his conduct very extraordinary in having so long withheld the particulars of his account, and his pretended ignorance on the subject. It is perhaps unfair to judge harshly but he certainly acted very oddly . . .'

Palmerston must also have made some general remarks about the need for economy, as the rest of his wife's letter contained this immediate and generous response:

'All I can say is that if you think we should spend less money this year by the family staying in the country and your living in a bachelor style in London, I have no kind of objection, for I have no wish to see London, and here I have no desire to see company. And I should want no horses in the country, never liking to go out in the carriage and always preferring walking. In short I beg you will adopt any plan you think most advisable and be assured there is none (even to the parting with Broadlands if you thought it right) to which I should even in *thought* have the least objection. As long as you and my children are well and happy, places are perfectly indifferent to me. And as I was never born to the expectation of the luxuries your partiality has placed me in the enjoyment of, the resignation of any can never be attended with a regret, save what I may feel at your being deprived of them. A deprivation which owes its origin from too much liberality and generosity towards me and mine. That reflection alone may call forth some melancholy ideas and be attended with regret, but it will be on your account not mine. Let me then request that you will never consider me in any plan you may form, for my greatest pleasure will ever arise from contributing in any degree to your comfort . . .

'Pray put this letter into the fire as soon as you have read it. I dread your leaving my letter on your table. The fire is a much more convenient place for them . . .'[25]

In fact Palmerston was faced with a period of acute financial embarrassment, which in due course called for drastic measures. His holdings in England managed to tide them over the worst of the crisis, which was brought to a head by a temporary cessation, due to the disturbed condition of the country, of his income from the family estates in Ireland.

At least their personal crisis had not prevented Palmerston from recording some of the current quips:

'*An old woman, asking why the price of her candles was raised and being told it was because of the war, desired to know whether they fought by candle light.*

'*When Mr Hey was going [as] Chief Justice to Canada, a friend advised him to carry over a good stock of shirts. "Sir," said he, "if I had a good stock of shirts I should not go there".*

'*An officer, being ordered by a court martial to ask another officer's pardon for having spoke ill of him, did it in the following manner: "Sir, I am accused of having called you a scoundrel, it's true; I am ordered to make you an apology, I am sorry for it."*

'*The late Lord Gage being asked by one of his friends, as remarkable as his Lordship for not paying his debts, who was his tailor? replied, "Your Lordship must excuse me, as I am certain the poor fellow cannot afford to work for us both."*

'*An author who had wrote a very dull play, having a quarrel with another author whose play had been hissed off the stage, reproached him with it. To which the other replied, "T'is true, your play was not hissed, but the reason is that it is not possible to hiss while one is yawning".*

'*Mr Palmer Robinson, going with Lord Pomfret in a hackney coach to Hyde Park to fight, just as they turned into the Park they met an empty hearse, upon which, Robinson thrusts his head out of the window and calls out with great generosity, "Here, you fellow with the hell cart, if you'll stay a minute or two, I'll give you a fare".*

'*A gentleman, giving a very strong dram to a person who complained that nothing he could take was warm enough, said, "If this won't do, you have nothing left but to fire a pistol down your throat".*

'*Cuckoldom is totally gone down in the world. It was formerly a situation in life and distinguished a man, but now it is nothing at all.*'

REFERENCES

1. B.1 10.XII.1794
2. B.1 11.XII.1794
3. C.44(a) 13.I.1795
4. B.1
5. B.2
6. B.1
7. B.2
8. B.1
9. B.2
10. B.2
11. B.1 10.XII.1794
12. B.1
13. D.9(b) 23.III.1795
14. B.1
15. D.8 30.IV.1795
16. B.1
17. D.6
18. B.1
19. D.6
20. B.1
21. B.1
22. C.66(a) and (b)
23. D.6
24. B.1
25. B.2

CHAPTER XI

IRELAND

Palmerston the absentee landlord – the Sligo estate – treatment of his tenants – the startlish Mr Hatch – Lord Charlemont and the Volunteers – Dublin Castle – Wolfe Tone and the United Irishmen – Fitzwilliam and Camden – revolt of the tenantry – the Hoche expedition to Bantry Bay – Palmerston's Irish revenues suspended

MORE than half Palmerston's income came from his estates in Ireland. Most of his holdings consisted of several thousand acres of farm land in County Sligo, together with a few small urban properties in Dublin. He was nominally a Member of the Irish Parliament from 1761 until the Act of Union in 1801, yet in all his life he spent but four brief periods in the land which had given his family its title. He never spoke once in its legislature, and left the extraction of his rents to agents, working through tenants, sub-tenants and under-tenants. He was, it is to be feared, a typical absentee landlord; not from malice – because on the few occasions when he took a personal hand in the administration of his estates the instructions he gave to his agents were not untinged with humanity, but because it was the pattern of the times and of the particular class to which he belonged.

He paid his first visit in November, 1761, not quite a year after attaining his majority. The first impression he reported to his mother changed but little over the years:

'The appearance of this country affords a disagreeable contrast to anybody coming from England on account of the great scarcity of trees, the quantity of bog and barren mountains and the great want of every kind of improvement, especially towards the western coast, in the province of Connaught, where I was. To say the truth, I think Sligo and the adjacent counties the most dreary waste I ever yet beheld, but I hope a few years will produce an alteration, as the linen manufacture, the only resource of this country, which has made the neighbouring

The entrance hall at Broadlands, showing part of the collection of antique marbles assembled by Viscount Palmerston

Benjamin Mee

province of Ulster rich, populous and even beautiful, and which must produce the same effects wherever it extends itself, is daily gaining ground there . . .

'The Parliament met the 22nd of last month, when I took my seat without any particular ceremony. Everything is mightily quiet here at present. The new Lord Lieutenant [the Earl of Halifax, who had succeeded the Duke of Bedford] is a universal favourite and, indeed, nobody ever filled that high station with more dignity and propriety and greater abilities or gained more upon the affections of a people than he has done in the short time he has been here . . .'[1]

No record has survived of the details of Palmerston's journey to Ireland between August and October, 1771, with the painter William Pars, apart from the bare summary in the overall diary, which mentions that he stayed with Mr Hatch, his agent, in Dublin, and at the house of his agent, Corkran, in Sligo. However, journals, letters and estate memorandum books survive for his two subsequent visits in 1784 and 1788. The estate books, in which supplementary entries were made from time to time in subsequent years, give in their laconic style a remarkable picture of the infamous system of land tenure, which for decades had allowed no native born Catholic Irishman, except on punitive financial terms, to take out a lease for more than three lives, or thirty-one years. Although Palmerston often gave vent to his exasperation at the wild complexity of the holdings, he was not without sympathy for the unfortunate under-tenants:

'Philip Byrne, Seneschall of the Manor of Ahamlish, an officer empowered to hold Courts for adjusting small claims and recovering small debts among the tenants. Mr Byrne, old and negligent of this office. In other hands it might be made of essential use. His bailiff used to collect money among the poor tenants for the Seneschall's dinner when the courts were held, which was very uncertain. This properly put a stop to by Mr Lyons [the successor or Corkran, who, the context of the entries makes clear, had proved inefficient and probably dishonest].

'Killculloge and the Tail. £140 and £2 2s. od. Tithes. 3 lives all in being. Mr O'Birne holds this and lets it out again at

M

exorbitant rents to wretched under-tenants. He is in arrear one year; is made to pay now regularly the growing rent, but does nothing to clear the arrear. This farm would produce a large profit rent to O'Birne if he was to let it out reasonably. As it is he probably loses much of his nominal rents. Mr O'Birne persuaded the tenants to make a quay and a road leading to it through the farm, pretending he had got a presentiment for it. This turned out false and the tenants were never paid. However, the road was an advantage to them and to the whole country. But Mr O'Birne charged a tax upon all vessels that came in and upon horses that came for the goods. This being unreasonable and without just grounds is discontinued.

'Mr O'Birne in 1777 objected to pay his rent, alleging he had not the number of acres he ought to have. A surveyor was brought down at a large expense and it was found he had 20 acres more. Many of his under-tenants pay from £1 1s. od. to £1 5s. od. per acre.

'Mr O'Birne, as a magistrate, used to encourage litigations and quarrels among the poor tenants. Mr Lyons put a stop to this by obliging the tenants to refer their disputes to him before they went to a magistrate. O'Birne likewise used to oppress them much by impounding cattle and taking exorbitant fees for releasing them.

'Clissony, etc. recovered from Corkran. Let to Ward for 31 years from 1763, for £105. Lease bought by Corkran. Now held by Mr Corkran's under-tenants at a very advanced rent of £224. They are excessively poor and paying in general very ill. Required to be new regulated, properly divided and a plan formed for letting it, the same as Mount Temple. Many bad arrears may be taken out in work for the benefit of the estate.

'Ardnaglasses. Held by Gelmartin and Co. under a promise of a lease at £60. Afterwards an abatement was recommended of £9 which makes it a very good bargain for them. Have never paid well and are much in arrear after allowing them the abatement. Cleriogh has been taken from them and let at 20 guineas to a very good tenant and his payments are carried to their account, notwithstanding all which they have incurred £30 arrear in the two last years. Their farm is a good land and would let to a good tenant for much more than they pay. These were people whom I wished to help by letting them their lands directly, at a reasonable price as being those who actually used it.

'These people seem to deserve no encouragement. The land should be advertised and let to a good tenant at a fair price.

'Grellagh, Cravykeel, Newtown, Kiltekeagh, and Googie [?]. This is one of the leases recovered from Corkran. Was let to him at £167 10s. 0d. per annum. The under-tenants stand at £279 13s. 11d.

'Kiltekeagh; a good farm held at near £50 by Corkran's under-tenants, who are too numerous and poor and cannot continue. It must be advertised.

'Derrylighane; another part let to Francis Crean at £12. He died last year in arrear £54 14s. 7d., which will never be recovered. Now held on by his daughter who cannot pay the rent, nor is capable of turning it to any account. This must be re-let. Something to be done for the woman . . .

'East Knocknaskeagh. Let by me in 1776 to Mick McCrehan and a number of others for 31 years at £60, reasonably let. Rent paid with some difficulty on account of their too great number, but are not in arrear. Have enclosed some part with a wall; 93 acres arable and pasture, 40 bog.

'Cloghbooly. Agreed to be let in 1771 to Patrick Mulvihil and a very large number of others for 31 years at £111. An abatement was afterwards made of £11, reducing it to £100, but the lease was never given. The land is set rather high and the tenants pay ill and are in arrear. This is more owing to their too great number and the badness of many of them than any other cause. The land is remarkably good. The number of tenants should be reduced, the best of them chosen out and some substantial persons got to join them. A further small abatement will probably be necessary, after which they may do extremely well . . .

'East Dromfad, Clysparrow, Edenreevagh, East Division of Mount Temple – all let to under-tenants.

'Let to Felix Gallagher from November, 1785 for 3 lives or 21 years, at £150. He is an improving tenant, resident at Dublin where he is a teacher of mathematics in the College, but goes to Sligo in the vacation. Uses a small part of the land himself. The under-tenants are encouraged and put in a good way by him. Has a fair bargain and pays well . . .

'Creevymore and Mills of Grellagh and Barnaderrig.

'Let to Phillip Byrne, Esq. at £83 for three lives. Owen, John and Henry Wynne, sons of Owen Wynne, Esq. of Hazlewood. Of these John is dead. Arable and pasture 103 acres; mountain and bog 224. The part of the farm to the left of the road to Ballyshannon is remarkably good ground, let out to an under-tenant. That on the right let to a great number of very poor people, totally unimproved. The tenants are compelled by their leases to bring their corn to be ground at these mills and great complaints have been made that Mr Byrne does not keep them in repair. He has lately done something to them. Sept. 1789: Byrne's profit rent, supposed, £102 per annum; lets it to one MacEntire, who has profit rent of £48 per annum. Both these are collected on the first instance and the poor tenants left to pay me, which they cannot do. Byrne died in June, 1794, leaving the farm to his widow for her life. Rent must be paid by Nov. 3rd. Farm wretchedly managed and likely not to improve under the present holder. Sept. 1796: arrears paid off, payments punctually made and mill kept in good repair.

'Under-tenants sadly oppressed. Rent paid and mills kept in good repair by Mrs Byrne's under-tenant, Mr Burke – 1800 . . .

'Moneygold Derry and Lisle

'Let to James, now held by his son, Tho. Soden, for three lives (all living) at £140. Contains 496 acres arable and pasture, 34 mountain and bog. Lands totally unimproved and let out to poor under-tenants. A very bad tenant never pays till forced to it. The lease so valuable that the rent and arrears can always be recovered. A considerable arrear has accrued. No further indulgence to be granted. Must be ejected. Ejectment served and must be settled in January, 1789. Ejectment turned out imperfect. New one brought; time would have expired in December, 1789, indulged till February, 1790. Money paid on the last day. Rent will be well paid in future as those who have advanced money will take care no further arrear is incurred. It would have been worthwhile to have bought in this lease, but

it is in settlement in Soden's family. A new arrear incurred,
fresh ejectment and the money paid by his creditor, Mr Jones,
treasurer of the county has got Soden's lease for almost the
whole and is likely to be a good manager of it – July, 1792 . . .

'May, 1797: Soden has got his land back and manages as ill
as before . . .'[2]

* * *

The American war had denuded Ireland of British troops,
and although their duties had been taken over loyally by the
Volunteers raised by the Duke of Leinster and Lord Charlemont,
this nationalistic body had been able to exercise considerable
pressure on the home government. By 1782 the Catholics had
obtained the right to purchase land. Restrictions on trade with
the colonies had been lifted and, with the unanimous support
of the Irish Parliament, Grattan had obtained legislative independence, but Irish ministers were still appointed by and
responsible to London. Legislative autonomy, without responsible government and electoral reform, lost all attraction and
discontent soon mounted again.

It is hardly surprising that this distressing and unpalatable
state of affairs found Palmerston happier amid the social delights
of London, and the complaints in his letters home about matters
Irish are leavened only by the accounts he gives of the more
fashionable houses he visited. The only comic relief in his
letters to his second wife during his tour in August and September, 1784, is provided by the well-meaning ineptness of the
ancient Mr Hatch:

August 13th. 'Not being willing to alarm Mr Hatch too
suddenly we lay at a hotel near the waterside and Mr Price
[a lawyer who had accompanied Palmerston] went up to his
house in the morning to inform him of our arrival. This news
flurried and alarmed him a good deal, and made him extremely
nervous; however he came down to me and we moved to his
house . . . As to his accounts, I believe from what I have been
able to learn that he has all the materials for making them out
and that he has no other reason for not having made them
out sooner, than his not having had courage to set about it. I

hope therefore we shall get them now in a reasonable time; and am likewise convinced that nothing but my coming over would ever have brought them to any conclusion.

'As to news I can send little, and that not good, as I find that the better sort of people here are disgusted and the lower sort very riotous. Tarring and feathering flourishes notwithstanding the Volunteers have declared against it. The freeholders of the county of Dublin voted a very insolent address to the King which I suppose you will see in the papers soon, as it is a curious one.

'Finding there was to be a Levée at the Castle on the day I arrived on account of its being the Prince of Wales's birthday, and that there were none in common at this season, I went to it, thinking it the shortest possible way of paying my civilities to the Lord Lieutenant [by that time the Duke of Rutland] and at the same time a good place to see everybody that might happen to be in or about Dublin. In the last expectation I was quite disappointed, for it was emptier than I could have conceived it possible, and I thought both the looks and the language of his Grace and his court very desponding.

'Dublin is emptier and duller than any place in the world. I have not seen any of my cousins yet . . . Mrs Siddons is still here, she has been ill but is recovered, and is to act two or three nights more.

August 19th. 'Mr Price and I have little to do here at present but to look about us and find what amusement we can, as we endeavour to keep Mr Hatch as much as possible to his work at making out accounts, and the person who under him manages my Sligo estate is not in Dublin but is expected in a day or two. I have no reason to suppose that there has been any mismanagement of my affairs except that which is in some degree a necessary attendant on delay. There are however several things which my presence will be extremely useful to settle and arrange . . .

'I dined yesterday at Mr Hutcheson's [*sic*] who is the present possessor of the family seat of Palmerstown [*sic*] where he resides and has laid out much money. It really is a fine place, and only wants to be finished and kept in the English way to be uncommonly beautiful for a spot within four miles of the capital . . .'³

[The 1784 estate book has more details of the vicissitudes of the estate from which Palmerston derived his title:

'Palmerston, house and domain, now belonging to Mr Hely Hutchinson. The house was built and the grounds laid out originally by Sir John Temple. His son, the late Lord P., some time in Queen Anne's reign sold it to Sir Richard Coxe, who was afterwards Lord Chancellor. He borrowed the money to pay for it of one Wilcox, an eminent banker at Dublin, and not being able to repay him, Wilcox became possessed of the house. Only 19 acres were sold with the house, but leases of large parcels of ground were granted at the same time, which Wilcox became possessed of. His descendants fell into poverty, the house was totally out of repair and inhabited by poor people when Mr Hutchinson purchased it of Wilcox, the representative of the original purchaser.⁴]

'The Duke of Rutland is settled at his summer villa in the Phoenix Park, which answers exactly to what Hyde Park is in London. He seems to wish to be very civil: I cannot say that I think she does; or at least if she does she is unfortunate, as she does not do the honours of her house and table in a gracious or pleasing manner.

'The political state of the country is very gloomy and disagreeable. There is a set of desperate people who are trying to throw everything into confusion under the pretence of reforming the constitution and protecting the manufactures. Unfortunately no experience is sufficient to convince people of the folly and mischief of giving in to these visionary schemes; even the well meaning people of the country seem but too much disposed to sacrifice to them all the benefits they might derive from the commercial freedom they have lately obtained and from the advantage they enjoy over England in the lightness of their taxes. These circumstances, if they would apply themselves with industry to make the most of them and endeavour to get the use of English capitals to trade with, might make this country rich and flourishing, instead of which they are neglecting all business for politics and idleness, and, by encouraging licentiousness and commotions through the country, deterring everybody from trusting any money with them that they can possibly draw out. One of their great plans is a non-importation agreement and scarce one day passes without some outrageous act of violence committed in Dublin upon some unfortunate man or other whom the mob suspect of having transgressed their edicts in this favourite point. Either from want of power or want of zeal no effectual measures whatever have been taken to stop these proceedings, and every tradesman and workman in Dublin is at this time liable to be taken out of his house at noonday by a handful of banditti and dragged through the streets to undergo the fashionable process of tarring and feathering which they have borrowed from their dear friends the Americans. These reflections are in everybody's mind and form the constant subject of all conversation and yet no means are found to produce the cure which everybody seems to long for; so that it is difficult to guess how far things must go before the enormity of the evil redresses itself. At present the prospect is sufficiently melancholy.

'Mrs Siddons has performed three or four times since my being here. I have taken the opportunity of seeing her much at my ease for I am ashamed to say that the houses have not been near full. She seems to have many enemies here and is constantly abused in some of the papers, so that I guess her expeditions to Ireland may probably not be very frequent in future. I have seen her in some new parts and among them in the Fine Lady in *Lethe* in which I think she succeeded very well, though it is the fashion to say not. Her singing is certainly bad and had better be omitted.

'You would have had this a day sooner as I intended coming home early last night to finish and send it away, but was detained at the Rotunda, a public room, for tea and music, something in the style of Ranelagh, by being desired to drink tea with the Duchess of Rutland, an honour which it seems is not to be refused and which kept me till the post was gone . . .

August 25th. 'The political state of things here is much as it was; some measures have been taken by the different parishes to prevent the continuance of the outrages committed by the manufacturers; and there seems to have been a cessation of them for some days. Great pains are taken by ill-disposed people to inflame the disagreements between the mob and the military to which the indiscretions of individuals give but too frequent occasions. Just before I landed, some young officers, among whom were Lord Harrington and some of the Lord Lieutenant's aide-de-camps, being very drunk got into a riot in a house where they behaved very ill and were in consequence very ill-treated. Mr St George has not been visible since. A few days afterwards one of the soldiers was attacked on his duty and maimed in a shocking manner peculiar to this country. Soon after that some soldiers went to rescue an officer who had been arrested. The bailiffs fired on them and killed and wounded several. Yesterday a man was publicly whipped for tarring and feathering. The mob began to pelt the guard that attended; some firing ensued and a man was killed. All these unlucky events serve to excite and inflame a very dangerous and disagreeable kind of spirit through the country. I hope and believe it is principally confined there. The country seems tolerably quiet and there are good prospects of plenty, which is the surest means of keeping it so . . .

August 31*st*. 'Mr Hatch . . . has a clever man under him who manages the Sligo estate and helps him here and I think when all the matters now to be fixed on are concluded I shall have good reason to be well contented with the situation of my Irish estate, if the turbulent spirits here will but let the country be at peace and enjoy its advantages. In this respect however I think things will mend. The spirit I have mentioned does not prevail through the country and what has appeared in this town will, I think, serve to alarm and put on their guard some who might otherwise have been led away.

'After I wrote last I went to Mr Conolly's at Castletown, which lies on the banks of the Liffey about 14 English miles from hence. It is an excellent house and reckoned the best in Ireland . . . He and Lady Louisa are the best humoured people imaginable and live in a very hospitable way. The Duchess Dowager of Leinster and Mr Ogilvie, her husband and many of her children and Mr and Mrs Siddons were there. The

Siddons went away to Cork. She was as usual proper and interesting and looked beautiful; he is less disagreeable than I expected . . .

September 7th. 'I long much to get away on my return to you and shall rejoice most sincerely when I see an end of the various businesses we have on our hands. Poor Mr Hatch is almost worried to death as he is now compelled to do in a month what he has been [un]able to do in thirteen years. He met with an adventure last Thursday which put a stop to everything for two days. On the morning of that day he was quite brisk and in spirits and so pleased with seeing a prospect of getting rid of us and our business that at dinner he proposed to Mr Price to go to some public gardens near Dublin where there were to be music and fireworks. We accordingly went. The evening was delightful and Mr Hatch, who had not I believe done so lively a thing for many years, was quite gay and gallant. But alas! the uncertainty of human felicity! all on a sudden, suspecting nothing, he tumbled over head and ears into a green canal which he had taken for a grass walk and to which from the immense quantity of duck weed with which it was covered I confess it bore some resemblance. I was not with him at the time, Mr Price luckily was and helped him out and sent him home. He did not venture out of his bed for two days and I began to be afraid we should see no more of him. However, the third he came out and is now tolerably well recovered but not what he was before, as his nerves, poor man, really have suffered from the accident and the lying in bed together . . .'[5]

Lord Charlemont was demanding parliamentary reform on a strictly Protestant basis, but the agitation of the Bishop of Derry, Lord Bristol, for the admission of Catholics to the franchise had split the Volunteer movement, which degenerated over the course of time from a respectable to a revolutionary organisation. Palmerston was over-sanguine in his prognostications:

'The political aspect of the country appears to me better than it did. Some little appearance of vigour on the part of government and of the inhabitants of Dublin in their parish meetings have put a stop to the riots, and the tarring and feathering committee have published that their proceedings are suspended for the present. The different trades are endeavouring to extend and enforce the non-importation agreements as far as possible. This however I believe must defeat itself from the inability to supply the demand at home, and as it is accompanied already with an advanced price and a demand for ready money I do not think it will long be very popular. The disturbances here have been carried on by a set of weavers and other manufacturers who inhabit an obscure quarter of the town and their proceedings are no more the act or the inclination of the people of Dublin or the country at large than the riots some years ago among the Spitalfields weavers were to be considered as the sense of the people of England ... As to the Aggregate Body, as they call themselves, of the city of Dublin and the freeholders of the county, who assembled to vote a most ridiculous address, it is difficult to say whether their numbers, their characters, their property or their abilities are most contemptible; and yet from a fatality that attends both countries these people meet and present addresses, circulate seditious letters, spread an extensive alarm, and are considered through Europe as a most formidable party ... The reform of Parliament is the point that has been chiefly dwelt on and declared for at the meetings that have been held in the country. It is a popular word and on that account few choose to declare themselves against it, they reprobate however all violent or unconstitutional methods in the attainment of it and I have much doubt whether it is really desired or not.

'The Volunteers, of whom we have heard so much and who have been so justly an object of jealousy and apprehension, are declining very fast, much faster than I supposed. Their numbers have been always immoderately exaggerated in all ways and particularly by the same men going about to half the reviews in the Kingdom and then by casting up the numbers at each review as the amount of the whole. Very few Volunteer uniforms are to be seen in or about Dublin ... If they could be kept out of politics, a few of them would be of infinite use in the remote parts of the country, where they have already done more to introduce good order and enforce obedience to the laws than has been done during this century before . . .'[6]

* * *

On his return visit in August, 1788, Palmerston prefaced business with two short excursions out of Dublin, noting in his journal:

August 24th. 'Kilcock, 19 miles; Kennegad, 19 miles; Pakenham Hall, 20. The first part of this journey lies through the country bordering on the Liffey, which is very pretty about Lucan and Leixlip. From there you pass the Duke of Leinster's at Cartown, which is a seat of considerable extent and some magnificence. After this the country is naked and affords no objects to excite the attention. At Kennegad you leave the turnpike road, which, however, is no inconvenience as the cross roads by which you pass to Pakenham Hall are very good, though the country is dreary, with many large tracts of bog. The grand juries have a power of levying money in their counties for making new roads, which power they exercise very freely, and though by this means large burdens are imposed and many jobs done, yet on the whole much good and useful road is made, and as the road is generally made to suit some particular person's convenience, it becomes that person's business to see the money well laid out and the road kept good afterwards, which may be easily done as the materials are hard, the road generally open and no carriages heavier than cars drawn by single horses are in use through the whole country. It is a circumstance particular to Ireland that the worst roads are the turnpikes, and the worst of all those near the metropolis . . .

August 28th. 'At Cellbridge, close to Castletown, is a house and garden belonging to the Bishop of Clonfert [Dean Marlay], who has lately laid out money to improve it. It is in a narrow vale on both sides [of] the Liffey, which tumbles over rocks through the midst of it. There are walks on both sides which communicate by a picturesque bridge of great antiquity, in the middle of the ground, and there are great numbers of fine old trees in all parts of the place. The house is done up on the Gothic style and is made comfortable and well suited to the place . . .'[7]

Either the ducking or the excess of business four years earlier had had a permanent effect on poor Mr Hatch, whom Palmerston now determined to replace, informing Lady Palmerston:

August 27th. 'I find poor Mr Hatch more nervous and dilatory and startlish than ever and, as I took for granted it would be whenever I came, have had nothing to do yet but to press him to make up accounts . . . He did not seem at all pleased with giving up the agency, though he did not directly say he wished to keep it on, but I am convinced he repents having said he would give it up. I believe he is fond of money to an excessive degree and that, as well as his peculiarity of temper, makes him live in the strange helpless way that he does. I have been rather distressed by his proposing at last that I should take a young gentleman in his place who has married his daughter and who seems to be a well disposed young man, but very young indeed and I believe unused to business. The consequence would have been that he must have depended on Mr Hatch and that Mr Hatch would have continued in fact to be the agent under another name and without the same responsibility. I had unluckily said that I had made no engagement though I had had several recommendations, so that I was forced to decline complying with the proposal upon the general grounds of preferring a person of more experience and knowledge in business and by saying that I had such a one in view though I had not absolutely engaged him. This happens very fortunately to be the case, for the Mr Stewart whom Lord Longford recommended to me seems, by all the accounts I can get of him and by the general voice of those who know him, to be as proper a man in every respect as I could have desired . . .

September 1st. 'My visit to Lord Longford has been very pleasant, I stayed two entire days. The house is comfortable enough but the place and country frightful. His mother, who lives with him in the country, is an excessive sensible and agreeable woman. She was a great friend of mine when I was first in Ireland and I used to live much at her house in Dublin, where one was always sure to meet the cleverest people of this country.

He is a very plain sensible worthy man and his wife a very agreeable woman. They have ten children. His brother, Tom Pakenham, whose pleasant character you have often heard of, lives just by him . . .

'The day after I arrived here I did a great deal of business. I called on Fitzherbert who asked me to dine with him to meet Cholmondeley and told me that if I came to the castle a little before dinner hour I might be introduced to the Lord Lieutenant [the Marquis of Buckingham had succeeded in 1787], which I was accordingly, and then went to Fitzherbert's villa in the Phoenix Park to dine . . .

September 3rd. 'The day after I wrote last to you I went to Mr Conolly's at Castletown where I stayed two nights and met Cholmondeley there, who stayed the same time. Conolly is the best creature that can be, but astonishingly tiresome so that it was no mortification to us that he was engaged out to dinner the second day. Lady Louisa is pleasing naturally and is made more so by the uncommon degree of goodness that appears to belong to her. I found at Castletown Mr Napier and Lady Sarah and all their children who are living there till a house in the village just by is ready for them. She is still very handsome in her face and captivating in her manner and seems cheerful and lively. He is excessively disagreeable; very solemn and very awkward, talks much and is very argumentative, with the roughest voice and the harshest Scotch accent I ever heard. I fancy he is become much worse of late, having I perceived applied himself in his retirement to many deep studies, upon which though his ideas are very confused his opinions are extremely decided. Cholmondeley and he had some arguments which were rather amusing . . .

'I dined last Sunday at the Marquis of Buckingham's, who has quitted the house in the park appointed for the Lord Lieutenant, which he thinks unhealthy, and has taken a small place by the sea. We had a large party and some of my brother peers whom I did not know before and who seem to be odd characters. Lady Buckingham is breeding, she seems to have lost much of her beauty. Lord Nugent was there and, except a pain in his face which persecutes him and which they cannot find out the cause of, holds out well at 84. The Marquis makes himself very disagreeable and sometimes very ridiculous by his economical reforms, in which I am told he is very apt to dwell upon trifles and let great things escape him. I believe however that he will do the country good, as the system of indolence and relaxation which prevailed under the Duke of Rutland very much wanted correction. There has been a great bustle in the Office of Ordnance which here, as well as in England, is liable to much suspicion of abuse. It is said great frauds and embezzlements have been discovered . . . [ms. torn] . . . the principal officers turned out and others immediately appointed. Among the latter is Tom Pakenham, who is made storekeeper, a place worth £400 a year and a house.

'I wish I could give a good account of the progress of my business here, as I grow most extremely impatient to return. Mr Hatch has not yet finished but I am told his accounts will be made up tonight. Indeed I believe he works as hard as he can, therefore teasing him can do no good and I have no resource but patience . . . I have seen Mr Stewart and settled with him as to his succeeding Mr Hatch. He is a very agreeable, genteel man and has entered into this line of business which it is not uncommon here for gentlemen to do, and has a regular office with proper persons under him to assist, which poor Mr Hatch never had . . . I suppose I shall have some trouble in getting everything completely transferred over on account of the confusion in which I suppose the papers are kept, but we must do as well as we can and take what pains we can to keep Mr H. in good humour, who I believe, poor man, is heartily vexed and I suppose will be more so when a man of business is brought in to take things from him in the state of disorder in which they probably are . . .

September 7th. 'A melancholy catastrophe has happened in consequence of the dismissions from the Ordnance. The late surveyor-general, Mr Ralph Ward, has destroyed himself, and unfortunately did not do it so decisively but that he lived some days after the deed. He was a man universally esteemed and beloved, had been many years in the office and bore an excellent character. He had had a paralytic stroke and was unable for some time past to attend closely to business. In such a situation I can conceive a man sinking under such a storm whether innocent or guilty, nor do I think either conclusion can fairly be drawn from it, though I have heard both attempted. I take it for granted the proofs of delinquency in his department are clear, otherwise Lord Buckingham has much cause to lament the severity of his proceeding . . .

'I cannot boast of the progress I make in my business . . . My situation is very unpleasant but had Mr Hatch and I both lived to the age of Methusalem nothing would ever have been settled till I had gone through what I am now doing . . .

September 18th. 'I took a most delightful ride last Sunday with George Jocelyn and Mr Fortescue, son of your friend Mrs Fortescue, for about twenty miles in the neighbourhood of Dublin, whose environs I really think are more beautiful than those of any town I know. Wherever you go you have the sea one way and a fine range of mountains at a proper distance the other, with the intermediate country rising gradually from the shore, sprinked over with white villas which have in general more ground belonging to them, and are more picturesque in their appearance than those in the neighbourhood of London. Dublin and its environs resemble London in the quantity of new buildings that are rising up, which I suppose must be considered as a proof of increasing ability; and indeed I believe Ireland may truly be reckoned to be in a state of gradual improvement as to wealth, trade and civilisation. At present there are no disturbances nor any particular distress throughout the kingdom and if we should be lucky enough to have no fresh disturbances, foreign or domestic, for some years I think a very considerable progress would be made.

'I am much entertained with the manners and discourse of the lower people as I walk about, though they are by no means what one would wish, but they are more merry, dirty, drunk and entertaining than any people I ever met with . . .

'I went to Castletown on Monday and lay there, and dined on Tuesday with Lord Charlemont, an old friend of mine who is the great General of all the Volunteers and reviews them annually, though they are now dwindled almost to nothing.

He is a zealous man in opposition to all governments, and if he was to make a government himself would certainly oppose it immediately. But at the same time he has a fund of good sense and right-headedness which not only keeps him from going to any dangerous lengths but enables him to prevent others and in that light I believe he was of great service to both countries by being at the head of the Volunteers ...

September 23rd. 'I am now extremely busy and have the comfort to see that things are in a train of drawing to a conclusion, but am totally unable to say exactly when. Mr Stewart is only just now beginning to have anything to do with the affairs. He will be as quick I believe in what depends on him as the other has been slow, but I must not depart till he is fairly settled and has got the necessary materials and information with which Mr Hatch must furnish him ...

'The fashion of suicide is mighty prevailing here at present, for besides one or two of inferior note, a Mr Bellingham Swan, a man of repute who held a place of £800 a year under government, shot himself on Sunday. He made his will the day before. He was a single man and it is said in good circumstances. His employment was Commissioner of Stamps and of Public Accounts united, and it is not supposed that any circumstances relating to that could have caused this catastrophe. As to Mr Ward, I believe Lord Buckingham is fully justified in the measure he took and that frauds and embezzlements of a very gross and disagreeable nature were very clearly proved upon him ...'[8]

The political situation in Ireland began to deteriorate catastrophically with the formation in 1791 of the 'Society of United Irishmen', by Wolfe Tone, aimed at uniting Protestants and Catholics for the purpose of overthrowing the English ascendancy. The Catholics were admitted to the suffrage in April, 1793, although they were still denied seats in the Irish Parliament. With the outbreak of the war against France, the English government sought to raise a compulsory militia in Ireland, which led to great unrest, of which Robert Lyons, Palmerston's agent in Sligo, sent a scarifying account to his master in Venice:

'Nothing material has happened since I last had the honour of addressing your Lordship. Many of the unfortunate insurgents have been shot by the military, and there are no less than 142 to be tried at Sligo, Leitrim and Roscommon in this month. Peace seems tolerably restored in the country, but no rents to be had as there is no money offered for either cattle, linen, yarn or corn, the staple commodities of the western counties. I hope things will mend for they can't be worse than at present . . .'[9]

At the beginning of 1795, Earl Fitzwilliam was sent to succeed the Earl of Westmorland, as Lord Lieutenant, with a brief that permitted him to grant further concessions if the situation deteriorated. Palmerston, back from his Italian sojourn, reported to his wife from London:

February 25th, 1795. 'What I said about Ireland is I believe pretty true. The disapprobation here I believe extends as much or more to some of the proposed measures as to the changes of persons. I understand the measure respecting the Catholics has been extended beyond what was meant but the repeal of the police and convention bills, on one of which the tranquillity of Dublin and on the other that of the whole country much depend, has received a flat negative from hence. What effect this will have on the Lord Lieutenant or his advisers I do not know, but any great disagreement or disturbance among them in the middle of a session would be very bad. I look upon Lord Fitzwilliam's talents to be more plausible and gentlemanlike than solid and substantial and I doubt he is surrounded by people who are full of spleen and violence, impatient for power and popularity and greatly too much connected with those of the same description here . . .

March 3rd. 'The Irish business seems a very unfortunate one. A letter has been received from one of the Churchills as late as the 26th. He is an aide-de-camp to Lord Fitzwilliam and says Lord F. has notified his resignation, that he intends to stay only to pass the money bills and come away as soon as possible. It is a strange business which nobody comprehends, and it seems quite incomprehensible that Lord F. should go away without a complete arrangement of the very points which had been so long in dispute or that he should act contrary to it

when made. What answers the ministers have received does
not seem to be known and some say that some very conciliatory
plans are sent over which will perhaps settle the matter, but
this is only report . . .

March 9th. 'Everybody continues very gloomy about the
Irish business and nobody seems to know what is to be done.
However the opinion seems to be that the Roman Catholic bill
must pass and that the matter will be patched up as well as it
can and that Lord Fitzwilliam will stay the session out. I have
heard that the bill was agreed to here (supposing it to be
necessary) before Lord Fitzwilliam went, but that the turned-
out people, when they came over, stated the mischief of it so
strongly as to have alarmed government here . . . The turnings-
out nobody justifies, being contrary to agreements and promises
of all kinds. The Marquis of Buckingham has totally renounced
Mr Pitt and is gone into opposition, which would not signify
much if that was the worst . . .'[10]

Fitzwilliam had found the situation so bad that he was
insisting to the Cabinet in London on the complete repeal of
all disqualifying laws, thus exceeding the extreme limit of his
brief. He was left no option but to offer his resignation. Lord
Camden was appointed to succeed him, and was accompanied
to Ireland by the Palmerstons' old friend, Tom Pelham.

March 10th. 'Nobody seems to approve much of Lord
C[amden] and I fear, as he is known to be quite Pitt's man, it
would be only making bad worse . . . I hope and trust that
there are many among the leaders of them [the Roman
Catholics] who do not wish for confusion and will endeavour
to restrain the others, but we are taught to look on them at
present as very dangerous as a body and likely to produce great
mischief if the indulgences proposed are not granted them in
their utmost extent. And if they are, the consequences are so
important and alarming that those even who think the measure
now indispensable tremble at the necessity . . .'[11]

Lady Palmerston, who was in Bath, commented in reply:

March 16th. 'The Irish [here] are vastly happy at Tom
Pelham's appointment. I consider Lord Camden as the auto-
matic chess player and Tom Pelham the man who moves the

figures. Poor Lady Camden, I fear, will suffer the fate of the sposa of Eneas and be lost in the crowd.

'Why did not Pitt send Lord Gower? His spirited conduct in Paris merited a reward and Lady Sutherland is formed for representation. She has all the grace and manner to make her admired in public and every domestic and elegant talent to render her equally captivating in private. I see I ought to be consulted . . . [end of letter missing].'[12]

On the day Fitzwilliam left Ireland, Lord Palmerston wrote to his wife:

March 25th. 'We were at the House till 12 last night. The division you will see in all the papers, 219, I think it was, to 63. The debate was very flat. Fox spoke well but it was the old hash over and over and people were tired of it. He brought in as much of Ireland as he could and stated as a reason for the enquiry that misconduct certainly had happened and that His Majesty's ministers either here or there must be answerable for it and though he did not doubt but Lord F[itzwilliam] would acquit himself, yet it made nothing to his argument on which side the water the blame was to be looked for. He passed great encomiums on Lord F. and on Mr Burke, expecting I suppose that this business would separate them from the Cabinet. Pitt stated the impropriety of the British Parliament discussing and prejudging matters that were to come before the Irish Parliament and with regard to blame, said that if any expectations had been held out, or hopes given, to the Catholics which were unfit to be realised, no blame on that score would be found to rest with him or any of his colleagues on this side of the water . . .'

On April 6 Palmerston continued:

'I send you down one of the papers in which is a large part of one of Lord Fitzwilliam's letters to Lord Carlisle. It does him great discredit and shows into what dangerous hands he was fallen, as it seems of the same manufacture with Grattan's speech and highly mischievous.

'There was a riot at Dublin in which the Chancellor was slightly hurt but was in considerable danger. Some windows were broke but on the troops coming it ended without any farther mischief on either side . . .'[13]

He received this spirited reply from his wife:

April 7th. 'I have seen Lord Fitzwilliam's first and second letter. He may perhaps have acted indiscreetly by having these letters made public, but he certainly has proved that he has been most abominably ill used, either by Pitt or the Duke of P[ortland]. In my opinion the whole blame will be found to rest with the Duke of P., who for feebleness of character, duplicity and I may add treachery has I trust not many equals. I fear, however, much mischief will ensue in Ireland which Lord Camden will not be able to subdue . . .'[14]

Her predictions were only too quickly confirmed. Robert Lyons wrote to Lord Palmerston from Sligo on August 13:

'I am sorry to say that the many executions and other punishments inflicted on this circuit, upon a vast number of those unfortunate wretches called defenders, have not in my idea quieted in any manner the minds of the lower order of the people. But I am happy to have it in my power to inform your Lordship that the Ahamlish people are perfectly quiet. I have been among them for some days, but I cannot help saying that there appears to me an unusual restlessness about them, and a very strong disinclination to pay their rents in the manner they used to do. I have not, nor shall not, in any manner change my conduct towards them, for there is but one way of treating that class of people – firmness divested of any tendency to cruelty of harshness suits untamed dispositions best.

'I wish your Lordship had been pleased to give me your directions about Arthur McKenna, as his conduct since he came home has not, I believe, served the tenantry; he having boasted in Ahamlish and here that your Lordship had immovably fixed him in his place, that he would shoot any man, even myself, if I dared to enter upon any part of his holding. To temporise in these times with a man of his temper and disposition will not do, for which reason I shall tomorrow morning take possession of the small rabbit warren he has thought proper to call his own, with which he never had anything to do but as Mr O'Birne's bailiff, and going about the country as a flax-dresser. I never, I hope, ventured to attempt to stop the stream of your Lordship's humane feelings towards any part of your

Lordships poor tenantry, as I hope I do not possess a disposition tending in any degree towards oppression, but allow me to assure your Lordship, McKenna's conduct since his return will in my mind be of the last disservice to the Ahamlish people. However, I shall not disturb him in his possession of his house until your Lordship desires it, even then I think he should be paid whatever it cost him . . .'[15]

The deterioration in the situation during the year that followed was one of the main contributory factors to the financial embarrassment in which Palmerston found himself from the end of 1796, a situation not helped by the failings of Mr Lyons. On December 21, 1796, Palmerston told his wife:

'I am now under a degree of uncertainty about what day I shall leave London on account of the old history of an Irish agent. After expecting Mr Lyons to return all the time I have been here, I received a letter from him two days ago to say he had been very ill but should set out on the 15th for England . . . I am sorry to say that Mr Lyons, though a very good humoured, obliging man and intelligent in business is not so regular as I could wish and I am often distressed about him, as it is unpleasant to have an agent who sometimes puts one in a state of doubt and uneasiness about him, though things always come right at last. On the other hand changing an agent of a distant property is an unpleasant thing and would probably be attended with very distressing consequences to him, which I should be very sorry to occasion without evident necessity . . .'[16]

Palmerston could at least report the failure of the French expedition to Bantry Bay under General Hoche:

January 2nd, 1797. 'You will see the accounts of the arrival of part of the Brest fleet at Bantry Bay in the south of Ireland. The accounts in the *True Briton* are very accurate. The French had totally eluded Colpoys, who not being able to learn anything of them, remained near Brest, where in very thick bad weather he saw and was near intercepting six ships of the line going in, which are supposed to be have been part of them separated and driven back. On the day after the sailing of those in Bantry Bay from thence, one of the severest storms came on that has been known in these seas and the officers who are come in since say it was weather in which they are persuaded none of that fleet could live out at sea. Much may be expected from that circumstance.

'The *Adamant*, which is just come in, saw the *Jason*, who had taken one of their transports with 250 men. The prisoners say the fleet was scattered and dispersed and that they know nothing of the main body of it; that the whole was destined for Ireland and that Galway Bay was the intended place. This would have been a very bad plan for them as it is a country very desolate, thinly inhabited, where they would have found much difficulty in getting provisions, the people not disposed to assist them and the nature of the country such that their progress, if landed, would have been easily impeded at the same time that they must have had a great way to have marched to have reached any part where they could have done much harm. Their force was much magnified, as you will see in Pelham's letter, by the accounts that first came to Dublin. Nothing can have been better than the conduct of the whole country as far as it is yet known, and luckily those who are their dear friends are too far off to help them. There seems now every reason to believe that this armada had met with the fate of its ancient predecessor and is entirely frustrated as to its object and that a great part of it may never get back, even supposing which, I fear is likely to be the case, that we have nothing to intercept its return, as Colpoys is come back and Lord Bridport not got out . . .'[17]

The situation in Ireland went from bad to worse, with letters from agents and tenants painting the blackest possible picture of anarchy and repression:

May 17th, 1797

'My Lord,

In the present critical situation of Ireland the magistrates of this county thought it their duty to meet and devise such plans as might be best calculated to prevent the troubles which disturb other counties from extending to this.

They have entered into resolutions, a copy of which I have the honour to enclose you.

The unanimous opinion of the meeting was that a stock purse and a secret committee to expend it in procuring information would be the most efficacious means of preserving us in peace. We therefore hope for your contribution, which will be received by Major Andrew Parke, Sligo.

I have the honour to be my Lord,
Your obedient and humble servant,
O. Wynne'[18]

May 23rd, Dublin

'Hearing on my arrival here that the lower part of Ahamlish was getting restless and bad I sent off directly to know the real state of the country from the Provost of Sligo. I beg leave to trouble your Lordship with his answer . . .

I have the honour to be my Lord
Your Lordship's most faithful
and obliged humble servant
Robert Lyons.'[19]

May 20th

'Dear Lyons,

You desired a full statement of the parish of Ahamlish. It is not easily done, Caldwell, Coun[r] Johnston, Jerry Glancy and sevral others were rob'd of their arms on Monday night, the insurgents went on Tuesday night to Coun[r] Dickson's but he had removed his arms on the day before, they desired to have them brought back on the succeeding night or they would burn the house. Hearing this I ordered a party in hopes of meeting them there. Mr Wynne with 24 of his troops and the like number of my company mounted behind them went there but the united brothers did not think proper to meet us. It had a good effect for the present, tho' since then they disarmed your warreners, to whom I had given arms at your request; in short, I cannot discredit the alarms and serious apprehension of danger in that country. Tom Jones of Mr Edw[d] had his hay-yard set on fire and burned. Arth[r] Irwin was served in like manner at Willowbrook but lost only one cock of hay estimated at 60 tons. James Henry's house at Strandhill is totally consumed, the loss is estimated at £500 but the cause is yet

doubtful. Threats and intimidation in all its shapes is held out
in the lower parts of Ahamlish, the upper parts are still loyal.
I am so taken up here that I cannot pay that attention to the
country I could wish. I have been apply'd to by the respectable
inhabitants to request a company of foot wd be sent there. I
will write by next post to you more fully ... The Militia
officers and all took the oath of allegiance Friday in the Market
Place. I am call'd away.

Ever Yrs,
T. Loden.'[20]

Lyons summed up the situation on May 30:

'The lower part of the county of Sligo (Ahamlish included)
is in the utmost confusion, I shall go down the moment I can
hold a bridle in my hand ...

'Forty of the military are ordered directly to Clissony I shall
get them accommodated as well as I can. The whole country is
a scene of confusion ...'[21]

Palmerston found his Irish revenues drying up and was
obliged to take drastic steps to restore some measure of financial
stability.

REFERENCES

1. C.17(a) 3.XI.1761
2. A.14 and 16
3. B.1
4. A.14
5. B.1
6. B.1 7.IX.1784
7. A.16
8. B.1
9. C.60 5.VII.1793
10. B.1
11. B.1
12. B.2
13. B.1
14. B.2
15. C.60 13.VIII.1795
16. B.1
17. B.1
18. C.60
19. C.60
20. C.60
21. C.60

CHAPTER XII

PARSIMONY AND 'PRINNY'

Palmerston £30,000 in debt – Broadlands mortgaged and English estates sold – Lady Palmerston offers to return her marriage settlement – his hospitality maintained – the friendships of advancing age – Count Rumford not received as Bavarian Minister – French invasion of Ireland and fighting on the Sligo estates – the prospect of Union – Palmerston petitions Pitt for an English peerage – the Palmerstons as intimates of the Prince and Princess of Wales

DURING the years 1797–9 Palmerston was weighed down by a load of debt, which by the middle of 1798 exceeded £30,000. To ease the pressure and meet the pressing demands of his bankers he was obliged, in due course, to sell two of his English estates and to take out a mortgage for £10,000 on Broadlands, and there is no record of this having been liquidated by the time of his death in 1802. In spite of the shifts to which he was put there is no evidence that the tenor of his life altered to any material extent, and the whole situation was redeemed by the wholly devoted and self-sacrificing attitude of his wife, whose letters on the subject give an insight into a quality of character to which her many friends paid incessant witness.

Palmerston's estates, even when he came into their full possession after the death of his mother in 1789, never produced more than £12,000 per annum. This was probably a tenth of the enormous incomes enjoyed by such great Whig magnates as the Duke of Newcastle, whose rent rolls alone ran into five figures. Even so, the purchasing power of money was probably ten times as great as it is today, and taxes a mere fraction of their present figure. The surviving account books, bank statements and agents' returns give meticulous details of Palmerston's income and expenditure. It is perhaps not without interest to record here an estimate he drew up in his own hand about this time of his gross and net incomes:

	£	s.	d.
From Ireland on an average	6,000	0	0
Hampshire, after all the deductions allowed, including repairs	1,100	0	0
Yorkshire – ditto –	460	0	0
Northamptonshire – ditto –	270	0	0
East Sheen, deducting taxes	200	0	0
House and gardens, and lands in hand, at Broadlands might let, exclusive of furniture for	800	0	0
Sheen – ditto –	200	0	0
London – ditto –	500	0	0
Copses	50	0	0
Funds	2,748	0	0
	£12,328	0	0

Less:	£	s.	d.			
Interest of debts	1,224	0	0			
Assessed taxes	262	0	0			
Parochial taxes	55	0	0			
London land tax	15	0	0			
Rent to City	7	0	0			
	£1,563	0	0	1,563	0	0
TOTAL				£10,765	0	0[1]

It is fairly clear from the account books and records that remain, which are by no means complete, that the above represented net figures after the deduction of land tax, rates, tithes and repairs, which in the case of the Hampshire estate amounted to something over £500 on the net figure of £1,100; the figure of £262 for assessed taxes, in case any connoisseur of such matters should be interested, was made up as follows:

	£	s.	d.
Window tax	7	11	0
Home tax	12	10	0
Additional ditto	3	5	0
13 male servants	39	0	0
Additional ditto	13	0	0
12 horses	6	0	0
Additional duty	5	10	0
Further ditto	11	10	0
Further ditto, 37 Geo. 3rd	3	0	0
6 husbandry horses		12	0
Additional duty		18	0
3 dogs		15	0
4 four-wheel carriages	28	0	0
Additional ditto	10	0	0
	£141	11	0
20% on ditto	28	6	2
	£169	17	2
Clocks and watches	1	2	6
	£170	19	8	Paid in London
	57	0	7	Paid at Broadlands
	34	0	0	Paid at Sheen
Total	£262	0	3[2]	

At the beginning of December, 1796, with the work at the
Hanover Square house, the fall in the value of public funds, and
disorders in Ireland all contributing to his embarrassment,
Palmerston wrote to his agent, Thomas Warner, at Broadlands to look out the title deeds of his properties, with a view
to raising mortgages. To this Warner replied:

'This morning, by permission of Lady Palmerston, I looked
into the box which contains the writings at Broadlands, and on

perusing them I think the shortest way will be to charge Broadlands estate only, being a very short title and which, in the year 1736, cost the late Lord Palmerston £24,300. This will be more than a sufficient security for the sum intended to be raised, unless your Lordship would rather charge the following estates – viz: Spurshott, which, I believe, cost £6,000; Painsfoot Hill, £9,000; Luyboro' [?], purchased of Mr Jeans for £2,175 and an estate at Toothill, purchased of Mr Chas. Godfrey for £1,235 – amounting together to £16,410.'[3]

By December 31 Palmerston was obliged to inform his wife that the problem had become urgent:

'There is another unlucky business which has vexed me a good deal lately, which is a sum of money I owe the banker [Drummonds] which I had of him some time ago, not to spend, but to employ in a manner that would have been advantageous and upon an idea, understood as I thought, that it was to remain as long as I wanted it. The excessive scarcity of money has now occasioned them to say that they cannot go on with it as it is, which is very distressing to me, for the same cause prevents me from being able to borrow it upon mortgage or any security, at least it is most extremely difficult and if I am obliged to sell out stock just at this time the loss to me will be very considerable. I must try to settle with them to call for as little of the money as possible and I am using every means to get money somewhere else. I have consulted Johnson [a nephew of Mr Godschall] about it, who is very kind and very intelligent about these matters and I hope we shall succeed in so great a degree as to make the matter easy, but for a few days I must not leave this part of the world, which I regret much . . .'[4]

Palmerston could not have asked for a more immediate and charming response from his wife, who offered, without a moment's hesitation, to return to him her marriage settlement, if it would ease his difficulties:

'I shall feel very anxious to hear that you have settled your business comfortable to yourself though I know at this moment it must be difficult and harassing. I think you have had lately a great many things to plague and worry you.

'You know there is nobody more ignorant than myself

about money affairs, but I know men sometimes, from being too generous and liberal to their wives, have suffered inconveniences not then in their power to remedy. After a very unpleasant morning passed previous to our marriage (except as it was an evidence of your affection and kindness) I was told that you had acted by me beyond what those who most loved me could even have expected. The particulars I begged to remain ignorant of, as I trust it will please heaven that I shall never be so miserable as to become possessed of that most dreadful of all knowledge. But I know enough to say that if it can be *now* or at any other moment more convenient for you to be liberated from that engagement (as far as relates to myself) you cannot I trust doubt with what pleasure I should assist in setting you free from a restraint to you and which you may wish did not exist. I beg you will believe me sincere in all I advance and to say the truth I do not mean or can I suppose you can imagine that I think I have any merit in making the offer or in executing this proposal whenever you wish and I flatter myself you will have the kindness never to hesitate in agreeing to it, if it can be of the least use to you.

'I hope next year to take away a great deal less from your annual bounty. But on this subject I will explain myself more fully when we meet, which I hope will now not be long, for I think I grow very anxious to see you . . .'[5]

On the same day, January 2, 1797, Palmerston was writing to say that his first attempt to raise a sum to meet Drummond's overdraft had been unsuccessful:

'Nothing can be more tiresome or unpleasant to me than remaining here or more vexatious than the cause of it. Every circumstance has conspired to increase the difficulty, and particularly the disappointment of a sum which I was to have borrowed of a friend of Mr Oddie's, which was the particular reason why I wanted my papers so much. Just when everything was settled, the man had a purchase offered him of an estate which he has been long trying to get without success, and of course he is off. Were I obliged to pay the whole to the bankers and could get no money from any other quarter my loss from the great depreciation of the funds would be a very serious one. The first however will certainly not be the case and I am in great hopes to be able to do something the other way very soon. The breaking off of the negotiation just now has been a very unfortunate circumstance, as the loan to which everybody who wished well to government felt a call to subscribe is by that means at a heavy discount and the payments upon it soon coming on. I hope in a very few days to be able to send or rather to bring better news as I regret being absent upon every account...'[6]

However, by January 13 he had succeeded in borrowing from Mr Francis, who was an associate in the City of William Godschall and his nephew, Godschall Johnson, the sum of £6,000 on bond at 5 per cent, payable at three months' notice, and on March 3 sold one of the farms on his Fairburn estate, near Ferrybridge in Yorkshire, to Sir John Ramsden for £1,975. His bank overdraft must have been well into five figures, as on April 7 he received from a Mr Baldwin: 'On mortgage of the Hampshire estate £10,000', and of that sum: '£6,000 was paid to Drummonds, the bankers, to discharge a loan and £2,000 to Hankeys, the bankers, to reduce an overdraft'. These transactions would appear to have settled his most pressing obligations, although between February 4 and November 25, 1797, he borrowed a dozen smaller sums, ranging from £200 to £500, amounting in all to £3,400, which may have been used to cover current expenses.[7] These small loans seem to have been raised through Thomas Warner, in spite of that gentleman's rather plaintive note on May 19:

'At present I see no probability of raising more money, but should an opportunity offer, your Lordship may be assured I will use my best endeavours to procure as much as possible...'[8]

Palmerston would appear, by his letter to his wife on December 8 to have been a little easier in his mind about the situation:

'You are very kind and considerate in what you say about reductions. I hope very few if any of those you are so ready to submit to are at all necessary. I think a good deal may be done, for a time at least, by care to avoid extra expenses without trenching into real and substantial articles of comfort; and least of all in the manner and degree you mention in what relates to yourself. Better regulation must be had with regard to the Romsey tradesmen, and Rutledge [the cabinet-maker] in particular, whose bills never diminish and make a very long and unentertaining volume every year . . .'⁹

A fortnight later further trouble was impending:

'I have been, as most people are, sadly plagued about money. I owe the Hankeys more than I ought, and must absolutely pay Francis back his £6,000 which he lent me last year. He is very civil about it but I know he wants to have it, and it is a point of honour as well as obligation that he should, as it was on that condition it was lent, and he gave me double the notice that was stipulated. Selling stock to any amount at this time is such a loss of income as is quite serious, and yet must be done if no other means can be found. What has vexed and provoked me is that I had been negotiating a large loan on mortgage which would have accommodated me well, and as the terms were settled to the perfect satisfaction of an eminent lawyer, who was in town as agent for the parties, who live in Lancashire, I thought everything concluded and only waited for their agreement as a matter of form, when to our great surprise one of the trustees (it being trust money) has refused his consent, objecting to the security without any grounds, whatever, as his lawyer says if what we offer is not good security, he does not know what is. He is gone down into the country and we are to hear from him again if he can prevail on the trustee to consent. Such an unexpected disappointment is really provoking . . .'¹⁰

Lady Palmerston's brother-in-law, Culverden, was even worse affected by the crisis. Palmerston, in his usual generous fashion, was doing all he could to help, noting in his engagement diary for 1797: 'Lent December 1st to Cripps and Francillon, on account of Mr Culverden, £100, together with £100 on Lord Minto's account, for which I took their note payable on demand to me; whenever it is paid I am to pay half of it to Lord Minto. Mr Culverden owed him £360, of part of which they were in the utmost want; Mr Culverden's affairs being entirely deranged, a composition is to be immediately offered to his creditors.'¹¹

Viscount Palmerston, 1801

Henry Temple, third Viscount Palmerston, aged twenty

The debt to Mr Francis was paid promptly in March, 1798, together with interest of £300, but there is nothing specific to show how this sum was raised; it must be assumed that Palmerston had found it easier to obtain accommodation from his bankers. A summary of his debts for some time in 1798 reads: 'Baldwin, £10,000; Bankers, £17,145; Hants, £3,400.'[12]

Palmerston had sold £1,900 of timber in 1798 and March, 1799, to a Mr Poore, but his bankers were becoming pressing again, and on April 3, 1799, he was obliged to dispose of another of his English estates, Great Houghton, near Northampton, to Henry Thornton, of the Bank of England, who paid him £11,000. The settlement of this business and the payment of the proceeds to Hankeys must have taken some time, as on October 3, 1799, we find Palmerston writing to his wife:

'I have been this morning to meet Mr Thornton and our business will be finished directly. A circumstance has occurred with the Hankeys which will very likely occasion and I think fully justify my leaving their house. I have been indebted to them for some time past £17,000, for which I paid them interest. The sale of an estate in Northamptonshire to Mr Thornton was to pay them the produce of it, viz. £11,000, leaving £6,000, which I thought and they seemed to agree, was doing handsomely by them and that what was left unpaid was no more than what a customer like me might reasonably expect as an accommodation for a longer time. But to my surprise the next day I received a letter from the house at large, calling on me to pay in the whole and advising me to sell stocks for the purpose which I do not choose to do. This I think a shabby proceeding, but as they have a right to be paid they cannot be surprised if I transfer my business to houses that will be obliged to me for it and ready to furnish me with such an accommodation. I shall be most happy to have a fair ground of getting rid of the Hankeys, whose situation is an almost intolerable inconvenience to me, who never go into the City. I think Mr Johnson's house, which is a most reputable one as to security, will be glad of this and I have written to him about it as he is out of town and I do not choose to go to any of the partners who do not know me. It is what he proposed last year

N

and therefore I suppose will be glad of it now. I expect his answer tomorrow. I shall do it without the least quarrel, merely upon the ground that as they want the money I must naturally resort to those who are willing to supply me . . .

October 4th. 'I have settled my business with the Hankeys upon a fair compromise that I pay them something more than I intended and they are not to call for the remainder unless they particularly want it and if they do, they are not to take it ill if I go to some other house who would willingly furnish it. I have had a letter from Mr Johnson, by which I understand they would be ready to do it if I wished it, but leaves me quite at liberty by saying he wishes to defer a positive answer till he comes to London. So I shall thank him and say I have settled it otherwise for the present . . .'[13]

Palmerston spent a week at Broadlands as soon as this business was concluded and must have had a series of heart-to-heart talks with his wife about the possibility of selling the estate. She wrote him on October 14, after his departure for Brighton, an enchanting letter which sums up, as no other, the happy and trusting nature of their marriage and her own qualities:

'The subject on which we were speaking previous to your departure this morning so entirely engrosses my thoughts that I cannot refrain from addressing you thus early upon it, as I am anxious to unite with you in endeavouring to rectify the evil before it becomes too serious.

'My attachment to Broadlands you will not doubt, even to the regretting the day that has passed since I know I have one the less to enjoy. Every delightful idea is connected with this place. Every object of my tenderest affection and fondest recollection so interwoven with the remembrance of Broadlands. Here I first perceived I had some share in your affections. Here I received the tenderest proofs of your kindness. This was the first habitation in which I had the delightful privilege of calling myself your wife. Every spot of ground here has been at some moment of their lives trodden by the feet of those much loved beings whose images can never be effaced from my mind and who are retraced in my daily walks from my

parents to my infant Mary. Here my beloved brother tasted
the last days of happiness he was ever permitted to enjoy, when
he saw me united to the most perfect of human beings. Here
also the fondest mother breathed her last sigh in peace, surrounded by every comfort that human assistance through your
kindness could offer.

'Such are the ties which bind me to this spot, but under all
these interesting and attractive points of view I feel daily regret
that they are solitary enjoyments, for to you it is a source of
constant uneasiness, and that you find no pleasure from being
here; on the contrary, the expense destroys every idea of
pleasure and that few things would concur more effectually
to establish your comfort than quitting it for ever. If I know
myself (and I do not consider that knowledge very difficult)
there is no deprivation of any convenience, less of any luxury
that would give me much pain, if I do not see those I love
affected by it. It is more painful to reflect that previous to your
marriage with me you had not a wish within the power of
fortune to obtain ungratified and that owing to the misfortunes
attending that connection that power has been daily diminish-
ing. The necessary increase of expense a married life must incur
under the happiest prospects makes a material change in every
man's situation and the circumstances of the times contributes
to nearly double every article of living since the last fifteen
years. All these considerations fill me with regret and takes
from the happiness I should otherwise enjoy without alloy in
this place. The continuing to pursue any mode of living that
exceeds our income can never answer. And the thinking on
every article of expense is also very wearying. It is far better
in my opinion to lay down some regular plan to bring our
whole expenses much below the annual receipts than to keep
on the stretch to be precisely within it. You are now living on
a great scale merely to allow me and the children to pass our
time in magnificence *without you*, for you seldom are here more
than three and oftentimes only two of the six months we spend
at Broadlands. For myself I sincerely declare with all my attachment to this habitation I should infinitely prefer living in even
the dullest place *with you* and seeing you possess health and

good spirits – you happy and I am completely so, you unhappy and I am wretched. My heart can know no quiet without yours is void of care. You know I never *loved* but you. I married *you*, not your fortune, and while I possess your affections and preserve your esteem every other consideration seems not worth a thought. Indeed after all in what ever way you might wish to live, it must be in a style of the highest affluence and beyond all my vainest wishes could have imagined.

'What would have been my fate without the aid of your fostering and supporting hand, worse than beggary. Then let me conjure you never to allow any feeling of delicacy on my account [to] operate in any determination you might wish to adopt. Had you married a woman of high birth and great fortune you might have some scruple in proposing any alteration. But to me every plan must place me so far beyond every expectation that fancy could even have suggested in her wildest moments that I think you cannot permit that consideration to hold a place in your mind.

'While we live here it is hardly possible to avoid seeing our friends till we have adopted some new plan, which must first commence in absence; and we may then return and follow it. The ideas floating in my mind are either to pass the rest of the winter in the West of England, Brighthelmstone, Sheen or London. The former would best suit your health, but I wish to adopt what would also conduce to your pleasure. If you prefer Brighthelmstone, house rent in winter is cheap and we might live at a small expense in comparison with living at home. I then should advise parting with Tagg and two kitchen maids and taking a quiet woman cook, keeping only two housemaids in future. Have only one pair of horses and when I am in London keeping a chair only for the evening and as I walk so much I have no want of a carriage in the morning. Part with the ponies, keep no second table. Get some clever man in Morgan's place if you allow him £20 a year annuity, for I believe with every honest intention he is the worst bailiff anybody ever had. In short, bring our establishment to one man out of livery, two footmen and a boy, one coachman, besides your own groom and stable man. Have the produce of the

kitchen garden sold at Southampton. In short, set apart what
sum you like to expend in the year and endeavour to draw out
a plan not to exceed it. But it will not be possible to do so
living as we are. And I think in this plan you would not
relinquish one comfort.

'Pray revolve all this in your mind and let us take some
active and early resolution and not go on in daily discomfort,
since our present mode does not afford you a momentary
pleasure, on the contrary, eternal disquiet. If you loved this
place you might find some hours of delight, though tinctured
with regret. But everyday spent at Broadlands is irksome to
you. Wherefore should you encumber your fortune for me to
set here and entertain company at your expense in your absence?
It is what in future I cannot allow myself to do. I have no claim
to such indulgence. If we could be fairly away from B. we
might make all our arrangements for our future plans, and
your not liking it is a perfect good reason for not living here.
I do not mean to suppose that you could save a great deal
in four months, but it will enable you to digest your plans
with more effect and we may then return another year on a
more confined and happier scale. I wish to lessen every
expense except what relates to my children's education and
their pleasure.

'After June I mean to lessen what I receive from you, before
that period I fear it will not be in my power, having lately laid
out more money in linen, etc. And having accustomed myself
to expend largely on others I cannot feel quite comfortable to
make an earlier change. It is impossible to live with you and
not to catch some spark of your benevolence. And from your
example, aided by your unceasing generosity, I have tasted the
happiness of adding some comfort to others, but it becomes
injustice to be depriving you of what should be reserved for
yourself.

'I have lately incurred some expenses here, in buying some
furniture for the bedrooms, which I now regret, but I assure
you I will expend no further and I will endeavour to be as
economical as possible in future. But as I have said before,
living in this place and accustomed to see it the mirror of

comfort within and without, I feel I cannot make much effectual change without some efficient plan of reform.

'If I was to ask myself in what consists true happiness I should answer that in my estimation it is to be obtained by living with those we love, and seeing them in the full enjoyment of health and tranquillity. The latter assuredly can only be attained by making, as Sir Ferdy [Poole, Palmerston's first brother-in-law] says, December shake hands with January. Life is too short, and too full of melancholy events to allow ourselves to add to the bitter drops by lessening our daily comfort from any false fear of the world's opinion when we act to ensure our own approbation. And long, very long, have I learnt to estimate all the luxuries of any situation as only transient possessions and those with which I have been surrounded so exceeding every ambitious expectation that the loss of any part can never much affect me. I have enjoyed it, but I hope not abused it, and the parting from any portion of these splendid advantages would not cost me one quarter of the regret I should feel seeing you uncomfortable or out of spirits.

'Forgive this long and tedious repetition, but I have thought I was talking with you and I fear I have trespassed beyond even your patience, but I knew how indulgent you are and that you will kindly forgive the errors of the head, being convinced that the heart can never form a wish but for your happiness. And that the desire of adding to it by adopting any plan most likely to ensure the possession has been the real motive for detaining you so long from your breakfast and I from my bed.

'Heaven bless you and believe me ever your most affectionate Mary.'[14]

Even Palmerston's dry literary style could not hide his gratitude:

October 24th. 'I have this morning received yours of the 14th ... the kindness, affection, feeling and consideration of which I cannot sufficiently admire, approve and thank you for. I am infinitely obliged to you for all that you suggest. Whether any and what part of it may be necessary and advisable will be a matter of future consideration and discussion. The increase of expense in almost every possible branch at the time when all circumstances of public and private situation rendered a diminution almost necessary, has certainly been a subject of uneasiness to me as well of surprise, when I know how ample the means I possess are compared with those of numbers I see, who appear to live at a greater expense in many most material points. Many of my expenses have been of a temporary kind, particularly the very heavy ones that have attended the house in London, which are hardly yet all defrayed. I hope soon to be able to form a better estimate than I can yet do of permanent income and probable permanent expense, after which we must regulate our plans accordingly.'[15]

* * *

The financial stringency of the time did not seem to make any appreciable difference to Palmerston's train of life. For a period in 1797 his social engagements were to a certain extent restricted to his immediate family and most intimate friends, but as the load of indebtedness came under control his life resumed its old pattern. Even so, there was a tendency in the engagement diary entries to hark back in advancing age to the friendships of his prime. He called on the declining Duchess of Devonshire and paid his respects to the widowed Lady Diana Beauclerk, living in semi-retirement and in her sixties. The entries for entertainment at the Catch Club had dwindled to a few pounds, as did the little sums for his gains and losses at cards.

Nevertheless he continued to attend to his parliamentary duties and kept Lady Palmerston informed of any aspect of events that affected their personal friends. With the abandonment of Corsica by the British fleet in October, 1796, Sir Gilbert Elliot had been obliged to relinquish his Viceroyalty and Lord Malmesbury was in Paris trying, unsuccessfully, to reach peace terms with the triumphant Directory:

November 18th, 1796. 'Emma [Godfrey] says that Lady Malmesbury has wrote her word that she has deferred going to Broadlands and that she is uneasy about Sir Gilbert [Elliot]. Government here know nothing about Corsica. I am afraid by the French accounts it is too probable that the evacuation has not been completed without some loss, but it appears by their accounts that Sir Gilbert and the principal part of the troops went to Porto Ferrajo where I suppose they are safe. Lord M[almesbury] and the Directory do nothing but snap [at] one another. I hope they will have vented all their ill humour before they come to business if that ever happens . . .

November 30th. 'I dined at C. Ellis's on Saturday with Canning, Frere and Sir H. Englefield, who desired a great many kind things to you. He grows enormously large.

'I am going today to Lord Lavingtons, who is as usual excessively kind and attentive. The last time I dined there one of the company was Mr Edgeworth who attended the poor King of France at his last moments. He is I believe a Frenchman by birth, though an Irishman by family. A very mild gentleman-like man. The company being mixed and all strangers to him, nothing passed that was interesting . . .'[16]

Political interest was absorbed by the death of Catherine the Great of Russia and Pitt's efforts to raise a loan for the continuance of the war. By this time Palmerston was his staunch adherent and an opponent of Fox:

December 8th. 'The House of Commons was over last night soon after ten . . . Nothing very remarkable passed in yesterday's debate. The taxes, as I mentioned before, do not seem to occasion any great uneasiness though the sum they are to produce is so enormous. Pitt's speech was clear and without any great appearance of exultation upon the loan or anything else. Fox and Grey attacked him where they thought they could. Fox endeavoured to put the subscribers to the loan in good humour with their bargain by stating it as highly in their favour as he could, which, as it has filled so well, seems to be the measure adopted. While it was uncertain how it would take, the measure was to represent it as extremely disadvantageous to the subscriber . . .

December 15th. 'We were till three this morning in the House. Fox's first speech I thought able. Pitt's reply was excellent and parts of it very fine. He established the necessity and good effects of the assistance given to the Emperor, which was a point which the opposition did not contest. He then proved very satisfactorily that much less benefit would have arisen to the Emperor and much more inconvenience to this country if it had been done in any other mode; and lastly he stated a great number of precedents in the proceedings of Parliament, in which various ministers from the Revolution to the present time had acted in a similar manner upon their own responsibility, and in which Parliament, upon subsequent consideration and information, had sanctioned the measure by their approbation without thinking it a violation of the constitution. This part of his speech seemed to give great satisfaction to a considerable part of the House who, though satisfied that it was right to do the thing as it had been done, thought it was unprecedented and ought to be the ground of a bill of indemnity. At the conclusion of Pitt's speech, he was very eloquent in an attack upon Fox, who had said he could see no motive for the conduct of ministry but a design to overturn the constitution. Sheridan made as usual a lively speech and Fox at past twelve got up to avail himself of an indulgence allowed by the practice of the House, contrary to its rules, to the mover of a proposition to close the debate by such observations as he may wish to make, upon what has been urged against him in the course of it. This indulgence I must say he tried to the utmost, by speaking till past two. The first three quarters of an hour about himself, and the remainder of the time in going over and over what he and everybody else who had spoke had exhausted before. It is a great pity that with all his abilities he is deficient in that great point of knowing when to have done and how to avoid fatiguing his auditors . . .

December 21st. 'The death of the Empress of Russia was as you see quite unexpected and I think in a public light unfortunate. From what I have heard I hope her successor will not take to the French. I do not know what his own inclinations may be but he is supposed to be much influenced by his wife and she being a Princess of Wurtemberg and sister to one of the late Empresses of Germany is supposed, as I am told, to be well disposed to the Austrian cause . . .

December 31st. 'I arrived in town yesterday and went directly to the House of Commons just in time for the business. Pitt's speech, though he had a very bad cold upon him, was very able and parts of it very fine. He spoke with great energy and vehemence for more than three hours, giving a complete and minute detail of everything that had passed, in which he placed in a very strong light the haughty, perverse and childish behaviour of the French Directory. He spoke very handsomely of Lord Malmesbury, without making a direct eulogium of him, by always stating him to have done what was wisest and best upon every occasion. Fox made a very long and I think a confused and certainly a most mischievous speech. Indeed it is not possible innocently to take the part the opposition do on this occasion by taking up the cause of France, justifying their conduct, blaming our government and furnishing the French with grounds of objection and motives of perseverance which their more intimate knowledge of the state of this country enables them to do in a manner that must be very useful to France and makes them in fact very useful allies. Erskine spoke, failed as usual, found he produced no effect and was little attended to after a vast parade of taking notes during Pitt's speech. So he had recourse to his usual expedient in the House of Commons of being taken ill and leaving off abruptly. Dundas's speech was very good, particularly his attack upon Fox, a tolerable good outline of which you will see in the Herald. I always liked Dundas for one thing, which is that he never is afraid to carry the war into the enemy's quarters, whereas in general government speakers are so tame and opposition so insolent that it rather provokes one. In general it is right to be so, as the contrary in imprudent hands would produce mischief, but Dundas always does it ably and with a laughing good humoured manner which is sure to succeed. Gray spoke tolerably well, but everything he could say had been forestalled. The opposition made a very poor figure as they had no real measure to oppose and nothing to propose but a substitution of words of an address, which none but their most determined partisans could agree with or approve. The House was not up till half past two and yet there were but four speeches, excepting Erskine's attempt, which I believe did not last above a quarter of an hour . . .

'I saw Lord Malmesbury last night at the House of Lords.

He looks very well and seemed in very good spirits. I am going to dine with him today at Charles Ellis's . . .'[17]

At the end of the year Duncan's victory over the Dutch fleet at the Battle of Camperdown had greatly eased Pitt's situation. Lady Palmerston had so far followed her husband's political conversion that she was able to rejoice in the Prime Minister's trouncing in the debates in the House of Commons of Tierney ['Such a reply as I have not often heard in point of severity and ability' commented Palmerston[18]], acting as leader of the Opposition, which had been reduced to a rump, by the temporary secession from the sittings of Fox and his immediate colleagues:

November 26th. 'It is impossible not to admire and wonder at Pitt's most extraordinary abilities. His head, in comparison with the rest of mankind (with few exceptions) in point of clearness is as our brilliant Test to the slow, muddy Severn. I enjoy his playing the baron upon Tierney's giving him a shake and throwing him upon his back so completely . . .'[19]

The House was debating Pitt's plan for financing the war with France during the coming year:

December 13th. 'The House yesterday, as you will see, did not sit by there not being members enough at 4 o'clock. How it happened I know not, whether by mischance or whether it was wished to put it off. It comes on today and I am just going down. The opposition are stirring every method to embarrass the business and intimidate Pitt to give it up. I have seen nobody today who could tell anything and am quite ignorant about it. If they do succeed I shall have a bad opinion of things . . .

'PS. I was at Brooks's last night for a little while, which seemed quite like a Jacobin club. The Prince was there. I understand Fox is to attend on the next stage of the bill after today.

December 14th. 'I am just going down to the House, the business was again put off yesterday upon some point of form. A great clamour is raised against the plan and friends do more harm by their way of talking than enemies. I do not however understand or believe that it is meant to be abandoned . . .

'Nothing can be more mischievous than Fox's speech (yesterday) or a more shamefaced abandonment of all former protestations that if France refused to treat upon reasonable terms the whole country would be unanimous in supporting the war. He said he should not attend the bill in the committee but might come again to oppose its passing and then return to his former plan of secession. Gray was not there.

'I have got a headache today which a full and long day at the House sometimes produces if I eat anything but bread and butter and tea. It is not however very bad and I hope will not prevent me from dining at Lord Lucan's today. I spoke to the Lavingtons about coming to Broadlands, which they propose doing if it is quite convenient to us, which I assured them it was . . .

December 22nd. 'I suppose this tiresome bill will finally pass about the middle of the week. The opposition to it is suspended while it is in the committee, where Pitt is allowed to fashion it as he pleases and one great push I suppose is to be made against it afterwards, to counteract which those who can attend to support it ought. However, if it goes much farther I shall leave it. Those who support it do it disinterestedly and from thinking this measure or something equivalent to it necessary, for it is made every day more burthensome to persons who have any property, as they now are to pay 5 times the amount of their assessed taxes and are precluded from any remedy when it exceeds a tenth of their income . . .'[20]

In Bavaria Count Rumford had again been called on to master a crisis:

February 13th, 1798. 'Here I am once more, involved in public business, and in business of the most disagreeable kind. On the 27th of last month, we received alarming accounts of popular disturbances and other symptoms of revolutionary frenzy, which had begun to make their appearance in Mannheim, and in several parts of Swabia, and private intelligence was received of emissaries being actually on their way to Munich with the friendly intention of opening our eyes and preparing our minds for the new doctrines of Liberty and Equality, and all their attendant blessings. On this emergency,

I was sent for by the Elector and desired by him to take it upon myself to prepare for the reception of these gentlemen and have things in readiness to give them such a reception as they deserve. H.M.I. Highness issued but one short order to the Council of the Supreme Regency, just informing them of my being charged with the preservation of peace, order and tranquillity in the country and directing them to co-operate with me in all cases, where I should require their co-operation or assistance. I have just put on my uniform, named my aides-de-camp and taken the command of the troops; but the military arrangements I am making are of little consequence, and require little labour compared with those of another kind which I have undertaken to introduce and carry into execution. The Elector has charged me with the police of the country in the most extended sense of that expression, with ample powers to alter what I find amiss and do all that is necessary to be done to introduce order and regularity in every department of the state and secure the peace, confidence and tranquillity of his subjects.

'You will doubtless wonder at my temerity in engaging in such an arduous undertaking, and at such a critical period. The fact is I could not avoid it. The proposal was made in so kind and so flattering a manner. The services I may perhaps render are so very important and the apparent necessity of the business being undertaken – and without delay – rendered it impossible for me to refuse devoting myself once more for the public good. I have done so, and have already had the satisfaction of receiving the most flattering proofs of the approbation of the public and the most touching marks of their esteem and affectionate regard. You will be able to form an idea of the confidence the Elector places in me, when I tell you that with the most unlimited powers which he has given – he has not given me any instructions in writing . . .'

This was his last and most considerable service to the Elector. Six months later he was able to write in much more tender terms:

July 4th. 'I have just returned to Munich from an excursion of fifteen days . . . After staying four days at Salzburg and visiting with great devotion the scenes on the mountain above the town, which we formerly admired together, we went to Berchtesgaden, where we stayed five days and saw everything you saw there, except your friend the Bishop, who was not there. From Berchtesgaden we returned by Reichenhall, Traunstein and Chiemsee to Munich. You cannot imagine how forcibly the various scenes I formerly saw with you recalled you to my recollection. When I came to the place on top of the mountain above the town of Salzburg where I lost you, the illusion was so strong as almost to overcome my reason. I was almost tempted to think you were still in the woods where you lost yourself and was very near exposing myself by calling out to try if I could make you hear me . . .'

As a reward for his services, the Elector had decided to appoint Rumford his Minister in London, but here a grave disappointment awaited him:

Royal Hotel, Pall Mall, September 23rd, 1798. 'I came here on Wednesday last, the 19th. I should most undoubtedly [have] written to you in one hour after my arrival had not Mr Canning done me the honour to wait upon me at the Hotel, half an hour after my arrival, to announce to me a most unexpected piece of news and of such a nature as totally to unfit me for all correspondence, except it be such as has occupied me ever since. You remember my reception the last time I visited this country.

'Fool that I was not to take the hint and never more set my foot on this ungrateful island. If you knew with what delight I looked forward to the comforts I thought to enjoy in the agreeable and honourable situation the Elector had given me in this country, you could then form some adequate idea of my disappointment and of my indignation at being refused. I am told that I am a subject of His Majesty and, therefore, cannot be received as a minister from a foreign court. If I had not myself seen a subject of His Majesty, Count Jennison Walworth, received as minister of the Landgrave of Hesse-Darmstadt, this reason might perhaps have appeared to me to have more weight. But it seems that there is still another objection to my being received. Some twenty years ago, I was under secretary-of-state and that circumstance, it seems, renders my reception doubly impossible.

'All my baggage, all my books – all I possess in the world – is packed up and on its way to England, and I cannot stop it. What is more provoking than all the rest is that I had taken the precaution, long before I left Bavaria, to sound the ground at the fountain head, and was encouraged to ask for the appointment and was promised the most gracious reception. Who then is to be believed? If people don't know their own minds six months – but no more on this subject.

'I shall go to Bath in a day or two and shall wait there in the most retired corner I can find, without seeing anybody, till I get fresh instructions from Munich. I shall leave the Royal Hotel tomorrow morning, having taken a private lodging in King Street, No: 4 St James's Square, where I shall leave the wife and child of my *valet de chambre* and the baggage I have with me. My daughter desires me to present her love to you. She longs to see you, but is outrageous at the people who have used her father so unkindly and, to tell the truth, we are both too much agitated by anger and disappointment to be fit to be seen in decent, quiet company . . .

No: 4, King Street, St James's Square, 1798 (undated). 'My situation is most embarrassing, but I must not lose my head. You may easily imagine my anxiety to receive answers to my letters to Munich. I have written in a pressing manner to the Elector to permit me to resign my case on the pretext of bad health. This I thought it my duty to do to prevent all disagreeable altercation between the Elector and this Court. In this request to the Elector, I have added another. I have asked his leave to visit America next spring and to spend a year in that country. In the meantime, I foresee that I shall be much embarrassed when my luggage arrives from Germany, for I have literally brought away everything I possessed there . . .'

However, a month later he had better news:

Brompton Row, No: 51, Saturday, October 27th, 1798. 'The letters I received from Munich of the 7th and 8th of this month by the last mail from Hamburg have relieved my mind from a state of the most painful anxiety. I now know my fate and am happy beyond any degree of happiness you can easily imagine. The scheme I proposed to the Elector in a private letter I wrote him immediately after my arrival in London, has met with his approbation and has served as the foundation of an official arrangement that relieves me from a most awkward and painful situation . . .

'I am on the whole, not sorry for all that has happened to me within the last two or three months. I am handsomely out of a bad scrape. All my private affairs are wound up and I am now a free, independent citizen of the world and your most attached friend and devoted servant.'[21]

His affairs thus settled, Count Rumford was able to turn to the project by which he is best known in England, the founding of the Royal Institution.

★   ★   ★

In Ireland rebellion and disorder had continued through the whole of 1798 and although repressive measures had restored a semblance of order by June, trouble flared up again with the arrival of the small French expedition under General Humbert on August 20. Landing in Killala Bay, the French forces at one moment were fighting over Palmerston's lands at Sligo. News of their surrender on September 7 did not reach France and reinforcements arrived off Lough Swilly on October 10, followed by a further small force which reached Killala on the 27th. Both these expeditions were routed before the troops could land. Lord Cornwallis, who had succeeded as Lord-Lieutenant in June, and had done all he could to restrain the ferocity of the government troops in repressing the rebellion, was already engaged in conversations with Irish leaders, which were to lead to the Act of Union less than a year later. Palmerston wrote to his wife from London:

October 16th. 'I met a Mr Elleson at dinner who is a clergyman and a principal man at Castlebar and who, being with the Bishop of Killala, was taken prisoner after going out with the rest of the clergy to join the military, who attempted to make a resistance, which with so very small a force would have been as well not attempted. The French used him as they did all their

prisoners, very well, and having carried him with them to
Castlebar he was at liberty when they left that place. The
inhabitants of that place gallantly and fortunately kept the
rebels out of it during the whole of the time that Lord Cornwallis left that country at their mercy. The French officers were
in constant expectation of reinforcements from France and said
they came to give liberty to Ireland and to annoy England and
were very indifferent as to their own fate. They soon grew
disgusted with their Irish followers and said that if the people
would not exert themselves in a more effectual manner and
were not disposed to receive the blessings they brought them
they could not help it; but seemed to think they had succeeded
well as an operation against England, and were not a little
proud of bringing out the Viceroy with his great army against
their small corps. The Irish Chancellor you see is come over.
He, I understand, is the only person with whom Lord Cornwallis
communicates, and whether he is in his full confidence or not I
do not know. A union is very seriously thought of, and in the
relative state into which Irish patriotism has brought the two
countries I believe it is the most desirable measure. To consult
upon this point I believe is the chief object of Lord Clare's
coming over. Pelham is I fancy going to meet him. A sense of
common danger is I believe likely at this moment to reconcile
many persons to this measure, whom the apprehension of the
loss of jobs, power and emoluments have always hitherto made
adverse to it, but still I fear it would be a very difficult business
to arrange . . .

October 25th. 'I hope before this reaches you we shall all be
rejoicing in the confirmation of the supposed victory on the
coast of Ireland, which will be a great thing for the present relief
and quiet of that country. The sooner Lord C[ornwallis] is got
out of it the better. It is unfortunate for himself at least that he
ever went there, as he has had full opportunity of showing his
want of ability both in the civil and military line so conspicu-
ously and lost all the credit which fortune more than merit
had given him. It has often been said and I believe with truth,
that his military conduct both in America and in India was
very poor. P[elham] showed me a letter from him yesterday

which I own surprised me, as he is not much in the habit of communicating his sentiments freely. He speaks with confidence of the probability of a considerable victory being obtained over the French fleet and their schemes of invasion at this time defeated. He then uses the most desponding expressions with regard to the general state of the country and says that a union *with the Protestants of Ireland, which would be the easiest of all points to carry,* as it would in his opinion be extremely pernicious, as it would throw an insurmountable bar in the way of a general admission of the Catholics to everything, which he seems to pronounce to be the most salutory measure. This, which is carrying Lord Fitzwilliam's and Mr Grattan's systems to the utmost, is very strange language for a Lord-Lieutenant to hold, who went over with no particular instructions from here but what related to promoting and trying to pave the way for a union, and who in the very few conversations he has held with people of consequence on political subjects has been rather indiscreet in opening his views and intentions too much in favour of that measure. Lord Clare, I understand, is strongly for the measure and thinks it perfectly practicable now, while the apprehensions of all people of property are so strong. A different situation of things might render them averse to it, and yet it seems to be the opinion of the best informed that without it that country, separated as it stands, can be nothing but a scene of turbulence and confusion . . .'[22]

This combination of circumstances – the possibility of Union and the temporary wreck of his Irish income – turned Palmerston's thoughts to the project he had mooted five years earlier of petitioning the Prime Minister for an English peerage, thus maintaining his social position and a seat in Parliament, without being put to the recurring expense of further elections to the Commons. On November 3 he drafted a letter to William Pitt:

'A considerable time has elapsed since I submitted to you my hopes of obtaining the honour of an English Peerage by your assistance and offered such grounds, as I presumed to flatter myself, might authorise the application and justify at least any attention you might be good enough to show to it. I was much obliged to you for the kind and encouraging manner in which you received this application, and at the same time not insensible of the obstacles you mentioned, which might prevent your compliance with it at that time. Those obstacles proceeding from former engagements have been diminished by the fulfilment of many of them. I have not, however, troubled you with any fresh solicitation, and not being willing to be an importunate suitor, should not probably have done so at present had not particular circumstances seemed to require it.

'The projected Union with Ireland which the relative situation into which the two countries are brought seems to have rendered desirable for both will, if it takes place, and should be modelled on the plan of that with Scotland, make a very essential alteration in the situation of the Peers of Ireland by laying them under an incapacity of holding seats in the British House of Commons. Permit me therefore, without delay, to renew my former application with respect to an English Peerage, or if that should not be at present attainable, allow me to solicit eventually, in case an Union should take place, the effectual support of government to be one of the representatives of the Irish Peerage in the British House of Lords.

'This application will not I hope be deemed unreasonable when it is considered in how many Parliaments I have held a seat in the House of Commons, that my property in Ireland is considerable and my family not unknown there, and that I have on every occasion, as far as lay in my power, shown an unalterable, and I hope I may say a disinterested zeal in the support of government and good order against the desperate attacks that have been made upon them.

'As it is to you only I mean to apply or wish to be indebted on this occasion, allow me to say that however I may have been withheld for a time at a former period by connections since dissolved and circumstances long passed away, from appearing under the same political standard with yourself, yet that my mind was early prepared for the opinion it has long since adopted that to your talents, your principles and your energy the public cause must be indebted, if it escapes the dangers of this alarming crisis.

'I feel no scruple in making this declaration though coupled with the solicitation of a favour because, let the fate of that solicitation be what it may, you will equally receive, in the great career you are pursuing, such support as I can afford in whatever situation I am placed. It was first given unbargained for and on full conviction and will be continued without a view to private advantage, which at a conjuncture like the present ought not, even in the calculations of self-interest, to weigh a feather in the great scale where everything we have to value is balanced against everything we have to dread.

'Forgive me for taking up so much of your time and accept the assurances of the high esteem and respectful attachment with which I have the honour to be,

dear Sir,

Your most faithful

and obedient humble servant,

Palmerston.'[23]

The approach did not succeed, although Palmerston was to return to the charge at intervals. During the remainder of the year he and his wife exchanged social tittle-tattle:

From Lady Palmerston, Broadlands, October 21st. 'In the evening we played at billiards till supper and Lord M[almesbury] was so particularly agreeable that we sat up till past two. I never saw him look better and he is exactly in his Grove Place happy spirits, entertaining everybody and appearing to be entertained by everybody. Certainly he is when out of his sombre mood the most captivating creature in the world for he never seems to wish to be in any other society than that one in which he is at that moment placed in . . .

London, November 29th. [Yesterday] 'Count Rumford, the Countess and my uncle dined upon a boiled chicken, mutton steaks and some Prince of Wales cutlets. In the evening Lord Minto [as Sir Gilbert Elliot had become], Lord St Helen's and Mr Quintin joined our party. Count R. looks sadly and both Lord M. and Lord St H. agreed the not receiving him was the extreme of ill nature. Count R. and his daughter will be at Broadlands next week. Lord Minto I am grieved to find has not pined in absence for he has grown amazingly fat . . . Lord

M. read me a delightful letter of Lord Nelson's to his wife in
May, the day after a dreadful storm which nearly rendered the
"Vanguard" a wreck off the island of Sardinia . . .

'This morning I am going on some business and visits, dine
at 4, – Countess Rumford, Mr Quintin and my uncle, on roast
mutton and my uncle's pheasant, and go to *Lover's Vows*,
where Lord Minto and his boys meet me and Lord St H. and
Sir Harry. I expect to eat no supper after the play. I have
taken complete possession of your apartment which is quite
beautiful . . .[24]

From Lord Palmerston, London, December 6th. 'I have had a
long visit this morning from Count Rumford, who I think
looks thin and seems a little hoarse, but says he is pretty well
and finds very great benefit from large quantities of strong
Burton ale which he begins to take in the morning as people
do asses milk and drinks little else through the day. This seems
an odd plan for a feverish man but I hope he will find it answer.
He seems better reconciled now to his lot than I imagine he was
at first and told me what his plans are of going to America and
making if he likes it a little establishment there, from whence
however he proposes after a short time to revisit England and
this Continent. He says that all things considered, however
severe the disappointment proves to him he is still very glad
the thing has happened as it has done rather than that he should
have remained as he was in Bavaria. Mr Quintin has likewise
been here. Both he and Count Rumford intend visiting Broadlands at some little time hence . . .

December 9th. 'I saw a new play last night of Mr Reynold's,
Laugh When You Can, which is very good advice to the audience, as they should lose no opportunity as if affords them
very few. It is I think worse than anything that has come from
that school before . . .

'Our troops are going as you know to Portugal. The French
are so urgent with Spain to do something against Portugal that
it may not be possible for her to avoid making some attempt
which will probably not be a vigorous one. Tarleton is to
command the Cavalry, but before he goes he is to marry Miss
Bertie, a daughter of the late Duke of Ancaster whom we saw

I believe with Lady Willoughby. She has £12,000. The Duke
of Bedford seemed to like her very much but she has taken
Tarleton. I suppose his wooing was like Othello's . . .

December 12th. 'I went to the House yesterday and was well
entertained. Tierney's speech was very well in its way and he
always keeps up something of decency and moderation in his
manner, which is more becoming and parliamentary than what
we have been used to for many years past. The only speech of
any consequence on [the] government side was from Canning,
who acquitted himself uncommonly well and gained great
credit which I am very glad of, as it was a fashion to run him
down as a speaker. The house was up by eight o'clock . . .[25]

From Broadlands Lady Palmerston responded:

December 12th. 'Mrs H. Drummond writes that Bath is
excessively full . . . One piece of news she heard as a fact surprised her as it has me – that you and Lord Malmesbury had
exchanged your Lordship's country seats and that you were in
full possession and residence of Park Place and Lord M. of
Broadlands . . .

December 14th. 'How could Miss Bertie wed Othello when
she appeared the object of so fair a Duke's admiration. I, certainly much as I love seeing new countries, had rather marry
the Duke of Bedford with all his faults and stay at home than
General Tarleton with all his virtues and go to Lisbon . . .

December 16th. 'Mrs H. Drummond tells me that Lady
Nelson's reception at the Pump Room proved that the Battle
of the Nile was not out of the recollection of the Bathites.
"Rule Britannia" was struck up and the applause was quite
affecting . . .'[26]

Palmerston's health had become progressively more troublesome during each winter and he kept an almost clinical record
of his ailments and of the terrifying specifics prescribed to cure
them:

Extracted from 1797 *diary.* 'At the beginning of the year I
weighed 13 stone 3 lbs in the morning, without my clothes,
and 10 pounds of which I had gained by relaxing from the
regimen by which I had lost 23 pounds since July. I had begun
to reduce myself again when on coming to town, 26th February,

I was seized with a violent cold, then universally prevalent. Not being feverish, I used evacuants and the common medicines to relieve the breath (which was afflicted for the first three days) and to quiet the cough. The disorder even became moderate, but as usual very tedious. I soon left off meat entirely, as well as all fermented liquor, and lived chiefly upon bread and milk and tea. By the 19th March, which was three weeks, I was reduced in weight to 12 stone 7 lbs, which was what I had been in the November preceding. No diminution of strength or spirits on either occasion. My cold gradually went off about this time, so much as to enable me to go about. I remained all spring and summer without any fresh cold, but with frequent sensation as if cold was coming on, which used to go off on taking small quantities of opiate. In October, I was attacked with a severe cold and some fever. For two or three days my breath was much affected and I was bled. Those symptoms soon went away and I got rid of the cold as usual in about three weeks.

'Some time afterwards, on walking on a frosty day, I found shortness of breathing and a nervous sensation of oppression in my chest, which I continued to feel at times and which returned again on walking in the cold air. My digestion was very weak with much flatulence. The abstemiousness I used in order to keep myself down in bulk seemed rather to augment this than diminish it. Purging myself regularly with rhubarb seemed to relieve me in both respects . . .

October 20th. 'Took at night two doses of James powder, five grains each. No sensible effect; lay in bed till 2 o'clock next day. Cough bad and feverish. Took another dose of the powder at night. Sent for Dr Mackay; pulse 90, was let blood. Found myself relieved. He ordered draughts with Tartarized Ant. 20 drops Squills Lac Ammoniacum. They made me sick and having the headache I did not take them, but took some rhubarb, which relieved me.

Monday, October 23rd. 'Feverishness much abated. Took some draughts by a prescription of Warren's. 12 drops Tartarized Ant. in them; Tuesday: Feverishness gone – cold remains very severe – head and breast.

'Friday, the 27th: Took Godbold's Medicine, as ordered on Friday night and Saturday, having taken some opening physic the day before. My cold at this time being considerably better, though seemed likely to continue some time.

'Saturday, the 28th: Find an effect something like the effect of opium. Think every time I take it that it irritates and rather increased the cough and oppression.'

Extracted from 1798 *diary.* 'At the beginning of the year I weighed 13 stone in the morning as I got out of bed. Having been six weeks in London and by great abstemiousness kept free from cold, I felt, however, some oppression on my breath, which seemed nervous, and as the abstaining much from meat and fermented liquors, which I was obliged to do to keep myself down in bulk, disagreed with my stomach, I thought the sensations I mentioned were in great degree nervous, which I was more convinced of when, upon living something freer on returning to Broadlands, they in great measure went off, though any quickness of motion still made me short breathed. I soon had some degree of cold which showed itself, as in 1796, by hoarseness, chiefly, but it went off soon. It is, however, necessary to reduce myself lower, as I weigh more than 13 stone.

'On February 23rd came to London, reduced myself to about 12 stone, 10 lbs. Continued free from cold and my breath quite well till the middle of April, when I got a cold, which lasted above a fortnight, but did not affect my breath.

'Went through the summer without a cold. One came on by degrees in December, while in London. Very oppressive in my head and turned into a cough. Let blood by Mr Walker's advice as my pulse was full, though I had no fever. Found myself better, but my cold continued to the end of the month, which was about a fortnight. Breath not affected . . .'[27]

* * *

These infirmities did not seem to affect his social life. During the last two years of the century Lord and Lady Palmerston attained a degree of social intimacy with the Prince and Princess of Wales, at their separate establishments, and Palmerston has left an amusing picture of 'Prinny' in all his convivial glory at

the Brighton Pavilion. The first entry to note this new relationship came in Palmerston's engagement diary for June 29, 1798:
'Went to the Princess of Wales at Blackheath at 3 o'clock; dined
in the garden at 5; music in the evening; supper in the greenhouse and the garden lighted. Came away at half past ten.'

In the autumn, as had become his custom, Palmerston followed
the *ton* to the fashionable seaside resort:

October 13th, 1798. 'I am very well lodged in the same hotel
we were in when you was here and have a very good bedroom
and parlour. I never saw Brighthelmstone so full or so pleasant.
You may guess how it looked [on] such a day as this had been,
with a fleet of ships and two or three men-of-war amongst
them in sight all the morning. I have been over today to Lewes
and never saw the Downs so perfectly agreeable. I found Sir
Ferdinand [Poole] in high health and good looks and desiring
to be most kindly remembered to you . . . I returned to dinner
at the Thompsons' and have been this evening at the play
where, with the help of Munden from Covent Garden, the
performance was very tolerable . . .

October 16th. 'The numbers of people of one's acquaintance
that are here is surprising; but it is like being in London with
them, as you only see them by going to their houses, where
everybody seems to remain, or at least if they get together it
is in very small societies . . . and I am afraid the Prince is
coming.

'Houses are at this moment so scarce and dear that Mrs
Hornley, who is come this morning, despairs of getting one.
The only one she has seen that she could possibly take is not
a remarkably good one and they ask ten guineas a week for
it now . . .

October 18th. 'Our weather here has been as delightful as you
describe it at Broadlands and the great warmth of it has been
a very pleasant circumstance both for wandering upon the
Downs in a morning or going about in the town at night . . .
I was out yesterday with the hounds and saw some very pretty
running. I rode my own horses, which do very well if one does
not think it necessary to attempt to follow up and down all the
steep hills . . .

Lord and Lady Sheffield called here yesterday when I was out and left a very kind invitation to Sheffield [Place], where they go tomorrow for a few days, which I believe I shall accept for a night as I shall be glad both to see them and the place . . .

Brighton, October 23rd. 'I returned yesterday from Sheffield to dinner . . . In the evening I went to the ball, which was much better attended than I expected. I find however that the Monday ball at the Castle has been tolerably kept up during the season. The Prince was there. He has been here these two days, chiefly to see his sister whom he has visited at Worthing every morning and has dined each day at Mr Concannen's, who is returned and established again here. The Prince seemed in good humour and in a pleasant style of behaviour and the interest he takes about his sister is very amiable. I am glad to hear that some change has taken place in her disorder which gives more favourable hopes of her recovery. It was quite impossible for her to bend her knee in the smallest degree from the violent anguish that any motion occasioned and it was supposed that the joint was become stiff. Lately, nervous spasms have come on, by which the knee is involuntarily bent at times in a great degree without any additional pain from that circumstance, which satisfies them there is no local malady or disease in the joint and that it is a disorder of the nerves or muscles, which though painful and tedious yet is far from hopeless, which if it had been a humour which had rendered the joint diseased would have been the case. The Prince is very anxious to have her moved to the Pavilion here, which I think would be the best plan if she can be moved at all. He tells people here that the King and family will certainly come down to see her and will lodge at the Pavilion, but I do not believe he has any authority for the opinion. The Prince is gone over to her today and sets out in the evening for London and is to dine with the King tomorrow . . .

October 25th. 'As soon as I had written my last letter I set out and rode to Lewes, where I found Sir F[erdinand Poole] sitting very comfortably drinking his wine and reading a novel after dinner . . .

'Yesterday morning, which, after some early storms, turned

out most delightful, I returned hither not by Lewes but by the sea coast, crossing the Lewes river near its mouth at Newhaven, where there is a good bridge erected since I was there. I reconnoitred Seaford and Bishopstone, a melancholy old place of Lord Pelham's which he usually lets. It was well known in the old Duke of Newcastle's time, who made it the scene of his Sussex electioneering parties and county hospitalities. The ride was quite beautiful as I went for 12 miles upon a terrace of chalk Downs immediately over the sea and came home through Rottingdean . . .

'The Prince set out in the night after supping and making some of the party very drunk on Tuesday evening at Mr Concannen's, in order to have a grave interview with the King before the Levée on Wednesday. It is not certain whether he returns here.

'I have not absolutely fixed my day for leaving this place but shall certainly be at Broadlands by the end of the month or the 1st November. I wish to see the bathing places along the seacoast and to call at Stanstead in my way . . .'[28]

During the following spring the Palmerstons dined twice with the Princess of Wales at Blackheath and on three occasions attended the oratorio and the play in the Prince of Wales' box. From June, 1799, onwards the Princess of Wales started to drop in, often unannounced, at their house at East Sheen, a habit doubtless launched on June 18 at an impressive dinner, attended by the Princess and her companion Miss Hayman, Lord and Lady Minto, Colonel and Mrs Drinkwater, Mrs and Miss Crewe, Mr Crewe, junior, Lord and Lady Lavington, Admiral Payne, Mr Canning and Mr Frere, an invitation repeated only a week later, when the other company consisted of Lady Malmesbury, Lord and Lady Minto, Miss Garth, Lord Amherst and Mr Cornwall. The next formal occasion found Palmerston confined in his Hanover Square house with a cold, obliging him to write to his wife:

August 7th. 'I have waited till the last moment before I could determine not to set out for Sheen; but my cold is so oppressive and, added to a headache, renders me so totally unfit for society and so unable to bear the air which everybody else would choose, that I think it a duty to remain where I am and not incommode at least those to whose entertainment I feel with regret it is not in my power to contribute.

'I trust to you to offer to the Princess of Wales these apologies for my absence, and to express how deeply I regret the not being able to partake of the honour and pleasure she is so good as to confer on us by her presence this day at Sheen . . .'[29]

His indisposition continued and although Lady Palmerston was in the Princess's company, either at Sheen or Blackheath, half a dozen times more during August, Palmerston was not able to be present. However, by October he was sufficiently recovered to attend the Brighton season again:

October 16th. 'It was rather late when I got here and the first and only person I saw here was Sir Charles Blagden, who sat with me for an hour. The place is still very full but not with quite so gay and pleasant a set as were here last year at this time. However the Prince's and Sir Godfrey Webster's dinners and Mrs Concannen's parties I fancy give some spirit to it. I went to the Pavilion this morning to leave my name. Neither the Prince nor the Admiral ["Jack" Payne] were at home but I immediately afterwards met the former who was very gracious and asked me to dine with him today, which I am to do . . .

October 17th. 'Our dinner party yesterday at the Pavilion went off very well, only somewhat too long, as he never gets up from table till past ten, which, as he sits down before six is rather too much. He never observes whether anybody drinks or not if they do but put the bottle by, which is constantly in motion and never passes unnoticed by him. Payne, Lord Egremont, Francis, General Dalrymple and myself were the principal guests. There were five or six more of his more constant party. He was in high spirits, excessive good humour, and remarkably agreeable, kept the conversation very much in his own hands and never let it languish, but told us a great number of very extraordinary histories and anecdotes, acting the different characters as he went on in the best style and with a great deal of humour. He had been over to Lewes in the morning and had invited Sir Ferdinand [Poole] to dine with him today and desired me to come and meet him, which I am accordingly to do. They are gone fox hunting today with Lord Egremont's hounds. I have not been out with the harriers yet. They go out tomorrow but I do not know whether I shall go as my new horse has cut his foot with a flint on his journey and is not fit to go . . .

October 18th. 'I dined again yesterday with the Prince and met Sir Ferdinand who is very well in health and spirits, but I am sorry to find has got the fashionable disorder of deafness to a cruel degree, so much as to hear little or nothing that is said unless it is spoken quite to his ear . . .

'I have been out today with the hounds, but could only ride my old mare, who carries me very safely so as to see a good deal of the hounds though not to keep with them . . .

'I do not hear of much gaiety in the way of assemblies or balls going on. Mrs Concannen is often at home in the evening and her house is, I fancy, the pleasure rest. She asked me just now to come to her tonight which I accepted . . .

October 20th. 'I have been these two nights at Mrs Concannen's, who is generally at home and her house very pleasant. The gentlemen's whist party assembles there and she has a half-crown casino party and sometimes a little music and a cold chicken and some sandwiches afterwards in a very comfortable way. I have met there Lord Archibald Hamilton, son of the present Duke. He is a very good humoured man but has got the fashionable complaint and is extremely deaf. Did we not meet him in Italy? . . .

'I only stayed two nights in the hotel where I first went and have got a very neat comfortable lodging . . . I have a sitting room and two bedchambers, all on the first floor with a very good side view of the Steine and no other lodger in the house. I pay $2\frac{1}{2}$ guineas a week and only engage for a week at a time. A fortnight from the time I came into it will carry me on to the end of the month, which will probably be as long as I shall wish to stay . . .

'The Prince and a large party are going in a few days to Petworth, after which I fancy he will not be much here. He appears to be perfectly recovered as to health and spirits. I do not understand that there was any foundation for the report of his parting with the Pavilion to Lord Carrington. Lady Carrington is now lying in here of her 9th or 10th daughter, I am not certain which.

'I have just been taking a long walk upon the cliffs in the most beautiful day I ever yet saw in this country, and with the help of the sea it put me in mind of the finest of all the fine days we saw at Naples. There is something in this air when the weather is fine that is uncommonly delightful . . .

October 22nd. 'On Sunday I dined with Mr Metcalfe, where our party was much broke in upon by sudden invitations from the Prince to several of our company to come and dine with him, which cannot be refused unless you have company at home, which was Mr Metcalfe's case, who was likewise invited. This is not a pleasant circumstance attending his residence here, for though his dinners are very good and sometimes very pleasant, yet people like in general to be able to dispose of themselves and depend upon their company, neither of which is the case among those whom he likes to have with him. I called in the evening at Lady Downshire's . . . [she] has generally a casino table every evening, but I am so little in the habit of playing and play so ill that I think half guinea casino quite deep play. Yesterday morning after a stormy and rainy night the weather was tolerably good and I had a pleasant ride after the hounds . . . I dined at the Francis's . . .

'In the evening there was a subscription supper and dance which was grafted on, in an odd manner I think, upon the common Monday ball, which now lasts till twelve, at which hour the subscribers went to a supper and then danced again as long as they chose. The Prince was there but I do not think it succeeded upon the whole well or was well imagined. The use of such an extra ball would be to give an additional night's amusement to the young people, who must in general find their evenings rather dull, as the balls are only attended on Mondays and there seem to be very few numerous private meetings even for cards. Now the whole effect of the subscription was to spoil the Monday ball, as most who did not choose to subscribe would not come to the ball and the supper was but a formal thing and the dance after it very thin and languid and

the whole over between two and three. There were so few
dancers that I found it right to dance and as there were but
four dances danced after supper and those short ones, I got
through it with great success . . .

'I am going to dine again by Mr Eyre's invitation with the
party at the Castle. Mr Francis, who goes with the Prince
to Petworth tomorrow, was to have dined there, but as it
happens to him two days out of three, he is sent for to the
Pavilion . . .

October 25th. 'I took a ride over yesterday to Sir Ferdinand,
whom I found very well and to my great satisfaction much less
deaf than when I saw him before . . . Wednesday and today I
have been out with the hounds and had very pretty chases both
days, of which indeed they scarcely ever fail. Sir Ferdinand
was so good as to send out a horse for me both days and today
he came himself for a little while . . .

'The Prince and his party went yesterday to Petworth. He
returns here no more for some time, unless for a day or two
as a visitor to the Duchess of Cumberland, who I understand
comes very soon. The pleasure the Prince seems to feel at
having got Payne with him again, and the unceasing attention
he shows him are very remarkable, and all the people who are
in the habit of living in his society are struck with the vast
difference of his cheerfulness and spirits since that time. Sir
Ferdinand's servant, Robert, is well acquainted with some of
the Prince's upper servants, and when Sir F. dines there Robert
comes with him in the chaise, and while he is waiting for
Sir F. is entertained by them. This was the case when I met
Sir F. at the Pavilion last week; at which time the servants there
assured Robert that the Prince is in correspondence with the
Princess and writes to her frequently. This they mentioned
with great pleasure and inferred from it that they would
soon live together again. Upon Sir F's mentioning this, I
asked Robert about it, who assured me it was exactly so. It
appears to me rather surprising, and as Robert has a little of
the fashionable disorder I cannot help thinking there is some
mistake in it . . .

October 31st. 'Most of the company here are upon the wing

and are preparing for their flight in the course of a few days. Others however are arriving and are to arrive and I understand that the houses on the Steyne are generally occupied till January. I am preparing for my departure tomorrow and shall be with you on Saturday, perhaps not till the evening and therefore not to be thought of as to dinner . . .'[30]

A month later, in London, Palmerston was invited to dine with the Prince again at Mr Francis' house at Sheen:

December 3rd. 'I have got a job on my hands for tomorrow which I do not much like but which I cannot well avoid. It is to meet the Prince of Wales and the Duke of Clarence, etc. at Mr Francis's, where they are to dine. I would gladly have been excused but I found it would not be taken kind and therefore I mean to go . . .

December 6th. 'Our party at Sheen . . . turned out very well. I was there before anybody. The Duke of Clarence came first. The Prince and Admiral Payne were there by a quarter past six. The rest of the company at dinner were Lord Bessborough, Sir Andrew St John, Mr Tierney, Elizabeth, Catherine and Phillip Francis and John Godfrey, who was in the house. The Duke of Cumberland was to have been there but sent an excuse and came next morning to make his apology. The Prince was perfectly civil and agreeable and took the lead and made the play in the conversation remarkably well and was extremely entertaining. I had no idea till the last two or three times I have dined in his company how much so he can be. His forte is relating anecdotes and conversations of people whose voice and manner he imitates in a most superior style. A good deal of wine was drunk but only by those who chose it. He sits too long, as he did not ask for coffee till eleven o'clock. We then went to the drawing room, where Harriet and the two Miss Bretons were expecting us. Music soon became the object. The Prince was much delighted with Phillip and Catherine's singing, with which he joined and sung with them without ceasing for full two hours, so the party did not break up till half past one, somewhat to the annoyance of the Duke of Clarence, Lord Bessborough, etc. who have not much relish for such sweet sounds. To say the truth, they were not the sweetest I ever heard, as Catherine was frighted and sung low and the Prince very loud, not always in tune, and, as he did not know many of the things he sung, was often out . . .'[31]

★   ★   ★

The entries in Palmerston's anecdote book had become more infrequent, but included a ribald piece of doggerel, to be sung to the tune of 'God Save the King', on Nelson's attachment to Lady Hamilton:

> *Also huge Emma's name*
> *First on the role of fame,*
> *And let us sing.*
> *Loud as her voice, let's sound*
> *Her faded charms around*
> *Which in the sheets were found,*
> *God save the King.*
>
> *Nelson, thy flag haul down,*
> *Hang up thy laurel crown,*
> *While her we sing.*
> *No more in triumph swell,*
> *Since that with her you dwell,*
> *But don't her William tell –*
> *Nor George, your King.*

A man being found fault with for contracting debts which he had no prospect of being able to pay, said he thought it an extraordinary idea some persons had that because a man had no money he was to have nothing else.

Sir John Shelley at Brighthelmstone used to be continually boasting of his great possessions in that neighbourhood, on which the people there said he was like the Devil, but not so good natured, for he was continually carrying you up to a high hill to show you his possessions, but never offered to give them to you.

o

REFERENCES

1. F.12
2. F.12
3. C.51(a) 15.XII.1796
4. B.1 31.XII.1796
5. B.2 2.I.1797
6. B.1 2.I.1797
7. A.3(b)
8. C.51(a) 19.V.1797
9. B.1 8.XII.1797
10. B.1 22.XII.1797
11. A.1
12. F.12
13. B.1
14. B.2 14.X.1799
15. B.1
16. B.1
17. B.1
18. B.1 25.XI.1797
19. B.2
20. B.1
21. D.6
22. B.1
23. C.69
24. B.2
25. B.1
26. B.2
27. A.1
28. B.1
29. B.1
30. B.1
31. B.1

CHAPTER XIII

THE LAUNCHING OF THE THIRD VISCOUNT

The Iliad and ferreting – Harry introduced to Pitt – commences to discuss foreign affairs in correspondence with his father – a Harrow monitor – his further education entrusted to Professor Dugald Stewart at Edinburgh – the second Viscount's last tour – rhubarb pills and devotion to the classics – Count Rumford and the Royal Institution – appraisals of Harry's progress – Harry helps the Duc d'Angoulême – Count Rumford's impressions of Bonaparte – the second Viscount's nostalgia at Sheen – with the Misses Berry at Strawberry Hill – Addington further solicited for an English title – final homily to Harry – death of the second Viscount – his widow distraught – death of Lady Palmerston – Malmesbury, Minto and Pelham appointed Harry's guardians – Lord Malmesbury becomes the mentor of the third Viscount

As the century drew to its close young Harry was making good progress at Harrow. On March 19, 1798, at the age of thirteen and a half, he was writing to a young friend in Bologna, Francis Hare:

'I am just recovered from the measles, which however I have had very slightly, and am now very well. I am sincerely obliged to you for your kind wish and trust that I make as much progress as boys in my situation at school generally do. I have begun Homer's Iliad which I did in that beautiful episode in the 5th book I think, in which Andromache takes leave of Hector when returning from the war to Troy to order a general supplication to Minerva, at this line ως αρα φωνησας απεβη κορυθαίοιος έκτωρ [his Greek calligraphy was not yet perfect].

'I suppose however that you have made considerable progress in your learning, more than is perhaps in my power, we having tasks regularly allotted for each day as long as we stay in each form or class. I am now doing Caesar, Terence, Ovid, Homer, Greek testament and a collection of Greek epigrams, and after the Easter holidays, which are now drawing near, I shall begin

Virgil, Horace and some more. I am perfectly of *your* opinion concerning drinking and swearing, which though fashionable at present I think extremely ungentlemanlike. As for getting drunk, I can find no pleasure in it ... I have begun to learn Spanish, I have also begun to read Don Quixote in the original which I can assure you gave me no small pleasure. Mr Gaetano, if you remember him, desires to be remembered to you. I can assure you I have by no means left off my Italian but keep it up every holidays with Mr Gaetano, who has published a new Italian grammar which has been very much approved of here in England. I cannot agree with you about marriage though I should be by no means precipitate about my choice. Willy [his younger brother] is come to Harrow and sends his love to you ...'[1]

Such mature thoughts did not seem to interfere with his schoolboy pleasures. Mrs Bromley had to elicit the aid of Lady Palmerston in a small matter of discipline:

'I shall feel much obliged if you will have the goodness to write a letter to Henry, entirely from yourself, and beg him not to go into the water as he does – the only good place for bathing, and where only the upper boys are allowed to go – is above two miles from Harrow, and when I consider how much my young friend must be heated by the time he gets there, and how little prudence boys have in those cases – I confess I have many fears on his account. I don't wish to appear in this business because it will come with more force from your Ladyship, and you may tell him you hear one of the boys (at Mr M. Drury's) has been very unwell from bathing improperly and has narrowly escaped a very serious illness ...'[2]

Lady Palmerston wrote to her son by return of post:

'This weather is magnificent but do not let it tempt you to go into the water when you are hot, and indeed I should think the less you did it the better till you have bathed in the sea. I have just heard of a boy who has suffered sadly from it, which has led me to give you this advice. Pray take care of yourself as I have no time to nurse anybody ...'[3]

In October, 1798, he was writing to tell his mother that he had acquired a half share in a ferret, with which he went out chasing rabbits – a practice greatly frowned upon by the school authorities. A month later his father sent Lady Palmerston an account of a more sophisticated pleasure:

'The boys are come home and are with me . . . I had a letter from Mr Bromley to say that it was rather unlucky to take them away just at this time as they are engaged in a Greek play and desiring me to send them back as soon as I can . . . We are going to dine early and then proceed to the play at Covent Garden, which is *Lovers Vows* with *The Jew and the Doctor* and I believe the Royal Family are to be there . . .'[4]

As soon as he was back at Harrow Harry had a pressing request to make of his father:

'I have a great favour to ask of you, which would make me quite happy, and that is to let me begin to shoot next holidays. I believe you have got a gun at Broadlands, or at least only to shoot the time that Kingsley is at Broadlands, for he most likely will bring his gun over with him and if, when he comes back here he tells the other boys that I do not shoot, I shall be most terribly laughed at, as it is reckoned almost a disgrace not to shoot and, indeed, there is hardly another boy of my age here that does not . . .'[5]

Palmerston told his wife of his encouragement of Harry's social accomplishments:

December 14th, 1798. 'The boys left Harrow yesterday morning and arrived here at five, looking both of them quite well . . . They seem very much grown but Fanny has outstripped Harry. I mean tonight to get Mr Bourne to exert his violin abilities and dance to his playing from eight till eleven. We can make up nine couple . . .

April 9th, 1799. 'I went to the play to Mrs Stanhope's and Mrs Robinson's last night. We did not stay late, except Harry whom I left and sent the coach for him. He seems however very well today and is going to dine at the Cornwalls' and has thoughts of hunting tomorrow with the Putney Hounds . . .'[6]

By the following June, Harry was slowly reaching the top of the school and old enough to tease his mother gently about her friendship with the Princess of Wales:

'The School now consists of one hundred and eighty-eight

boys, which is about seventy more than there were when I first came, and it most likely will be increased by ten or fifteen more after the holidays. Drury has put six more boys into the sixth form, by which means there are but eight before me in the fifth form . . .'[7]

'I never heard of anything so grand as your style of living; one day you dine with the Princess, another day she dines with you. The next thing, I suppose, will be that she will occupy the state green velvet room, and her picture will be hung up with Queen Caroline's . . .'[8]

During the summer holidays he accompanied his father on a horseback tour of the south coast bathing places. 'Harry is a most agreeable companion', Lord Palmerston wrote to his wife:

Romney, September 4th. 'We got to Sandwich . . . and rode to Deal, Walmer Castle, and over the cliffs by the sea coast to Dover . . . We saw the French coast very distinctly all the day, and a little privateer looking out for some of our vessels which happens continually. The people at the signal house were giving the alarm to some of our ships at Dover, who went out to try to catch the privateer but with very little chance, as they are too nimble and keep at too great a distance . . . went to Mr Payne's at the York Hotel, who is better bred and dearer than any innkeeper I have met with . . . Today we had as fine a ride as yesterday through Folkestone and Sandgate to Hythe . . . Between Folkestone and Hythe is Sandgate, a small place on the sea shore full of bathers . . .

Brighthelmstone, September 10th. 'We are both well and the delightfulness of the weather makes our tour very pleasant . . . There are some people here of my acquaintance but not many. On Sunday we dined with Lord Malmesbury and passed the evening at Lady Lucan's, where was Lady Clermont, Mrs Brown and some other people. Yesterday we dined at Lord Pembroke's with the Malmesbury's and Lady Pembroke . . . In the evening we went to the ball, which, it being Monday night was as usual, but after the expiration of the common time allotted to it, was a fine supper by subscription and a renewal of the dance without limitation. Harry took a good dance, but as we both had quite enough we came away before the supper . . .'

Picking up William at Broadlands, the holiday ended for the boys with a memorable first sight of the House of Commons:

September 24th. 'I have sealed the boys in the House, which is pretty full and Mr Shaw Lefevre is moving the Address . . .

'The House is unluckily up without any debate, which I am sorry for. All I could do for the boys was to show them Mr Pitt, whom they were very curious to see and Harry had the pleasure of shaking hands with him . . .

September 25th. 'The boys went off early this morning to Harrow very well. Though the House of Commons failed in supplying them with debates, it succeeded adorably in beef steaks and in order to show them the humours of it completely we went and dined upstairs where the members usually assemble during long debates. We sat close to the gredina[?] and had our steaks hissing hot from it and very good they were. At a table close to us was a party of opposition such as Mr Grey, Mr Tierney, Sir Andrew St John, George Ponsonby from Ireland, etc. and I was rather amused now and then by the scraps of conversation that fell from their table. They seemed somewhat comforted by the failure of the attack on Holland and wore the particular sort of melancholy face when they talked of it that people put on when they make a thing, and wish it, ten times worse than it is. I carried the boys from thence to the play where we sat in Lord and Lady Lavington's box and they brought us home . . .'[9]

October 20 was Harry's birthday, and Lady Palmerston revealed herself as a doting mother:

'My dearest Harry,

This is a day which has made me so happy for *fifteen years* that I cannot refrain from offering my wishes that it may be continued equally so for years to come and that the fair prospect of all we may expect from all we have experienced may never be blighted and that your charming natural character may never be hurt by age or the world . . .'

[*No date*] 'I hope you will have received the money which

was to go by the carrier. If not, borrow 3 guineas of Mr Bromley, take 2 and give one to Willy. If you want more let me know.

'Shall I send you some tea and sugar, I think that might help, or chocolate? Inform me of all your wants, for nothing can afford me more real happiness than complying with any of your and Willy's wishes ...'[10]

In his letters to his father Harry was already showing an intelligent interest in foreign affairs. His comments had a remarkably mature ring:

October 23rd. 'There was a report spread over the school yesterday ... that Buonaparte and Berthier had got back to France: that while the army was blockading Sir Sydney Smith in Alexandria, Buonaparte got into a very swift sailing frigate, and escaped from two English ones which pursued him. If it is true, I think the expedition had better follow his example, and come over to England as fast as they can, for of course he will take the command of the army in Holland, as I should think the French would not mind letting Suvorov gain some small advantages if they could destroy our army, and put an end to the project of these proud islanders, as they call us ...'[11]

Palmerston approved his sentiments:

'I agree with your politics and heartily wish our army may get back from Holland as safe as Buonaparte has from Egypt. I fancy we shall now be convinced that our proper element is the sea and that we had better leave Continental fighting to others and that it is both cheaper and better even to pay people for fighting their own battles than to go over and fight them for them ourselves ...'[12]

By the summer of 1800 Harry had reached a milestone and on June 29 was able to inform his mother:

'We are both very well, and I am a monitor. It very often happens that when one of the monitors is ill soon before the holidays and the head of the sixth form is going after the holidays, Drury makes him a seventh monitor; this is my case. Pepys is gone home very bad with the mumps, and as it is near the holidays and I am going away, Drury made me a monitor yesterday ...'[13]

The time had come to consider the next stage in his education. The normal procedure would have been to broaden his
mind further by a period of residence abroad, but the military
triumphs of Napoleon made it impossible for young Englishmen to visit the European centres of learning, and some
alternative had to be found. The last two years of the second
Viscount's life were devoted to his principal claim on the
notice of history: the preparation for life of the son who
became one of the outstanding Foreign and Prime Ministers
in British political life.

Living almost at the height of his reputation in Edinburgh
at the time was a considerable figure, Professor Dugald Stewart.
A staunch Whig and an academician of European renown,
Stewart had shared with Charles James Fox strong sympathies
with the early revolutionary movement in France, and as
incumbent of the Chair of Moral Philosophy at Edinburgh
University was the outstanding authority on philosophical
topics in Great Britain. A man of unimpeachable personal
character and one of the great orators of his time – James Mill,
the historian, not a great admirer of the philosophers, said that
neither Pitt nor Fox, whose best efforts he had heard, was
nearly so eloquent – Stewart admitted two or three sprigs
of the aristocracy at a time to live in his own home. Ten
years earlier he had married, as his second wife, Helen d'Arcy,
third daughter of the Hon. George Cranstoun, and sister
of Walter Scott's friend, the Countess Purgstall, and his
wife helped to make his house a centre of the best society in
Edinburgh.

On June 19, 1800, the second Viscount made a formal
approach to the Professor:

'My son, who was fifteen years of age last October, has risen
nearly to the top of Harrow School and has given me uniform
satisfaction with regard to his disposition, his capacity and his
acquirements. He is now coming to that critical and important
period when a young man's mind is most open to receive such
impressions as may operate powerfully on his character and his
happiness during the remainder of his life. At this time, therefore, I think it of the greatest consequence that he should be

judiciously directed through such a course of studies as may give full exercise to his talents and enlarge his understanding, and that he should converse as much as possible with persons to whose opinions he must look up with deference, and in whose society his manners would be improved and his morals secured. These objects I have always thought unattainable by boys remaining in the upper class of a public school, who can only pursue the common routine of classical instruction, and who must associate principally with companions from whom they can derive no improvement. It has therefore always been my intention to place my son, when he should attain the period to which he is now arrived, in some intermediate situation between school and an English university, if that should be his future destination: and after much consideration and enquiry, it is the united wish of Lady Palmerston and myself, with a direct view to all those points I have enumerated, to place him under your direction, and in the family of yourself and Mrs Stewart, whose character, you will, I am sure, allow me to say, has very considerable weight in our determination . . .

'You will find him perfectly tractable and disposed to conform himself with cheerfulness to all such regulations as you shall think fit to prescribe to him; and though he is forward enough in all good points, he is still a boy, and has not assumed the airs and manners of a premature man . . .'[14]

To this Professor Stewart replied:

'I . . . feel myself highly honoured by the intention you express of entrusting Mr Temple to my care. The flattering terms in which your Lordship has been pleased to convey your wishes on this subject are the more gratifying, both to Mrs Stewart and myself, that we know how much we are indebted for your favourable opinion, to the kind partiality of Lord Warwick, and of Lord Brooke.

'The account I had received from Lord Warwick of Mr Temple's abilities and dispositions was so completely satisfactory that I was preparing to write to your Lordship at the moment when your letter reached me. It will give me great pleasure indeed if I shall be able to contribute anything to forward your views at this important period of his education;

and the high character which he bears disposes me to look forward to much satisfaction in our future connection.

'Our academical business commences with the month of November; and it would be rather more convenient for me if your Lordship could delay Mr Temple's journey till that time; but if this should interfere with any of your previous arrangements, I shall be happy to receive him the beginning of October . . .'[15]

Count Rumford accompanied Harry and his parents on the journey north, which provided Palmerston with the opportunity to fill his last travel journal:

September 13th, Burghley. 'Much has been done and great sums expended by the last Earl, in improving and fitting up the inside, laying out the park and pleasure ground and making a very large and beautiful piece of water, all under the direction of the late Mr Brown, who was employed there at least twenty years and laid out between forty and fifty thousand pounds . . .

September 16th. 'Clumber, belonging to the Duke of Newcastle . . . The [late] Duke took great pride in this place and made vast purchases so as to be by far the greatest land proprietor in Nottinghamshire. By this means, however, and by the great sums he laid out in his building and works, he left his estates encumbered with a debt of near £200,000 and no ready money, so that when the present Duke, who is a minor, comes of age, he will be obliged to sell a part of his property in order to discharge a debt which swallows up so much of his income. He has five seats in Parliament, which he can sell in perpetuity, and he has the Castle of Nottingham and the park, which would sell to great advantage. These, if sold properly, would go a great way towards clearing the estate, without any great diminution of income . . .

September 19th, Worksop Manor. 'The property of the Duke of Norfolk . . . The present Duke seems totally to neglect the place, suffers the grounds to lie in a rough and neglected state, and is sending away the best pictures and most valuable furniture to Arundel Castle, which he is repairing and fitting up at a great expense . . .

October 6th. 'The town of Langholm and all this country

belongs to the Duke of Buccleuch – that is to say the lands are held under him and pay him a small sum annually, which bears no proportion to their value, nor do I understand that he has any power to raise the rent arbitrarily or to turn out the holders if they make their payments. He is greatly beloved and esteemed in the country, with great reason, as he has done much to improve it and is the promoter and encourager of every beneficial plan . . .

October 17th. 'To Stirling by the Carron Ironworks – 11 miles . . . They are not usually shown, and letters of introduction seldom succeed. By stopping ourselves at the gates and applying personally to the director, we were admitted with much civility, and saw what happened then to be going on, which was the casting [of] cannon. I do not understand that there is anything in these works to distinguish them from others, but their size and extent. The vast beds of coal that are flaming and smoking in order to be converted into coke; the rattling sounds of the steam engine which raises four tons of water at each stroke and the roaring of the cylinders made use of as bellows to blow the furnaces, united to a dark stormy day, formed a scene particularly awful and impressive.

October 18th. 'Glasgow makes little appearance as you approach it this way. It is a large commercial and manufacturing town, in which are a great number of persons who have acquired wealth and have built handsome houses within the town and in the adjacent country. The principal streets are wide, and formed of good houses, most of which are new. The old parts of the town are very bad. There are some handsome public buildings, but nothing particularly worth notice. The inns, as is usually the case in populous manufacturing towns, are large, noisy, dirty and dear . . .

October 20th. 'Loch Long was full of fishing boats catching herrings, and the transition of quitting the lonely and desert scenes of Loch Lomond and finding ourselves in so short a time on what is in fact the sea shore, and amongst the bustle and animation of a fishery, produced a singular effect. The inn to which we came is a single house, belonging to the Duke of Argyll, and fitted up by him and established as an inn . . .

October 21st. 'The storm which began in the evening continued with great violence, accompanied by heavy rain the whole night. In the morning the rain ceased, but the wind continued. We were surprised to learn that the herring fishers had been out during the whole of the night, which it seems is the only time for them to fish. The season lasts not more than three months. The coming of the herrings up these lochs is very precarious and often interrupted for some time, which has been the case lately and, therefore, the people lose no opportunity of which they can avail themselves. The herrings which they catch during the season are their great dependence, as the whole country subsists on herrings and potatoes at least half the year, and is in great measure maintained by the produce of what they send out, salted and pickled, to other places. The method of catching them is merely letting down a net of some length across the channel, in such parts as they think the fish most likely to frequent, and then waiting till a shoal comes against it. Great numbers entangle themselves in the meshes and when the fishermen think the net is pretty well loaded, they draw it in and take them out. Such numbers are sometimes caught during a night in one net as to load the boat to which it belongs quite to the water's edge. In ordinary seasons the herrings fresh caught are sold from two to three shillings per hundred . . .

October 23rd. 'The Duke of Argyll has a large farm in his hands, which he cultivates at a great expense on a most liberal plan, so as to make it useful to his neighbours by the employment it furnishes to them, by the agricultural improvements it exhibits to them and the supply of the various articles it produces, afforded them at a reasonable rate in times of scarcity. A part of the farm lies in a valley near the castle, called Glen Shyra, where there are two magnificent ranges of buildings resembling, at a distance, great monasteries, and which consist of various barns, not for storing only, but for drying hay and corn, which in so very rainy a situation as that of Inverary, is extremely useful . . .

'Having walked about the grounds and drove up Glen Shyra in the morning, we dined and passed the evening at the castle, where we found the Duke, who rarely leaves Inverary, in good health and spirits, passing the close of a very long life surrounded by his children, grandchildren, dependants and neighbours, and occupied in the amiable and respectable employment of endeavouring to make them all happy ...

October 24th. 'At Cairndow we were attracted by the sound of music to ascend a kind of ladder to a place like a hayloft, where we found an itinerant master teaching the neighbouring children to dance, some of whom had shoes and stockings and some were with naked feet. They were learning reels and country dances with great alacrity.

'The lower, and I might say the middling class of people, go much without shoes and stockings, and those who have them, in general, only wear them occasionally, when they wish to appear better dressed than usual, and are not likely to spoil them.

'The Gaelic, or Erse, language is spoken in general among the inferior people, but a traveller meets with few who do not speak English likewise ...

October 28th. 'Dined at Hamilton House, or Palace, as it is called by ancient custom. It is a large and ancient mansion in a good park adjoining to the town of Hamilton. The house is ill-placed and the apartments ill-disposed and dark, which is particularly unfortunate as they contain the best collection of pictures in Scotland, of which, for want of light, we could obtain but a very imperfect view. Some of the best of them, particularly portraits by Vandyck and a celebrated picture of Daniel in the Lions Den by Rubens, have been long there. The remainder have been brought down by the present Duke, who as well as his son, the Marquis of Douglas, has been a considerable collector ...

November 7th, 8th, 9th. 'During these days we remained at Edinburgh and finally settled Harry, much to our satisfaction, in the house of Professor Stewart, under whose care he is to pursue his studies and attend the lectures of some of the professors in the University of Edinburgh ...'

Before they left Palmerston made a few notes about Professor Stewart's establishment:

'Lectures are read in the College at Edinburgh in various branches of science, by the respective professors, to all who choose to attend them. No students reside in the college, nor are they under any kind of regulation or discipline.

Mr Stewart is the only professor who receives pupils. He has never had more than two or three at a time. He has, at present, Lord Ash[burton] and Harry, besides his own son, who is about Harry's age, and pursues the same course of study. We understand that he has lately declined taking any additional pupils, but we have no certain knowledge of the fact, or what his intentions really are. Mr Stewart takes considerable pains with the young men under his care, if they are disposed to be industrious and, in that case, they may, by his assistance, get much forwarder and draw much more advantage from the lectures of the other professors than they could otherwise do. He sometimes, as an evening amusement, encouraged the young men in his house to debate before him upon some subject previously agreed on.

'Mr Stewart's terms are £400 per annum, for board and for his own instruction. The payment to other professors, which are inconsiderable, and the expenses of masters, are not included.

'The principal lectures, read by the professors, are upon Mathematics, Algebra, Natural Philosophy, Chemistry, Botany, History and Moral Philosophy. The latter are by Mr Stewart. There are classes, as they are called, for Latin and Greek, but they are not fit to be attended by young men of a certain age, who have already made any progress in those languages . . .'[16]

His wife, in a mother's note, made this entry in her own diary:

November 10th. 'At ten o'clock Lord Palmerston, Count Rumford and myself set off from Edinburgh, having bid farewell to my dear Harry. The pain I felt at bidding him adieu made me so wretched that I had no spirits to enjoy a very fine drive, for I wept the whole way. It is impossible to leave so amiable a being without regret, and when that being is one of the most affectionate sons, the pain must be acute . . .'[17]

Harry was still not fully robust and in a description of his studies had a somewhat worrying account of his health to give his father before the month was out:

'I tried the riding in the manège three times and twice it

gave me a sick headache preceded by that dazzling in my eyes. I fancy it was owing to riding round in a small circle very fast, I find it has that effect upon many people, and I think it more likely as I never have been used to that kind of riding. I pretty well got rid of my last manège headache last week, but I have been troubled with one for these two or three days. I took some rhubarb yesterday and the day before, which has done me good, though I still feel a sensation which reminds me that I have a head. I have seen Dr Rutherford, who says it proceeds from the stomach (which to be sure I could have told him), and that I shall get rid of it in a day or two ...

'I like Mr and Mrs Stewart amazingly, it is impossible for anybody to be kinder than they both are, Lord A[shburton] improves upon acquaintance, though his oddities and whims are surprising. He has a surprising dread of squinting and he thinks that the study of optics must bring it on; therefore as Mr Stewart in his lecture about the sense of seeing described the anatomy of the eye, he would not go to college that day ...

'My hours at college are from 9 to 10, 12 to 1, 2 to 3, Mr Playfair's, algebra or second class; Mr St., moral philosophy, and Mr Tytter's historical lectures. The hours are rather awkward, as no two lectures come together. In general the students manage it so that once going up to college serves for all, but as I breakfast before nine, I have the two hours from 10 to 12 perfectly free. The only part of the day which is lost is from 1 to 2, for in a bad day if I return to Lothian House, I have no time to do anything before it is time to go back again to Mr Tytter's lecture. I intended to have employed that hour three times a week in riding, but as that does not seem to answer, Mr Stewart proposed my taking a lesson of drawing. There is a very good master who lives very near the college, and he can give me from one to two twice a week, Tuesdays and Thursdays. I believe he would give me an hour on Saturday, but as that is our holiday, I had rather have it perfectly unengaged. I like the plan very much if you have no objection. ... Three times a week you know I read Latin and Greek with Mr Williamson from 3 to 4. As I have not much leisure time I do not get the lesson before he comes, indeed it is perfectly

understood between us. I am reading at present Sallust's con-
spiracy of Catiline (part of which I read for my own amusement
at Harrow, indeed it is as easy as an English book), and
Xenophon's Anabasis, which is I believe the easiest Greek book
there is. I get on very well with Mr Stewart in Euclid, I am
nearly through the first book. I should have been through it
already if we had gone on regularly every night, but when my
headaches were bad he would not let me do any . . .'[18]

His father's reply is an almost fulsome example of paternal
solicitude. Rhubarb pills and devotion to the classics was the
second Viscount's recipe for physical and mental health, and it
must be assumed that the future third Viscount followed these
maxims to the letter, as his long life never found him short of
vitality or an apt quotation:

'I received your letter with very great satisfaction, and likewise that which you wrote to your mother which she sent me
up from Hampshire. Few things can give me truer pleasure
than to know that you are doing well, and are at the same time
happy and comfortable. I feel every day more and more satisfied when I reflect on the situation in which you at present are
placed, which I am persuaded will afford you advantages that,
with your happy disposition and talents to avail yourself of
them, will tend most essentially both to the comfort and credit
of your whole life. I am rejoiced to find that you are so well
pleased with Mr Stewart. His character stands so very high in
the world, and both he and Mrs Stewart appeared to us so
thoroughly amiable and kind, that I had no doubt but that you
would all of you be equally well satisfied with each other. I
approve very much of the disposition of your time, and shall
be particularly glad to have you apply at [sic] leisure hours to
drawing, for which I really think you have a turn and have
made some progress, which it would be a great pity to lose.
Does the master you are to attend teach figures? I think you
ought to practice them as well as landscape. I hope the Latin
and Greek will not be neglected, and that you will go on to
more difficult authors. You have made so great a progress
towards being a good classical scholar that I trust you will
not fall short in the end, but that you will acquire so much

facility in reading the best authors as to find an amusement in familiarising yourself with their works. Nothing contributes more to set off and ornament natural talents than a ready acquaintance with the classics; and the being known to be a good scholar gives a young man a reputation even beyond its real value, which is however very considerable . . .

'I am very sorry you have been plagued with sick headaches after riding on horseback. Pray when you write again let me know whether you have had them at all in the same manner when you have not been riding. I have all my life been troubled with headaches at times, proceeding from a stomach that was always liable to be disordered by the slightest excess in eating, and still more in drinking, as wine always disagreed with me particularly, so much so that two or three glasses in addition to the two or three which I commonly took was sure to make me uncomfortable for the whole day, and often to give me a headache for 24 hours. About your age I often found the same effects that you do from riding, particularly from hunting or riding a hard trotting horse; and all the early part of my life I suffered much from continually feeling unwell in a manner which I could neither account for nor describe. The advice of physicians never did any good, and whenever they advised any thing bracing or strengthening they did harm. By degrees I found out that the only method to be pursued with advantage was to reduce the quantity of food and fermented liquor as much as was practicable, and whenever nature had more to do than she could manage, which she never failed to give me notice of by various uncomfortable feelings, to assist her by doses of rhubarb. By these means I entirely got rid of those kind of unwell feels which I used to have so continually; and when I felt out of order the remedy I had recourse to never failed to succeed. I mention all this because I think there is a similarity between your case and mine which is very naturally to be looked for; and I would strongly recommend to you, if you find these headaches return, to eat less than you have been used to do and to get a box of rhubarb pills and whenever you find yourself with any symptoms of headache or otherwise unwell, to take a sufficient quantity to produce a considerable effect. If you do not do that you may as well do nothing. And I am sure it is better to take a smart dose now and then when it is wanted, than to take small quantities often . . . You must remember that as your life at present is somewhat more sedentary than it has hitherto been, a diet somewhat more abstemious is probably necessary, especially as your constitution seems to give you very intelligible intimation that it does not bear to be overloaded . . .'[19]

Back in the south Palmerston had resumed his social round. One invitation came on November 25 from Mary Berry, the friend of Horace Walpole:

' 'Tis an ill wind that blows nobody good. By some tickets having been returned we are enabled to have the pleasure of your company at our representation on Monday, for which I enclose a ticket which Mrs Damer desires me to say she has much pleasure in being able to send you.'[20]

Lady Palmerston had returned to Broadlands, leaving her husband to his parliamentary duties in London. The account of her journey contained one note which will bring a nostalgic sigh to those seeking Georgian furniture from twentieth-century antique dealers:

'When I arrived at Epsom the people at the Spread Eagle insisted that the road by Leatherhead was impassable and that I must go by Dorking . . . I am certain the motive for their care of me was that they may charge 18 miles instead of 15 . . .

'At Dorking I stepped into Mr Hyde's, the cabinet maker, who, by the way, has left off business and his successor is named Cheseman. There I saw two tables which I think would suit the book room and saloon. The largest, a remarkable handsome table, mahogany with a satinwood border, steady claw, etc., 4 feet 8 by 3 feet 8, shape rather inclined to oval. Price five guineas and a half, and I really believe you could not meet with one in London equally handsome under 8 guineas. The other, octagon, 4 feet by 3 feet 2, three guineas and a half, a very pretty table. He sends his goods to London, paying himself the carriage . . .

'PS. They charged £1 18s. 3d. from London to Epsom, is that right?'[21]

Palmerston resumed his budget of London gossip with news of old friends:

November 25th, 1800. 'I have been out this morning and called on the Hamiltons, whom I found at home. He is still thinner and yellower than he was when we saw him but in other respects seems much the same and seems occupied with the same pursuits as usual. She is grown much larger and her face broader and her features stronger than they were. She was dressed in a white wrapping gown which made her look of very large dimensions, but so completely took away all shape that I cannot judge what her figure would be in a common dress. She has a little more conceit and affectation than she had, which is very natural, but has the same good humoured manner that she used to have. Her attentions to Sir William do not seem to have relaxed in any degree and they both talk of Lord Nelson in every other sentence. His bust is in the room and Sir William says his friendship and connection with him is the pride and glory of his life . . .

November 27th. 'I am sorry you met with so many difficulties in your journey. I hope the remainder of it was easier and somewhat cheaper. The prices of post horses from London are enormous. They charge now, as they have done for some time past, eighteen pence a mile, which with the saddle horse and two miles addition for the stones to the 16 which they charge from Westminster Bridge will I believe amount nearly to what you paid . . .

November 29th. 'I have been with Count Rumford this morning at the [Royal] Institution. The works are in forwardness. The lecture room will be very good if the lecturer is well and distinctly heard, which I cannot judge of till it is tried. I own I dread the example of all our theatres which have been spoiled by magnificence and enlargement. I hope however this will not happen here. It is a misfortune that by crowding so much building together all the lower part is dark, particularly the large kitchen and workshops. I am particularly sorry for the latter, which I think will be rendered entirely useless for the proposed purposes . . .

December 2nd. 'I returned to Sheen yesterday [in] time enough to get my tea and set out for the play [at Strawberry Hill] and arrive there in very good time. The theatre was very well done up and the seats very comfortable and not crowded. There were not many people I knew. The chief were Lady Mount Edgecumbe, Mrs Webbe, H. & C. Francis who were staying with her at Twickenham, Mr Fauquier from Hampton Court and Lord Glenbervie. The performance opened with a prologue written and spoken by Lord Mount Edgecumbe which did very well. The first performance was *The Old Maid* which went off very well. Miss Berry acted Mrs Harlowe with whom Clerimont has fallen in love, supposing her to be Miss Harlowe. She did it extremely well and looked it still better. Mr H. and his sister Miss H., the old maid, were done by a Mr and Mrs Burn from Lisbon, with whom Mrs Damer was much acquainted during the winter she passed there. Mrs B. acted extremely well and Mr B. very decently. The India Captain who was to have married Miss H., but is discarded when she thinks Clerimont is in love with her, was done by Mr Berry who looked the character very well and except a little over-acting did it very tolerably. Clerimont was Lord Mount E., who is very much like an old actor and seems quite at home. He would do very well if it was not for the insignificance of his figure and the lisp of his voice, which are circumstances that make it rather unfortunate he should have chosen acting as a favourite amusement.

'The second piece was *The Intriguing Chambermaid*, a very poor performance of Fielding's, stolen from twenty other pieces but particularly taken from a French piece called *Le Retour Imprévu* . . . Mrs Damer acted the chambermaid, which is the only material part. Now and then she was very well but in general she did so much too much and distorted herself about so violently that one sat quite in a fright and an alarm for what she would do next. Miss Berry did not act in this. Agnes [her sister] did the young lady, which is a wretched part, but there were two or three little speeches she spoke excellently well. As there are more parts to be filled up they had got a Mr Campbell and a Mr Hervey, who were deplorable. Mrs Damer spoke an epilogue in the same unequal style with her acting. The lines are pretty, written by Miss Bailing . . .'[22]

The interior of the House of Commons was being remodelled, and on December 5 Lord Palmerston revealed in a remark to his wife, with distressing clarity, how he had come to view his duties as a back-bencher:

'There is nothing to be seen at the House of Commons, which is all rubbish and workmen. By taking away what one may call the inner case they will get room for many more within the same walls, and they will open large recesses of windows which will be good sleeping places. I think it probable the effect upon the voices of the speakers will be bad . . .'[23]

Three days later Lady Palmerston received from her son somewhat more reassuring evidence of assiduity:

'I learn drawing. The man's name is Walker, and though he is not a very good artist himself, yet he is a remarkably good teacher. I like him very much. He certainly made me begin from the beginning, for the first thing he set me to do was to draw half a sheet full of straight lines; but, however, I have got on faster since, for the last lesson I took, he gave me some ruins (only outlines) to do at home. He can only as yet give me two lessons a week, an hour each, from one to two – on Tuesdays and Thursdays . . . In a month's time he will be able to give me three days a week, Monday, Wednesday and Friday. I might now have Saturday, but as that is our only holiday, besides Sunday, I like to keep that disengaged, either for skating, shooting or walking. It freezes today pretty hard, so it did indeed all last week, except Saturday and Sunday, and I am in hopes of having some skating on Saturday . . .'[24]

On December 9 Palmerston wrote an account to his wife of the reaction in London to the ending, in fact on November 28, of the armistice between France and Austria on the Continent. By the time he wrote, the French had crushed the Austrians at Hohenlinden on December 3, and Pitt's second European coalition had collapsed. In the shadow of these grave events Palmerston attended the reappearance on the London stage of George Cooke, the drunken actor of genius, whom many theatregoers considered, in his sober moments, to be the legitimate successor to Garrick:

'You will see by the papers nearly all that came by the Hamburg mails. Hostilities have commenced between some auxiliary corps in a kind of way that does not seem to make it quite certain whether they will be absolutely begun seriously between the two armies or not, though it is not improbable, as it is understood that the negotiations at Lunéville do not come to any agreement. The dispatches from Lord Carysfort at Berlin say that that Court has no hostile intentions towards us. A person is said to be coming over from the Court of Sweden who it is believed, besides whatever Swedish matters he may have to treat upon, is to negotiate on the part of Paul [Czar of Russia] with whom, unless by some such round about way, we have no communication. His conduct seems tantamount to a declaration of war and the extravagance of his manifesto is only to be equalled by the absurdity of it. The seizing the property of the English, making all the crews of the ships prisoners, and sending them by tens into the interior country because Malta had surrendered to us, and as he says he does not know whether we intend to give it him or not, is more like the politics of Morocco than anything that calls itself a civilised country. The convention he alludes to was, as I understand, never signed, but if it had, his having broke through all the conditions on which it was founded, withdrawn himself totally from the alliance and entered into an agreement with the common enemy to receive Malta from them, and to transport the garrison to act in Egypt, leaves him no claim whatsoever to the fulfilling of it on our part, which in the present moment could never be thought of.

'I went yesterday to see *Richard III* performed by Mr Cooke, whom you have read so much of in the papers. He certainly has great merit. I do not recollect anybody in that part but Garrick, with whom he will not certainly bear a comparison and in the striking and most difficult passages where Garrick's excellence is so strong in one's mind he was very inferior, but in several scenes of less consequence which require quiet intelligent acting and an attention to a number of little circumstances and a great deal of what is called *jeu de théatre*, and in which one has almost forgot how Garrick performed, he is very excellent and seems to have studied the part with great care and success. He is an elderly man and an old actor, but is such a drunken, worthless fellow that the London managers have always been backward to engage him . . .'

The next day Palmerston saw a much more popular public figure:

'I have been this morning visiting Lady Spencer whom I found at home with quite a levée of people coming in and out. What I thought myself in luck in was meeting Lord Nelson with all his fine presents of every kind which he had brought there to show. It is melancholy to see him, himself so shrunk and mutilated. The worst is that his only eye is so weak as sometimes to give great alarm. Jack Payne was there, who seems pretty well. He says the Prince advises him to stick to Nelson for that he looks like a stout man by Nelson's side . . .'[25]

Harry had better news of his own health for his father:

'I have not had any return of my headaches since last Monday week, the day after I returned from Dalkeith. I was troubled almost the whole of the week before I went there, with a headache, which, though it was not immediately caused by riding (nor indeed was it preceded by that dazzling feel which I never had except after riding), was I think a continuation of the last manège headache. I have got a box of rhubarb pills, 4 grains each, so that a few of them, 8 or 9, are sufficient I should think. I do not think that my headache was at all owing to wine, as I hardly ever drink any at dinner, and never more than two glasses after, indeed in general but one, for we never sit after dinner. I think we generally leave the eating room an hour and a half after we sat down to dinner, sometimes sooner. I think however it is very likely in part owing to eating supper, or rather to drinking a glass of that ale, for I never eat more than a potato. It is a great nuisance that there is always supper at ten, and it seems unsociable not to come down when everybody else does and when one is there it is difficult to hinder oneself from taking a potato and a glass of ale. But however, as I find that I am much better without it, I shall in future never eat or drink anything . . .'[26]

Nothing but praise came from Professor Stewart in Edinburgh about his young charge:

'I would have done myself the honour long before now of writing to your Lordship, if I had had anything to mention of Mr Temple, but the uniform and exemplary propriety of his conduct. On this head I know your Lordship does not stand in need of any assurances on my part, as his good sense and the uncommon steadiness of his character cannot fail to relieve his friends of any anxiety about his welfare, in so far as it depends on himself.

'It is equally unnecessary for me to say that his abilities are excellent, his temper most amiable and his industry unremitting. Indeed, I don't know any young man of whom I am disposed to think more highly, or who unites in one greater degree all the qualities to be wished for at his age . . .'[27]

However, in a letter to his father in the new year Harry made it clear that he was successfully combining pleasure with work:

'Last Saturday I was out a shooting with Mathew and another boy of the name of Brown. It was a terrible day. When we set out between nine and ten it was snowing very hard, and nothing would have tempted me to have gone out, but that I had a terrier upon trial who, among his other numerous good qualities (such as drawing badgers, killing cats, etc.), was recommended as a good one for finding rabbits, and I, having heard of a place where there were some, wanted to try him. As it happened it was lucky we went out, for though the snow and cold had driven all the rabbits (if there were any), into their holes, and we could not find them, yet it made the larks and small birds flock together, so that we killed between two and three dozen of them, of which we afterwards had an excellent pie made . . .'[28]

'I have begun German, I like the master very much and I think that the language, as far as I can judge, is much easier than I expected, indeed I do not think there seems to be any great difficulty at all in it . . .'[29]

The energy of the new generation found little echo in Palmerston's account to his wife of his attendance at Parliament:

'I write this from the House of Commons where I came

early to avoid being taken into custody for not attending a fortnight ago. However, I only came to vote in a large majority that no farther notice should be taken of us defaulters . . .'[30]

On the other hand, it must have been a source of delight to Palmerston to find that the last young man of promise whose abilities he was able to foster was his own son. They exchanged correspondence as between equals on the major events of the day. In his letters to his son Palmerston expressed great satisfaction at Nelson's victory at Copenhagen and its attendant developments:

April 14th. '. . . last night an account arrived which I believe is perfectly to be depended on that the magnanimous Paul has finished his mad career and is actually dead. I have not heard any particulars but if I can collect anything before the post goes out I will add it at the end of my letter. Accounts likewise come from the Danes themselves that our fleet passed the Sound (I think) on the 30th and from the various stories they tell it seems probable that the passage was effected with little loss on our part. Rumours likewise seem to have been in circulation that an attack was made on Copenhagen on the 1st, but the event was not ascertained at Hamburg. This latter part however seems very doubtful. I hope before I close my letter to be able to speak with more certainty . . .

'PS. I can learn nothing material beyond what I have mentioned. I believe a Russian messenger arrived with despatches for Count Woronzoff, the former minister from Russia, who was still remaining here and is at Bath. He brought a few letters from individuals to individuals here, by which the account of Paul's death is ascertained and likewise a copy of a proclamation issued by the new Emperor. This messenger is said to have declared that the new Emperor had immediately ordered the release of the English vessels and crews. Paul died, it is said, suddenly and it seems probable he may have been poisoned . . .

April [?]. 'I congratulate you on the account which is arrived this morning of a complete victory by our fleet over the Danes. Every ship or floating battery which composed the line of defence for Copenhagen is taken or destroyed and their batteries silenced. After this a cessation of arms took place and Nelson, who commanded the attack, went on shore and after being received with shouts of applause by the people of the town, dined with the Hereditary Prince and his Minister, to whom he told such truths as they were not likely to hear from anybody else.

'Our terms were stated and the Danish Government requested to accede to them, which they had not quite made up their minds to on the 5th, and Lord Nelson says if they do not we shall proceed tomorrow . . .

'I have ordered a Gazette to be sent you if it comes out in time. The post is going.'[31]

Harry replied on the 18th:

'Many thanks for your two very entertaining letters which I received yesterday and this morning. The intelligence they contain is indeed excessively interesting, and I think has made a material alteration in the face of affairs. The northern confederacy, by the death of Paul and defeat of the Danes, has received a blow from which I should think it will not easily recover. Buonaparte must be terribly annoyed by the death of Magnanimous [the Czar]. I see in the papers this morning that his physician writes word to a Russian merchant here that Paul died of an apoplexy. It seems it is a family disease. There is a report here this morning, though I believe void of foundation, that a revolution has taken place in Sweden. I think it is a very odd circumstance, that our fleet in its passage was not fired at from the Swedish side although the King was on the coast . . .

'I am now reading the first volume of Moral Tales just published by Miss Edgeworth. The first contains one story called "Forester", the scene is laid in Edinburgh, and this Forester, an Englishman, is come to a Doctor Campbell to continue his studies. I am sure that the character is meant for Ashburton, it is him exactly, only he is much more eccentric and differs in many respects from *Ash.* especially in his contempt for gentlemen, as Ashburton has very high notions of rank and old families. But I am persuaded that he furnished a great many hints for it, and this is the more probable as Lovell Edgeworth, who writes jointly with his sister, resided for some time at Edinburgh . . .'[32]

A letter to his mother on May 15 was in lighter vein:

'I have not yet been able to muster up a sufficient number of fellows to have a game at cricket, as it is a game the Scotch know nothing of, but, however, as a substitute for it I have begun to play at golf, which on the other hand is a game I believe perfectly Scotch, and which is scarcely ever played in England. The object is to strike a ball with a kind of bat, into a certain number of holes successively, which are made in an open common at 3 or 400 yards distance from each other. It is a poor game compared to cricket, but better than nothing ...'[33]

Another good end-of-term report came from Harry's Professor on May 20, making it clear that Palmerston's wishes concerning the education of his son were given the fullest consideration:

'With respect to Mr Temple's classical studies, if I had thought that your Lordship had wished his attention to have been directed principally to them, I should certainly have advised him to attend Mr Dalzel's lectures on Greek, and put him under the care of a classical tutor. As this plan, however, must necessarily have interfered with the other studies in which he was engaged last winter, it appeared to me more advisable on the whole to avail myself of the short stay which I understood he was to make at Edinburgh, in attempting to give him some general idea of those branches of education which he may find it more difficult to supply elsewhere. If I were to be consulted hereafter about the plans of any young man who wishes to unite the advantages of an English and a Scotch University, I should strongly recommend the example of Lord Webb Seymour, who after remaining for several years at Oxford, has finished his academical studies at Edinburgh. The uncommon maturity of Mr Temple's mind will, I am persuaded, render in *his* case a departure from this plan, of immaterial consequence, more particularly as I flatter myself that his classical knowledge, if not increasing so rapidly as it might have done if it had been his chief object, has not been suffered to decline since he left England. I intended, during the remainder of Mr Temple's stay in Scotland, to have kept the same plan in view, but as I am anxious, in everything which concerns him, to be guided by your Lordship's judgment, and as it is very possible that I may overrate some of my own favourite pursuits, I shall, if you signify your approbation, put him under the care of a tutor who attended Mr Ward greatly to my satisfaction and who, I will venture to say, is one of the best scholars in the island . . .

'After what I have repeatedly mentioned to your Lordship with respect to the propriety of Mr Temple's conduct, it is sufficient for me to add that every day confirms the favourable opinion I formerly expressed.'[34]

Later in the year Harry showed that he was developing a useful sense of the services that could be rendered by the right word in the right place, when he wrote to his father:

'The Comte d'Artois and his family are coming down here and they are preparing Holyrood House for his reception. Mrs Stewart told me yesterday that she had been in search of a person who was acquainted with the Marquis of Abercorn, for some friend of hers had shown her a private letter from the Duc d'Angoulême, in which he said that his greatest ambition was to get Dudiston, Lord Abercorn's house near Edinburgh, and that it would be the greatest happiness in the world if he could. Now it just happens very luckily that Lord Abercorn has let it to a Mr Campbell, who is now in India, and Mrs Campbell, who used to live in it, is just dead, so that there would not be any difficulty about turning out the tenant. I should think that as my mother is so intimate with Lady Bessborough and Lady Abercorn she might just mention the circumstance to one of them, and I daresay that Lord Abercorn would have no objection to oblige the Duke. The place is not a large one, but it would be particularly convenient for him as it is out of the way of everybody and a short walk from Holyrood House, so that he could whenever he chose, come over to see the Comte d'Artois, and at the same time have a house of his own . . .'[35]

★ ★ ★

Count Rumford, whose patron, the Elector of Bavaria, had just died, was obliged to pay his respects to the new Court, and embarked on a journey which was to keep him, with brief exceptions, until the end of his days in Paris, where he married the widow of the guillotined French scientist, Lavoisier. Lady Palmerston remained his confidante:

Brompton, September 9th, 1801. 'My passport, signed by the King, is in my possession, and I have leave by it to pass either from Gravesend or Dover and to go either to France or to Holland. M. Otto promises me a passport from Paris in a few days . . .

'I go now to Munich with the determination to be back in London by, or before, the middle of December. To make my permanent stay now impossible, I take nothing with me but a small portmanteau. I go to pay my court to my new Sovereign and to settle with him, if possible, a reasonable plan for the rest of my life. I shall try hard to arrange matters so as to divide my time between England and Bavaria. My house at Brompton and a summer lodging at Munich. That is my scheme. In all events, I must get leave to return to England and spend the winter in London, for the important purpose of finishing the Royal Institution, and settling my own private affairs. I have great hope of being able to carry that point, at least Sir Joseph [Banks] and Lord Pelham approve much of this new plan, but Sir Charles [Blagden] is not quite sure it is right. He never yet approved of any plan I communicated to him . . .

Munich, October 3rd. 'I arrived here last evening, have seen the Elector and have every reason to hope that everything will be settled exactly as I could wish. Nothing could possibly be more friendly than the reception I met with from the Elector . . .

Paris, October 26th. 'You will, perhaps, be surprised at receiving a letter from me dated from this place, but I hope you will not disapprove of the alteration I have been induced to make in my plans. Circumstances have greatly altered since I saw you and I thought I might without any impropriety indulge my curiosity.

'Curiosity, however, was not the only motive which induced me to come here. The Elector wished it, and charged me with dispatches of some importance for his Minister here . . .

November 1st. 'I find it quite impossible to leave Paris so soon as I intended . . . I dined yesterday at M. de Talleyrand's country seat . . . I am to dine tomorrow with Senator Laplace at a dinner made for me, where I shall meet all the philosophers of the first distinction now at Paris . . . I have seen all the Consuls but one, and him I shall see on Friday next . . . The preparations for the Fête de la Paix are immense. Temporary temples are now building at the Place de la Revolution, which will vie with those of Greece and Rome in size and grandeur. The whole of the Seine is to be illuminated and all the bridges . . .

November 10th. 'I pass my time here most agreeably, my mornings in seeing the sights and my evenings in the first circles of genteel company . . . Both gentlemen and ladies are well dressed in all the first circles, and democracy is quite out of fashion. The word "Citoyen" is never heard in good company, and as to the word "Liberté", it seems to have become quite obsolete. I have been presented to the First Consul, and was received by him with marked attention. Many foreigners were presented at the same time and some of them of high rank and distinction, but I was the only foreigner, except the foreign ministers, who was invited to dine with Bonaparte. I met him the next evening at the National Institute; he came and rested himself near where I was sitting. There was but one person (Lagrange) between us, and I had a fine opportunity of observing him for more than an hour. He made a speech of some length – as a member of the Institute – and acquitted himself very well indeed. I was quite surprised at his knowledge in science and his eloquence. I am going this morning to pay my respects to Lord Cornwallis . . .'[36]

* * *

Cornwallis was in Paris as British plenipotentiary to negotiate the Treaty of Amiens. Nelson's triumph at Copenhagen had produced only stalemate in the war with France. On March 14, 1801, Pitt had resigned over the question of Catholic emancipation and Addington, the Speaker, had been appointed as George III's pliant First Lord of the Treasury in his place. His was a weak ministry, and, as Palmerston wrote to his wife, rumours of a dissolution of Parliament were rife. It seemed a good opportunity to resuscitate his plan of obtaining an English peerage:

November 3rd, 1801. 'I suppose we shall have a long day in the House and probably an entertaining one. There is much talk of dissolution soon, but I am quite of the opinion of your informers that it will not take place till next summer. Whenever it comes it will probably be the termination of my parliamentary career, which has been a pretty long one, as I have sat in seven Parliaments and do not now find myself desirous of throwing away a great sum of money for the satisfaction of continuing any longer, nor in the situation in which I now stand would it be either proper or even justifiable for me to do so. I wish to make some farther attempt in the line you allude to but hardly know which is the best method of going about it. I thought perhaps when Lord M[almesbury] came over he might be of some assistance and that perhaps if you (as you said you had taken up the measure) was to have some conversation with him and Lord P[elham] upon the subject, it might answer better in the first instance than my going to Lord P. and Mr A[ddington]. You will let me know your thoughts on the subject. I think that having taken the same line with Lord M. and Lord P. in 1793 gives me a claim to their assistance and had I been in England at the time probably something of the kind would have been acquiesced in and obtained . . .

November 4th. 'We were at the House till between three and four this morning, when the address of approbation, which was modestly worded, was voted without many dissenting voices and without a division. You will see some account of the debate. Lord Hawkesbury made an excellent speech. Pitt spoke strongly and completely in favour of the preliminaries, thought the Cape of more value than Lord H. did, but admitted that it was not probable more could have been obtained and rated very high the value of both Ceylon and Trinidad. Fox as usual got up at past twelve and made a long speech when the House was much fatigued. He spoke decidedly for the peace and commended the ministers who had made it. He was on the whole moderate and though he argued pretty much at length to prove that the war was unnecessarily undertaken on our part, he did not go into any violent invectives against Pitt or the late ministers. Tom Grenville and Lord Temple were the principal people who condemned the peace. Much was expected from Wyndham, whose opinions were frequently alluded to in the debate. He did not rise till very late and then merely to say that he had not altered his opinion but that indisposition, fatigue and the lateness of the hour hindered him from entering into the question. Many people seemed to wish to speak but found it too late. Doctor Laurence got up at three o'clock, which occasioned such universal horror and consternation that the whole House seemed to rise against it, which luckily put him in a passion and down he sat. The arguments against the peace appeared to most people weak and inconclusive, because though they established what everybody admitted, that France is left in a situation extremely alarming and dangerous to this country, yet scarce any argument was advanced to show that we could have obtained better terms or that any effect was to be expected from continuing the war, but that of exhausting in fruitless and childish efforts all the resources that remain to us and which we shall have so much occasion for if the present gloomy apprehensions should be realised. The comfort we have is that no political predictions ever are verified and therefore I hope these will not be the first . . .

November 6th. 'Mr Rose called on me yesterday. I fancy he is pretty much in the knowledge of what is going on. He assured me that a dissolution of Parliament during this winter was utterly impracticable and never had been thought of. That he understood it had been under consideration whether it would be best to dissolve next spring and that after having [been] for some time inclined to adopt that intention, the ministers had given it up and do not at present think of dissolving even next year. The Parliament may continue till August or September 1803 . . .'

The nostalgia of advancing age were beginning to affect Palmerston, and in an affectionate and charming letter to his second wife he ranged back over the years to his undimmed recollections of the first:

P

November 8th. 'After I wrote on Friday [the 6th] I went late to Sheen and . . . remained . . . all yesterday till the evening, which was not my original intention, but the leisure and solitude of the place led me to indulge without restraint or interruption in a train of melancholy recollections and the mournful luxury of reviewing the affecting memorials of long departed worth, tenderness and attachment. The images of things so dear and so respected do not present themselves, nor is it fit they should, at every turn amidst the bustle of the world and its ordinary occurrences, but they dwell as it were enshrined in the recesses of the heart, and come forth with redoubled energy at suited seasons and in moments of serious recollection. Time that soon wears away the sharpness of affliction has no influence on these sensations, or only serves to increase them. More than two and thirty eventful years have passed away since the melancholy period to which I refer, yet never has the loss I then sustained or the distressful scenes I passed through been more tenderly or deeply felt than at the present moment. As far as relates to myself alone, that loss, which I long thought irreparable, has been compensated by similar merits, equal affection and a far! far! more fortunate attachment, but selfish and unfeeling must I be if I did not on that very account cherish with redoubled tenderness the memory of a being the most perfect of her kind, who lost everything on this side the grave, and much she had to lose, by her ill-fated partiality to me.

'I will not apologise for entering with you into such a subject, which I hardly intended when I begun; but my thoughts are too full of it just now to dwell upon anything else, and not to feel a relief in disburthening themselves by communication with a friend. Nobody is so formed as you are to enter into these feelings, and I know you will take the being entrusted with them as the highest mark of confidence and affection. I have long wished at various times to enter on this subject, and to make you acquainted with some faint traces that I have preserved of a character in so many points resembling your own. This I shall at a proper season have a real gratification in doing, for though it would be a kind of profanation to treat such subjects lightly and unworthily, yet I cannot conceive why one is never to speak of what one has felt the most, and why the subjects that lie the deepest in one's heart and are the dearest to one's remembrance are to be eternally banished from one's lips.

'Adieu! Give my affectionate love to those around you and believe me ever

faithfully yours, Palmerston.'

Palmerston persevered with his request for a seat in the House of Lords:

November 26th. 'I have seen Lord Pelham, who was as kind and as friendly as possible. I am to write to Mr A[ddington] and desire to see him and at the same time explain on what subject, as it is better the application should be made directly to him as a principal, but between my writing to him and seeing him Lord P. has promised to speak to him on the subject and enforce it as much as he can . . .'[37]

Lady Palmerston approved wholeheartedly of the project:

November 27th. 'I am glad you have spoken to Pelham. I never could doubt his wishes to have an opportunity of manifesting his gratitude to you for all your kindness and steady friendship which you have so invariably shown to both himself and brother and what ought to increase his zeal is the reflection he cannot fail to make that hitherto he has not paid you all the attention you certainly merited to have received both from Lord P. and his family. Addington, I do not doubt, will be glad to give his interest with Pelham, the only person who I have any doubt about is the [illegible] himself and I should not have had that idea but from its not being done before. However, if I was you I would follow it up now and if you do not succeed I shall say more shame for those who prevent it . . .'[38]

At the end of the month Palmerston duly made his last effort. Pelham himself was not encouraging:

'Addington seems to have made it a rule not to give any encouragement to applications for peerages. I fear, therefore, that his answer to you will not be so satisfactory as I could wish, at the same time I am inclined to think that he will favour your pretensions, but that he thinks it safer to refuse any one, than to make a selection until the time shall arrive when he must come to a determination.

'I can only add that whenever an opportunity offers that will enable me to forward your wishes, you may depend upon my employing it with zeal and sincerity.'[39]

The draft of Palmerston's letter to Addington was almost an *apologia pro vita publica sua*:

'I have now sat in the House of Commons about 37 years and have brought myself into seven Parliaments, during which period I trust my conduct has been that of an independent man and a zealous supporter of our constitution as it at present exists. I passed through those situations of office at the high and respectable Boards which have usually been considered as leading to some marks of favour and distinction. Favours of a lucrative kind I have not solicited. The point to which my views have been directed has been a seat in the House of Peers; which becomes every day a more interesting object to me, as I have sons growing up who give a well-grounded promise of not disgracing any situations in which they may be placed.

'I flatter myself my pretensions to a peerage cannot be deemed presumptuous with respect either to my property or family. The first is not inconsiderable and it is unencumbered; as to the latter, it has been not unknown or undistinguished in both parts of the United Kingdom. The elder branch of my family, that of Lord Cobham, is extinct in the male line, and the property is gone in the female line to the Grenvilles; mine, therefore, may be considered as the principal remaining line of the Temples.

'The present Parliament is necessarily drawing towards the conclusion, after which the seat I now hold in it can no longer be mine, and after so many years attendance I feel no inclination to engage afresh in the trouble or expense of electioneering pursuits.

'On these grounds, therefore, I can no longer defer making this application, to which I am strongly prompted by several of my most respectable friends. Permit me, therefore, to intreat that through you and by your kindness I may be recommended to His Majesty for the honour of a peerage before the opening of the next Parliament. If I am fortunate enough to succeed in this request to you, I shall consider it as a very high and lasting obligation and entertain a sense of it beyond what I can easily express.

'Allow me in the meantime to assure you of my grateful remembrance of past kindness and of the sentiments of sincere respect and high regard with which I have the honour to be,

dear Sir, your most faithful and most obedient humble
servant,

Palmerston'[40]

The Prime Minister replied:

Downing Street, November 29th, 1801

'My dear Lord,

If perfectly convenient to your Lordship, I shall be happy to have the honour of seeing you in Downing Street on Wednesday morning at half past eleven o'clock.

Believe me to be, with sincere regard,

my dear Lord,

Your most obedient and faithful humble servant,

Henry Addington'[41]

But nothing came of the conversation for the time being, and soon it was too late; Palmerston had barely five months to live. The last exchange of correspondence of which there is record was, appropriately enough, with his son, who received this affectionate – and prophetic – homily, dated January 6, 1802:

'I should have written to you before had I had anything particular to say, but you have so many correspondents here that you are informed of all our transactions in the greatest detail and with the utmost exactness; and you leave me little opportunity of enlarging upon the usual topics of fathers' letters, which are reproofs for the past and good advice for the future. The first you take care never to deserve, and the latter you stand so little in need of that instead of holding out to you, as is often done, the example of some other person as a rule for your conduct, I am perfectly satisfied with entreating you to

P*

persevere as you have begun in a line so well calculated to make you happy, respected and beloved. Your good talents and your application have smoothed to you those difficulties which are often insurmountable to those who are deficient in those qualities. And as to what remains before you, your love of knowledge, a just disdain of being insignificant and an honest pride not to disappoint the general good opinion and expectation of the world will, I trust, induce you never to relax in your efforts to secure those attainments of which you will feel the advantage to the latest period of your life.

'I received a few lines from Mr Stewart while at Dunglas in which he speaks of you in a manner highly gratifying and satisfactory to me; and such as proves that you have gained his affection as well as his approbation.

'I do not hear anything from him or from you with regard to the person who was to attend you for classical study. Pray let me know whether anything has been done about it or whether you are going on as last year. I am anxious on this subject as I think it a very material part of a young man's acquirements and though perhaps not so intrinsically valuable as the various branches of science, yet as it is by no means incompatible with them it should not be neglected even for them; and in the common intercourse of life there is nothing so ornamental or that so often comes in play and gains a man so much credit as a general and ready acquaintance with and taste for the classical authors. Of this I believe you are thoroughly sensible and as you made so good a progress in them at Harrow I strongly recommend you not to omit in some way or other going on with and improving yourself in them while at Edinburgh . . .

'We have a very agreeable party here, among whom are the Miss Berrys who are extremely pleasant, and Sir Charles Blagden and Count Rumford. The latter is just returned from Bavaria where he went at the earnest desire of the Elector, and where he has made arrangements and engagements with the Elector to pass several months in each year in superintending many parts of the affairs of that country. He reserves to himself a full privilege, which I hope he will not fail to use, of coming over to England every year. But I fear if he gets deeply engaged and interested in plans to be carried on in Bavaria he will feel less disposed than he now thinks to make such frequent absences. Besides which, Paris will now divide his attentions with London. He passed about 5 weeks there in his return and the many objects of curiosity and the flattering attentions he met with from all sorts of people have made a great impression on his mind . . .

'Count Rumford thinks Buonaparte a very extraordinary character, full of energy, and intense and constant application; gloomy, reserved and cold in his manner, forming no friend-ships, placing little confidence and entering into no amusement or free society. His whole time and thoughts seem to be occu-pied with business and his dependence for the support of his Government seems to be on the popularity of his measures and the general desire of peace and quiet through the country; and for his personal security he trusts to his troops, to which he pays the greatest attention, and with whom he seems to be greatly in favour. His body of guards are all picked veterans and he seldom trusts himself out of their protection. They were till lately commanded by one General of the name of Lannes, a man of high character as an officer; but Buonaparte thought he was caballing and making a party of his own, in consequence of which he removed him and has divided his command among four. Nothing can be more despotic than Buonaparte's authority is or than all the quiet people wish it to be; seeing in it their only security against all the horrors and all the absurdities to which they were so long exposed. This is a fine lesson for intemperate reformers, and proves to all who wanted such proof that violent and hasty revolutions necessarily lead to a state of things so disastrous and an anarchy so dreadful and complicated, as to admit of no remedy but that of having recourse for protection (which is the principal object of real liberty) to a despotism far more absolute and complete than that which it was thought worth risking all these mischiefs to overturn.

'A government like Buonaparte's when first established is generally popular with the country at large, because it is a refuge from worse evils and because the man who has abilities enough to obtain such absolute power is likely to have sense enough to wish to reconcile people to it by a mild and temperate use of it. But it is a melancholy consideration for those who have been honestly treading this miserable circle to find themselves come round at last to a point full as remote from liberty as that from which they set out, and to know at the same time that even the temporary security that serves to reconcile them to it, depends on the arbitrary will and precarious existence of a single man ...

'I forgot to mention that the splendour and expense of Buonaparte's Court, the magnificence of his table, servants and *liveries* seems to exceed that of any court in Europe...'[42]

Harry replied two days later:

'As I have never told you exactly what classes I attend, and what I do, and as I thought you would most likely wish to know it, I send you a kind of list of the hours I am regularly employed, besides which, I have a good deal to do at home, in writing out the notes I take at the chemistry and at Mr Stewart's lecture, and doing the algebraical exercises Mr Playfair gives us, and reading Latin and Greek for Mr Christison ... Ashburton, Mathew and myself are deeply engaged in chemistry and burn our fingers and tables with acids most delightfully...'[43]

A letter to Harry, dated March 5, describing the death of the great Whig magnate, the Duke of Bedford, is the last manuscript extant in Palmerston's hand. At least he had the satisfaction of knowing that his son had become a universal favourite. In a letter, dated January 4, 1802, their old friend, Sir Henry Englefield, told Lady Palmerston:

'I must not conclude without quoting to you a passage from a letter from my nephew to his mother which she sent to my mother and so I saw it, which *he* could not know I should. Having spoken of some silly fine gentlemen and other boorish students, he says, "Temple is however a proof that it is possible to unite the manners of a perfect gentleman, with the utmost attention to science". Praise from equals is of high value. I wish he may have ever thought of my nephew in the same light...'[44]

Within the same week she had received this comment from

another intimate of many years' standing, Sir Gilbert Elliot, first Earl of Minto, whose son and namesake had joined Harry at Professor Stewart's establishment:

'Harry is as charming and as perfect as he ought to be; I do declare that I never saw anything more delightful. On this subject I do not speak of my own judgment alone. I have sought opportunities of conversing with Mr and also Mrs Stewart on the subject, and they have made to me the report which you have already heard from others, that he is the only young man they ever knew in whom it is impossible to find any fault – diligence, capacity, total freedom from vice of every sort, gentle and kind disposition, cheerfulness, pleasantness and perfect sweetness – are in the catalogue of properties by which we may advertise him if he should be lost . . .'[45]

Palmerston's engagement diaries show that the weather continued to be uncommonly cold and frosty right into the middle of March. Having spent the first seven weeks of the year at Broadlands, where his guests had included the Misses Berry, he returned to Hanover Square on February 20. His diary entries for the first two weeks in March show him engaged in his usual round of social functions, attending the opera and the theatre as well as numerous parties. On March 13 there was the Speaker's dinner for the Lord Chancellor, which he went to despite 'a bad cold'. The next day's entry shows him 'at home with a severe cold'.[46]

That was the last diary entry he ever made. The rest of the book is blank. At the end of the month he was stricken with what contemporary records describe as 'ossification of the throat'. Although very ill, he remained in good spirits, cracking his jokes and reading from morning to night. Of the Treaty of Amiens, he remarked to Minto, in the phrase Wilkes had used in 1762, 'that it was certainly the peace of God which passeth all understanding!' On April 14, Harry was sent for, and on the 16th his father died. Lady Palmerston asked Lord Minto to meet her son. On April 19 this old family friend wrote to his wife:

'I went to Barnet on Saturday afternoon [the 17th]. Gilbert [Elliot] and Harry arrived there this morning at 7. Harry was

not at all aware of the extreme danger and had, therefore, a
greater shock than I hoped he might have. I had taken great
pains to tutor both my own servants and the Palmerstons', not
to speak to Harry before he had seen me. But Hunter mistook
Gilbert for Harry, brought him up to my room saying "Here
is Mr Temple, my Lord", and then ran down to Harry and told
him the event as a piece of news. It was in reality the same
thing, as I must have told him the moment after; yet I was
provoked at it as I had stayed there two days to perform the
office myself . . .'[47]

The distraught widow went to stay with her sister, Mrs
Culverden, at Lavender House, Sheen, and as soon as she had
sufficiently mastered her grief wrote to Lord Malmesbury:

'In this solemn hour, when the anguish of my heart too
plainly proves the instability of our existence, I cannot permit
another day to pass without consigning to your friendly bosom
the last wishes which I may not long be permitted me to
express. In case of my death (no previous arrangement having
been made by my ever dear and most lamented husband) I
appoint you, Lord Minto, Lord Pelham, Mr Culverden and
my sister guardians to my children . . .

'I wish Harry to return into Scotland with Lord Minto to
make a tour, and return into England if he likes in the summer,
but the next winter to pass with Mr Stewart, such I know being
the wishes of his dear father, and when the classes are over to
come up to be entered at Cambridge and placed under the
care of the most eminent man as tutor. In the long vacation I
could wish he would make some tour with some intelligent
clever man to point out all that is worthy of observation, to
improve his knowledge, open his mind to the advantages his
country possesses and give him an insight into the manufactory
and the various excellence of England – What a friend, what
a companion has he lost! One whose judgment was so perfect,
whose taste so refined and who imparted the knowledge he
possessed with that clearness, that good humour – with that
affectionate kindness – that no one could pass a day, nay hardly
an hour, with him without learning something and gaining a
degree of pleasure no other society ever could bestow. But

alas! Such happiness can never beam on me or my children again. I would wish Harry to see Ireland before he goes abroad and, having passed his minority and in possession of his fortune, I advise him to choose some amiable friend – may it be Gilbert [Elliot] or James [Harris, Lord Malmesbury's son] – and pass two years abroad seeing with the eyes of a traveller who wishes to improve by viewing other nations and other countries and not living with his own countrymen, despising those who are the object for which he travels. When he returns I hope he will come into Parliament and there act, as I am sure he will on every other station – with all that perfection of excellence – he has inherited from his father. With respect to William, I wish him to remain at Harrow till he is sixteen, which will be in February twelve month, then to go for three years to Mr Stewart's, but as he would lose the classes he must quit Harrow the end of October so [as] to be in time for the opening of the classes in November. I hope he will make a choice of a future profession in which he will give all his time and talents to shining in whatever line he chooses for himself. I have no right to hope – the Church is perhaps the one most suited to him, but as he is to decide I will only advise that he will consult you and his other guardians on the subject and my wishes for his success must ever await his choice . . .'[48]

[Sir William Temple was to become one of the most respected ambassadors of his country, spending many years at the Legation Sir William Hamilton occupied for so long at Naples.]

Lady Palmerston wrote in similar vein to her son's other guardians, but in her letters to Lady Malmesbury she was still almost hysterical with grief:

'The sight of your hand writing is ever most consolatory and to say the truth I think I never felt more strongly in need of consolation than at this moment when my heart is so loaded with sorrow that I hardly know how to support myself. Remember that it is only to you and Emma [Godfrey] I can open every secret thought – and I can depend on both your fidelity never to betray my confidence. It is a painful proof of regard but alas! if I do not unburthen my sorrow to some

friendly bosom my heart will surely break. I could have bowed
in silent resignation to my loss had it been the will of Heaven,
but oh my dearest friend, he died for want of care, and had I
shot him with my own hands I should not have been more
guilty of his death than I feel I now am. What a return for
years of unceasing kindness. What did he not do for me! I
brought misfortune on him, but it seemed to bind him still
stronger to me. He became the support of all who fell into
affliction around me. To my dear brother he was the firmest,
the tenderest friend. To his tenderness and generosity I owe
the prolongation of a mother's existence and saw her breathe
her last surrounded by every comfort his fortune could bestow.
Misery overwhelmed my sister when his ready hand raised her
again to comfort. In every sorrow his affection reanimated and
gladdened life and taught me that he had the power to give a
second spring to happiness. And how have I requited all this
store of benefits – suffered him to expire for want of the
common assistance he would not have spared the servant who
attended him. That he might have been alive at this moment
(perhaps walking on that very hill now in my view): I have no
doubt. And when I look on my poor children and think how
cruel I have been to them, whose affection to me adds to my
self-reproach, the sensations I feel are too painful to be conceived but by one who has deserved them.

'Never can peace revisit this sad heart, for when can guilt be
happy – I wonder that so much kindness can be shown to one
who deserves to be scorned and neglected by everyone who
loved my dearest husband – the object of my unceasing regrets.
Do not attempt to tell me the fact is not as I have stated it, for
I am certain of the truth of all I have asserted. I might plead
the judgment not the heart was in fault, but that is no excuse
and the remembrance of my sins will last me to the end of my
existence . . .

'Let me entreat you to burn this letter as soon as you have
read it – No, send it me back that I may never forget my crime
or my remorse and that when time has softened all other
feelings that of my conscious guilt shall remain undiminished.
I can have no better wish to offer than that your heart may

never feel the wretchedness that dwells in your afflicted
friend's . . .'[49]

Lord Minto became the tenant of the forsaken house in
Hanover Square, the third Viscount returned to Edinburgh, and
Lord Malmesbury assumed the duties, so admirably performed
by his father, of guiding the young man's brilliant mind:

November 23rd. '. . . respecting the mode in which you are
pursuing your studies. I approve of it most intensely and I am
sure, my dear Harry, that I on my part both in compliance with
my duty as a guardian and from the affection I bear you,
cannot do better than to let you trace out for yourself the
different branches of literature and science to which you wish
to apply. I am a very great friend to mathematics, they accustom
the mind to get at and to determine truth; while logic teaches
it to reason and argue . . . Political economy is a very important
and interesting subject. From everything I hear of Mr Stewart
I have no doubt he will teach it on its right principles and in
the way which can the best tend to qualify you to act as becomes
in you in the rank you hold in life and in the part you will
probably be called upon to act. The classics never should be
forgotten, besides the taste and elegance they give to our habits
of thinking and modes of expressions, they are an inexhaustible
and constant fund of invaluable reading and late in life when
other studies fatigue too much, you will find in the reverting
to them the most pleasant of all resources . . .

Saturday, March 5th, 1803. 'The plan of your studies appears
to me to be as good as possible and such a one as to lay in for
you a store of useful and amusing information. I only fear when
you get to Cambridge you will find yourself with nothing to
learn, or rather that your tutors will know nothing with which
you will not be previously acquainted. I, however, hear from
every quarter St John's so well spoken of that if it should only
prove a quiet and comfortable residence for a year or two which
you may dedicate to reading, it will answer the going there
perfectly. You may, I find, enter by proxy and it is not necessary
for you to go to Cambridge yourself till you leave Scotland
entirely . . .'[50]

Lady Palmerston made a dispirited attempt to gather together the threads of her existence. She even endeavoured to carry on the practice of her late lord of keeping a copious diary of her activities:

Friday, May 13th, 1803. 'I went out with my sister in the King's Road. It always makes me feel melancholy in the extreme, but where can I go that his dear image does not present itself with the memory of happy hours passed together, nor would I, if I could, annihilate one recollection in which his idea is interwoven, for only can I by recounting past happiness support present deprivation. I forever think he is only gone out for a few hours and that I shall see him come in to tell me what is passing – alas! he arrives not! and I have to weep my sad, sad loss . . .

Sunday, May 15th. 'There was a great riot in Kensington Gardens. Two well dressed women, whose dress attracted notice, were mobbed and grossly insulted by men like labourers in Sunday clothes. Lord Camelford, at the head of a party of gentlemen, went to their assistance at last; a scuffle ensued and he knocked down everyone in his way, giving them his card . . .

May 16th. 'Took out Miss W[hitworth?] with us, airing towards Hampstead – walked, though very cold. Received a proof of natural civility from a man not far removed, by his dress, from a very low class. In getting under a rail to go into a field we were obliged to stoop and there being a ditch to step up it was rather difficult. The man was at a little distance. He came up quickly and gave me his hand to assist me. I only mention this circumstance as a different demeanour has of late appeared in the lower ranks of people since the fatal Revolution . . .

May 21st. 'The Royal Institution, I fear, is on the decline by the ill-management of the present managers. They have subscribed £100 each. Their abuse of Count R[umford] is atrocious. Sir J. Banks thinks of withdrawing from it . . .'[51]

The sparse entries soon petered out, but her devoted admirer, Count Rumford, remained constant, telling her of his marriage and the new eminence he was attaining as a scientist and philosopher in Paris:

February 8th, 1804. 'How does the Royal Institution go on?

What do the philosophers in England say to my late experiments on heat? Do they continue to believe in Caloric? I am quite sure that it has no real existence. I am now very busy in making preparations for a new set of experiments on the subject of heat. The French philosophers begin to waver in their opinions upon that subject. The chemists still hold out, but the natural philosophers (physicians) express their doubts freely. I think I shall live to drive Caloric off the stage, as the late Monsieur Lavoisier (the author of Caloric) drove away Phlogiston. What a singular destiny for the wife of two philosophers!

July 5th, 1804. 'I wrote to you a few days ago by the way of Germany. An opportunity now offers, which seems to be safe, of sending a letter directly to England. I am extremely anxious to hear from you; knowing you to be ill, and not knowing what is the matter with you is a very painful situation for me. Pray write to me soon and let me know how you are and tell me how long you have been ill and what the doctor says of your complaint. I am really very anxious about you and you must contrive to let me hear from you often . . .'[52]

Lady Palmerston was indeed mortally ill. From Lord Minto's letters to his wife it would seem she developed cancer. In December, 1804, she wrote to Lady Malmesbury from Broadlands:

'I hope I may amend, but if I do not, I trust my spirits will be restored to enable me to bear with fortitude whatever evil I am to suffer; for there is something to me quite wicked in repining at whatever may be our lot in this world and I have had my share of happiness and health.'[53]

The next month she died. 'To us', wrote Lord Minto, 'she is the greatest loss possible out of our own family – the oldest, fastest, safest friend'.[54]

With both parents dead, it was their other intimate for so many years, Lord Malmesbury, the wise old statesman and diplomatist, who offered himself *in loco parentis* to the future Prime Minister of England, then still nine months short of his majority:

Monday, January 21st, 1805. 'It is, I am sure, my dear Harry, quite superfluous for me to take any pains to express to you my feelings. Neither should I have thought of giving you the painful task of reading a letter at this moment, was I not persuaded it would be less distressing to you and to your dear sisters to receive in writing rather than in words the assurance that, as far as lays in my power, it shall be my endeavour to replace the irreparable losses you have sustained. I consider the doing it as one of the most sacred duties imposed on me, strengthened by the remembrance which will never fail me of that kind and confiding friendship that thought me worthy of so important a trust and heightened by the truest and best deserved affection I bear you, William, Fanny and Elizabeth, all of whom, as long as I live, will be looked upon by me as my own children, and I hope you and they will equally look on me as on an indulgent parent. This comprises everything I can say. I shall be at Broadlands on Wednesday about 1 o'clock. God bless you, my dearest Harry. Give my kindest love to your sisters and believe me most affectionately yours,

Malmesbury.'[55]

REFERENCES

1. E.1(b) 19.III.1798
2. D.8 12.VI.1798 .
3. D.9(a) 15.VI.1798
4. B.1 5.XII.1798
5. C.72(b) 9.XII.1798
6. B.1
7. D.9(b) undated, 1799
8. D.9(b) 28.VI.1799
9. B.1
10. D.9(a) 20.X.1799
11. C.72(b) 23.X.1799
12. C.72(a) 27.X.1799
13. D.9(b) 29.VI.1800
14. C.71(a)
15. C.71(b) 16.VI.1800
16. A.21
17. A.22
18. C.72(b) 28.XI.1800
19. B.1 undated
20. C.74 25.XII.1800
21. B.2 25.XII.1800
22. B.1
23. B.1
24. D.9(b) 8.XII.1800
25. B.1
26. C.72(b) 10.XII.1800
27. C.71(b) 23.I.1801

28. C.72(b) 3.II.1801
29. C.72(b) 22.III.1801
30. B.1
31. C.72(a)
32. C.72(b) 18.IV.1801
33. D.9(b) 15.V.1801
34. C.71(b) 20.V.1801
35. C.72(b) 6.XI.1801
36. D.6
37. B.1
38. B.2
39. C.76 November 1801
40. C.75(a) November 1801
41. C.75(b)
42. C.72(a)
43. C.72(b) 8.II.1802
44. D.2
45. H.20
46. A.1
47. H.20 Vol. III p. 247
48. D.18 29.IV.1802
49. D.18 2.V.1802
50. E.3
51. A.22
52. D.6
53. H.20 Vol. III p. 351
54. H.20 Vol. III p. 350
55. E.3

LIST OF SOURCES AND BIBLIOGRAPHY

A. DIARIES AND JOURNALS

1. 34 engagement diaries for the years 1765-67, 1769, 1771-92, 1795-1802
2. Overall diary covering the years 1765-1795
3. Four account books as follows: (*a*) account and notebook, 1760; (*b*) account book, 1785-1798; (*c*) travelling account book, 1791; (*d*) travelling account book, 1789-1794

Journals as follows:

4. 1758 – Tour of South of England
5. 1760 – Tour of North of England
6. 1763-64 – Grand tour of Holland, France, Switzerland and Italy
7. 1765 – Tour of South-West England
8. 1769 – Tour in South of England and South Wales
9. 1770 – three journals: tour of France, Switzerland, Italy and parts of Germany
10. 1775 – Tour of West of England
11. 1777 – Tour of North of England
12. 1779 – Tour of West of England
13. 1783 – Tour of South Wales
14. 1784 – Journey to Ireland and Sligo memorandum book
15. 1787 – Tour of West of England
16. 1788 – Tour of Sussex, journey to North of England and Ireland and Sligo Estate roll
17. 1789 – Tour of Holland and Germany
18. 1791 – Paris journal of Constituent Assembly
19. 1792-94 – 12 journals of tour on the Continent:
    (*a*) July 28, 1792 – November 27, 1792, London – Rome
    (*b*) April, 1793, excursion to Capri and islands of the Bay of Naples
    (*c*) May, 1793, excursion to Tivoli, Frascati, etc. Journey to Rome from Naples

(d) June to December, 1793, from Rome, touring Northern Italy and Switzerland

(e) January, 1794, around Naples, description of Pompeii

(f) May–June, 1794, Rome to Venice

(g) June, 1794, continuing to Verona, Innsbruck, arriving Munich, July 1

(h) July, 1794, short tour to Chiemsee and description of Cassel

(i) Four notebooks describing Rome and various parts of Italy

20. 1796 – Tour of West Country

21. 1800 – Tour of North of England, Lake District, Edinburgh and Highlands of Scotland and notebook for this journey

22. Lady Palmerston's journals of 1800 journey and 1803

23. Lady Palmerston's engagement diaries for 1788, 1790, 1798 and 1799

B. CORRESPONDENCE BETWEEN SECOND VISCOUNT PALMERSTON AND HIS SECOND WIFE, MARY MEE, 1782 – 1801

1. 339 letters from Lord Palmerston written between the years 1782 and 1801

2. 106 letters from Lady Palmerston written between 1782 and 1801

C. LETTERS TO AND FROM SECOND VISCOUNT PALMERSTON

1. (a) 8 letters from Frances Poole (first wife) before marriage, 1767

   (b) 8 letters to Frances Poole before marriage, 1767

   (c) 14 letters from Frances Poole, Lady Palmerston, 1768–69

   (d) 10 letters to Frances Poole, Lady Palmerston, 1768–69

2. 6 draft letters from France, Switzerland and Italy, 1763–64, 4 to Mrs Howe and 2 to unidentified correspondents

3. 6 letters from Mrs Howe, 1761–64

4. 1 letter from Mme Geoffrin, 1763
5. 8 letters from Lady Charlotte Burgoyne, 1763–65
6. 1 letter from Mrs Greville, 1764
7. 1 letter from Helvetius, 1763
8. 1 letter from Voltaire, 1765
9. 5 letters from Gavin Hamilton, 1764–66
10. 7 letters from the Rt. Hon. Hans Stanley, M.P. for Southampton, Paultons, nr. Romsey, 1763–76
11. 2 letters from Sir William Hamilton, 1764, and 1773
12. 9 letters to and from Mr White, agent at Broadlands, 1757–63, with various schedules and inventories
13. 3 letters at Dublin to lawyer, Timothy Waldo, London, 1762–64
14. 1 letter from John Hatch, Dublin, to Timothy Waldo, 1762
15. 4 letters from Mr Arden, 1764–65
16. 45 letters from Mr W. Daman, bailiff and agent at Broadlands, 1768–80, with some documents
17. (a) 20 letters to his mother, the Hon. Mrs Henry Temple, 1761–88
    (b) 6 letters from his mother, Mrs Temple, 1761–63
    (c) 1 letter from Mrs Temple to William Godschall (uncle of second wife), 1763
18. (a) 18 letters to William Godschall, 1767–92
    (b) 3 letters from William Godschall, 1797–99
19. 3 letters from Christ. Arthur (? solicitor), 1767
20. 8 letters from H. Vernon Sadleir, 1767–69
21. 1 letter from Charles Townshend, 1767
22. 1 letter from William Pitt, Lord Chatham, 1767
23. 1 letter from Charles le Gay, 1768
24. 1 letter from De Saussure, 1769
25. 1 letter from Earl Harcourt, 1770
26. 1 letter from Mrs Isabella Poyntz, enclosing epitaph by Rousseau for translation, 1771
27. 1 letter from Viscount Nuneham (later 2nd Earl Harcourt), 1771
28. 1 letter from Lord Huntingdon, Paris, 1771
29. 1 letter from Mlle Julie de l'Espinasse, 1771

30. (a) 1 letter from M. Frenais, Paris, 1774
     (b) 1 copy of draft reply to M. Frenais, 1774
31. 1 letter from General John Burgoyne, 1775
32. 1 letter from Sir James Burrow, 1775
33. 2 letters from the Earl of Pembroke, 1776–78
34. 2 letters from David Garrick and 1 from Mrs Garrick,
     1777–78
35. (a) 17 letters concerning Madame Gallina
     (b) 5 accounts of expenses connected with Madame Gallina
36. 1 letter from Lancelot ('Capability') Brown, 1779
37. 1 letter from William Pitt, 1779
38. 2 letters from Mrs Cholmondeley, one of 1780, another
     undated
39. 1 letter from George Crabbe, 1781
40. 1 letter from Lord Banbury, 1783
41. 1 letter from Valentine Morris, 1784
42. 1 letter from M. Kersaint, 1785
43. 1 letter from George Colman, 1785
44. (a) 21 letters from Benjamin Mee (brother-in-law),
     1785–95
     (b) 7 letters to Benjamin Mee, 1788–91
45. 1 letter from Sir Joseph Banks, 1786
46. 1 letter from the Marquise de Gleon, 1787
47. 1 letter from R. B. Sheridan, 1788
48. 2 letters from Sir Gilbert Elliot (afterwards Lord Minto),
     1788
49. 17 letters from Sir Charles Blagden, 1788–1801
50. 1 letter from Sir Henry Englefield, undated
51. (a) 20 letters from Thomas Warner, agent at Broadlands,
     1789–99
     (b) 2 statements of accounts from Thomas Warner
52. 1 letter from Beckmans at Antwerp, 1790
53. 1 letter from Sir Joshua Reynolds, 1790
54. 1 letter from the Hon. Thomas Pelham (later 2nd Earl of
     Chichester), 1791
55. 1 letter from Mme de Boufflers, undated
56. 1 letter from M. de Flahaut, Paris au Louvre, 1791
57. 1 letter from M. Lavoisier, 1791

58. 1 letter from Sir Ralph Payne (afterwards Lord Lavington), 1791
59. 1 letter from Godfroi, Duc de Bouillon, 1791
60. 11 letters re Sligo Estate – mostly to and from Mr Lyons, 1791–97
61. 1 letter from Sir John Acton, Bart, 1793
62. 1 letter from Godschall Johnson, 1795
63. 1 letter from Hare Naylor, 1796
64. 1 letter from Mr John Woodburn, 1796
65. 1 letter from Mr Clark at Naples, 1796
66. (a) 2 letters from Mrs Anna Pitt, 1796
     (b) 1 draft reply to Mrs Anna Pitt, 1796
67. 1 letter to Lord Cholmondeley about books for Prince of Wales, 1796, and list of said books
68. 1 letter from Vicomte du Giron-Grenier, 1797
69. 1 draft of a letter to William Pitt, 1798
70. 1 letter from, and a draft reply to, William Sewards, 1799
71. (a) 1 letter to Professor Dugald Stewart, 1800
     (b) 6 letters from Professor Dugald Stewart, Edinburgh, 1800–02
72. (a) 7 letters to elder son, Henry Temple (afterwards 3rd Viscount Palmerston), 1799–1802
     (b) 13 letters from elder son, Henry Temple, 1799–1802
73. 1 letter from Madame la Comtesse de la Bourdonnaye de Cléry, 1800
74. 2 letters from Miss Berry, 1800–02
75. (a) 1 letter to Mr Addington, 1801
     (b) 1 letter from Mr Addington, 1801
76. 1 letter from Lord Pelham, 1801
77. 1 letter from Thomas Bouchier, 1801
78. 1 letter from le Comte de la Tour d'Auvergne, 1801

D. LETTERS TO AND FROM MARY MEE, LADY PALMERSTON

1. 3 letters from Lydia Denty, 1787–88
2. 4 letters from Sir Henry Englefield, 1790–1802
3. 119 letters from William Godschall, 1790–1802
4. 27 from Sir Charles Blagden, 1791–1804
5. 29 letters to Benjamin Mee, 1792–93

6. 66 letters from Count Rumford, 1793–1804
7. 11 letters from Peter Quintin, 1794–99
8. 23 letters from Mrs Bromley (wife of the housemaster at Harrow), 1795–1803
9. (*a*) 40 letters to her son, Henry Temple, 1796–99
   (*b*) 68 letters from her son, Henry Temple, 1789–1801
10. 2 letters from Frances and Elizabeth Temple, undated
11. 3 letters from Caroline Douglas, and her maid, 1801
12. 6 letters from various French Emigrés, 1801–02
13. 1 letter from Lady Lavington, 1802
14. 1 letter from Mr Bennet, 1802
15. 1 letter from Henry Drummond, 1802
16. 1 letter from Hans Sloane, 1802
17. 1 letter to Lord Pelham, 1802
18. 7 letters to Lord and Lady Malmesbury (one to Lord Minto), 1802
19. 1 letter from Thomas Heaphy, 1802
20. 1 letter from Henry Addington (afterwards Lord Sidmouth), 1803
21. 7 miscellaneous letters

E. LETTERS TO AND FROM HENRY TEMPLE, THIRD VISCOUNT PALMERSTON

1. (*a*) 1 letter from Francis Hare, 1798
   (*b*) 1 letter to Francis Hare, 1798
2. 3 letters from William Godschall, 1801–02
3. 5 letters from Lord Malmesbury, 1802–05
4. 1 letter from John Flaxman, 1813
5. 1 letter from Thomas Heaphy, 1840

F. MISCELLANEOUS DOCUMENTS AND LETTERS

1. 16 engagement books of 1st Lord Palmerston, 1736–56
2. 1 diary by 1st Lord Palmerston of rentals of estates settled on his grandson, Henry Temple, 1740–50
3. 1 notebook, extract of 1st Lord Palmerston's will and estate, 1754

4. Receipt from Lady Palmerston's executrix, December 1, 1762

5. (a) Account of expenses of 2nd Viscount Palmerston at Cambridge, 1760
    (b) Regulations about Honorary Degrees at Cambridge, in the hand of 2nd Viscount Palmerston

6. 4 documents relative to Broadlands, 1757–58

7. Documents relating to family, mostly Poole's, about six pieces

8. (a) 8 letters from Earl Delawar (1693–1766) to Miss Poole, circa 1750
    (b) 7 letters from Lady Di Clavering (daughter of Earl Delawar) to Miss Poole, circa 1756
    (c) 32 letters from Lady C. West (later Johnston) to Miss Poole, 1754–69

9. Poem by Voltaire, Portrait du Dieu du Goût, undated

10. 5 miscellaneous verses

11. Draft of parliamentary speech on American Colonies

12. Documents concerning banking arrangements with Messrs Drummond and Messrs Hankey – about 17 pieces – 1782–1802

13. Certificate of Long Annuities, 1780

14. An account of works proposed at Broadlands, 1788

15. 1 draft letter, by Lord Palmerston, to a neighbour at Romsey

16. 1 letter from Sir John Day to the Hon. Sir William Jones, 1784

17. Names of persons who signed address to Prince of Wales at Romsey, when he visited Broadlands, 1789

18. List of the Channel Fleet under Earl Howe, 1795

19. List of Books bought in Paris (Le Gros), 1796

20. List of addresses (Paris)

21. Abstract of will and codicil of 2nd Viscount Palmerston

22. List of allowances made by executors of will of 2nd Viscount Palmerston to Lady Palmerston for maintenance of children, 1802

23. Record book of political anecdotes

G. PAPERS RELATING TO PAINTING AND SCULPTURE
COLLECTED BY SECOND VISCOUNT PALMERSTON

1. Notebook on pictures purchased, 1764–92
2. Pictures at Broadlands and Hanover Square, by room, giving dimensions, undated (1 notebook, three folios)
3. One folio of drawings bought at Mr Barnard's sale, February, 1787
4. Statement of account at Christie's, 1774
5. Two lists of sales of Sir Joshua Reynolds' drawings at Poggi's, and the Duke of Argyll's
6. List of sculpture and pictures bought in Italy, 1764
7. List of pictures in dining-room at Broadlands, in 3rd Viscount's hand, undated
8. Catalogue of Christie's sale, June 10, 1844, and note of prices fetched, in 3rd Viscount's hand
9. Catalogue of Christie's sale, November 5, 1850, and note of prices fetched, in 3rd Viscount's hand
10. Note of pictures sold by the Hon. Evelyn Ashley, about 1890, in late Lord Mount Temple's hand
11. List of pictures, drawings, furniture and china in Lady Palmerston's apartments at Broadlands, started by her in 1797 and continued until 1803
12. Two lists, in the hand of 1st Lord Palmerston, of his pictures at East Sheen and in St James's Square, 1724 and 1726
13. List of portraits at Sheen, in the hand of 2nd Lord Palmerston
14. List of family pictures from Sheen to be hung in the billiard room at Broadlands, after 1757
15. Scraps of paper with the same list of pictures for the billiard room at Broadlands
16. Two lists, of the 2nd Viscount Palmerston, of cost of pictures bought abroad 1792–94 and supposed values

H. BIBLIOGRAPHY

1. *Alumni Cantabrigiensis*, part II, volume V, J. A. Venn
2. *Boswell on the Grand Tour*, 1764, edited by Frederick A. Pottle, Heinemann, London, 1953

3. *Poetical Amusements at a Villa near Bath*, Lady Miller, 1775
4. *New Foundling Hospital for Wit*, 1784
5. *The Wreath of Fashion*, Tickell
6. *Notes and Queries*, 1st, 3rd and 4th series
7. *Life and Correspondence of the Rt Hon. John Burgoyne*, E. B. de Fonblanque, 1876
8. *Diary and Letters of Madame D'Arblay*, edited by Charlotte Barrett, Macmillan & Co., London, 1904
9. *Memoirs of Dr Burney* by his daughter Madame d'Arblay, Edward Moxon, London, 1832
10. *Life and Times of Sir Joshua Reynolds*, Leslie & Taylor, John Murray, London, 1865
11. *History of the Works of Sir Joshua Reynolds*, A. Graves and W. V. Cronin, London, 1899–1901
12. *Discourses*, Sir Joshua Reynolds, 1842
13. *Private Correspondence of David Garrick*, Henry Colburn, London, 1835
14. *Boswell's Life of Johnson*, volumes V and VI
15. *Miscellaneous Works of Edward Gibbon*, 1796
16. *Letters of Edward Gibbon*, 1896
17. *The Devonshire House Circle*, Hugh Stokes, Herbert Jenkins, London, 1917
18. *Georgiana*, edited by the Earl of Bessborough, P.C., G.C.M.G., John Murray, London, 1955
19. *Beckford*, Guy Chapman, Jonathan Cape, London, 1937
20. *Life and Letters of Sir Gilbert Elliot, First Earl of Minto, 1751–1806*, edited by his great-niece the Countess of Minto, Longmans, Green & Co., London, 1874
21. *Diaries and Correspondence of First Earl of Malmesbury*, London, 1844
22. *Journals of Horace Walpole*, 1771–83
23. *Letters of Horace Walpole*, edited by Toynbee, 1905
24. *Englishmen in the French Revolution*, John G. Alber, Sampston Low, Marston, Searle & Rivington, London, 1889
25. *Talleyrand*, Duff Cooper, Jonathan Cape, London, 1932
26. *Voyage d'Italie*, M. Cochin, Paris, 1769
27. *Works of Benjamin Thompson, Count Rumford*, American Academy of Arts and Sciences, 1870–75

28. *Despatches of Earl Gower, together with the Diary of Viscount Palmerston in France during July and August* 1791, Oscar Browning, London, 1885

29. *Dugald Stewart, Lecturer on Political Economy,* 1753–1828, 1855–56

30. *Memoirs of William Hickey,* edited by Alfred Spencer, Hurst & Blackett, Ltd, London, 1925

31. *The Structure of Politics at the Accession of George III,* Sir Lewis Namier, Macmillan & Co. Ltd, London, 1929

32. *Life of Viscount Palmerston* by Sir Henry Lytton Bulwer, completed by the Hon. Evelyn Ashley, M.P., Richard Bentley, London, 1871–76

33. *Palmerston,* Philip Guedalla, Ernest Benn, London, 1926

34. *The Grenville Papers,* being the correspondence of Richard Grenville, Earl Temple, K.G., and the Rt Hon. George Grenville, William James Smith, London, 1852

35. *Political History of England,* Volume X, William Hunt, Longmans, Green & Co., London, 1905

36. *Catalogue of Royal and Noble Authors,* Horace Walpole, edited by Parli, 1806

37. *Beauties of England and Wales,* Brayley & Britton, London, 1805

38. *Nollekens and His Times,* John Thomas Smith, Turnstile Press, London, 1949

39. *Anecdotes of Painters,* Edward Edwards, London, 1808

40. *Artists and Their Friends in England,* 1700–1799, William T. Whitley, The Medici Society, London and Boston, 1928

41. *History of the Society of Dilettanti,* Lionel Cust, Macmillan & Co., London, 1898

42. *Anecdotes of the Arts in England,* the Rev. James Dallaway, London, 1800

43. *Ancient Marbles in Great Britain,* A. Michaelis, Cambridge University Press, 1882

44. *English Architects,* 1660–1840, H. M. Colvin, John Murray, London, 1954

45. Autograph letters of Mrs Sheridan to Mrs Stratford Canning by permission of the Victoria Art Gallery and Municipal Libraries, Bath

INDEX